The Challenge of Democracy

The Challenge of Democracy

To Achieve a Global Plus-sum Game

Gustav von Hertzen

© Gustav von Hertzen
Layout by Oy Nord Print Ab, Helsinki, Finland 2008

ISBN 978-952-92-4856-8
Library of Congress Control Number 2008910854

Preface

This book takes the measure of democracy and reaches out to all concerned citizens. It is not an academic treatise with pretensions of scientific objectivity, but plainly mirrors the views of the author. The limited critical apparatus will refer to the most important sources and serve as an aid to further study. No attempt is made to cover the literature in a systematic way.

The only work I want to mention at this point is *La Démocratie en Amérique*, by Alexis de Tocqueville. It appeared in two volumes in 1835 and 1840, and was based on personal observations made during a voyage around the United States in 1831. The author had just reached the ripe age of 26 and was not burdened by the baggage of scientific merit. We may well ponder the fact that almost two centuries later we have been unable to significantly increase our understanding of the essence of democracy.

The subtitle of this book, *To achieve a global plus-sum game*, requires a short commentary. A society exists in order to produce added value for its members through fruitful cooperation. The internal rules of the game should therefore promote value-enhancing plus-sum games and minimize futile zero-sum play. Destructive minus-sum games should be totally unacceptable. By defining these interrelations in mathematical terms, game theory becomes applicable and fundamental insights can be gained. The reader will, however, be spared formulae and derivations.

The focus is on modern, large-scale democracies; historic and prehistoric precursors are discussed only in relation to the main theme. Neither have I tried to pin down a definition of democracy or to deal at length with the advantages and disadvantages of democratic government. The superiority of democracy is taken for granted. The interested reader is referred to an earlier work (*The Spirit of the Game*) where these questions are taken up in a broader context.

The Spirit if the Game appeared in 1993 and carries the subtitle *Navigational Aids for the Next Century*. In the present book the aim is the same: to try to warn and to guide, to point at dangers and pitfalls while shedding light on resources and opportunities. Our challenge is to shape the future, without false presumption but with firm conviction.

Contents

Introduction

The history of mankind can be perceived as an extended tutorial in plus-sum games, slowly learning the art of productive cooperation between individuals, groups, tribes and recently even nations. Constructive collaboration always requires a certain amount of trust, which implies a moral foundation. As communities grow, so too does the scope for free-riders, and cheating tends to proliferate. A corresponding increase in moral resources becomes imperative in order to uphold voluntary, democratic cooperation. The alternative is an autocratic, even totalitarian society.

Lately, the democracies have gone from strength to strength, politically as well as economically. Today, we regard democratic societies as self-evidently superior, which may well be right. But we are laboring under a dangerous delusion when such self-conceit leads to presumptions about the final supremacy of democratic countries. Democracy is not only the best – or the least bad – mode of government, but also the most demanding. It rests on foundations that are constantly exposed to erosion.

A short flashback to our recent history serves as a lesson in humility, particularly for us Europeans. In the shadow of Hitler and Stalin, very few futurologists would have bet on democracy in the early 1940s, at least in our part of the world. The almost universal retreat of the intellectual establishment from democratic ideals is particularly depressing even in retrospect. Sundry variations on socialism and a planned economy were dominant even in liberal circles. The admonitions of Karl Popper and Friedrich von Hayek fell on deaf ears, when they warned against the imminent totalitarian threat of sweeping government control.

Even in the bright light of hindsight, the resurgence of democracy in the post-war period seems nothing less than miraculous. The leftist intelligentsia proclaimed in unison the inevitable victory of socialism, while the conservatively minded were inclined to accept it as a fact with a sigh of resignation. The majority of mankind was already in the grip of decidedly un-democratic regimes and the home front was undermined by devoted communists, Maoists, pacifists and assorted fellow travelers. The concept of democracy itself was prostituted and began to lose its meaning. The market economy became a term of abuse.

Fortunately, ordinary people retained a healthy skepticism toward the blessings of world revolution. Ex-communists offered testimony of the actual practice of socialism and social democratic politicians repeatedly demonstrated the courage of their convictions in the fight against communist infiltration. Even so, the game would have been lost without the resolute foreign policy and military readiness of the United States. The gradual re-structuring of Europe could take place only under cover of the US nuclear umbrella.

Socialism was finally discredited by the implosion of the Soviet Union. This was not due to the attractions of democracy, but to the self-destruction of the planned economy. The self-organizing dynamics of the market economy eventually created a decisive competitive advantage, both politically and militarily. The decay of the Soviet state and the disasters of Maoist policy laid bare the inherent contradictions of Marxism. Dearly bought experience turned the minds of Mao's successors, and they have tried, with some success, to combine control and repression with the evident benefits of free markets.

We would like to see democracy and the market economy as a global panacea against all the ills of society, or at least as guarantor for economic efficiency and competitiveness. The obvious strengths of democracies are openness and transparency, adaptivity and creativity, even if the practice of democracy will remain constantly in dispute. The question stands: do people in general have the will and the capability to accumulate and maintain the moral capital which is indispensable for sustained democratic rule?

This is the challenge of democracy, which will be examined from a variety of angles. A foretaste of the problems is provided by the current wave of nostalgia for 'good old socialism', which has found a fuzzy focus in the anti-globalization movement. Democratic learning is indeed a slow process, where emotions and inherited attitudes usually prevail. The democracies, on the other hand, have a wonderful capacity to integrate even the most radical dissidents. Puerile thought experiments, containing a few grains of truth, are eventually refined into sensible contributions to the political process, and young rebels may over time become pillars of the community.

The health and vitality of the democracies is certainly our primary interest, but the challenge of democracy also has a missionary aspect, as it were. Our entire system of values is questioned, not only by fundamentalist fanatics, but by millions of less articulate people around the world who cling to their traditional ways of life. As immigrants, particularly Moslems have difficulties in accepting democratic ideals and mores. The multitude in the less developed countries is an even greater challenge.

Human progress is reflected in the realization of ever greater, value-generating plus-sum games. Honesty and transparency are the key to success. Only by leveraging our scant moral resources can we hope to inculcate fair play and create the preconditions for worldwide democratic cooperation. Whatever the outcome, democracy is the only political system worthy of man. Whether or not mankind can live up to this dignity remains an open question.

Part I

The foundations of democracy

The first part of the book recounts the emancipation of man into a socially competent and morally sentient being.

*The human psyche comprises a number of invariables that can neither be eliminated nor ignored. But we can control and, at best, even exploit these forces of nature.

*The fruitful interaction of technical and commercial endeavors can be consistently played out only in a market economy, featuring private property and a stable monetary value.

*The rise of democracy can be understood as a reduction to practice of basic Christian values. The renaissance, the reformation and the enlightenment were steps on the way to the liberation of the human intellect.

* The crises of democracy in the first half of the twentieth century taught us a hard lesson about the consequences of a moral breakdown.

*Ultimately our halting ethical evolution is dependent on an elusive, spiritual inspiration. Democracy as such is an empty vessel which must be filled with meaningful content.

Chapter 1
Human nature

Human behavior is the product of the interaction between genetic nature and self-made culture.[1] Evolutionary psychology tries to unravel the influence of our inherited nature as it has been formed by millions of years of social experience. Group selection gave rise to new, innate rules of human interplay that allow efficient cooperation within the group. This inherited morality allows the members of a tribe to combine internal competition with trustful collaboration. Humans are well adapted to pass on the crucial cultural heritage to the next generation. However, great difficulties are encountered when the moral capital must be enhanced in order to allow for value-creating plus-sum play in large, heterogeneous populations.

1.1 Nature or culture

What is man? How does he or she react to fellow human beings? How are they shaped by their environment and genetic heritage? We urgently need at least provisional answers in order to understand the workings of human societies. Veritable verbal wars have been fought over these questions, with the opposing parties deeply entrenched in their emotional positions. Now that some of the furor has settled, verifiable causalities can be discerned. In most cases we are confronted with genes *and* environment, heritage *and* culture in varying proportions.

The science of psychology has long been searching for a solid foundation. Psychoanalysis and behaviorism are two examples of pseudo-empirical theories that have lost their plausibility. Neurophysiology produces ever more detailed insights into the fundamental mechanics of the human psyche, but the leap to understanding *Homo sapiens* as a free agent appears insurmountable. Under these circumstances, evolutionary psychology offers a fresh point of view.

The basic premise is that natural selection has impressed universal patterns of behavior on our genome. Human emotions have been forged by evolution and are open to interpretation by analyzing how they might have improved fitness under ancient conditions. Strong internal competition has shaped our genetic heritage. Each individual is closest to him- or herself; family comes next and the tribal community claims the remaining reserves of altruism. Nothing is spared for the rest of humanity.

> Human nature has been seen variously as completely unchangeable or utterly malleable, depending on the ideological point of departure. The truth is that it evolves, slowly but faster than anticipated. According to C. Lumsden and E.O. Wilson (in *Promethean Fire* 1983) it takes about fifty generations to genetically stabilize a cultural breakthrough. New dog breeds with highly disparate behavior can be developed in about twenty generations. The fast evolutionary change can be explained by extra-genetic modifications of gene expression, which does not require mutations of the DNA.[2] Such epigenetic divergences could partly account for the difficulties of primitive peoples to adapt to civilization.

Man, like other social carnivores, has an innate hierarchical reflex. Respect for seniority and expertise is universal in human societies and an elevated status is very desirable, particularly in the male line. But we are also devoted to equality, evident in the few remaining stone-age societies. Our distant ancestors seem to have been radically democratic, albeit one should avoid overhasty conclusions on that score. A stronger hierarchical reflex may well have been a prerequisite for growth and prosperity, displacing the egalitarian tribes to the fringes.

The territorial instinct is another trait we share with many animals. Hunting or feeding grounds are marked and defended against members of the same species, and the struggle for group territory can lead to all-out war.

> Researchers have been particularly interested in the behavior of chimpanzees. The males often cooperate when hunting baboons and the team spirit is strengthened when the band is on the warpath. Inferior groups are attacked without provocation and sometimes the conflict resembles ethnic cleansing.

At best, aliens are viewed as competition and treated with suspicion. In humans, evolution has produced ethnocentrism. We have an innate tendency to look at the world from the viewpoint of the in-group. Differences in appearance, language or behavior trigger rejection. In many languages the word for humans is reserved for the natives. All outsiders are by definition nonhuman.[3]

Fundamentally we are all racist; xenophobia has been a survival factor. Humans do, however, have some freedom of action and are not tied to stereotyped reflexes. Many indigenous people have strong traditions of hospitality. The peaceful stranger is welcomed as a bearer of information and as a potential trading partner. The sharing of food and drink is an ancient way of creating affinity and long-term reciprocity. Sooner or later the roles might be reversed.

> Among isolated tribes, such as the Inuit, Sami and Chukchi, hospitality even extended to putting their women at the disposal of the guest. This can be interpreted as insurance against the risks of inbreeding – very long term reciprocity indeed!

Our strongest emotions and inhibitions have deep roots. Incest has been taboo in most cultures, the very few exceptions being royal personages with divine status. Incest has always been rare, but not because it was forbidden by law. It is a well-documented fact that humans have an innate aversion to sex with close relations. The same tendency is evident in many mammals that instinctively minimize the genetic burden of inbreeding – the so-called Westermarck effect. Also the clear difference between male and female sexuality has a logical explanation in terms of evolutionary psychology.

> Both men and women are programmed to maximize the number of offspring. But a woman's investment in pregnancy, as well as breastfeeding and infant care, is much greater. Even granted that a father is naturally disposed to care for his children, the man has an even greater interest in getting a free ride by planting his genes far and wide. A woman does not have a similar interest in the quantity of sexual encounters. Instead she puts a great value on quality and wants to pick and choose. Infidelity may be justified if the temporary partner is attractive enough. A nice husband who takes on responsibility for the children, and a lover with high status who sires them, can be bingo in the genetic lottery.

We will be obliged to return to the gender question, an issue that for better or for worse is very current in modern democracies. Here I will only point out that the family is and always has been a central element in the social fabric. The future of society is at stake if men won't take responsibility for their offspring. Edward Westermarck (1862-1939) was the first scientist to show that the family institution was not a modern invention but a human universal with very deep roots.[4]

Evolutionary psychology has of course many other strings to its bow. A propensity to conform – a herd instinct – is certainly part and parcel of our psychic set-up; there is even talk of genes for religion[5]. Well-known phobias, such as an aversion to rats, snakes, spiders etc., probably go still further back to distant, pre-human ancestors. A major part of our psychopathology can, perhaps too easily, be explained in evolutionary terms. Surprisingly enough mild depression, widespread in our civilization, is open to interpretation in terms of evolutionary fitness.[6]

> Monopolar depression can be understood as a personal protest against an environment that has exposed the self to stress, disappointment, trials or lack of empathy. Depression may be a deeply seated, instinctive reaction that puts pressure on the human environment to care, to help, to show sympathy. The sufferer simply goes on strike, which may improve his or more often her inclusive fitness.
>
> Indulgent concern is our spontaneous response which of course is the subconsciously intended effect. This may alleviate the symptoms but can impede the inevitable personal processing of grief. Conditioning therapy is the clinical complement of evolutionary psychology. Sigmund Freud (1856-1939) was on the right track when confronted with a hysterical woman who refused to get up. He shouted "fire", at which the deeply depressed patient immediately got to her feet.

Most phobias may be overcome by resolute therapy; deep-rooted prejudices too are open to self-conditioning. The need for human contact is another redeeming feature of our psychological heritage. The isolated human is not only materially powerless but emotionally amputated as well. The family and the community are the womb of the psyche; the campfires of distant times still retain their age-old attraction. Great literature often relies on deep insights into evolutionary psychology.

> In *Madame Bovary's Ovaries*, David and Nanelle Barash reveal the background to the intrigues of famous (and some less famous) works of literature in terms of evolutionary psychology. The classical Greek tragedies as well as Shakespeare and Chekhov abound in clashes of archetypal, psychological forces to great dramatic effect.

The most important conclusion of evolutionary psychology is that the human psyche comprises a number of invariables that can neither be eliminated nor ignored. On the other hand, we can control and, at best, even exploit these natural forces. The accelerating development of our culture constantly creates new tensions between inherited emotional attitudes, social norms and rational decision-making. We are doomed to live in this state of emotional maladjustment, a never-ceasing well of embarrassing conflict and painful creativity.

1.2 Group evolution

Charles Darwin (1809–82) speculated on group selection in *The Descent of Man* in order to explain the evident unselfishness in human relations even outside the immediate family circle. This view suggests that not only the individual (and his or her genes) but competing groups as well can be subject to natural selection. Altruistic behavior, which benefits the group, could then be genetically established, even if it is detrimental to the immediate interests of the individual.

Over the years, group selection became an all too popular explanatory model. Any evolutionary issue that seemed troublesome was thoughtlessly placed under the heading 'for the good of the species'. Although such cheap 'explanations' have subsequently been discredited by scientists, they are still accepted by the laity. But evolution follows a more sophisticated logic.

> Family ties are the natural basis of social relations. W.D. Hamilton (1936–2000) introduced the concept of 'inclusive fitness', to measure the influence of kin by quantifying the selfishness of genes.[7] The altruism of insects of the Hymenoptera family, like ants and bees, is explained by the fact that the males are haploid, that is, they have only a single set of chromosomes. This means that sisters have ¾ of their genes in common and are therefore more closely related to each other than to their own offspring, which inherently promotes social cooperation. The physiological and social development of ants was arrested some 50 to 100 million years ago and is one of many examples of evolutionary stalemate. Every genetic move will mean a change for the worse.
>
> Evolution, however, rarely follows narrow predestined routes. Most Hymenoptera species do not build communities but are solitary or only tenuously social. Moreover, the workers of a beehive are not full siblings, since the queen usually mates with several males; even so, their cooperation is close to perfect. Furthermore, termites are not members of the order Hymenoptera and possess a normal, diploid set of chromosomes. Notwithstanding, termites are very social but they constitute the only exception among such insects!

The widespread abuse of the concept of group selection made it an anathema to biologists who, like the economists, prefer to dismiss altruism as a causative influence. Individual selection is and will remain the dominant factor, but group selection has nonetheless regained its legitimacy.[8] During human evolution, productivity and efficiency – that is the capability to play plus-sum games – became an important competitive weapon and thus the subject of selection. The evolution of indispensable group morality will be discussed in the next section, but first we will take a look at a simple game-theoretic model that illustrates the conflict between self-interest and benefit to the group.

Social and cooperative morality always requires some sacrifice or at least risk taking, a reduction of personal fitness for the good of the community. This conflict of interest is illuminated by a simple game matrix which for historical reasons is called the 'prisoner's dilemma'.[9]

> Two opposing players each have two alternatives for their move, honest cooperation or deceit. Cooperation gives the greatest added value, each player benefiting equally. Defection produces a better outcome for the deceiver, but the deceived player suffers an even greater loss and thus the added value of the game has decreased. If both players choose deceit, the value of the game is zero. The underlying logic can be illustrated using a market transaction. If the seller chooses deceit, for instance by supplying goods of inferior quality, he makes an additional profit, but the buyer's loss is much greater. If the buyer delays payment and the seller has to rely on recovery, the situation is reversed. If there is mutual distrust, the transaction is aborted and no added value will be produced.

The dilemma arises because deceit is the dominant strategy for both players. Defection always gives the better outcome regardless of the opponent's move. The somewhat paradoxical consequence is that the potential added value will remain unrealized due to the lack of trust between the players.

The primary function of society is to create and maintain the conditions for productive interplay. The destructive, egocentric logic of the prisoner's dilemma must be overcome or circumvented. The solution should be voluntary, self-organizing and based on the long-term self-interest of the players or at least be compatible therewith. The situation is more manageable if several games are played in succession. The defector can expect a superior gain only once since the potential benefit of all subsequent games is forfeited – the customer relationship is destroyed. The problem is to get the plus-sum game going. The first steps are risky for both parties, until sufficient trust capital is accumulated.

> One game strategy, called tit for tat, has proven very successful in computer tournaments with a great variety of competing programs. All programs play repeatedly against each other and 'remember' the outcome of previous confrontations. Tit for tat has only two instructions.

-In the first confrontation, choose cooperation.

-In the following confrontations, imitate the opponents move in the previous confrontation.

Tit for tat is an 'honest' program but it will be fooled only once by the same player. It never gets the upper hand but is successful with other plus-sum players and best of all with itself.

Computer simulations have shown that 'honest' software, such as tit for tat, can be successful even in a deceitful environment, depending on the parameters. Thus a cooperative morale can be built from scratch, at least in silico. A prerequisite is a minimum proportion of honest players. Otherwise the potential plus-sum game cannot take off. Moreover, the game sequence should be extended and of indefinite duration. A specific end point would undermine the mutual trust of the players, which is assumed to be based exclusively on self-interest. It always pays to deceive in the last game and as this applies to both players, the deceitful gambit is carried back to the penultimate game and so on....

Dishonest strategies waste time on fruitless zero-sum games. They can only gain at the expense of the opponent. Poker is a typical zero-sum game where players try to deceive their opponents or at least to withhold all information. War is a destructive minus-sum game and calls for similar ploys – secrecy, deceit, surprise and ruses. In contrast, success in plus-sum games depends on openness and honesty. This always involves risk-taking since the opponent may switch to deceit at any moment and thus appropriate the lions share. Therefore the mutual trust between the players is an essential resource that accumulates slowly, but can be wiped out in no time.

1.3 The roots of morality

The deceitful free-rider takes advantage of cooperative efforts but does not contribute to the cost, thereby improving his (or her) relative fitness. Such individuals must be kept in check; otherwise social morality and the propensity for playing plus-sum games cannot be imprinted on the genome. How has this been possible?

Once more we find interesting clues in the study of our nearest relatives, the chimpanzees. The key concept is reciprocity. Among chimpanzees the rule is literally "scratch my back and I'll scratch yours". Deceit doesn't pay; the only result would be missing out on delousing. The same principle holds coalitions of male chimpanzees together with the aim of maintaining or improving their position in the hierarchy.

After a hunt, the kill is distributed according to a system of spoils, but nobody is completely left out. Useful 'inventions' can also be passed on to the next generation. Chimpanzees, in short, show signs of human behavior in a rudimentary form.[10]

The ancestors of the chimpanzees and humans separated about five to six million years ago. Our own palaeontological history is fairly well documented, but we know next to nothing about the chimpanzees. Probably they haven't undergone any radical change. The chimpanzees are well adapted to their stable rain forest habitat and are not subject to significant evolutionary pressure.

Brain volume is the best palaeontological yardstick for human development. What then was the reason behind the rapid expansion of the brain? After all, it comes at the cost of difficulties in childbirth and a higher metabolic rate. The modern brain accounts for one fifth of our energy consumption at rest and runs the risk of overheating in a tropical climate – probably a contributing factor to our hairlessness.[11]

> The evolution of mammals in the tertiary period (the last sixty million years) reveals an interesting parallel. The size of the brain of both predators and their prey has increased slowly and in step. Competitive pressure has been a pervasive driving force in the development of the central nervous system.

In humans, competition between fairly isolated groups has probably been instrumental. Constructive plus-sum play emerged as the key survival factor, rewarding group cohesion and morality. The development of language was both a cause and a consequence of intensified cultural competition. The communication capacity or bandwidth, to use modern terminology, increased dramatically and the scene was set for unbounded human interplay.

> The dynamics of cultural evolution exceed those of biological evolution by several orders of magnitude. For the inferior variant, there is no escape to a safe ecological niche. The dominant culture is hard on the heels of the weaker one with a minimum of delay. That is why there is only one surviving representative of the genus *Homo* – all others have succumbed under the pressure of merciless competition.

Group selection through cultural competition brings moral capital to the fore. We have already certified that honesty and openness are basic conditions for a plus-sum game. Furthermore, the added value per individual grows with an increase in group size. But so does the opportunity and temptation to cheat, which intensifies the quest for cooperative morals. Even so, internal competition was not eliminated; indeed the reverse is true.

> Internal competition for status and the attendant perquisites certainly increased the pace of human cerebralization. Insidious lies, cheating and misrepresentation call for a great deal of intelligence, and to expose the deceit requires as keen an intellect. In this contest brain was more important than brawn.

In a computer simulation, tit for tat software has to find out the intentions of the opponents in a laborious process – one by one. Humans, on the other hand, are capable of observing and communicating the outcome of a great number of confrontations within the group. The unmasked cheat is detested and branded whereas a good reputation is a valuable resource. In order to administer this ancient justice we have early on been endowed with an exceptionally keen memory for faces.

> Humans can effortlessly distinguish up to a thousand individuals, particularly if they are members of the in-group. (The racial divergence of strangers can make for difficulties in identifying individuals; to the naïve observer all Chinese look alike.) Our memory for faces is located in a very small area of the brain, which suggests selection at an early stage of evolution. If this area is disabled (a condition called prosopagnosia), the individual will be unable to recognize even the people that are closest to him while other memory functions remain intact.

Humans have never been altruistic exemplars. Far from it. But eventually the self-interest of our ancestors was adequately coordinated to serve the common good. The crucial factor is strong reciprocity, which Robert Trivers aptly calls moral aggression.[12] An elementary sense of justice emerged, and group members were conditioned to react strongly towards deceit and cheating, even at some cost to themselves. Competition was tempered by cooperation, self-esteem by team spirit. Particularly among young men, collaboration developed into comradeship that shows no mercy to defectors.

> We spontaneously abhor treachery as the blackest of crimes; in Dante's inferno, Judas is placed in the deepest, ninth circle of hell, together with Cassius and Brutus, the betrayers of Caesar. Tattle-tale and squealer are still among the most offensive insults. In times of war, the spirit of comradeship is vital, since the key to victory is troop morale. The Indo-European peoples featured an extensive network of militant

brotherhoods, which may well have contributed to their rapid expansion between 3000 and 1000 BC.[13] The street gangs of our cities are
their modern successors.

Our psychological makeup has over hundreds of thousands of years
been molded to promote mutual solidarity. Any breach of loyalty
caused the indefinite unease we call pangs of conscience. All latter-
day ethical superstructures are dependent on this inborn propensity
which unfortunately can be repressed, but which may also be refined
in a variety of directions.[14] Our culturally conditioned conscience is an
invaluable resource, a measure of the available moral capital.

1.4 From generation to generation

The step from one generation to the next is a critical moment in the
progression of genes. Fatal faults may enter the genetic script, multiple proof-readings notwithstanding. Gene duplicates may appear and
genes may be transposed to different locations. Entire chromosomes
may trip up in the complex choreography of meiosis. This is all grist
to the mill of genetic, DNA-based evolution. On the other hand, epigenetic adaptation has gone to great lengths in order to improve the
odds of survival.

> Nausea and vomiting are well-known early indicators of pregnancy. In
> the first months, the fetus is very sensitive to teratogenic toxins, such as
> thalidomide, that can cause severe malformations. Such toxins occur
> frequently in plants, particularly in wild varieties, but are normally of
> little concern. Overall, humans have an astonishing adaptability when
> it comes to foodstuffs. Cattle-rearing populations have repeatedly de-
> veloped the inheritable ability of adults to utilize lactose. Normally the
> secretion of the relevant gut enzyme ceases in childhood.[15]

Until very recently there has been a measure of doubt about paternity
and to ensure paternal bonding, the resemblance of father and infant
is pronounced during the first months of life. The commitment of the
mother is even more important. The close physical contact between
mother and child immediately after birth stimulates maternal feelings
and ensures good child care. Ignoring this kind of fundamental interactions has certainly caused much harm in so-called civilized societies.
To set aside ancient rules of the game carries a heavy penalty.

The number of offspring is not decisive for propagative success; what
really counts is the number of grandchildren. It is therefore in the

best interest of parents (and their genes) to improve their children's long-term viability by transferring experience and wisdom to the next generation. Our singularly prolonged childhood and extended old age provide the opportunity for comprehensive indoctrination of the younger generation. Grandparents are in a good position to contribute a great deal to the prosperity of their descendants, even though, or rather because, they no longer breed themselves.

> When growing up a child absorbs language, customs and norms without reservation, but puberty marks a change. During the maturation of the teenage brain, respect for the parents diminishes and often turns into its opposite (cf. chapter 15.1). Trivers was first in viewing the generation gap in the light of genetic conflicts of interest.[16] Primeval priorities still dictate the behavioral patterns of our youngsters.

In the heyday of behaviorism in the 1920s, researchers often neglected heredity and believed that a growing human could be manipulated at will.[17] Faith in the power of upbringing is still strong. Nevertheless, extensive research has shown that genes account for about half of the behavioral variability in the young of an average middle class family. More upsetting is that differences in upbringing seem to account for only ten per cent of variability. Close to half of our children's social conditioning depends on other influences.[18]

> Experiments with rhesus monkeys show that the peer group can be even more important than motherly care. Only the interaction within the peer group guaranteed adequate social competence of the adult monkey. In contrast, the mother could be replaced by a rag doll, without irrevocable consequences.[19]

The influence of the peer group is a well known phenomenon among humans as well. Its values often compete successfully with the moral code at home. The old chestnut about youngsters, led astray by bad company, has more than an ounce of truth in it. The peer group does, after all, represent the environment he or she must master as an adult. But the home environment is, on the other hand, decisive for the choice of friends. It is not easy for the sociologists to disentangle all the relevant variables.

In order to keep young men in particular under control, most societies have created demanding initiation rites to mark the acceptance of the teenager into the world of adults with its responsibilities and privileges. In the modern state, the school system is expected to perform the same function. The societal need to integrate and even regiment the young finds its expression in the unabashed ethnocentrism of the education plan. Myths and symbols, flags and national anthems are applied by modern societies in order to fortify the concord of their citizens, mobilizing our inherent tribal solidarity.

Basically, each generation re-creates the whole human genome but harmful mutations continue to make inroads on our genetic capital. Has modern medicine then done away with natural selection? Is our civilization threatened by incessant genetic degeneration? Similar questions were already raised by the ancient Greeks.

Plato (427–347 BC) prescribed strict regulation of reproduction (with concurrent segregation), and John Dalton (1766–1844) was the first spokesman for systematic racial hygiene. Nazi ideology thoroughly discredited these ideas, and the eminent biologist W. D. Hamilton made himself unpopular when he attempted to re-introduce the subject in the 1980s. He foresaw a dystopia, where the post-modern human is becoming completely reliant on medical intervention.

These fears may be exaggerated. Most non-viable variants are weeded out early on at the ovarian stage or by misscarriages in the early embryonic phase. Natural selection has been mitigated, not eliminated. In a not too distant future we will in any case be able to correct human genomes, if this is found desirable. Apart from artificial intervention, we can expect the continuous evolution of the human genome.

Natural (or unnatural) selection through alcohol abuse has for millennia been operating in agricultural societies with an abundant supply of fermentable carbohydrates. A mutation that changes the metabolism of alcohol is quite common among civilized nations. Acetaldehyde, a toxic intermediate, is burned at a reduced rate which leads to its accumulation with subsequent hangover symptoms. Primitive peoples have not been subjected to this selection factor and have a normal metabolic rate. The warning signal of a hangover is much weaker and alcoholism is often endemic.

In *A Farewell to Alms: A Brief Economic History of the World* (2007), Gregory Clark traces back the English industrial revolution to a persistent genetic change during the preceding centuries. In contrast to other peoples investigated, the affluent English had more children surviving into adulthood than the population at large. Under stagnant economic conditions, this meant that many of them ended up in straightened circumstances, squeezing out the common indigent by their cultural-cum-genetic competitiveness. Clark maintains that the slow change in genetic endowment was the mainspring of the subsequent economic development. By the same token, the less developed countries are in for a long haul. These controversial conclusions have so far evoked only muted reactions.

Today drug addiction affects our genetic heritage, which is certainly subject to a number of other influences, most of them unknown. The conventional wisdom that human nature is essentially immutable must be qualified. Slight modifications of the cybernetics of the genome can achieve remarkable hereditary adaptation in a short time frame. Our culture may have a noticeable impact on our nature over a period of less than ten generations.[20]

1.5 The route to high culture

We have acquainted ourselves with a number of mechanisms that facilitate long-term cooperation between individuals with a strong self-interest, preparing the way for successful plus-sum games. But this is not the whole story. Contingencies have played an important part in the evolutionary process.

> If a small group is isolated, they may by accident be carriers of a deviating, genetically based behavior. This 'founder effect' can provide an opportunity to develop better cooperation and thus enhance the competitive edge of the group. The *Homo sapiens* genome is exceptionally uniform, which suggests that our male and female ancestors have passed through one or more population minima. Some 200,000 years ago, the original population in Africa supposedly counted no more than a few thousand people. During migration to other continents, the bottlenecks were probably even more constricted.[21]

There is no royal road to cultural development but instead an abundance of dead-ends. These can be traced back to the egalitarian ethos of ancient social bonding which only under protest yields to the demands of efficiency and competitiveness. Under pristine conditions, a human group holds only 150–300 members before splitting up.

> Conventional anthropology distinguishes the following schematic stages of development.[21]
> -The small band does not have a clearly defined territory, and family hierarchy is the only repository of authority. Neighboring groups may occasionally combine forces to tackle demanding projects, but only on an ad hoc basis.
> -Related families coalesce in a clan with a common, often mythical ancestor.

-The clans merge into a tribal community where 'big men' from prominent families have considerable influence.

-Chiefs are appointed but their mandate is restricted to times of war.

-Prominent chiefs establish permanent authority and the tribes may combine in loose confederations, but central control is still quite limited.

- A kingdom is founded when power is concentrated in one person at all times; ultimately the succession is controlled by the king. In addition to kinship, merit also begins to influence positions in the hierarchy.

Primitive agricultural societies may have been matriarchal even if the archaeological evidence is controversial. It stands to reason that when the importance of hunting declined, the status of males was undermined. The queen became a key figure and kings were degraded to prince consorts with a short life-span. The emergence of patriarchy is reflected in Greek mythology. Bold heroes abound, displaying great feats and cunning when they topple the pre-existing matriarchal power structures.[23]

In a small group implementing justice is no problem. Everyone, save the defendant and the plaintiff, is part of the jury and there is no right of appeal. But social integration creates friction between loosely allied clans and tribes. In the absence of adequate societal structures, every family or clan has to look out for itself when asserting its rights, which inevitably leads to escalating blood-feuds. Vengefulness is a specifically human emotion, reflecting an elementary sense of justice which certainly enhanced survival during the hominizing process. The craving for retribution prepared the ground for strong reciprocity that calls for fair play regardless of personal interests or injuries.

Competitive strength generally increases with group size, provided a hierarchal structure that can suppress destructive internal conflicts. But in the long-term, stability is always called into question. Kingdoms suffer from unremitting inner tensions. The best cure for disunity is to look for a fight with your neighbor. Warfare between neighboring states has been the staple of history writing, but in the shadows tribal conflict has been equally vicious.

The Pueblo Indians of South-Western USA have always been considered peaceful, and that is why it came as a shock that their predecessors, the Anasazi Indians of the 13th- and 14th centuries practiced genocidal warfare. The ultimate reason was probably a deteriorating climate that caused starvation and all-out competition for scarce resources.[24]

The Yanomamo Indians are the classic example of bellicosity as part of everyday life. Neighboring villages attacked each other ceaselessly, in order to kill enemies and capture their women. If the maximum group size of about 150 individuals was exceeded, the group split up in two and were soon at war. The entire population constantly lived in a state of emergency.[25]

To escape the exigencies of the primitive condition, humans had to break with age-old rules of the game. The corresponding values – the chromosomes of culture – are by definition resistant to change. Rare leaps of faith may initiate a virtuous circle of development although just a tiny fraction of such cultural mutations have borne fruit. We know little or nothing about pre-historic fiascos, but some recent failures can be investigated in detail.

> In the nineteenth century, the ideas of Charles Fourier (1768–1830) and Robert Owen (1771–1858) inspired the establishment of a number of socialist collectives on pristine land in the new world. Their average lifespan was somewhat less than two generations. The Chinese worker's communes of Mao Zedong are the latest eruption of communal utopianism; they were disbanded after a couple of decades.

In the end, self-interest cannot be suppressed by futile ideologies and the new generation habitually distances itself from the founders' precepts. The Israeli kibbutzim are a unique case. Their socialism is watered down to be sure, but they have become a national institution, shored up by pseudo-religious Zionism. Religiously based collectivism has proved rather durable. For centuries, Nonconformists have established exclusive societies in the wilds; the greater part of the North-American colonies were founded by British dissidents of differing hues with a democratic bent. In contrast, the fate of the Jesuit state in Paraguay demonstrates the frailty of a top-down approach.

> The Jesuits were horrified by the brutal treatment of the natives and in 1608 they were empowered to convert and administer the Guarani Indians in a large territory, centered on present day Paraguay. Despite repeated incursions from Portuguese slavers, a self-sufficient community was created with its own municipalities, churches, workshops, schools etc., all paternalistically run by benevolent, incorruptible and highly motivated Jesuit brothers.
>
> The Jesuit state was a collective run from the top, without private property or industry. When the Society of Jesus was suppressed in 1768, the Jesuits were driven out and the population of close to 150,000 was completely disoriented. The social capital evaporated as the natives were unable to maintain the societal plus-sum game. Under a new in-

competent regime agriculture declined, the artisan skills were lost, the missions dissolved and the people dispersed.[26]

In a hierarchal system of government, the stabilizing factor is the legitimacy of the rulers. The Jesuits of Paraguay invoked the highest possible authority and established their credibility by their irreproachable conduct. But the natives were treated as children, their emancipation was curtailed and hence their ability to shoulder social responsibility. Despite the best of intentions, the heroic efforts came to nothing – a tragic example of misdirected community building. In the long run you can't protect people like animals in a game reserve.

Throughout history rulers of all hues have made a point of disassociating themselves from ordinary mortals by their clothes, conduct and ceremony. A well-used ploy is to claim divine, or at least semi-divine status. The European monarchs have ruled by God's grace and the Chinese emperors received their mandate from Heaven. Naked coercion has been necessary, of course, but without legitimacy the power structure would be shaky.

> Kings, emperors and sultans have worked under severe stress. Capital mistakes, famine and epidemics could lead to serious dissent, not to mention conspiracies and assassination. Despite or rather because of his elevated status, the autocrat was responsible for all ills that befell the population. When the drive of a dynasty diminished, the operative responsibility of government was handed over to a minister, vizier, shogun or major domo, who was expendable if circumstances so required. Power without responsibility is, however, an unsustainable situation. Sooner or later the divine figurehead would be dispatched to the heavenly domains, either literally or figuratively.[27]

Whichever way the mighty turned, their power rested on an insecure foundation. A productive plus-sum game could flourish under good government, but the added value tended to end up in the wrong hands and to be invested in unprofitable projects – splendor and parade, pyramids and palaces. Misrule sooner or later ended in revolt and a power shift which rarely produced permanent improvements. If the entire plus-sum was squandered away, the justification for an autonomous state vanished and it dissolved into its constituent parts, or fell prey to rapacious neighbors.

Republics, governed by aristocratic elites, were in a better position to adapt to internal change and secure the commitment of significant constituents/major interest groups. Sparta, Carthage and Rome are textbook examples of the ability of a republican constitution to mobilize society in the long term. Still, they too dug their own graves one way or another. Athens executed a unique experiment in linking an expanding high culture with democracy, albeit with severe limitations. The attempt failed in a maelstrom of philosophic speculation, self-deceptive oratory and foundering triremes.

Only in the turbulent Europe of the Modern Era has the protracted historic reiteration been disrupted. The competition between national states was not only a military issue, but was extended to trade, the economy and ultimately to the form of government. In contrast to China, no single European state was able to achieve hegemony. In this mêlée of conflicting influences and interests, a new set of rules for societal plus-sum play was taking hold. Democracy was on the march.

Chapter 2
The material base

From the beginning, technology and trade have been the driving forces of economic progress, with social development as a decisive background factor.[1] The level of cultural achievements is strongly correlated to the size of the population involved. Prosperity has been contingent upon the protection of private property and a stable monetary value. A centralized barrack economy may work in times of crisis or war, but inevitably falls out of gear under normal circumstances. The market economy is the only way to identify consumer priorities and to allocate resources in a rational manner. Within a sound social frame of reference, the plus-sum game of a market economy works as a self-sufficient welfare generator. In the final analysis, each nation has the economy it deserves.

2.1 Technical ingenuity

Tools are not a human prerogative; a number of birds and mammals, notably the chimpanzee, occasionally put external objects to good use. As far as we know, however, our ancestors were unique as tool manufacturers. Over millions of years, a progression of ever more sophisticated stone tools marks the development of our species and human culture. These artifacts were certainly supplemented with utensils made of perishable material, such as wood, plant fibers, bone, animal skins and sinew.

The quality of stone tools shows a definite correlation with the increase in brain volume, beginning with the australopithecines some 3.5 million years before present (BP), all the way to *Homo erectus*, who appeared about 1.8 million BP, equipped with well-formed stone axes. *Homo erectus* was the first hominid to migrate from Africa and to spread all over Eurasia. The brain of *erectus* was almost the same size as ours and yet there is little evidence of cultural evolution until *Homo sapiens* makes its appearance some 200,000 BP. Why this plateau? This is one of many question marks in the evolution of hominids.

Internal competition drove *Homo sapiens* to migrate to every continent except the Antarctic. The pioneers probably preferred the shoreline, and some form of craft was certainly invented early on. More advanced rafts or canoes may have been necessary for the leap to Australia some 50,000 years ago.

Modern man relentlessly pushed aside earlier hominids. Even though they co-existed for millennia, DNA-analyses of Neanderthal bones do not indicate any interbreeding. In Europe *Homo neanderthalensis* died out only about 25,000 BP, and a recent discovery on the Indonesian island of Flores puts a pygmy form of *Homo erectus* in the area some 18,000 before present.

Superior technology was the key to the success of our ancestors. Technical development was in all likelihood connected to a strengthening of social ties, based on linguistic capabilities, division of labor and trustful cooperation. Cultural development accelerated, overshadowing genetic evolution.

> Dramatic climate changes accompanied and probably hastened the cultural evolution. Severe ice-ages alternated with relatively short inter-glacials, which rewarded fast adaptation through cultural advance. There is, however, also a discernible genetic adaptation. In contrast to the tropics, a short and robust body improved the chances of survival in an arctic climate. Dark winters and misty summers forced a decrease of the skin pigmentation in order to safeguard the supply of vitamin D. The pygmies of the African rain forests are another example of rapid genetic adaptation. The brain volume is close to the human norm even though growth during puberty is otherwise greatly reduced.[2]

Humans could survive in every climatic zone and learned to exploit all available sources of food. Early hominids used fire and made clothes from animal skins, but the innovative power of Homo sapiens was far superior. The productivity of fishing was greatly increased by traps, nets and barbed fishing hooks. Big game hunting was facilitated by a short spear thrower (atlatl) that improved the precision and reach of the weapons. When, about 20,000 years ago, the bow was invented and man adopted the dog as a hunting companion, the efficiency of the hunt drove a number of game animals over the brink of extinction.

> The carnage was worst in the New World, colonized by man about 15,000 before present. The unsuspecting native fauna were confronted with sophisticated hunters and the resulting slaughter wiped out an estimated three quarters of the big mammals (over 40 kg) in a few thousand years. The mammoth, mastodon, camels, rhinoceros, horses and

several species of deer all became extinct, as did their highly specialized predators. Australia, too, suffered severe extinctions; the aborigines seem to have relied on systematic torching of the vegetation. In Tasmania the carnage was delayed due to the later arrival of humans.[3] In Eurasia, the decrease in biodiversity was less dramatic but still significant while Africa was almost untouched.

Obviously Paleolithic man was capable of undercutting the very basis for his own existence. The human race may have comprised only about one million individuals, but in many places it exceeded the carrying capacity of the ecosystem. Man was forced to adapt, and in a few instances new, more sustainable methods of subsistence were discovered. Over the generations, edible plants were protected, cared for, cultivated and bred. Valuable prey was subjected to a similar process and turned into cattle. Slowly but surely the new technology and its adherents spread in ever widening circles.

In *Guns, Germs and Steel*, Jared Diamond maintains, with splendid hindsight, that agriculture and animal husbandry sprang up wherever there were plants that could be grown or animals that could be domesticated. This theory is a bit thin. Cultural evolution is an enigmatic process with many variables; neither biological reductionism nor ecological determinism provides a tenable doctrine. Man had to undergo a comprehensive cultural and genetic adaptation when switching to a sedentary existence. Even today, it is no easy task to tie down freely roaming hunter people to the daily drudgery of a settled life.

Ceramics and textiles are early examples of human creativity. They were followed by metalworking; copper, tin, lead and bronze. Irrigation, urbanization and writing worked as mutual catalysts in the first high cultures around 3000 BC. Iron and steel followed before 1000 BC, but then technical development seems to abate. For sure, existing knowledge was disseminated and refined, but great leaps of technical innovation do not occur. Apart from the limited exploitation of water and wind power, new sources of energy emerged only in the eighteenth century with the advent of steam power.

Pre-Columbian America remained to all intents in the Stone Age, despite impressive achievements in agriculture, architecture and art. But on the other side of the globe, China had already in the fourteenth century become an industrial power based on technical innovations. China obviously enjoyed the external pre-conditions for sustained cultural development, but something was lacking in the social dynamics.[4]

Anno 1400 China was the only great power in the world, with the largest population and the best education, the strongest economy and the most advanced technology. The country could well have gone on to instigate a global trading network and the industrial revolution. But after several successful voyages of discovery that reached Eastern Africa, further expeditions were prohibited – ocean sailing ships were outlawed. The ruling class concluded that they already possessed everything they needed; outside influences would only create disturbances. At the same time, the promising industrial development was arrested and China sank into a quiet regression, disturbed only by occasional uprisings and invasions.

> Gunpowder is a Chinese invention and a very special source of energy, but it had social consequences only in late mediaeval Europe. Roger Bacon (ca 1220–92) was the first to publish a recipe for gunpowder and the significance of artillery increased at the close of the Hundred Years War 1337–1453 between England and France. Warfare has always been a driver of innovation.

Revolutionary innovations require vision, risk-taking and capital, which have been in short supply at all times. In addition, innovations are often disruptive and provoke resistance from vested interests that may nip any change in the bud. Without a certain measure of missionary faith, the old mold cannot be broken. Technical progress and cultural evolution in general are by no means self-propelled. Backsliding is the rule rather than the exception. Empires crumble, hard-won knowledge is forgotten, only the most basic practical skills are preserved.

Neolithic man had to pay a high price for his agricultural exploits and the attendant population explosion. In the densely packed settlements, diseases spread quickly and became endemic while pests and vermin multiplied. New plagues tormented mankind and put a brake on the population increase.

> Most pathogenic organisms have animal hosts besides humans, and they were quick to exploit the new opportunities. Traditional remedies were of little use; the only defense was genetic adaptation which, by remorseless selection, achieved at least partial immunity. When the Europeans colonized America, smallpox and other contagious diseases became terrible biological weapons. The smallpox virus appeared as a mutation of a related animal virus about 8000 years ago. As it happens, it is a specifically human pathogen and was finally eliminated in the 1970s because it cannot 'hide' in an animal species.

High cultures were confronted with a number of ecological problems. Domestic plants and animals were also susceptible to disease. Intensive farming threatened the fertility of the fields and the recuperation of pastures. Deforestation through slash-and-burn practices is another age-old blight. Water supply and salinisation of irrigated areas must have been a constant headache. Small wonder then, that most cultures were not equal to the challenges. Technical problems are usually solved with better techniques, but this requires an adequate social structure. Otherwise human creativity is curtailed and the plus-sum game fades away.

2.2 Commercial enterprise

The manufacturing of tools and the exchange of goods are specifically human activities. Trading flint-stone and other necessities goes back all the way to the Paleolithic period. Ever since, commerce has grown to become an increasingly important value-creating activity. Exchanging goods and services is the best example of a simple plus-sum game, driven by the division of labour. The traded item must always be more valuable to the buyer than to the seller, otherwise there is no trade. The distribution of the added value is a zero-sum game, however, which is reflected in haggling over price and terms of delivery. The interference of plus-sum and zero-sum aspects engenders a moral ambiguity which often taints commercial relations.

Trade and technology in mutual interaction forms the economic foundation of society. The vicissitudes of long-distance trade generated writing, one of the most important innovations of mankind.

> Around 3500 BC, the traders of Sumer were using bills of lading to document their cargoes in long distance trading. Each consignment was accompanied by a number of small clay figurines that symbolized the type and quantity of the goods. In order to avoid fraud, the tokens were enclosed in a shell of burnt clay. The recipient broke the receptacle and checked the delivery against the tokens. Still, the middlemen could not inspect the bill of lading. This problem was solved by marking the shells with the contents of the bill of lading prior to burning. Each figurine was represented by a set of wedge-formed impressions on the surface of the shell. The cuneiform script was born!

Over the years the Sumerians simplified their script until they had replaced the original pictograms with a syllabic alphabet that is the source of our phonetic alphabet. Other cultures independently developed their own scripts, but of their origin we know next to nothing.

Increased trade leads to a superior division of labor and makes room for innovation, which in turn is the mainspring of higher productivity and an improved standard of living. Whereas technical innovations and insights tend to become public property, trading transactions can be tightly controlled. Then the added value ends up in the hands of monopolistic middlemen or commercial centers of power.

In a time-honored manner, the Dutch East India Company maintained a monopoly on the trade with their colonies. The reorganization of the nutmeg market is a flagrant example of ruthless colonialism. In the sixteenth century, nutmeg was considered a cure for fever, stomach illnesses, headaches, halitosis and impotence. Nutmeg grew principally on the small Banda islands in the Portuguese-controlled Moluccas archipelago. After the Dutch had forced the Portuguese out in 1621, the Dutch East India Company established strict control over production and export; punitive expeditions cut down all unauthorized nutmeg trees. Recalcitrant natives were deported or massacred with the aid of Japanese mercenaries. Small wonder then, that profitability was excellent but eventually the commercial position eroded and the company went bankrupt in 1800.

The cost of transport restricted trade, but the rapaciousness of officials was even worse a problem, not to mention open robbery along the trade routes. In the Middle Ages, the incipient contact between China and Europe was periodically cut off. Empires usually allowed rather free commerce within their territory, which stimulated trade and gave the government an objective reason for existence. Similarly, the Hanse in northern Europe and Venice in the eastern Mediterranean maintained a modicum of order in the 14th and 15th centuries.

By the mid eighteenth century, Great Britain had superseded Spain, Portugal and the Netherlands as the leading commercial power. The British colonial empire eventually spanned the globe, and a wide network of naval bases made worldwide operations possible. Pax Britannica guaranteed free trade on the seven seas and was backed up by a robust navy. Foreign policy bore the mark of the liberal values of the British establishment, and the Parliament did not hesitate to introduce legislation that chastised abominable international commerce.

The slave trade has ancient roots; gaining slaves was often a motive for warfare, or at least a by-product. All the old cultures accepted slavery in some form as part of the natural order. In principle, Christian Europe disliked slavery, but unfortunately the trade was very profitable. The West Indies-England-West Africa triangle route, controlled by

British merchants, was particularly lucrative. It took decades of political struggle to persuade the British parliament to criminalize trading
with slaves in 1807. Thereafter the navy set about suppressing the slave
trade and eventually stamped out the filthy business.[5]

The nineteenth century saw a great rise in free trade, followed by unprecedented prosperity and technical advance. It was a time of globalization – of markets, of technology and of capital movement. Despite
stiff competition for colonies and raw materials, the world enjoyed a
century of relative peace, unlike previous and subsequent periods.

Trade tends to create and maintain good relations. The origin of
commerce was a system of reciprocal gifts. Our Christmas traditions
reflect the need to reinforce togetherness through an exchange of material tokens of affection.

> In primitive tribal communities anyone was allowed to claim a desired
> object, but the claimant then had to assume a reciprocal commitment.
> Successful individuals were in a position to enhance their social stand-
> ing with elaborate gifts, but were also jealously watched. Sometimes
> the situation exploded in a rage of generosity and even public destruc-
> tion of valuables, as was the case at the ceremonial potlatch feasts of
> the native Americans of the northwest.

Good trading relations are both cause and effect of peaceful co-exis-
tence between clans, tribes and nations. In his classic *Essai sur le Don**,
Marcel Mauss (1872–1950) shows how gifts create a permanent social
connection between the parties. If there was no real object of commerce, people took recourse to ritual exchanges.

> Bronislav Malinovski (1884–1942) has documented the Kula system,
> which maintained peaceful relations in an extensive archipelago east
> of New Guinea. Locally crafted necklaces (soulava) and armbands
> (mwali) circulated as gifts and return gifts throughout the islands; the
> soulava in clockwise rotation and the mwali counter-clockwise. The
> ornaments were not meant to be kept by the recipient, but to be passed
> on in a continuous string of visits. The main purpose was to maintain
> peaceful relations over great distances, even when a visit didn't have
> any apparent purpose.[6]

It bears repeating: commerce is a plus-sum game that creates and maintains peaceful relations to mutual advantage on every level. Where the
trading links are strong enough, nobody can gain, or even imagine

---

* In English *The Gift: The Form and Reason for Exchange in Archaic Societies* gaining, from warlike adventures; aggressive plans are shelved at an early stage. The European Union wisely started the integration process by removing trade impediments step by step, and hence, for all practical purposes, excluded a relapse into militant chauvinism. The on-going globalization should be interpreted as the first hesitant steps toward a permanent state of global peace.

2.3 The value of money

Exchange is the original form of commerce. The use of money works as a catalyst for trade, but requires general acceptance and at least a core region with a stable social structure. Market oriented high cultures, such as Mesopotamia and ancient Greece, were monetary economies whereas strictly centralized, authoritarian states tend to marginalize the use of money. The Inca Empire seems to have managed without any kind of currency.

Anything useful or rare can be used as payment to facilitate trade. The world of commerce has only lately given up the concept of real value and accepted money as a pure convention, based on trust.

> Flint and obsidian must have been used as tokens of value long before recorded history; grain and cattle were obvious means of payment in the Neolithic period. In parts of Africa a male slave has periodically been the currency standard. The concept of monetary value has variously been represented by sea shells, cocoa beans, tobacco, pieces of leather, arrowheads and particularly metals – gold, silver, bronze, copper and iron.[7]

Each choice of a measure for material value has drawbacks. Utilities are often bulky, heavy or subject to decay. Precious metals lack these problems, but have no practical utility or intrinsic value. Rarity, however, turned out to be a decisive advantage. In order to maintain its value, money must always be in short supply. Otherwise inflation and economic collapse loom.

Thus gold and silver became universal currencies at an early stage, with copper in a supporting role. Inscriptions from Ur III in Sumer (c. 2000 BC.) instruct payments in standard pieces of silver. The earliest known metal coins were minted in Lydia in Asia Minor in the seventh century BC. The profile of the ruler guaranteed the quality of the coin. Unfortunately, the problem of inflation didn't vanish. Unscrupulous rulers debased the coinage by adulterating the precious metals, and coins were painstakingly cut with scissors by professional cutters.

The debasement of money reflects the ups and downs of the Roman Empire. Augustus (ruled 30 BC to 14 AD) restored the coinage after the upheavals of the civil wars. Nero (54–58) initiated the adulteration of the silver coinage; by the time of Septimius Severus (193–211) the value of the denarius had dropped by 50%. Then the inflationary pace increased. Around 250 AD, the silver content was about 5%, and under Claudius II Gothicus (268–270) it had declined to 0,02%!

Diocletian (284–305) was unsuccessful in his attempts to stabilize the currency and tried to check the runaway inflation with rigorous price controls. Like so many after him, he fought in vain against the power of the market. The money economy broke down and taxes were paid in kind. Constantine the Great (306–37) introduced a gold coin, the solidus, which maintained its value in the Byzantine Empire for centuries, but this stability was not extended to the silver and copper coins in daily use. In Western Europe large areas regressed to a barter economy. In the fifth and sixth centuries, no coins were circulating in England.

A solid currency is no guarantee against rising prices, a phenomenon that has periodically plagued most economies. When the supply of goods is reduced, say by war or a failed harvest, a temporary rise in prices is inevitable. But in the sixteenth and seventeenth centuries, Europe was subject to an unprecedented inflationary wave. The stream of gold and silver from America depressed the value of precious metals in an unheard of way. The purchasing power of gold was halved and that of silver decreased by 80%.

A gold or silver standard also has the reverse problem. If the economy grows faster than the supply of money, the liquidity crisis leads to deflation, which puts a brake on the economy. This occurs only when economic development has reached a fairly high level, and consequently China was first to encounter this problem. The solution was paper money, i.e. an undertaking by the state to honor the paper bill with payment in metal coinage at the nominal rate.

A shortage of precious metals caused Emperor Hien Tsung (Tang dynasty) to issue paper currency in the early ninth century. Two hundred years later, inflation was out of control and reached astronomical heights until Kublai Khan, the first Mongol emperor (1279-94), restored the value of money. A further roller coaster of monetary value forced the Ming dynasty (1368-1644) to give up the use of paper currency altogether. Still, the deflationary pressure called for continuous imports of silver that could not be met, the Spanish deliveries from America notwithstanding. This created an incredibly profitable arbitrage opportunity in the seventeenth and eighteenth centuries. In China, gold could be bought with silver at half the European rate.

The first public institution in Europe to issue paper currency was the Bank of Sweden in 1661, followed by the Bank of Scotland in 1695. A similar attempt in France failed when, after an initial success, the bill and securities issued by John Law crashed in 1720. Paper money is totally dependent on confidence in the issuing government, and is a sensitive gauge of social stability. After the First World War, the copious inflation in Germany and other Central European states created economic havoc and foreshadowed World War II. The all-time inflation record is held by Hungary.*

Printing money can temporarily solve the problems of the public purse when resources are furtively transferred from trusting depositors to state coffers and sharp speculators. But when ordinary people become privy to the inflationary mechanism, the game is over. Hyperinflation sets in and the economic plus-sum game is paralyzed by the dissipation of the trust capital. With few exceptions, everybody is a loser.

Under conditions of hyperinflation, society reverts to bartering. Assets as well as precious metals are frozen and no credit is available. For an economy to work, money must stay in circulation and the available surplus should be invested productively. To that end, banks are needed which can be entrusted with accumulated savings.

> Somewhat surprisingly banking is ancestral to minted money. As early as 2000 BC, the temples and palaces of ancient Babylon received deposits of grain, cattle, agricultural tools and precious metals. This suggests a financial market with a measure of competition. The business climate was harsh. Defaulting debtors were forced to sell their children as slaves – sometimes even themselves. The same draconian practices were current in Greece, until Solon (638–559 BC) abolished debtor's slavery.

A shortage of capital precipitates heavy sanctions against light-hearted indebtedness; otherwise the credit would dry up. Collection methods have become more human since antiquity, albeit debtor's prisons persisted well into the nineteenth century. Despite collateral, collection has always been problematic for banks, particularly in their relations with recalcitrant rulers.

---

* It stands at an unbeatable 42 quadrillion % per month, which not even Zimbabwe can threaten.

The Medici family of renaissance Florence had major problems with the Holy See as debtor. The house of Fugger in Augsburg received a 50% cut of the papal income from the indulgence trade in Germany, but foundered on the unreliability of princes. The Fuggers generously financed generations of Habsburgs, and the election of Charles V as Holy Roman Emperor in 1519 was backed by Jakob Fugger, the richest man in Europe, to the tune of 850,000 florins. Charles V paid back his debts, but his son Philip II did not, and in 1596 Spain was declared bankrupt. His grandson, Philip III, went bankrupt in 1609 which toppled the house of Fugger.

The interest rate reflects the risk exposure and the availability of capital. Annual interest rates of 20-30% are indicated by mathematical exercises preserved on old Babylonian clay tablets. In ancient Athens, 10% was the normal rate of interest for a low risk investment. Roughly the same rate applied in England around 1600.

Usury was strictly forbidden in most countries, but the Catholic Church and Islam categorically prohibited all forms of collecting interest as a violation of their respective Holy Scriptures. This did not worry the Lombard and other Northern Italians who, in fierce competition created a modern banking system; in a landmark decision in 1403, a Florentine court legalized interest on debt. If necessary, interest could be defined as a delivery charge, a risk premium or a share in profits – a convention still current in Moslem countries. No prohibition against interest existed in Judaism, and consequently the Jews became active as bankers in mediaeval times.

For a long time, earning money was considered a shabby traffic, not acceptable to the upper crust. Princes and aristocrats were perfectly happy to rob and loot, but taking a direct hand in economic transactions, commerce or technology, was not on. Aristotle (384–322 BC) made himself spokesman for the intellectual arrogance of antiquity, with his condescension toward trade and industry. The Catholic Church adopted this attitude and affected to despise all worldly things, although the practice hardly matched the message. A reformation was needed to create due respect for work, thrift and economic activity in general.

2.4 The formation of capital

There is a long-standing, misguided usage of the word capitalism as a pejorative label for a market economy. But every society is dependent on accumulated capital, though eventually most of them switch from accumulating to wasting. The sustained accumulation of productive capital is an exception in human history.

> When capital is well invested it grows with interest on interest, an exponential formula that also applies to biological growth under favorable conditions. With a modest rate of interest, say 1% per annum, the value of the initial capital is increased only by about 11% in ten years but grows 27-fold in a hundred years and 20,000-fold in a thousand years. (In biological processes the interest is not added annually but continuously, and growth is even more spectacular.)

The key to the creation of capital is trust, not to say faith in the future. Uncertain conditions are detrimental to confidence and preclude long-term risk taking. If the economic environment – the government, customers, debtors and suppliers – is deemed unreliable, then nobody is keen to invest, except possibly in short-term, speculative ventures.

Any order is preferable to anarchy and general unrest. The ultimate consequence of this logic is the complete order and predictability of a totalitarian state. Utopian thinkers from Plato to Thomas More (1478–1535), Tommaso Campanella (1568–1639), Karl Marx (1818–83) and H.G. Wells (1866–1946) have envisaged comprehensively administered societies, where an enlightened and well-meaning elite governs evermore for the good of all. (Marx and Engels imagined that the state would eventually wither away.) Later, we will discuss these questions in more depth. Here it suffices to say that all attempts to reduce to practice such flights of fancy have failed, not least because of insufficient, or even negative, capital formation.

Our aim then, is to define an order that achieves decentralized economic decision-making combined with a sensible central government. Every successful variety has one thing in common – private property. The earliest form of property is the possession of a piece of land. Primitive tribes defend their territory collectively and the territorial reflex is also widespread among animals.

> Animals that defend their territory seem to have a psychological advantage over the interloper, who usually retreats if the animals are anything like matched in strength. John Maynard Smith (1920–2004) suggested an interesting explanation in terms of game theory. In a territorial conflict, the individual can either act as an aggressive hawk or a timid dove. But the best strategy is bourgeois: play hawk in your own territory and dove in your neighbor's. This way, extended conflicts are avoided and in the long term everyone is better off.[8]
> Defense of territory has a parallel in evolutionary biology. Most spe-

cies of plants and animals have their own competitive survival tactic, an ecological niche (not primarily a physical territory) to which they are adapted and where they can hold their own against invading species. If two or more species are confined to the same niche, only one will survive. This causality is called Gause's Law after the Soviet biologist G.F. Gause (1910–86) and applies equally to business economics. If several companies compete on the same market with identical products and strategies, only one company will survive. Diversity in nature and the economy spring from the same logic.[9]

Homo sapiens does not occupy a specific niche; each group copes with the problem of survival in its own competitive way. For the ambitious individual it is imperative to demarcate his (or her) personal possessions from the collective, where most things are held in common. This is an initial step in the transition from a static tribal community to dynamic social structures. Protection of private property is a universal prerequisite for sustained capital growth as well as for individual freedom.[10]

An elementary condition is that people can save their hard-earned coins without risk of bandits or the government (not infrequently the same thing) laying their hands on all available cash. At the next stage the capital can be deposited with interest in reliable savings institutions. When society stabilizes with established rules of the game, the future is fairly predictable and business enterprises can take off, founded on personal or borrowed means.

Our deep-rooted egalitarian reflexes cry out against significant differences in income and property, and put a strain on the social relations of the community. The emotional burden of being poor and confronted with the riches of others may be harder to endure than being even poorer, but without any object of comparison. Differences in wealth will always and everywhere cause resentment. The vulgar logic perceives the economy as a through and through zero-sum game, where the acquisition of wealth is possible only at the expense of people of lesser means. Property is theft exclaimed Pierre-Joseph Proudhon (1809–65) as a young anarchist, although he later changed his mind.[11]

Anyway, populous societies are bound to live with their internal tensions if they want to enjoy the associated benefits. As could be expected, there is a strong correlation between population base, division of labor, productivity and cultural level. The size of the population, and hence the richness of the cultural fabric, is to a great extent dependent on the available territory. This is evident when comparing isolated island communities of varying size.

> R.L. Carneiro has mapped out the correlation in a wide range of native populations. New Zealand with 750,000 Maoris showed the greatest social differentiation, whereas the 40,000 Andamanese featured much less cultural complexity. The Tasmanians are an interesting exception. They occupied the lowest slot, actually without any division of labor, even though Tasmania is an extensive, wooded country.[12]
>
> Some 13,000 years ago the Tasmanians were cut off from Australia by rising sea levels and fell into a vicious circle of cultural regression. When the Europeans arrived in the early nineteenth century, some 5,000 Tasmanians were subsisting mainly on shellfish, and had lost most of their technical skills. They couldn't resist the British colonists, neither could they adapt. In 1824, the odd survivors were moved to the uninhabited Flinders Island, nearby. (The original Flinders Island natives became extinct 4000 years ago) In 1847 the remnant, 46 individuals, were brought back to Tasmania; the last pure-blood Tasmanian died in 1876.[13]

The accumulated intellectual capital, knowledge and skills, is more valuable than the so-called real capital. Material goods can always be replaced, but lost skills, not to mention social mores and morals, are much harder to regenerate.

Important inventions and innovations have frequently been the subject of great secretiveness. Valuable seeds, plants and animal breeds could be perceived as national property and kept out of reach of strangers. The know-how of mining and metallurgy was the joint possession of industrial brotherhoods, and the mediaeval guilds made it a point of honor not to divulge their occupational secrets to outsiders. Military technology has been particularly well guarded.

> Greek fire was the terror of the Moslem navies of the eighth century and the Byzantine fleets won a number of naval battles by setting fire to enemy ships. The napalm-like substance was self-igniting and very difficult to put out. The secret of Greek fire was so well kept that the Byzantines, after half a century of success, seem to have mislaid the formula. Later versions are distinctly less effective.[14]

Economic development is enhanced by the dissemination of valuable technology into the public domain; after all openness is one of the prerequisites of successful plus-sum play. The dispersion of new technology does not merely bring immediate welfare effects, but also promotes new development, sometimes in unexpected directions. Secret knowledge is always stagnating knowledge. On the other hand, the inventor should have the right to enjoy the fruits of his innovation. The patent institution is one solution to this dilemma, although less than perfect. The inventor gains an interim monopoly on his invention, provided he makes all attendant secrets public.

> In 1449, Henry VI granted the first English patent for the process of manufacturing colored glass. Queen Elizabeth granted about fifty patents, though the water closet could not be patented, for reasons of propriety. In 1769 James Watt (1736–1819) applied for his first patent for an improved steam engine. Parliament granted an extension of 25 years for his patent in 1775, and Watt was in a position to make a commercial breakthrough, together with his business partner Matthew Boulton (1728–1809).

The protection of intellectual rights increased the motivation of innovators and facilitated the industrial revolution of England and Scotland. The copyright Statute of Anne (1709) signifies a corresponding support for freedom of speech in Great Britain. Authors were no longer exclusively dependent on rich benefactors or powerful overlords; free public opinion could gain momentum.

Private property is one of the mainstays of sustainable capital growth; taxation is another. Without publicly financed administration, the wealthy have to defend their property against all comers. Apart from the basic task of defending the realm and maintaining internal peace, taxation has been used and abused for a variety of different ends. Warfare, the splendor of princes and the redistribution of income and wealth have been never-ending drains on the treasury.

Taxation has an inexorable tendency to ascend toward a maximum yield. There are an unlimited number of more or less deserving objects of government spending, irrespective of the system of government. Taxation is increased until tax evasion and capital flight reaches a level where any tightening of the screws becomes counterproductive.

> The decline of the Roman Empire is reflected, in parallel, by galloping inflation and the burden of taxation. For several centuries, Rome supported itself by extracting the wealth of conquered provinces, but escalating misgovernment led to a crushing level of taxation. When no more money was available, the taxes were arbitrarily collected in kind. It went so far that the Emperor Valens in 368 AD had to issue a decree banning the practice of submitting to serfdom in order to escape taxation.

Easing taxation can actually lead to increased tax revenues. When Russia halved the income tax from 26 to 13 per cent in 1999, the revenues went up immediately; it no longer paid to be involved in intricate and risky tax evasion. It is safe to say that the long-term, dynamic effects were positive too – a high tax rate distorts the economic plus-sum game.

Confiscatory taxation backfires. Capital growth is curtailed, petty bureaucratic control paralyses enterprise and administrative costs skyrocket. Legitimacy is a prerequisite of efficient taxation. Taxpayers have to accept, albeit reluctantly, that they have to pay up for common endeavors. In a small community, public expenditures are easily understood and tightly controlled. With the increase in population and an expanding territory, tax collection becomes more challenging. Transparency suffers and administrative wastage mushrooms.

The objective need for tax revenues tends to increase as society develops. Even if income transfers are set aside, society requires ever more resources for long-term investments in diverse areas – communication, health care, education and science. In principle, however, market related self-financing should be preferred. A rise in the tax rate requires a corresponding increase in the moral capital, to avoid negative consequences. And we have every reason to economize on morality, the scarcest of resources.

Ultimately any accumulation of capital is a matter of postponing the satisfaction of a need – good old-fashioned thrift. When our ancestors made the transition to agriculture and cattle-raising, it was no longer feasible to live from hand to mouth. The same applies to us, their distant descendants. Even if we could contrive to live beyond our means, we would be betraying our responsibility for future generations. A sound economy is a moral imperative.

2.5 The market economy

We have established that a commercial transaction creates an added value that serves both parties. Dividing the joint profit can be a problem, however, and may lead to endless negotiation. A market with many buyers and sellers dealing in the same type of product is a self-organizing system which will establish a generally accepted price level, dependant on supply and demand. That is the theory. The reality is sometimes different.

A taxi service should do as a prototype for a smoothly running market. There is an abundance of clients and service providers, barriers to entry and exit are low, the service is standardized and competition should accordingly be close to perfect. And yet, the taxi service is strictly regulated in most major cities, even in countries that embrace the market economy. Why? A simple answer is provided by game theory (see section 1.2). In a major city a client is unlikely to encounter the same cab driver more than once. The driver therefore has little to lose by fleecing his customer, if the opportunity arises. In a small community where everyone knows everyone else, this is out of question, and it is logical for a driver to uphold his reputation by playing fair.

Like any plus-sum game, a well-ordered market thrives on a measure of trust. A small interacting group can build up their trust capital, particularly if the relationship is long-term, but an open market with many unknown participants calls for an outside authority. Order must be kept, weights and measures must be controlled, counterfeiting prosecuted and so on. All this carries a cost, but in mediaeval Europe markets meant profitable business and competition between rival markets was fierce.

> Market towns levied tolls at the gates as well as various other charges designed to cover administrative costs, and then some! Local artisans had a lively trade and the inns had customers in plenty. A market day was a big feast and the occasion to go on a spending spree. The time and place were decided by the authorities; generally markets were not permitted in the countryside.[15]

A market was usually strictly regulated and organized to serve the interests of tax collectors and the burghers. Free trade was an unknown concept; excessive competition was not tolerated. This attitude is deep-seated. Corporative authority was practiced by sundry fascist states and military juntas in the twentieth century, with trade unions and employers' associations replacing mediaeval guilds. Up to this day, free trade is sometimes curtailed, even in the leading democracies. Everybody likes competition, except when they are exposed to it.

> Competition is in no way limited to the market place. On the contrary, it is even fiercer in politics and within the hierarchies of civil and business organizations. The difference is that a sound market economy is open and honest as is fitting a plus-sum game. Other sectors are obsessed by zero-sum play and the competitive weapons are thus less appealing. Everybody strives for power and money – a place in the sun. Only democracies can keep insolent human self-interest within reasonable bounds.

Rulers and power brokers have habitually distrusted market forces which impudently limit their exercise of power. A market represents incorruptible objectivity that doesn't often serve the particular interests of the powers that be. Ordinary people, customers and consumers, will enjoy a long-term benefit from the market economy, but they are rarely consulted. Anders Chydenius (1729–1803) and Adam Smith (1723–90) were among the first to elucidate and speak up for the common good. Their views gained momentum in Sweden and Great Britain respectively, and contributed to the advance of trade and industry on their home turf.

> Anders Chydenius deserves to be remembered by historians of the market economy. In 1766, ten years before Adam Smith, he wrote *Den nationella vinsten*[*], a well-argued presentation of the advantages of free trade and occupational freedom. As a member of parliament he also introduced legislation that was designed to promote religious tolerance, the freedom of the press and improved working conditions.[16]

The market knows no pity. It can be brutal and strike quickly. Above all, the market is risky and unpredictable. It often affects the weakest in society, but also the privileged and wealthy. The market is an incorruptible bearer of bad news, and hence it is no wonder that the market economy has often taken the blame for real or, more frequently, imagined shortcomings. It calls for continuous change, but people take exception to such strain and effort – the market is never popular.

> Joseph Schumpeter (1883-1950) coined the concept of creative destruction.[17] Economic growth requires change, which unavoidably means that certain products, services, enterprises and trades become obsolete. In a modern economy about ten per cent of the jobs disappear each year, but they are replaced by roughly the same number of new jobs.

What are the alternatives to a market economy? Over the years, planning, regulating, regimenting and rationing have been tried in different combinations. Under severe stress – war, famine or natural disaster – there is often no alternative. Survival is then the highest priority and the outside threat mobilizes solidarity and self-sacrifice which make a planned economy possible. Trade and industry are simplified and schematized, freedom of enterprise and entrepreneurship are set aside.

A barrack economy was (and still is) the more or less conscious ideal of socialist regimes. The military nomenclature is revealing; labor was organized in brigades, great offensives were undertaken, the

---

[*] The National Profit

government acted against saboteurs and enemies of the state, menaces were painted in garish colors. All this may work at a pinch as long as the adrenaline of society is peaking. But the ambitious plans became straightjackets and personal initiative disappeared in a bog of bureaucracy. Sooner rather than later corruption spread its tentacles and value destruction grew to monstrous proportions. Without a grey zone of de facto market economy – barter, garden lots, the black market – daily life would have been unendurable.

> The formation of queues is a certain sign that the market economy isn't working – the Soviet Union is the classic example. Money has lost its value and no longer coordinates the welfare preferences of the economic actors. In other, more understandable words: the fluctuating needs of individuals create a demand that must be balanced against the similarly fluctuating supply in such a way that everyone is as satisfied (or as little dissatisfied) as possible.

After World War II economic planning became fashionable. In the newly independent former colonies, a planned economy in the socialist mould was introduced with verve – with catastrophic consequences. The outcome was much better in Japan, South Korea, Formosa and Singapore, where a framework plan was deemed sufficient and implemented in cooperation with vigorously competing enterprises. However, when a nation is reaching parity with the leading economies it becomes increasingly difficult to set up unambiguous goals. Central direction loses its legitimacy and companies have to shape their own future.

> From the very beginning, the developing countries have received massive aid in the form of advanced technology which has been developed with great effort. They are also in a position to model themselves on successful economic and political systems, though this is a greater challenge. The aforementioned Southeast Asian countries have shown the way and are now at the forefront of development.

A market economy is a complex, self-organizing system, an immense plus-sum game with independent actors who compete and cooperate within a generally accepted legal framework. The ideal market economy distributes the added value in relation to the achievements of the actors; the profit then stands in direct relation to the public benefit. A market is self-regulating and self-cleaning; poor play leads to bankruptcy – what goes around, comes around. Basically, a market produces relevant information about human needs and aspirations, information that cannot be gained any other way.

Like most complex systems, market economies are subject to instabilities, expressed as business cycles. A substantial number of independent actors may have misjudged future supply or demand. They may have invested too much or too little, which, through a series of chain reactions, can lead to drastic price fluctuations, widespread bankruptcies and unemployment. Professional speculators are often accused of making instability worse, but in reality the opposite is true. Profitable speculation always lessens volatility in a market by creating a stabilizing feed forward signal, based on future expectations.

National governments try to adjust their fiscal policy and the interest rate to make remedies, but sometimes the cure is worse than the disease. Wrong timing only increases the oscillations that the government attempts to dampen.

> The time span between a macroeconomic measure and the response of the economy (the dead time) varies from 12 to 18 months which means that in a boom, restraining action usually comes too late. Correspondingly, in a depression the stimulating effect often arrives only when business is already recovering. The trick is to monitor the underlying disturbances and apply pre-emptive action. When in doubt it might be better just to wait and let the self-regulating processes run their course. Restraining rapid change is usually a safe policy, but freezing the status quo will only give rise to destructive economic quakes. These conclusions are even more pertinent for politics where our ignorance is far greater.

As a market grows, so does its complexity but stability does not necessarily suffer. The great depression of the 1930's became a disaster only when the world market was thrown into disarray by new trade obstacles. Today globalization has eliminated local shortages which are a source of inflationary instability, and has also taken to task a great number of local monopolies. The self-propelled machinery of the market economy is reducing poverty and raising prosperity around the globe. Those who have put themselves beyond the pale of globalization are not in an enviable position – North Korea and Myanmar serve as warning examples. In the final analysis, each nation has the economy it deserves.[18]

Chapter 3
Political foundations

Before the Reformation, democracy was unknown in Europe (and the rest of the world), apart from a few free cities and isolated farmer republics. Religious emancipation, Enlightenment ideas and the precedents of Antiquity, paved the way for democratic development, culminating with the American Revolution – actually an evolution. The French revolution was a disseminator of democratic impulses, but it also drove them off course. World War I was the harbinger of a deep crisis. Successive totalitarian regimes put the democracies under severe pressure but, despite an impressive display of power, they fell into their own trap; the all-out commitment of the United States turned the tables. Democracy is the least bad form of government, but also the most demanding; success is directly proportional to the available moral capital.

3.1 The roots of democracy

We have observed that egalitarian reflexes have deep roots, whereas democratic institutions have a shorter ancestry. The early agrarian societies were probably self-governing, but eventually they were overrun by feudal lords, counts and barons, kings and pharaohs. The peasants were bound to the land as more or less dispossessed crofters, serfs or menials. The traditional independence of farmers survived only in distant or inaccessible areas. In Scandinavia the liberty of farmers has a long history; Iceland survived for over 300 years as an agrarian commonwealth, dominated by local chiefs.

Irish monks inhabited Iceland early on, but moved away when the Norse arrived in 874 AD. In 930 the chiefs established the Althing, probably the first Parliament in the world. In the year 1000 (or 999) Iceland converted to Christianity by an Althing decision. But the homespun democracy deteriorated, whereupon internal strife and natural disasters precipitated an economic breakdown. By the middle of the thirteenth century the social order had collapsed and Iceland submitted to Norwegian rule in 1264.

> The Icelandic democracy was probably typical of independent agrarian commonwealths. The chiefs were descended from powerful families and dominated the Althing, ordinary farmers held little sway. Common people were subject to the will of their master, menials and thralls were virtually devoid of any rights.[1]

Switzerland is another example of the self-determination of free farmers, periodically stimulated by the incursions of feudal lords. In 1291, the original cantons united in a defensive league and gained one military success after another. Subsequent history was played out as Europe in miniature – internal strife and warfare, conflicts of language and religion, conquest and retreat. Finally, in 1848, a loose federation was born – a portent of, and a prototype for, the European Union.

The Greek city-states and the republic of Rome were sources of inspiration for the builders of modern democracies. Ancient Greece was a testing ground for virtually any conceivable kind of government; Aristotle presents a lucid typology and a detailed analysis of the alternatives in *Politica*. He disapproves of the democracy of his day – direct popular rule – and arrives at what he calls lawful democracy where errant public opinion is constrained by a strong constitution.

> Aristotle tries to make an objective evaluation of the contemporary political systems, with a view to specific recommendations. He makes a heroic effort to combine his axiomatic assumptions with a wealth of empirical material in order to reach valid conclusions regarding the utility of different forms of government. Revolutionary propensities, female emancipation, musical education and foul language – sundry issues great and small are grist for his mill and re-emerge in fluent writing. As with his expositions on physics, the reader is unsettled by a descriptive superficiality. The occasional profound insight tends to drown in the detailed rendition of self-evident trivia – a characterization that also fits much of today's sociological writing.

All political practices were tried out in ancient Greece; demagogues, aristocrats, oligarchs, as well as tyrants[*] had the opportunity to test their brand of government. Carefully reasoned constitutions were applied but real stability remained elusive. Women, foreigners and slaves were in any case excluded from the political arena. In Athens, no more than ten per cent of the male population had full civic rights. Pericles (c. 495–429 BC) introduced a law in 450 BC, stipulating that to qualify as an Athenian citizen, both parents had to be Athenians.

---

[*] In Ancient Greece a tyrant was just a ruler who had seized power and he often enjoyed popular support.

In contrast to the Greeks, the Roman republic favored evolutionary progress which started well before 509 BC, when the Etruscan overlords were expelled. Tradition was the guiding light; if in doubt *mos maiorum*, the way of the ancestors, was normative. The unwritten constitution of Rome proved very durable and magnificently weathered the enormous strain of the Punic wars (264–146 BC). In the end, the successes proved the bane of the republic. Social tension erupted in civil war (88–82), a slave rebellion (73–71) and an extended power struggle between the leading military commanders (49–31). From there, only a short step remained to imperial autocracy.

> Rome never came close to democracy, neither in the Greek nor the modern sense. Originally, power rested with three hundred senators; the people's representatives played second fiddle, though they had a right of veto on certain issues. But an unwritten code curtailed the abuse of power among senators and patricians. Moreover, the rights of Roman citizens were protected by detailed statutes and courts of law of reasonable integrity. Plebeians were free to earn money and make a career, and new families could be introduced to the senate. Cicero (106–43 BC) was such a *novus homo* and rose to consular rank despite the handicap.
>
> The political system was buttressed by a considerable amount of social capital. People with political clout or wealth were supported by a large number of clients, who formed the political basis of their principal. And the principal, often a senator, had a personal responsibility for the welfare of his clients, a kind of social security with deep roots in human prehistory. To win wider support among the population you had to be generous in your dispensation of entertainment and sumptuous food and drink. Early on in his career, Julius Caesar (100–44 BC) went deep into debt in order to bolster his popularity.

The barbarian invasions eventually crushed western Rome, but introduced a more democratic form of government amid the chaos. The Germanic peoples were used to electing their own chiefs and kings, and their primitive sense of justice protected the rights of free men. The linguistic, political and legal interaction between the Roman and Germanic heritages was to put its mark on the future Europe. Byzantium and its successor, the Turkish Empire, did not foster any democratic impulses, nor did Russia under Mongol domination.

The last Germanic incursion into Italy came 568 AD and the invading Lombard governed most of the region until 774, when they were defeated by Charlemagne (742–814). Self-governing city republics appeared in northern Italy in the early Middle Ages. The first Doge of

Venice was elected in 727 but political power soon gravitated to the merchant aristocracy. The same pattern was repeated in Genoa, Milan, Florence, Pisa, Padua, Ferrara and Bologna which, unlike Venice, all had their origins in Roman cities.

The city republics of northern Italy became a fertile ground for economic and political innovation and an inspiration to the budding trading cities north of the Alps. Soon, most of them were able to establish relative independence from regional feudal lords. In Germany, many Hanseatic cities became sovereign states in the nominal Holy Roman Empire. The cities were a refuge for undesirables and dissenters; the jurisdiction of the regional princes ended at the city walls. The Hanse even managed to create a strong international confederacy and faced down both kings and emperors.

In the late Middle Ages social unrest increased. In the fourteenth century the climate deteriorated, most arable land was already under the plough and the economy stagnated. War and famine took their toll. To top it all, the Black Death descended on Western Europe in 1348. An estimated 25 million people, a third of the population, were struck down. Popular risings erupted in France (1358) and in England (1381), where the revolt took on religious overtones.

> In 1376 John Wycliffe (1324–84) began his sermons against the wickedness of the times, the profanity of the church and the corruption of the popes; the Bible ought to be the supreme guide. He was accused by the church authorities, but influential patrons achieved his acquittal. The Bohemian Johannes Hus (1369–1415) embraced the ideas of Wycliffe, but was less fortunate; he was duly burned at the stake for heresy. After two decades of fighting, the moderates among his Czech followers reached a modus vivendi with the Emperor and the Catholic Church in 1436.

From Wycliffe and Hus a straight line can be drawn to Martin Luther (1483–1546) and John Calvin (1509–64). The Reformation carried a democratic message, but served initially as a tool for the kings in their attempts to centralize power. In the sixteenth and seventeenth centuries the nation states managed to incorporate the old free cities, though many important privileges were preserved. In the Netherlands though, the cities took over most of the political power and established a liberal merchant democracy.

> The seventeenth century were the glory days of the Netherlands. Despite constant warfare on land and at sea, the Dutch became the leading trading and maritime power as well as the vanguard of political

and religious tolerance. Newspapers gained wide popularity and censorship was light, in stark contrast to the neighboring countries. Political power, however, was the reserve of the wealthy burghers.[2] The Friesian agrarian republics were more democratic – the old saying "every Friesian is an aristocrat" speaks for itself – but they lacked political influence on the national stage.

The Reformation galvanized the quest for democracy. The Dutch war of liberation from Spain was also a fight for religious independence. In England too, the struggle against royalty took on religious overtones. Charles I was beheaded in 1649 and the date marks the first parliamentarian seizure of power, although the democratic legitimacy of the Rump Parliament was questionable, to say the least.

The Restoration of 1660 notwithstanding, the House of Commons eventually established its authority. But far into the nineteenth century, the franchise remained very limited with a heavy bias against the cities. At the onset of the French Revolution, Great Britain was, along with Sweden, the only constitutional monarchy of any dignity. Together with republican Netherlands and Switzerland, they formed a rather unimpressive platform for democratic development in Europe.

3.2 The democratic breakthrough

The Renaissance saw the re-birth of classical antiquity in new and revolutionary forms. The equality of all men before God was implicit in the message of Jesus, but it was not clearly stated until the Reformation. Later on, the evolving humanism reinterpreted the charitable message of the gospels. Scientific advances enhanced the skepticism and rationalism of the enlightenment philosophers. All this and more besides combined to prepare the ground for a fundamental decentralization of political power. This did not, however, take place in Europe, but in the virgin soil of the British colonies in North America. Actually it was not a revolution, but a carefully reasoned evolution.

In 1776, the Americans declared their independence and simultaneously, human rights were proclaimed as the basis of democratic rule. The following year the articles of confederation for the United States of America were approved. A federal constitution was adopted in 1789 and is still in force. The constitution limited the powers of the Union to certain clearly stipulated tasks. The state governments retained most of the political decision-making, including electoral legislation. The right to vote was quite extensive but, as a matter of course, did not include women or slaves.

Subsequently the US Constitution has been augmented with twenty-seven amendments. The first ten, called the Bills of Rights, were approved straight away en bloc in 1789. Slavery was abolished in 1865 and women were given the vote in 1920. The senators were originally elected by the state assemblies and served as a kind of Ambassador to the capital, but have been elected by popular vote since 1913.

The French revolution broke out in 1789 when the third estate, mainly representing middle-class taxpayers, took over the government and displaced the king, the nobility and the church. The peasants or serfs, forming the great majority of the population, had no representation, but egged on the revolution together with the urban proletariat of Paris. The revolution was a consequence of financial mismanagement, the incredible blindness of the upper classes and the fatal hesitation of Louis XVI. The revolutionary ideas got a boost from the American struggle for independence, which had enjoyed the enthusiastic political and military support of France – mainly to annoy Great Britain.

The overthrow of the government immediately acquired a brutal character when the weak regime proved unable to maintain order in the capital. An excited mob took to the streets and decided to force their way to the Bastille, releasing seven prisoners and massacring a number of jailers who had already laid down their weapons.[2a] It was not the last time the street parliament would be used for the ends of the extremists.

In *The Old Regime and the French Revolution* (written in 1856), de Tocqueville depicts how the revolution was the ultimate consequence of administrative centralization, which started already in the sixteenth century and led to the deterioration of local self-government. Hasty and half-baked reforms on the final stretch only made things worse. He says: "I cannot help feeling that had this revolution, instead of being carried out by the masses on behalf of the sovereignty of the people, been the work of an enlightened autocrat, it might have left us better fitted to develop in due course into a free nation."

This is not the place to dissect the drama of the French revolution, instructive though that may be. Suffice to say that irrespective of the wildly fluctuating opinions, political power inexorably drifted from the National Assembly into the hands of ever smaller coteries, committees and directorates to land in the lap of Napoleon Bonaparte (1769–1821). The revolution further accentuated centralization and France still struggles with the ills of the traditional concentration of powers.

After a deluge of self-deceptive oration, new constitutions, ruthless bloodletting and new ladies fashions, the French had exchanged one incompetent monarch (Louis XVI) for an even weaker specimen (Louis XVIII). On the credit side we must recognize the metric system, a better judicial system (the Code Napoleon) and an improved administration. The peasants gained possession of the land they tilled, and the interests of the middle-class could no longer be ignored but the social tensions remained. In France, the revolution was sacrosanct until 1978, when François Furet deflated it in *Penser la Révolution Française**. He declared tersely: "The revolution is over."

The French revolution put the ideas of enlightenment into undeserved disrepute and did democracy a disservice. Europe was saddled with the reactionary Holy Alliance and even worse, a romanticized revolutionary ideology that poisoned reform efforts, particularly in the more backward countries. Idealistic self-sacrifice, intellectual arrogance and fixation with physical terror were to erupt time and again in senseless acts of violence. When a revolution is necessary, it is unfortunately impossible and when it is possible it is unnecessary – the powers that be are already open to reform.[3]

> The fate of the Russian revolutionaries in the 19th century is the most depressing and also the most fatal example of misguided idealism. Revolutionary self-righteousness was acted out to the hilt against the representatives of the Tsarist government – the more reform minded they proved to be, the harder they were hit. The best and the worst of East and West created a witches' brew that eventually threatened civilization itself.
>
> National fanatics have other goals, but their methods are identical and the result sometimes equally catastrophic. Finland had one lonely assassin, Eugen Schauman, who in 1904 committed suicide after shooting Bobrikov, the Russian governor general. The deed was inconsequential, whereas the Black Hand, a group of Serbian conspirators, launched the First World War when they assassinated the crown prince of Austria on 28 July 1914. Anyway, a suitable *casus belli* would have presented itself sooner or later.

Democratic ideas may have achieved wide dissemination through the French revolution, but practical democracy was sorely neglected. Napoleon introduced advanced constitutions wherever he went, but as Benjamin Franklin (1706–90) pointed out in his confrontation with the British Parliament "No power, how great so ever, can force men to

---

* In English *Interpreting the French Revolution*

change their opinion." When Europe receded to become a democratic backwater, the United States was the obvious vanguard, and thence the twenty-six year old Alexis de Tocqueville (1805–59) traveled in 1831. *La Démocratie en Amérique* was published in two volumes in 1835 and 1840.[4]

> de Tocqueville had secured for himself and his friend, Gustave de Beaumont, an official mission to study the local prison administration. They did write a detailed report, but the real objective was to study the democratic form of government and its potential application in Europe. The two friends traveled all across the United States for nine months, covering 11,000 kilometers including a detour to Canada.

de Tocqueville shows a deep understanding of the spirit of democracy, its prospects and advantages as well as its pitfalls and limitations. Despite his clear political convictions, he approaches the subject matter with commendable objectivity. We will return to de Tocqueville's observations and conclusions on a number of occasions. For now it suffices to quote his dry comment on the fact that not even free Negroes had a vote: "The majority claims the right not only of making the laws, but of breaking the laws it has made."

In 1848 all of Europe came down with revolutionary fever, beginning in France. After a relatively bloodless revolt, the constitutional monarchy was replaced with a liberal democratic regime which declared universal suffrage. (de Tocqueville served a short term as foreign minister in 1849). After various pirouettes, the democratic disorder was replaced in 1852 by a new emperor, Napoleon III. A military defeat at the hands of the Germans was required to restore democracy, but only after serious convulsions during the Paris Commune of 1871 which aimed at the establishment of a socialist republic.

Other countries were spared traumatic events of this magnitude, but one country after the other enacted reforms in a democratic direction. In Great Britain, a Reform Bill was passed in 1832, but it still excluded two thirds of the male population from the franchise. In 1867 most males with a permanent residence were granted the vote; in 1918 women over 30 years of age got the franchise but complete equality was gained only in 1928.

The expansion of elementary education was an advance comparable to electoral reform. Widespread literacy is a precondition of modern democracy; there is a striking correlation between the level of education and social progress. In Europe, one country after another introduced obligatory education for children.

Scotland was first in the field in 1561 when the newly established Protestant Church of Scotland proposed free education for the poor. In 1633 the Scottish Parliament translated words into deeds by introducing a new tax to finance the project, and at the turn of the century the greater part of the population was literate. The Scottish Enlightenment followed in due course half a century later, featuring luminaries such as David Hume (1711–76) and Adam Smith. The American Puritans, too, valued basic education and appreciated higher learning as well. Harvard College was founded in 1636, sixteen years after the pilgrims landed in Massachusetts.

Up to the First World War (1914–18), Europe was the scene of unparalleled prosperity. The Great Powers had divided the colonies between them; world trade expanded under Pax Britannica; industry, art and science flourished; social integration proceeded at an increasing pace. The arrival of democracy and the democracies seemed an irreversible fact. The twentieth century thoroughly disproved this optimism. Democracy was facing a momentous challenge.

3.3 Democracy in crisis

How could things go so wrong in Europe? In retrospect, the First World War seems a completely meaningless event, an orgy in irrational minus-sum play. The United States had its own cataclysmic experience in the Civil War of 1861–65, but then at least the clash of interests and opinions was serious and easily understood.

If we rank the belligerents according to the degree of democratization, a pattern can be discerned. The most authoritarian regimes, Austria-Hungary and Russia, were also keenest on starting a fight; both harbored hopes that a popular, external conflict would augment the tattered prestige of the respective dynasties and put a lid on internal ferment. Austria was particularly keen, although it wasn't anticipating a great European war. Serbia had to be punished though, preferably by conquest, and Austria would not be restrained by its German ally. Russia was allied with France, but had actually no interests of its own to protect. Yet the Serbs were a sister nation and the Tsar would have lost face if he had not intervened.

Germany had nothing to gain from a war; the war aims were invented only after the fact. Wilhelm II had close relations of family and friendship with both the Russian and the British royal houses and at the last moment wanted to stop the outbreak of hostilities. But the German Chief of Staff, von Moltke, announced coolly that the mobilization could not be interrupted. To change the Schlieffen Plan in order to attack Russia rather than France was even more impracticable. The Emperor gave in. His prestige would not have survived an about-turn, which in any case might have spelled military disaster.[5]

War broke out with a seemingly inevitable inner logic. France was naturally obliged to defend itself and a spirit of revenge after the 1870–71 defeat was also evident. Great Britain, the most stable democracy, needed more time to reach a decision. The probable victory of Germany and its overt ambition to challenge British naval supremacy finally decided the issue, and the British Empire went to war in order to preserve the continental balance of power; the German occupation of neutral Belgium made manipulating popular opinion all the easier. The United States only joined the conflict in 1917, provoked by the German submarine offensive, and brought the war to an end.

Although all the belligerents came to see the futility of war, there was no way to make a reasonable peace. Victory presented the only way to compensate, at least psychologically, for the enormous losses. The democracies survived the ordeal relatively intact, while the three empires that caused the misery, all crumbled. Semi-democratic Germany survived as an unstable democracy, but Austria-Hungary fell apart. Russia was subjected to social collapse and sank into barbarism.

> I have dwelt in some detail on the First World War because, on account of its boundless stupidity, this conflict is a symptom of a deeper malady. When war broke out, the enthusiasm was great in the capitals of the belligerent nations, except for London. Young men viewed war as a test of manhood, a way to escape the boredom of the daily drudgery. The war can also be viewed as an atavistic paroxysm that reduced a looming over-population and gave vent to suppressed, sexually charged aggressions. But such pop-psychology only scratches the surface. A thorough diagnosis is high on my wish list.

The war in Europe was followed by hunger, unemployment, inflation, social unrest and the Spanish flu, which swept across the world and killed tens of millions of people, many more than the war. The communist dictatorship won the day in Russia, even if the world revolution stopped at the borders of the Soviet Union. But the fear of communism promoted fascism, first established in Italy. In Germany and Japan, democracy succumbed in the wake of the great depression. Totalitarian ideologies started to penetrate the remaining European democracies. Young people were not attracted to soft humanism or bland democracy, and the will to defend their country touched rock bottom.

In contrast to its predecessor, World War II (1939–45) seems inescapable. The treaty of Versailles was an open invitation to revenge; the United States chose isolation; the League of Nations was an empty gesture. The clash between peaceful democracies and dictatorships bent on world domination was inevitable. Fortunately, a test of strength between Joseph Stalin (1879–1953) and Adolf Hitler (1889–1945) was just as unavoidable, the Molotov-Ribbentrop pact notwithstanding. Even so the summer of 1940, when Winston Churchill (1874–1965) alone and isolated defied the enemy, indicates the darkest hour of democracy.

In the autumn of 1939 Finland was in an equivalent position, alone against a formidable enemy but without the sea or a navy for protection. I remember very well how, on the 30th of November the first day of the winter war, I watched the Soviet bombers approaching Helsinki from bases in Estonia, only fifteen minutes away. But a democracy, large or small, is a difficult adversary if the people believe in their cause. The Soviet Union had to content itself with a partial victory. Finland survived and pulled through the war and the vicissitudes of the post-war period avoiding occupation and with an intact democratic system.

Without a heroic military effort (92,000 fallen) the country would not have survived, but in the end diplomacy proved decisive. Between the world wars, Finland had gained considerable goodwill in the west. Particularly in the United States, Finland was known as the country that pays its debts – rarely have amortizations produced a better payoff! When Britain and France threatened to come to the rescue in 1940, Stalin decided to avoid friction with his future allies. In the summer of 1944 a similar scenario was played out, only now Stalin's concern was the United States. Finland could wait for a more propitious moment. It never came.[6]

Churchill was justified in his faith in victory. When Hitler and Stalin finally clashed in the summer of 1941 and Japan had pulled the United States wholeheartedly into the war, the outcome was evident. The atom-bomb arrived only to deliver the coup de grace to Japan. The democracies were not out of danger, however. Stalin only paused for breath and proceeded to get his own nuclear weapons. Eastern and central Europe were under Soviet domination, Western Europe was bombed out and wide open to communist infiltration. Even Britain was subject to radicalism.[7] Later on, China fell to communism and most of the third world seemed headed in the same direction.

Without the United States and President Harry S. Truman (1884–1972) the game would have been up.[8] He realized that a reiteration of the isolationist policy after World War I would have left Stalin an open field and eventually put the United States in an impossible position. The Marshall Plan and NATO gave Europe a shot in the arm, while a resolute re-armament put paid to Soviet military advances. The resolution of the United States was tested in Korea, where Truman brought communist aggression to a halt and also drew a line to warfare by refusing General MacArthur the use of nuclear weapons.

Truman's containment policy was not spectacular. It required both patience and firmness, but would prove surprisingly successful. The erstwhile mortal enemies, Germany and Japan, not only came into the democratic fold but turned into the best of allies. Overall, the expansion of communist dictatorships was stopped, with Cuba as an irritating exception. The Vietnam War (1964–73) was an embarrassing failure, a mini-crisis where American arrogance brought on a fiasco.

> An American business acquaintance told me at the time; "see how powerful we are, we conduct a war on the other side of the Pacific but live in peace at home." That's precisely what went wrong. A democracy can't make war offhandedly, particularly not with conscripts. A democracy wants to hit with all its might – here I am paraphrasing de Tocqueville – get it over with and the boys home as soon as possible. Students were mostly exempt from military service and had no way to maintain their dignity apart from opposing the whole business on principle. Mercenaries are good for limited policing operations, but conscripts can fight only if they feel at one with the nation.

During the Vietnam War a latent anti-Americanism first came to the fore in Europe, but the Soviet menace muffled the protests. Despite the tension, the democratic front held, and eventually began to push the Soviet Union on the defensive. Despite domestic and European protests, President Ronald Reagan (1911–2004) put increasing pressure on the Soviets, who had forced themselves into a political and economic dead-end.[9] The denouement of the Soviet empire came surprisingly quickly and the whole enormous structure collapsed like a house of cards. The world was safe for democracy and the long-standing crisis was over. At least, that's what Francis Fukuyama stated in 1992 in *The End of History and the Last Man*.

3.4 Democratic weakness and strength

Between the world wars, democracy was challenged by totalitarian movements that advocated direct, violent action and the absolute supremacy of the party. The attraction of Fascism and Nazism was based on anti-Semitism and a narrow-minded nationalism. On the left, the mainspring of Marxism and communism was class hatred, that is, institutionalized envy. The pseudo-scientific nature of Marxism also attracted unworldly enthusiasts and intellectual snobs. The democracies exhibited inexplicable irresolution and pitiful confusion when confronted with these totalitarian challenges.

> European intellectuals fell for the leftist ideology almost to a man. It offered a shortcut to power, an irresistible allure to excitable souls with a superiority complex who despised democratic bickering. It was a small price to ignore awkward facts and take everything at face value, thus safeguarding the good conscience of a devoted pioneer of humanity. A long progression of pilgrims to the Soviet paradise weren't deceived, really – they merely saw what they wanted to see. This state of mind can best be described as conscious self-deceit.
>
> While the great number of fellow travelers can be forgotten, the few exceptions are worth remembering. André Gide (1869–1951) traveled to Moscow in 1936 as a communist, but severed his links to the party on his return by publishing a biting criticism, *Retour de l'U.R.S.S.*[*] George Orwell (1903–50) always had his heart on the left, but that is precisely why his sarcasm is so scathing in *Animal Farm,* and why *1984* is such a realistic totalitarian dystopia.
>
> In *Darkness at Noon* Arthur Koestler (1905–83) delivered an eloquent testimony on the fall of communist ideology. He was originally a Zionist, became a communist in the 1930s and worked enthusiastically for the Soviet propaganda machinery. Koestler was disillusioned by the show trials in Moscow, but nonetheless joined the republicans in the Spanish civil war. Only several years under constant threat of execution in Franco's prison provided enough distance to finally settle his accounts with communism.[10]

Nazi ideology represented an atavism, a regression to primal social forms. Communism claimed to stand for a great leap into the future, but in reality found its driving force in the same soil. Practical politics also followed joint totalitarian principles: boundless leader-worship, complete social control, extermination camps, the whole society on a war footing, institutionalized lying – the extremes were converging.

> The extremist threat was met by incredible indulgence. Perhaps agitation and rabble-rousing must be tolerated in the name of freedom of speech, but the revolutionaries were generally handled with kid gloves. In Italy, Benito Mussolini (1883–1945) could unimpeded pursue terror tactics prior to his coup in 1922. One year later, Hitler tried to follow

---

[*]   In English *Return from the U.S.S.R.*

his example. Hitler failed and was sentenced for his bloody putsch, but released after a round year in prison. The communist threat wasn't taken seriously either. Infiltration in labor unions and the civil service hardly met with any countermeasures.

The inborn conservatism of people – political inertia, pure and simple – served as the passive defense of the established democracies. In contrast to the intellectuals, ordinary people were not taken in by the ideological mirages. The man in the street had more confidence in their well-known leaders than in revolutionary demagoguery. To a certain extent, the violent attacks from right and left neutralized each other. Still, the political infection was malignant and many nations succumbed irrevocably.

> Totalitarian ideologies can be compared to infant diseases. A naïve population will inexorably be infected. Long-term immunity ensues if the disease is overcome, but it eventually falls off. Recurrences are usually less serious, but democracies are always prone to new, unknown infections. Unfortunately, there is no way to stamp out demagoguery and populism, lies and deceitful half-truths. We just have to put up with them.

Strong democracies are good at integrating their dissidents. After a few decades, even the angriest of young men may find themselves among the pillars of society. Democracies have a way of exploiting their worst critics, to extract the incipient value and thus neutralize the destructive effect. The best democrats were often former communists, disenchanted with their ideology and therefore best suited to expose it.

> Among politicians we could point at Ernst Reuter (1899–1953), Willy Brandt (1913–92) and Aneurin Bevan (1897–1960). Milovan Djilas (1911–97) was Tito's second in command and supported him in the conflict with Stalin. He made a break with communism in 1957 by publishing *The New Class,* a reckoning with the thoroughly corrupt nomenklatura.
>
> Immediately before the Winter War Arvo Tuominen (1894–1980), the Chairman of the Communist Party of Finland, left Moscow in 1939 to stand by his native country. His defection was an example to the domestic communists and unified the resistance against the Soviet attack.[11]

A democratic society implies continuous, collective learning. Like evolution, it advances by trial and error, step by step even if diverse shortcuts to a brilliant future are eagerly presented and promoted. Ultimately, only experience can give a definitive answer and the feedback is often negative. Stable democracies don't change tack every time the winds of political fashion twist and turn. The most sensible response is often to wait and see.

In spite of an innate conservatism, democracies generally adapt fairly well to both internal and external change. But unlearning is more trying than the learning of new habits, and the best democracies can sometimes be stuck in self-satisfied stagnation. To surrender time-honored but outmoded precepts can be a blow to the occasionally exaggerated self-assurance and calls for a long grieving process.

> Switzerland is an epitome of democracy, but for that very reason it is unwilling to divest itself of traditions, abandon the alpine fortress and join the EU. Norway is also aloof, and complacent to boot but the Norwegians can afford it, thanks to their oil and natural gas. In Sweden, the welfare state has become a holy cow, an object of worship that may not be questioned, much less slaughtered or even subjected to a slimming diet. Swedish neutrality is an unassailable icon, out of touch with current realities. All three countries are convinced they are exemplary democracies, which only makes it harder to adapt to the new realities.

Democratic strength can turn into a weakness, or at least a severe limitation. But ostensible weaknesses, such as tolerance, openness, eternal compromising and slow decision-making hide an underlying strength. When it really matters, the democracies can become formidable opponents. At the dawn of the second World War, the dictators of the day did not expect Britain and the United States to stand up to the burdens of war, but indulged in wishful thinking about depraved and degenerate democracies. Were not the citizens of the democracies loudly testifying to defeatism, social evils and discord in stark contrast to the exemplary discipline at home?

Later on Stalin and his successors had more respect for American power, but were still convinced they could outmaneuver and wear out their main opponent. Stalin had lost his faith in world revolution at an early stage, and based his expanding empire on Soviet military power and political centralization. The monolithic power could not but impress surrounding countries and many, perhaps the majority in Europe, prepared mentally for a communist victory. The defenders of democracy deserve all the more respect. However, the dejection of the cold war and a deficit of civil courage are still lingering. Europe has not yet regained her mental strength.

3.5 Democratic self-organization

The power of the governed over the governors, the circularity of power, expresses the principle of democracy in a nutshell. But the power of the people is open to many abuses – the tyranny of the majority by arbitrary and unjust government. Early on Aristotle made a distinction between law-abiding and lawless democracies. Constitutions provide a limited number of fundamental rules that may be changed only after repeated deliberations and/or by a supermajority. This is to prevent strong but fleeting emotions or miniscule majorities from turning the helm of government to and fro.

> In ancient Athens, all serious matters were subject to an open vote by the citizens. Thucydides (460?–404? BC) tells us how, in 427 BC the popular assembly, egged on by Cleon, decided to punish a revolt in Mytilene by killing every man on the island and selling the women and children as slaves. The next day, calmer counsels prevailed, and the new decision arrived just in time; the assembly deemed it sufficient to execute only one thousand prominent Mytileneans. But a decade later, the sovereign people took the 'Cleonian' view when dealing with a revolt on the island of Melos.

The notorious inconstancy of the Athenians contributed to Plato's misgivings about democracy. This skepticism has been shared by other notable thinkers such as Thomas Hobbes (1588–1679). The idea that the ignorant people might be capable of ruling themselves was deemed absurd.

The American Revolution put these pundits in the wrong. In 1780 all the colonies (later, states) adopted their own constitutions. The existing local self-government was thus transformed into full sovereignty. The step to a union was more difficult. But the hardships of the War of Independence had created a strong feeling of shared destiny and the loose confederation of 1781 was replaced in 1789 by the present system of federal government.

> During the constitutional convention in Philadelphia, the delegates of the sovereign states disagreed on most things, particularly on matters concerning the balance of power between the federal and state governments. But rarely has a political discourse attained such a high standard. After a four-month debate in 1787, a text was drawn up that won general approval. (Rhode Island sent no delegates and subsequently refused to sign.) Ratification required nine states out of thirteen to approve the federal constitution. In many states the fight ran very close

and Rhode Island only ratified the constitution in 1790, after George Washington (1732–99) had already been elected President.

The hard struggle over the constitution ended only when the federalists agreed that it would be supplemented by an unequivocal declaration of civic rights. The ten first amendments to the constitution (the Bills of Rights) were all enacted by the first federal congress and taken together they meet this objective. The citizens are guaranteed freedom of worship and of speech, the right to bear weapons, security of property and trial by jury.

The US constitution follows the principle of a tripartite division of power between the legislature, the executive and the courts, applying the ideas of Charles Montesquieu (1689–1755) presented in *De L'esprit de lois** It puts heavy emphasis on the checks and balances between the different spheres of power. The might of the majority is also modified by the fact that every state is represented by two senators, regardless of the size of population. The senate has considerable powers and a longer mandate than the directly elected House of Representatives.

The US constitution has served as a model for good governance in many countries, particularly in Latin America. We will return later to the question of why the quality of government nonetheless is so variable. Obviously no amount of fine-tuning of the constitution is likely to be helpful.

> James Madison (1751–1836), 'the father of the constitution' and the fourth President of the United States, anticipated Churchill when he looked back on his life's work: "Our government was far from perfect, but less bad than all the others." Modern game theory would have been a consolation to Madison. It shows that a complex set of rules cannot be free from contradictions. It follows that no constitution can provide an unambiguous interpretation in every situation.[12]

The electoral process and the control thereof has always been a stumbling block to democracies. Psephology, the science of electoral proceedings, teaches us that there is no such thing as a perfect electoral process. Every variety has its pros and cons. A democratic choice of the electoral procedure is no solution, because the forms of this election remain arbitrary. There is no uniquely just method of appointing democratically elected representatives for a large collective.

---

*   The Spirit of the Laws

In *Social Choice and Individual Values* (1951), Kenneth Arrow analyses the fundamental difficulties of joint decision-making. He proves that it is impossible to construct a democratic voting system which would unambiguously select between three or more alternatives if certain reasonable democratic criteria are to be fulfilled.

More important than the election protocol, is the integrity of the election. Voter registration, the secrecy of the vote, ballot box supervision, the counting of votes – at every point cheating is possible and mere suspicion is a blow to the credibility of the election. The will of the people comes under a cloud if the sanctity of the election is violated.

We know from experience that neither advanced constitutions nor electoral subtleties decide the viability of a democracy. On the other hand, centuries of learning from joint plus-sum play can create a civic spirit, which is the critical resource of a democratic society. Robert Putnam has produced empirical proof of this causality in a pioneering study.[13]

Putnam compared the efficiency of regional administration in various parts of Italy in the 1970s and -8os, after a major decentralization of the administration. The differences were great, but the reasons remained a mystery until he began to study the historical background. It transpired that the northern regions of Italy, primarily Lombardy and Emilia-Romagna, had a tradition of self-government dating back to the early middle ages. By contrast, southern Italy had been subject to serial repression by Byzantine, Arab, Norman, Imperial and Spanish overlords, without the opportunity to develop even a rudimentary local administration. The correlation between historical experience, civic responsibility, the efficiency of regional government and, ultimately, economic welfare was quite astonishing. Apparently the recipe for successful democracy is the same as for English lawns; just let them lie for a few hundred years.

The Achilles' heel of government is implementing the constitution and protecting vital human rights; even Stalin's Soviet constitution was immaculate. Therefore, the organization and quality of law enforcement, from the Supreme Court down to daily police work, determines if a democracy is to be or not to be. Jurisprudence can be influenced by an all-powerful executive, by wealthy tycoons or by ruthless criminals. The inherent sluggishness of the legal machinery doesn't improve the situation – a court ruling may be endlessly delayed.

Freedom of speech is the cornerstone of democratic government and the media have been the scourge of the rulers ever since the eighteenth century. Even to the point that one might ask whether the fourth estate lacks checks and balances. de Tocqueville says it concisely: "Nothing is worse than a free press, except censorship, of course." Every democratic country has the press it deserves. Media abuses ought to be taken with the same equanimity we reserve for extremist opinions – we just have to suffer them, get used to them and maybe by and by get rid of them.

If the media sometimes go overboard, it is a trifle compared with their important function in society. An early, laudable example is a series of 85 newspaper articles in support of the new federal constitution, published in New York 1787–88 by Alexander Hamilton (1757–1804) and James Madison. These so-called Federalist Papers are a timeless reminder of the problems of democratic society.

> A short passage in the article number 51 is worth quoting. It concerns the concentration of too much power in a few hands: "Ambition must be made to counteract ambition. The interest of the man must be connected with the constitutional rights of the place. It may be a reflection on human nature, that such devices should be necessary to control the abuses of government. But what is government itself, but the greatest of all reflections on human nature? If men were angels, no government would be necessary. If angels were to govern men, neither external nor internal controls on government would be necessary. In framing a government which is to be administered by men over men, the great difficulty lies in this: you must first enable the government to control the governed; and in the next place oblige it to control itself." Apparently, the French revolutionaries did not pay attention to these reflections.

A working relationship between the ruling elite and the great majority of citizens is the key to the democratic plus-sum game. It is the task of the elite to initiate and lead development through an intensive internal debate. If the people fashion their opinions on their own, any change is unlikely. The majority will prefer the old, the safe and the well known, be it a question of the constitution or the system of weights, measurements or money. If the elite is corrupt, depraved or merely passive, it forfeits its legitimacy, loses the initiative and is outflanked by populist movements.

Democracy is the most demanding form of government and it presupposes continuous learning and as well as unlearning. Success is directly proportional to the available moral capital. In the following chapters we will try to come to grips with these elusive but decisive causalities.

Chapter 4
The foundations of morality

Basic morality cannot be derived from long-term self-interest or from fundamental principles.[1] The myth of innocent man, good by nature, is a related illusion that has resulted in many evil deeds. Social capital can structure a small community, but is insufficient as a moral surety for large societies. Human rights touched rock bottom during the French revolution; when the ends justify the means, both liberty and equality are doomed. Karl Popper and Friedrich von Hayek punctured the delusion of an almighty human intellect, and delineated the limits for scientific understanding; tolerance and pluralism are logical consequences of human fallibility. Morality is the minimum factor for success at all organizational levels; a democracy gets the politicians it deserves. Everything can be purchased for money except morality, which has to be employed economically, although it is free of charge.

4.1 Rational morality

Ever since Socrates (469–399 BC) the philosophers have excelled at speculating on the nature of morality and truth. The great ambition has always been to derive, from first principles, a rational morality or rather a more abstract category called ethics. The problem is that impeccable logic tends to deteriorate into a circular argument. Proof of the hypothesis is covertly included in the basic assumptions. Alternatively one ends up with empty tautologies that go nowhere. This is not to say that classical philosophy is lacking in penetrating thought and noble conclusions. But in reality the conclusions first came across as self-evident. Only then did philosophers employ subtle reasoning to deduce the desired inferences from crystal clear assumptions.

The mediaeval scholars perfected this art of sophisticated self-deception. Starting from first principles and supported by the writings of Aristotle they went to great lengths to prove the existence of God and the rationality of Christianity. Baruch Spinoza (1632–77), a non-denominational, excommunicated Jew from Amsterdam, became the unlikely fulfiller of the scholastic program. In his posthumously published *Ethics,* he presents in geometric formalism a consistent worldview and a rational theology, which somewhat paradoxically arrives at a mystical pantheism.

In contrast to his mentor Descartes (1596–1650), Spinoza propounds a metaphysical monism; body and soul are two sides of the same reality. In very general terms, he derives the human psyche from primary forces, such as self-preservation, the will to power (or freedom) and self-realization. The highest form of human happiness is realized through intellectual love of God. Spinoza manages to combine fundamental determinism with an overly abstract code of ethics that, unfortunately, cannot give us much guidance for our daily existence. In an unfinished manuscript he also makes a logically stringent case for the superiority of democracy as a form of government.

Logical flaws notwithstanding, the philosophers of the seventeenth and eighteenth centuries propagated new attitudes and values. Erasmus of Rotterdam (1466–1536) was already a devoted proponent of enlightened humanism, whereas John Locke (1632–1704), David Hume and Immanuel Kant (1724–1804) represent a modern, skeptical view of the world. The so-called Philosophers of the Enlightenment, Voltaire (1694–1788) in particular, were distinguished by their strong social and political commitment. They were the inspiration of both the American and the French revolution and only Marx is their equal in political influence.

Jean-Jacques Rousseau (1712–78) is often regarded as an Enlightenment philosopher, but could as well be placed in a utopian tradition that began with Plato and ends with Marx. Rousseau's thesis of the supremacy of emotions met with the approval of a public that was sick of the rationality of the Enlightenment. Back to Nature became a fashionable slogan, shepherds and shepherdesses were chic, and there was no limit to the idealization of primitive peoples.

> Rousseau is a hyper-exponent of romanticism in all its forms. The myth of the golden age or the lost paradise, populated by moral innocents, is deeply rooted in the psyche of cultured humans. Alas, all attempts to actually return to nature have failed miserably. Nonetheless this particular form of self-delusion maintains its popularity.

In his main political work, *Le contrat social ou principes du droit publique**, Rousseau developed the romantic view of nature into a theory of government. The notion of a treaty between citizens as the foundation of government goes back to ancient Greece (in stark contrast to Rome). Rousseau's social contract is based on a utopian level of

---

* In English *The Social Contract*

morality when all citizens can agree on the common good. He ignores such democratic subtleties as the electoral system, courts and constitutions; decent people live in harmony without such fancies. When it comes to the system of government, Rousseau is remarkably tolerant. Aristocracy, even a monarchy is acceptable, provided it implements the will of the people, the public consensus, *la volonté générale*.

The French revolution was strongly influenced by Rousseau's idea while the fathers of the American Union had fewer illusions about the selflessness of human nature. From Rousseau's social contract a winding but fairly visible path leads to the totalitarian states of the last century. To be sure, the unanimous will of the people was realized in its purest form through a power wielding dictator. The illusion of limitless freedom consistently turns into its opposite.

In modern times John Rawls (1921–2002) has in *A Theory of Justice* made a respectable effort to infer an unimpeachable social morality from fundamental principles. He presents a 'thought experiment' with citizens debating the shape of an optimal society. In order to safeguard objectivity they (or Rawls) assume that there should be no foreknowledge of the health, wealth or social standing of the individual. Under the veil of ignorance the assembled citizens will, according to Rawls, arrive on rational grounds at a set of rules that reflect justice and fair play.

> The rights of the individual are the primary concern, but they are complemented by the Difference Principle. Differences in wealth are acceptable only provided those who are worst off can profit from them. Thus equality is given a definite weight; an improvement in the standard of living is legitimate only if the poorest share in the added value.

Rawls was accused, with some justification, of conducting a circular argument. The carefully deduced conclusions are all too politically correct, and fit perfectly into a liberal democratic frame of reference. Robert Nozick (1938–2002), who in *Anarchy, State and Utopia* represents a more conservative line, was the foremost critic of Rawls, and compelled him to modify his position.

The intellectual adventures of the great philosophers are instructive blind alleys. Only Ludwig Wittgenstein (1889–1951), the premier exponent of analytical philosophy, put a stop to this splendid series of philosophical self-reflections. He pointed out the limitations of everyday language in the context of logical reasoning: "Every honest philosophy is self-destructive." Solely mathematics, and above all formal logic, can maintain the absolute mental purity that is essential to avoid logical fallacies. In *Tractatus Logico-Philosophicus* (1921) Wittgenstein methodically demolishes the hope of deducing anything but tautological truths from a priori arguments. The final conclusion has gained fame: "Wovon man nicht sprechen kann, darüber muss man schweigen."*

> A few years earlier Bertrand Russell (1872–1970) and Alfred North Whitehead (1861–1947) had published *Principia Mathematica,* a grandiose attempt to explain the foundations of mathematics in mathematical terms. Wittgenstein pulled the rug from under their reasoning. No system is self-explanatory, but rests on axiomatic faith. In 1933 Kurt Gödel (1906–78) followed up this insight by deducing mathematically that no interesting formal system (e.g. the number system) can prove its internal consistency – that is its reliability.[2]

I claim that it is impossible to arrive at a tenable ethics on purely rational grounds, just as it is impossible to pull oneself up by the hair. Still Wittgenstein was himself a peripatetic morality. For him the insistence on intellectual honesty was absolute and he strived to follow that precept in his own conduct. At Christmas time 1937 he approached his friends in Cambridge to confess hypothetical infringements. Among other things he may have dodged his Jewish origins. When he met with the incredulous exclamation "What is it? You want to be perfect?" His reply was "Of course I want to be perfect."[3]

4.2 Social capital

Social structuring takes place in any group, where individuals have an opportunity to build mutual trust. As the group grows it tends to split up, just as spontaneously; there is no longer room for all the inflated egos. To keep a large group together, a sufficient joint interest is called for. In addition you need either a charismatic personality or an ingrained ethic to subdue conflicts and keep the free-riders in check, safeguarding the plus-sum game.

> Water distribution on Bali is a classic example. Water is a scarce resource, which is channeled to the rice paddies. In the rolling landscape water allocation is a potential source of conflict and cooperation is essential. The distribution system is managed by a *subak,* a self-organized group of about 200 rice-growers who cultivate a total of about 50 hectares. They have their own democratically elected functionaries who take care of channel maintenance and water management. The

---

* Whereof one cannot speak, thereof one must be silent

subak decides on planting, fertilizing, pest control, seed purchasing etc. The farmer at the end of the water channel is preferably elected distribution manager.

The *subak* is an ancient organization and is still involved in religious ceremonies, pilgrimages to holy places and harvest festivals; a hermaphrodite rice deity is included in the ceremonial. The water cult was served by priests and temples who stood for the legitimacy of the regulations and who arbitrated between the *subak*s in times of drought. The government wisely did not meddle in this smoothly running system. The *subak*s have proved very adaptive. They accepted the short stemmed 'miracle rice' with enthusiasm even though they had to change the methods of cultivation, harvesting and storage. Traditional technology has given way, but the cooperative spirit has survived.[4]

There are plenty of similar examples of low-level self-government. Common land and communal fishing rights have often been exploited in a sustainable way by applying mostly unwritten rules for collecting firewood, pasturing or fishing. One example, studied in detail, is the lobster fishing in Maine where the quantity and quality of the lobster catch has been preserved by self-organized fishermen.[4a] The so-called tragedy of the commons – the senseless over-exploitation of resources held in common – is actually a variety of the prisoner's dilemma. It is avoidable if sufficient social capital can be deployed. Unfortunately, unfettered grazing and slash-and-burn agriculture is destroying the very basis of cultivation in many developing countries.

Easter Island in the Pacific, some 2000 km from the Chilean coast, is a dramatic example of social self-destruction. According to the latest chronology the first inhabitants arrived from eastern Polynesia to an earthly paradise around 1200 AD. But overpopulation, deforestation and soil erosion led to ecological disaster and internal strife. When the Europeans arrived in 1722, all the colossal stone statues were overturned and the local alphabet, the only one in Polynesia, was forgotten. The population had shrunk to a fraction of previous numbers and cannibalism was not uncommon.[5]

Why did things turn out so disastrously? Was the maximum population of about 10,000 individuals too large for the available natural resources? Similar societies have managed very well in Polynesia. Was the island too isolated? The Hawaiian archipelago is just as far from the nearest land. The cultural regression brings to mind the Tasmanians, who declined with their environment intact. Perhaps we should not view the ecological disaster as the reason for the social collapse, but rather as the consequence.

In a broader context social capital may intensify existing conflicts. A street gang has a tight internal discipline, but the significant social capital is rarely applied for constructive purposes. The strong social bond switches to open hostility when you move on a couple of blocks; without superimposed structures, social capital can turn destructive. The political party system is a hotbed for similar minus-sum games.

> In the first decades of independence, political passions threatened to break up the new North American union. The violent party infighting made the first US Presidents despair. In his farewell address, George Washington warned the listeners of the ruinous effects of the party spirit. "It exists under different shapes in all Governments, more or less stifled, controlled, or repressed; but in those of the popular form it is seen in its greatest rankness and is truly their worst enemy."
>
> In 1805 John Adams (1735–1826), the second President of the United States, is querying the state of the Union: "… are ambition and greed, flattery, pettiness, avarice, lust for riches, contempt for principles, the spirit of party and faction the governing motives and principles?" Not for the last time would a standard bearer of democracy feel disgust at democratic practices.

Social capital comes into its own in a small community by structuring human cooperation and providing safety and support. Workplaces can both generate and destroy social capital, depending on the corporate culture. The number of voluntary associations – religious bodies and trade unions, party organizations, societies, clubs, guilds etc. etc. – are seen as a measure of the social capital and should also correlate with the political viability of a society. The traditional democracies are abundantly blessed in this respect.

> In 1831 de Tocqueville wondered about the proliferation of voluntary organizations in the United States. He says: "In my opinion, nothing deserves more attention than the educational and moral associations of America." In 1997 there were 22,901 nationwide voluntary organizations registered in the US. The local associations must number in the millions. The Nordic countries are not far behind. In 2000, Finland, a country of about five million people, had 115,000 registered voluntary organizations with a total membership in excess of 15 million.

Thus democracy seems to be thriving in its old, core countries but the activity, enthusiasm and commitment of the citizens can't be discerned from these figures. In *Bowling Alone (2000)*, Robert Putnam analyzes the changes in the social capital of the United States in recent decades.

He finds discouraging trends in civic engagement. Particularly the re-shaping of family life by protracted television viewing has had a nega-tive impact.

While Putnam can only see a few bright spots, Richard Florida pres-ents a rejoinder in *The Rise of the Creative Class* (2002). The social capital is replenished by footloose but gifted youngsters – high bo-hemians – gravitating to centers of attractive diversity. Putnam and Florida may both be right when describing the present social dynamics from diverging angles. Neither takes the Internet seriously as a new source of social contacts; whether it will build up social capital is in-deed an open question. In any case, Americans still appear willing to volunteer for social work.

> In the late 1980s I was invited to the home of a business acquaintance in a small Long Island town. In the middle of Sunday lunch, the fire bell rang and the host ran out to join the local fire brigade. He was back in three quarters of an hour. A false alarm as it turned out.

Alexis de Tocqueville asserts that local self-government was at the root of American democracy. A closely circumscribed society, where every-one knew everybody, took full responsibility for the management of local issues. There were no self-evident leaders; all functionaries were elected. Leadership did not necessarily bring any material gains, and corruption was unthinkable due to the strict social control. The com-munity practiced democratic self-organization based on the available social capital, which in turn increased in a virtuous circle of communal learning. All of this was founded on ancient Anglo-Saxon tradition and was supported by a puritan faith.

> Latter-day communitarians, such as Amitai Etzioni, construct a nos-talgic social philosophy around the merits inherent in a small com-munity. *The Spirit of Community* (1993) and *The New Golden Rule* (1996) emphasize, as the titles suggest, the importance of morals and cooperation. Yet the darker side of man is passed over. In *From Empire to Community* (2004) Etzioni extrapolates his visions to a world com-munity – a misguided attempt. (cf. chapter 14.4)

As a rule social capital has only a limited range; it is a necessary but insufficient precondition for a strong democracy. Extended states re-quire something more to prevail – broadly accepted values, a consti-tution, common aims or enemies. Social accord captures the entire nation only in times of a national crisis, like war. Then we are all close together, all in the same boat, displaying spontaneous solidarity. Conversely, a crisis exposes the actual loyalty structure of a country.

> In the 1850s the political divide in the United States over the slave question became an open sore. The dividing line between federalists and anti-federalists had been there all along; loyalty to the home state was strong. Before the outbreak of the civil war in 1861, President Abraham Lincoln (1809–65) offered Robert Lee (1807–70) the post as commander-in-chief of the Union army. Lee wanted to think it over. He was a federalist (a Whig) and did not appreciate slavery, but first and foremost he was a Virginian. When Virginia joined the Confederacy, he followed the flag of his native state and became the greatest general of the South.[6]

Perhaps social capital could best be described as a network of personal relations and loyalties. The network may be tight and strong, but when turned in on itself it does not strengthen society at large. The essential, nation-building networks are extensive and varied. They not only cross party, class and occupational categories, but also country boundaries. Moreover, they transcend workaday relations and special interests. It takes a certain amount of idealism, an urge to improve the world, for social forces to be translated into constructive political activity.

4.3 Freedom and human rights

The first draft of the American Declaration of Independence was written by Thomas Jefferson (1743–1826), who later became the third President of the United Sates. In the solemn introduction he had included equality among the human rights, but that part was deleted. The colonial delegates felt it sufficed that everybody was born equal and had an inalienable right to life, freedom and the pursuit of happiness.

> Even this wording was stretching current reality, a fact that could not have been lost on slave-owning Jefferson. The situation is typical for democracies in general, and in particular for the United States of those formative days. Uncomfortable questions were brushed under the carpet, and the unattainable was not touched upon in order to save the achievable. The best is often the enemy of the good.

The French revolutionaries had no such inhibitions. They wanted to realise their fantasies immediately and had a boundless faith in the power of the human intellect. They were also overestimating the moral capacity of man. Or rather, following Rousseau, the revolutionaries felt that morality was irrelevant in the coming ideal society, since man was good by nature. Freed from repression, hunger and other ills, he would spontaneously use his liberty to maintain equality and live in brotherhood. Humans, in short, were perceived as misunderstood angels.

The great leap has failed time and again in human history, ending up in regression and cynicism. Without firm institutions and a credible political foundation even the most engaging visions are defiled by selfish and power-hungry cynics. Human rights without the corresponding obligations, is just so much empty verbiage. In order to realise rights, there must be a mutual trust between the parties concerned; solidarity depends on reciprocity.

> To receive help without resentment is even more difficult than helping without compensation. In the long run, one-sided dependence will lead to the moral degradation of both parties. Only children and the acutely distressed can receive unconditional help without a feeling of shame. In a welfare society social support is marketed as a right, and is thereby easier to accept. Even so the outcome is an unhealthy relationship that corrodes self-esteem, reducing the individual to a supplicant.

de Tocqueville has the following to say about the ability of a future democratic society to repress its citizens and to demote them to dependent serfs: "The power of the state is absolute, detailed, regular, considerate and mild. It would be like the authority of a parent if, like that authority, its object was to prepare men for manhood; but it seeks, on the contrary, to keep them in perpetual childhood... the government provides for their security, foresees and supplies their necessities, facilitates their pleasures, manages their principal concerns, directs their industry, regulates the descent of property, and subdivides their inheritances: what remains, but to spare them all the care of thinking and all the trouble of living?"[7]

de Tocqueville blames the principle of equality, which we already have marked as an obstacle on the road to social development. If equality is not balanced with freedom and cooperation with competition, even a democratic society stagnates and crumbles. Politics then prevents the individual from interfering in his own affairs.

> In Europe, modern labour laws intrude upon the right of the individual employee to decide on his or her work efforts. Detailed rules govern the amount of overtime, stipulate vacations, impose breaks etc etc., supposedly to protect the workers from ruthless exploitation by employers. This was once a legitimate aim, but now the justifications are

turning to protection from stress and burnout. The recklessly industri-
ous worker must be shielded from himself; society and its bureaucrats
always know best. But there are indications that people are becoming
fed up with the protection.[8]

Fortunately the authorities are frequently less than diligent, which
makes room for a grey area of generally accepted but, strictly speaking, illegal behaviour. This can have serious consequences. Public morals degenerate into hypocrisy, the rules are bent, the cheats gain sway.
In short, liberty loses its legitimacy.

Political freedom is a catchphrase like equality, and the excesses of
liberty can be equally destructive. A significant part of our legislation
serves to protect the weak from assault by people who are physically
or financially superior. The laws both curtail and safeguard freedom
– they attempt to resolve the collisions between the rights of different
individuals. Equality before the law is a democratic imperative, but
does not solve the complicated equation of liberty and equality. Equity
can only be laboriously achieved in everyday politics and court decisions which, ultimately, are a reflection of the moral foundations of a
society.

Personal freedom is our most precious possession and it is scrupulously guarded by all democratic constitutions. But freedom requires
self-discipline. Otherwise discipline is imposed from the outside, ultimately via the negative feedback of society. The parents, first of all,
should with firm and loving consistency prepare the growing individual for personal freedom. Even with the best available upbringing, there
is a disconcerting time lag between our mental and physical maturity.
Surprisingly often young people abuse their newly gained freedom in
willful self-destruction.

> How far do we have the right and duty to interfere with or prevent
> juvenile play with life-threatening behavior? Can we and should we
> try to shield grown up people from their own mistakes. Should they
> take full responsibility for the consequences of their actions? Where do
> you draw the line and how do you handle the crossover from child-
> hood restrictions to adult freedom? These, and many other questions,
> problematize personal freedom, even when he or she is not infringing
> on other people.

Any parents wish their children well, but they cannot protect them
from freedom. We can try to teach, to show an example and to impart
fundamental values to steer the children away from the slippery slope,
but the price of liberty always includes an inestimable risk. Societal ac-

tions are needed to compensate for parental shortcomings and also for sickness, disability and other blows of fate. But when the inalienable basic rights include housing with all modern conveniences, foreign vacations, a broadband Internet connection and regular sex – a life of undisturbed tranquility – we are not far from de Tocqueville's dystopia.

> The welfare society has managed to increase the citizen's dependence on government care, but has failed miserably in their upbringing. The impertinent welfare consumers continue, against all advice, to increase their consumption of unhealthy food, alcohol and drugs. The only vice that is definitely declining in the western world is smoking (girls and young women excepted). We've simply had enough of it. As usual the upper classes show the way, for better or for worse. And among them, it is no longer socially acceptable to smoke.

The life style of some individuals may have negative personal or social repercussions but does it justify state interference in strictly private matters? Do not human rights include the predicament that each and everyone is allowed to be unhappy in his or her own peculiar way? When we consider suicide and assisted death these issues come to a head. If someone really wants to die, who are we to refuse that choice? Here freedom is not confronted with equality but with caritas – human concern, empathy. But when care is mired in government bureaucracy, it can assume grotesque shapes. The individual is reduced to a mental case that is incapable of comprehending his or her own good.

The unlimited freedom of any individual will by necessity intrude on other people. Apparently an indisputable truth – or so one might assume. A committed anarchist would disagree, however. For certain, anarchy is generally understood to mean lawlessness and disorder, but the anarchist ideology only claims complete freedom from authority and social structure in general. Orthodox anarchism is a variety of the back-to-nature concept with its fictional solidarity in peace, happiness and freedom.

> When nineteenth century fanatics began a series of attacks on prominent people, the practice of anarchism did not violate the freedom of fellow citizens, but instead their life and limb. The latter day red brigades were responsible for a similar wave of assassinations in Germany and Italy, inspired by the student uprisings of 1968. Marxism too aimed at a society of plenty, where government had withered away. The outcome was a government machinery that took over everything. The eminent ant researcher E.O. Wilson puts it succinctly: "Good idea, wrong species."

With depressing regularity Utopian visions metamorphose into a brutal contempt for every human right. The magnificent objective justifies any and all means. The Founding Fathers of the United States, for their part, exhibited profound insight into the predicament of state-builders. Our circumscribed freedom and our limited comprehension should be focused on the choice of the fundamental rules of the political game. The aims that are achievable and worthwhile will materialize during the democratic process in their proper priority. In this context at least it is the means that justify the end – not the other way around.

4.4 Core values

But which are the good means? High-flying phraseology may easily turn into smoke screens for eminently selfish purposes, as we have seen in the preceding chapter. Core values should act as palpable guidance for society. Laws and norms regulate our daily life, whereas values are less determinate but superordinate rules of the game. They direct lawmaking and serve to inform us in the choice between right and wrong. Core values structure a chaotic social environment where the final consequences of our actions are basically unforeseeable.

A functioning democracy presupposes not only respect for, but the daily application of, these fundamental meta-rules. Otherwise human rights, constitutions, laws and regulations will remain a long, long row of dead letters. The situation is worsened by the inherent contradictions of all abstract rule systems, which opens the door for intellectual self-deception. In general, crude self-interest can rather effortlessly be reconciled with things fair and square.

> A single inconsistency in a mathematical system has the consequence that anything can be proved and the whole system becomes meaningless. The ambiguity and fuzzy semantics of ordinary language provides ample opportunity for the accomplished polemicist. Outside the realm of rigorous mathematics, logic becomes a poisoned weapon.

We sorely need to admit our inherent fallibility and tendentious egotism. Want of humility blocks the way to peaceful coexistence as well as to scientific insights. Karl Popper (1902–94) constructed a complete philosophy of science around the fallibility principle. He also came forward in defense of democratic values in *The Open Society and its Enemies* (1945).

The book is a reckoning with totalitarian doctrines starting with Plato. (By the age of sixteen, Popper was actually a convinced communist but one year later he left the party.) According to Popper, the fallacies are linked to a delusion he calls historicism. The course of history is assumed to follow established laws and thus becomes predestined and predictable. This is related to the misdirected ambition of the social sciences to reach out for the strict causality of natural science. Of course Popper does not deny historical connections but the future is always indeterminate and open to human influence.

In an essay, *On the Sources of Knowledge and Ignorance*[9], Popper analyses the all too human attitudes which hamper or even prevent the acquisition of knowledge. At issue is an unscientific stance inherent in the human psyche. We refuse to call prevailing beliefs or established authority into question and stay comfortable in the safe cocoon of public opinion. Ironically, elderly scientists often have great difficulties in adjusting to the radical ideas of younger colleagues.

Complexity is the key concept in understanding the limits of our insight. The calculable portion of reality comprises only a small fraction of our sphere of experience. Most of it is embedded in complexity of varying degrees, precluding any detailed analysis and long-term prediction. Knowledge of the fundamental rules of the game is of little avail when the complexity of the system overwhelms all imaginable computing power. The potentially chaotic nature of most complex systems aggravates the problem. Minimal differences in the initial conditions then exert an immense leverage.[10]

The weather is an instructive example of a chaotic system. Tomorrow's weather cannot be foreseen in detail. But it can be approximately simulated by collecting a sample of data on the present weather and play out the well-known physical interactions in a suitably programmed computer. Extending the time horizon increases the uncertainty and the forecast soon becomes meaningless. Even if we could observe every single atom in the system, quantum physical uncertainty would spoil the calculation.

World history is without doubt an enormously complex process and therefore unpredictable. Even if we can assert a satisfactory understanding of the interplay of natural forces, *Homo sapiens*, the main actor, will remain an enigma. In human affairs, cause and effect as well as fault and merit are permeated by uncertainty, and irrevocable judgments should be adjudicated only with great discretion. Thus tolerance and freedom of expression are singularly well-founded meta-rules for human intercourse. In democracies they ought to be inviolable, but in a crisis they are often heavily compromised.

> In the United States the internment of American-Japanese citizens during the Second World War serves as an example of basic democratic principles being set aside in a putative emergency.[11] The overreaction of McCarthyism has created much more hullabaloo, notwithstanding the real danger of communist infiltration, compared with a Japanese fifth column after Pearl Harbor.

Although social tolerance became generally accepted, the totalitarian fallacy encroached on trade and industry. After the First World War, economists were impressed by the performance of the centrally planned war economy, and after the Second a fresh wave of socialism swept through Europe. It was not understood that a modern dynamic economy is a complex system, which cannot be micromanaged without a serious loss of efficiency, not to mention creativity.

Friedrich von Hayek (1899–1992) was the first to touch this sore spot. He showed that only a free market – the interplay between supply and demand – can deliver the vital information which is required for setting prices and directing production, investment and product development in a sensible manner. Only the market can coordinate the needs, priorities, decisions and resources of millions of people. Like political democracy, the market is an emergent phenomenon, which calls for a legal framework, just as a democracy needs a constitution.

> Hayek was among the first to understand that communism and Nazism (or socialism and fascism) are kith and kin. In *The Road to Serfdom* which appeared in 1944, he demonstrated how economic regulation step by step leads to restrictions in personal freedom and a totalitarian regime. The *Constitution of Liberty* (1960) is an apology for freedom, an intrinsic value which deserves the highest priority and must be protected at any cost. *The Fatal Conceit* (1988) is Hayek's last work, a definitive reckoning with the fallacies of socialism.
>
> Hayek is a renaissance personality with exceedingly broad interests. He was a pioneer not only in economics, but also in political science, psychology and the methodology of science. Hayek perceived clearly the dissimilarity between the natural and the social sciences, including economics. Scientism is his label for the presumptuous abuse of the methods of natural science in the study of human interactions. Physics envy is a brutal expression for the same circumstance.

Popper's historicism and Hayek's scientism both tackle the inability of social scientists to understand and admit the complexity of their research object; science is the art of the explainable. Popper and Hayek were good friends and shared core values (and a Viennese background), but even so they disagreed in many respects. Together they illuminate the problems of complex reality from slightly divergent points of view. Under magnification this approach becomes an expression of pluralism, which not only accepts but welcomes a multiplicity of aspects, opinions and values in order to secure a comprehensive and objective inquiry. Pluralism is tolerance in a positive perspective.

> In politics, objectively reasoned decisions are elusive, despite the incessant weighing of arguments. Politics is the art of the possible; that is the art of making compromises. Conflicting interests have to be resolved and, what is even harder, irreconcilable values must somehow be reconciled. Compromise is tolerance reduced to practice. If a single party controls the parliament the government may look monolithic, but the unavoidable compromises are then made backstage, within the party hierarchy or between party fractions. Moreover, democratic decisions have to be acceptable to the opposition, albeit with much gnashing of teeth. Only dictators are not obliged to compromise.

On the surface, practical politics is all about zero-sum play but at bottom it is a very demanding plus-sum game (see chapter 6). Honesty and openness are therefore highly rated. Linguistic usage reflects our understanding of the political game and its actors. Horse-trading is a zero-sum game where the parties usually extract a gain at the expense of the taxpayer. Statesmen are perceptive plus-sum players, whereas run of the mill politicians myopically look for temporary advantage. Democracies have a tendency to despise their politicians, but the truth is that parliaments and politicians faithfully reflect the moral level of the electorate. A democracy has the politicians it deserves.

4.5 Morality – the critical success factor

Honesty prevails is an old maxim which according to many of the worldly-wise has been thoroughly falsified. Even so I dare to insist that it holds, at least approximately, but under two conditions. Firstly the societal rules of the game have to meet a set of reasonable criteria, which are adequately fulfilled in modern democracies. Secondly society must hold a sufficient proportion of honest people. These conditions are dynamically coupled. Men and women of good will produce good rules of the game, which accordingly foster honesty.

Unfortunately the dynamics also act in reverse. If societal morality falls below a critical level, corruption will escalate and the cheats and tricksters take over. Then dishonesty prevails in all its sundry varieties, and the state and democracy enter a vicious circle. Undemocratic societies inexorably descend into corruption, which may give democracy a chance. Devoted plus-sum players can find each other in small coteries and initiate reforms. Alas, the upshot is often rebellion and revolution when power-hungry cynics take over and only make things worse.

The cogency of democracy depends on its powers of self-purification and self-renewal. A relatively modest amount of moral capital is sufficient to start a virtuous spiral of self-improvement. In a democracy it is not necessary for the majority to possess remarkable civic virtues. Neither does the socially committed minority face superhuman moral demands. But more and better morals go hand in hand with societal success and prosperity. This thesis is empirically validated.[12]

> Morality is difficult to gauge but the level of corruption in a country certainly stands in inverse proportion to the moral standards. On the other hand, the negative correlation between corruption and the gross national product is statistically valid within a broad margin. Thus the level of morality correlates with the economy and the overall state of society. It is no coincidence that Finland has persistently been vying for the top ranking as both a corruption-free and a successful, business-friendly country.
>
> All these estimates are liable to substantial error and the economists have yet to appreciate the decisive role of morality. The fashion has been to ignore important but hard to measure factors, thus preferring precise but erroneous computations to approximately correct cogitations. Nevertheless, the importance of civic virtues is nowadays generally accepted and is beginning to affect the policies of development aid; nowadays the World Bank links the eligibility for soft loans to the perceived corruption level. It is high time for common sense to prevail.

Small groups rarely encounter problems with cooperative morale but when an organization grows, morality becomes a scarce resource. The demand for moral capital grows with the size of the community. Conversely, the moral resources set a limit for the attainable size of an organized group if it wants to preserve its integrity and competitiveness. A socialistic society presupposes an unrealistic level of morality among its citizens; the moral demands are directly related to the degree of socialism.

> Communism and anarchism are vain attempts at abolishing human egotism; only angels can make a success of a communistic state. Even the first Christian congregation in Jerusalem could not sustain its origi-

nal collective community; St. Paul had to come to the rescue with financial assistance from other, less unworldly congregations.

The Swedish welfare society has been erected on the foundation of a stable, Lutheran morality, which has been inculcated by generations of preachers and stern government. This strong moral base has made possible a high tax level and public care from cradle to grave. But the rot is now setting in. Sick leave is abused on a grand scale, and cheating is touching the apex of a society which used to be beyond reproach. A slow retreat from socialism is in the offing, but if it does not succeed social decay will propagate irrespective of administrative countermeasures.

A successful plus-sum game, not least a democracy, will always provide scope for free-riders who sponge off the loyal players. In a small community free-riders are easily identified and get short shrift. But when society and the state machinery grow, so does the temptation to cheat despite intensified public supervision. In an expanding society bureaucracy anyhow tends to proliferate, which open the gates for inefficiency and corruption. A far-flung, complex community cannot take on extensive social responsibilities without weakening its moral spine and thus its future prosperity.

From the very beginning the constituent states of the federation of The United States of America jealously guarded their rights, and the subsidiarity principle was scrupulously observed. Everything which was not explicitly a federal concern was managed by the states. Latterly the balance has, in the name of equality, shifted towards joint responsibility. Accordingly the federal welfare programs are about to inundate the taxpayer. It is politically very difficult to decentralize by pushing responsibility back, closer to the consumer of welfare services.

The European Union has so far kept income transfers within reasonable bounds, and social policies are, for the time being, the unequivocal responsibility of the member states. A healthy competition is emerging in the area of taxation and social benefits; in the end the efficiency of the public sector is on the line. But the pressure is increasing within the Union to synchronize tax and social policies. Demands for global income transfers are also on the rise, never mind the political corruption they have fomented in the receiving countries.

Morality is a success factor in all big organizations. Skeptics may take exception especially in the case of profit-seeking companies. But I maintain that in a modern market economy the moral capital of a company is the decisive competitive resource.[13]

A corporation is an island of planned economy in a sea of uncontrollable market forces, a small society where morality is indispensable for the efficiency of the internal plus-sum game. High morality reduces control requirements, improves motivation and encourages creative cooperation. It facilitates delegation and activates under-utilized resources. The organizational hierarchy is flattened, which promotes flexibility and adaptability; the company can promptly adjust to changes in the business environment. Better morality brings higher productivity and profitability – the well being of the personnel is thrown into the bargain.

The crucial qualities for a leader of such an organization are honesty, fairness, integrity – three words which encircle a single concept – morality.[14] A good leader selects and attracts competent and honest people. He assures fair play and administers the vital trust capital, internally and externally. Cynical climbers, schemers and slanderers are dismissed or reined in. All energy is concentrated on the task at hand, customer satisfaction and the success of the company.

> I have myself tried to apply these management principles as chief executive and later on as chairman of the board in diverse companies. To write them down is simple but their implementation is anything but problem-free. In my experience it was much easier to direct a fruitful internal plus-sum game as a vice-president. Executive power isolates; you are not the same team member as before. The information flow is censored and essential knowledge concerning the personal qualities of your associates is weeded out. The most onerous task is to fire a close friend, the most difficult one is to check your own ego; you are yourself the source of the moral deficit.[15]
>
> In the 1990s I had the opportunity, as Chairman of the Board, to contribute to the creation of a vast and very successful corporate structure in the former Soviet Union, centered in Russia.[16] From the very beginning we understood that expatriate management would not work and went for delegation to local management. This was a 90% success and the auspicious emancipation of the local leaders is one of the most rewarding experiences of my career. They were happy to have escaped the old Soviet style of management – I am boss, you are stupid – which has its adherents in the West, too. Genuine leadership incorporates full respect for all subordinates as fellow human beings; you must never repress, ridicule or humiliate.

The reduction of sustainable business success to a single factor – simple morality – is indeed a bold hypothesis.[17] I hasten to add that it can hold strictly only in the ideal case where the rules of the game are perfectly tuned to the common weal. But I maintain that our present democracies are close enough to the ideal for good morals to pay off handsomely. Even so we must take into account the weakness of moral sentiments in comparison with inveterate self-interest.

"Economize on love" says the Nobel Laureate James Buchanan, one of the founders of the public choice school of economics.[18] The Founding Fathers of the United States followed this prescription when they carefully worked out the checks and balances of the constitution. 'Love' stands here for morality and work ethic, which are always in short supply and are not to be wasted. To avoid overburdening our scarce moral resources, the self-interest of company executives as well as of politicians should, as far as possible, be aligned to the greater good. The personal advantage of the chief executive or the management must not conflict with the corporate interest, and this should in turn serve the long-term prosperity of the whole society. The rules of the game should create a firm link between corporate profits and societal benefit.

> To preserve a sense of fairness and to support our fragile morality, material incentives and sanctions must be thoroughly balanced; otherwise they can become counterproductive. Incentive pay can be a poisonous chalice for company executives. Some mechanisms induce even the civic-minded to act as if they were selfish. In general, high pay as such is not a dependable motivator, but unfair payment is unfailingly demotivating.[19]

Thus morality is a bottleneck, the critical success factor in the development of society as well as business; success stands in direct proportion to the available moral capital. Fierce competition in an open market guarantees that, in the end, most of the added value flows back to the consumer. Successful economic development eventually generates an abundance of fixed capital creating more room for other investments – education, science, art – which again drive capital formation. Scarcity of capital does not fetter entrepreneurship any more. Money can provide access to key production factors like technical know-how, efficient marketing and professional management. Money can buy everything – except morality. That comes for free.

Chapter 5
Spiritual foundations

Faith in man, despite his moral frailty, is the specifically democratic utopia. Evil is due to lack of goodness – complacency and passivity – which gives egomaniac fraudsters free play. Despite severe setbacks, Western society has during the last centuries undergone a moral evolution. Its finest expression is the success of science; truth is what remains when all untruths have been exposed. "You shall not bear false witness" is a commandment which does not presuppose full insight, only good will. The craving for truth will always call faith in question but they both have the same root; the intrinsic value of truth is a question of faith. Christianity ennobles the ancient golden rule, which is a reformulation of the reciprocity principle. The command to love your neighbor, enemies included, defines a mission well worth failing. God is what he is – after all idols have been peeled away.

5.1 Faith in man

What is this? Hasn't there been enough harping on morality and ethics? Maybe, but we are now looking for the sources of morality, casting about for answers to the knottiest questions. How does morality arise? Why does it tend to fall off? How should we generate or rather regenerate this vital resource?

We just certified that morality is for free. Yes, in the same manner as fresh air, clean water, personal freedom or equality before the law. When they exist we don't take note, but their absence is all the more distressing. In its societal aspect morality may be free (it is not taxed after all) but, in contrast to the immoral, the morally burdened individual is always giving up some real or at least potential benefits. There is no morality without a readiness to sacrifice, without something more important than oneself. Our selfish interests are without doubt the overwhelming factor in our decision-making, but we are in pursuit of the small remainder of altruism which goes beyond rational self-interest.

Moral cowardice, lack of civil courage, is the original sin of democracy which undermines its very existence. 'Why me?' asks the dispirited man. 'Why not you?' is the appropriate answer. We are all responsible but the person in charge must not expect any thanks; unselfish efforts are their own reward. Harry Truman once said: "It is amazing what you can accomplish if you do not care who gets the credit." Benedict of Nurcia (354–430), the founder of the Benedictine Order, introduced a shorter formulation: "Pray and work".

Homo sapiens is according to all Christian doctrines evil by nature. The Protestants with the Calvinists in the lead are faithfully following the Church Father St. Augustine, and hold that man is incapable of doing good on his own, that is to maintain his morality. The Catholics are less unconditional and the Orthodox are even more lenient. Socialists of all hues have, on the contrary, unanimously agreed that man is good by nature. There is nothing wrong with man. All evil is due to unfavorable circumstances or historical encumbrance.

The empirical fallout is unambiguous. Credulous trust in a faultless man inspires the worst in him (somewhat less in her), whereas man convinced of his moral decrepitude paradoxically is capable of taking responsibility for himself and his environment. I have already referred to the contrast between enlightenment-oriented, but Christian, Founding Fathers and Rousseau-inspired French revolutionaries.

On the whole, the Enlightenment philosophers were anti-clerical but not anti-religious. 'Crush the Infamous' exclaimed Voltaire and meant the church, not the faith. The Catholic Church always carried totalitarian aspirations, and the struggle with the Protestants hardened the conflict with the freethinkers until the Jesuit Order was dissolved in 1773 (it was resurrected in 1814). In the turmoil of the French revolution, the wholesale abolition of received religion became *de rigueur*. In a vain effort to fill the spiritual void, a cult of Reason was introduced. It was soon followed by the short-lived worship of a Superior Being concocted by Maximilien Robespierre (1758–94), the incumbent dictator.

When allied with the state, Protestant churches could be quite intolerant, but the American colonies were not encumbered by nobility or an established clergy. Many States had their own religious order but in the Union, state and religion were strictly separated. The leading Union Fathers were freethinker Christians without dogmatic liabilities.

Benjamin Franklin serves as an example. He was a pacifist ("I never heard about a good war or a bad peace") and was in 1752 already laboring for the merger of the colonies under British supremacy. As a young man he decided that truth, sincerity and honesty should be his guiding stars. Franklin is the archetype American, who coined the expression 'Time is money'. He was an optimist systematically working on his self-improvement, and a pragmatist with the ambition to practice his Christian faith with a minimum of fuss.[1]

In our time, totalitarian doctrines have consistently preached the un-limited sovereignty of man, his will and ability to implement the good society all on his own. Communism and Nazism both did their utmost 'to practice the absence of God', to use an expression of C.S.Lewis (1898–1963). Socialism tries to apply Christianity without God; com-munism did the same but with the additional feature of atheism as the state religion.

The myth about the intrinsic good of human nature builds on self-deception at the highest level. Its proponents actually imply that *their* good will is above any criticism. The masses are backward, simple-minded and do not understand their own good. Well-intentioned or not, they are exceedingly undependable and must be controlled by ideological masters.

> Here another paradox emerges. Totalitarian regimes are utterly con-temptuous of the common man and his opinions. Nevertheless José Ortega y Gasset (1883–1955) in *La rebellion de las masas** (1930) demonstrates that dictatorships represent the true will of the People, broken down into its smallest common elements. Anti-Semitism, chau-vinism, class hatred, everything which appeals to the lowest instincts of man is exploited to keep the masses in check. The arduous learning of democracy – the pursuit of 'love' – has turned into its opposite; the elite and the people are actively engaged in a vicious circle.

Elites typically feel ambivalent towards the people, and not without cause. The people are by definition ignorant and stubbornly conserva-tive as has already been noted; the great majority acts as a keel, but also as a drag to the ship of state. There are often good reasons to set aside the will of the people. Democracy is always inconvenient for the elite; it is tiresome to laboriously seek approval for policies which appear self-evident.[2] Superficially elitism is not compatible with democracy but a self-defined elite of morally responsible citizens is in-dispensable for the survival and progress of democratic states. Yet the Nietzschean individualism of an Ayn Rand must be rejected.[3] Its em-phasis on exceptionalism and personal heroism leads into a dead end.

Democracy cannot be built on pure reason. From the beginning the Christian message was an incitement to democracy, especially in its Protestant version. Before the face of God we are all equally valuable, equally sinful. Additional leaps of faith were required before the po-

---

* In English *The Revolt of the Masses*

litical equivalence of men was accepted, step by step. Faith in democracy equals faith in man and – considering his manifest shortcomings – faith in a superior power. Democracy was the only option in sustaining the hope for a society fit for human beings, a city on the hill.

> Blaise Pascal (1623–62), theologian, physicist and mathematician (he constructed the first calculating machine) is famous for his wager argument. Irrespective of God's existence it pays to wager on His actuality; there is everything to win and nothing to lose (Pascal worked out the argument in more detail.)[4] A similar argument can be presented for the belief in free will; if it is counterfactual nothing is lost. This desperate and uncompromising train of thought reflected the plight of democracy at the time.

Edmund Burke (1729–97), a British statesman, sympathized with the struggle of the American colonies but detested the intellectual presumption of the French revolution. He stated that "people are qualified for civic freedom in exact proportion to their moral inclination to restrain their desires". But what is the source of morality, indispensable for our vital self-control? Egotistic desires can be controlled only if something better, more valuable and more interesting is in command. Absolute freedom is a meaningless chimera. Man is in chains if he believes himself to be completely free. But if he humbly gives up his position at the center of the universe, he has the liberty to choose the cause he wants to promote and the master he wants to serve. Then, and only then, will the moral capital of society increase.

Once again de Tocqueville is ahead of his times. He infers that democracy in the United States relies on the religious inheritance, and boldly generalizes this conclusion to a universal hypothesis: "I am inclined to think that if faith is wanting in him [the citizen], he must be subject, and if he be free, he must believe".

5.2 The so-called evil

Konrad Lorenz (1903–89) has in an eponymous book (*Das sogenannte Böse*) elaborated on animal aggression and its inhibition. The hierarchy of social animals is upheld by ritualistic fighting and submission reactions in order to minimize the costs of injuries and waste of time. According to Lorenz, laughter is a specifically human way of relieving aggression and preserving the coherence of the group. On the whole he tries to relativize evil by identifying it with primitive 'animal' drives, which must be managed competently.

Hate, vindictiveness and greed are distinctly human vices, whereas egoism, self-assertion, lust for power, jealousy and envy are part of our animal legacy. The problem is that negative propensities usually are vital survival factors. The challenge lies in channeling these primary energies into constructive, cooperative play. In game-theoretic terms, evil can be identified with destructive minus-sum games where the aim is to cause havoc, pain and misery. War is the archetypal minus-sum game, a dirty handicraft wide open to self-righteous condemnation.

> Extreme 'principled' pacifism is an oversimplified, self-delusive doctrine – an all too easy intellectual shortcut. Violence is always the last resort, but giving up this option only provides free scope for evil play in all its diverse forms. The dedicated pacifist denies the reality of evil. Evil deeds are just errors, aberrations or delusions of good people, a chain reaction which can be interrupted if we all rise to the occasion.

The right to self-defense is hard to question and without policing, no civilized society can exist. War is justified only if it can be understood as an extensive police operation which maintains or establishes rules for constructive plus-sum play. In other words, war must serve an overarching interest. In the absence of a binding international order, war is always a controversial matter.

> In the eighteenth and nineteenth centuries, the border zone between western civilization and indigenous peoples was a scene for extended conflicts; war emerged as a natural force. The settlements and cattle in the border zone invited unprovoked raids, while the march of colonization was difficult to restrain. It was often impossible to pin down an authoritative negotiation partner on the native side. Bloody punitive expeditions became the best security policy. A superior culture cannot be hemmed in.
>
> In ancient times the shoe was usually on the other foot, though. Over and over again, barbarians robbed and laid waste the existing centers of culture. The Roman attempt to seal off their territory by a fortified line of colonies (the limes) ended in disaster. The barbarian peoples poured over the Roman realm in wave after wave. To take a purely defensive position is to invite attack.
>
> The warring parties have generally had God on their side, even if Hitler and Stalin rashly renounced this ally. Justified interventions are not easily distinguished from self-seeking expansion even with the hindsight of history. The participation of the United States in two world wars is approved, not least because they ended in victory. The Korean War was also widely accepted, whereas Vietnam was considered unjustified even if the mission was the same.

The emergence of conflicts and concomitant wars are spontaneous processes. They dominate the chaotic state of nature by their dismal logic. For inveterate zero-sum players, personal success is wholly dependent on the setbacks of their fellow human beings. Evil is a symptom of the absence of good; it is indifference extrapolated – banal in the terminology of Hannah Arendt (1906-75)[5]. Evil is the default position of nature – if in doubt it is safe to defect. The minus-sum game takes over without anybody actually embracing it.

> Evil is an immensely subjective concept. Everything which threatens us or our dear ones is demonized and perceived as evil, starting with natural phenomena, like hurricanes or earthquakes, to malevolent snakes, bacteria and cancerous tumors. A hated enemy is deprived of all human features and perceived as the personification of evil, while we are quite unaware of any evil if we have the upper hand.

Does evil then possess any objective reality? The theologians have for millennia struggled with the theodicy, but never thought of the possibility of defining away evil from the world. Now, our relatively secure position of strength has changed the perspective. It has become psychologically possible to analyze inferior enemies without hostility (though soldiers in the field probably feel differently), to regard violence and sundry bad behavior as symptoms of mental disease (police officers certainly feel differently) and to blame most that goes wrong on bad upbringing or, as a last resort, on bad genes.

Nevertheless our all-pleasing humanism is open to unpleasant disturbances. Sudden death is not abolished and terrorist attacks bring us intermittently back to reality. We still have to endure the ailments of old age, and cancer remains a major health problem.

> Cancer is a fair model for the metaphysics of evil. The soil for malignant growth is prepared when a cell loses its capability to commit suicide if it goes astray. (Stem cells are inherently immortal and may be a common source of cancerous growth.) A sequence of genetic changes can then transform the immortal cell into a monster, which ruthlessly propagates at the expense of the whole. It becomes unresponsive to cooperative signals from neighboring cells, deceives the immunological system and secures the delivery of nutrients by inducing the growth of new blood vessels. Colonizing cancer cells roam freely, forming fresh metastases. The end result is the proliferation of unstructured blobs of parasitic cells. They have no justification for existence and are the product of blind self-realization – naked cellular egoism destined for death.

Furthermore we are stuck with unequivocally evil individuals, mass murderers, sadists and other tormentors. Many, maybe most of them, are pathologically callous with mental defects which predestine malevolence against others. But the most interesting cases, psychopaths like Hitler, Stalin, Mao & Co., would not have achieved notoriety under normal circumstances. The moral breakdown of society prepared the ground for the cancer-like rise of evil which temporarily became organized, taking over the state machinery.

> The face of evil is exposed in the hellish concentration camps – it is not 'so-called' any more but a naked actuality. When systematized, evil becomes a terrible, commonplace reality. "Arbeit macht frei"*, the motto at the entrance to Auschwitz was in its grotesque hypocrisy a measure of human baseness. In Vorkuta the corresponding text read; "In the Soviet Union work is equal to honor, pride and heroism".
>
> Without belittling millions of other victims of torture and summary executions, Auschwitz, Treblinka, Dachau, Buchenwald, Katyn, Kolyma, Magadan, Vorkuta....stand out as remainders of the unthinkable that must not happen again. But evil always rests under the surface, waiting for our morals to break down.

Most of the people taking part in these crimes against humanity had few scruples to begin with and went morally downhill in the fierce competition with likeminded souls. In such an environment the survivors are paranoids, the first in applying the poisoned cup, the dagger-stab or the neck shot. Habit soon blunts any feelings of guilt while success sanctions all outrages. Let us hope that in Europe this belongs to history, but in Africa we can still witness similar pageants live in the media.

> Liberia was founded by American abolitionists as a haven for liberated slaves. In 1847 the country declared its independence. It was governed with moderate success as a semi-democratic one-party state by American-Liberian powerbrokers. However, the tribes of the hinterland had never been integrated and the discontent erupted in 1980 in a coup d'état. President Tolbert and his closest associates were murdered and Samuel Doe of the Krahn tribe was installed as President. Doe was tortured to death in 1990 by Yormie Johnson of the Gio tribe. The procedure was videotaped and spread for propaganda purposes. Charles Taylor, a man of mixed provenance and the force behind the coup against Doe, took control in 1997 after a drawn-out civil war,

---

*   Work shall set you free

but international pressure forced him to resign. He is now facing trial before an international court for crimes against humanity.[6]

Such events are not restricted to Liberia. Worse atrocities, for instance the mutilation of children, have occurred in other countries, but there the blame can conveniently be thrown on colonialism. The share of bad people is hardly higher in Africa than elsewhere, but in the absence of an adequate political structure they often have a free rein. I am throughout emphasizing the importance of a personal commitment, but under extreme conditions even the most devoted plus-sum players come to grief.

> Ruthless dictators like Stalin can and will keep the lid on. After his death, a slight loosening of the ties provided some wriggling room for determined dissidents. We have every reason to honor the memory of people like Andrei Sakharov (1921–1989) and Alexandr Solzhenitsyn (1918–2008) who time and again put themselves on the line, at high personal risk.

Well-meaning psychologists trace back the evil impulse to an inferiority complex which craves compensation in the form of spectacular deviations from current norms. In *Evil, Inside Human Violence and Cruelty* (1999) Roy Baumeister argues for a contrary interpretation. Evil is linked to a human superiority complex which is wounded by the least affront. His (rarely her) greatness must continuously be affirmed and he can never win sufficiently acknowledgment for his incomparable merits. Human pride and vanity are magnified into megalomania and self-deification.

> Most extremist movements, including Islamic fundamentalism, can be understood from this premise. Islam (or Anarchism etc.) is seen as the manifestly superior doctrine, but real life overflows with humiliations and stands in infuriating contrast to the eschatological expectations. The emotional balance can be restored only by spectacular shows of strength and the attendant publicity.

The perverse logic of evil permeates all minus-sum games and predestines a parasitic, self-punishing course. Evil has no future; left to itself it comes to an inglorious end. But neither can the plus-sum game be perfected without losing its inherent creativity. Perfectionism is not of this world; dishonesty and injustice, anxiety and ill fortune can be minimized but never abolished. All bodily infirmities may be eliminated in the future, but we can never get rid of our spiritual sufferings. Setbacks, privations and sorrows are unwelcome but mandatory – they are part and parcel of human existence.

5.3 Moral evolution

In Chapter 1 we got acquainted with the genetic starting capital of human morality. During the last 5000 years the major part of humanity has managed to organize itself into societies which by many orders of magnitude surpass the population of the original tribal communities. Previously we have established that the minimum demand for moral capital is proportional to the size of the community. It follows that we have achieved a more efficient use of the starting capital and/or we have created additional moral capital during this journey.

Military units have since times immemorial utilized the spontaneous loyalty of young men in prolonged close contact. The hierarchy of the Greek phalanx and the Roman legion can be found in modern armies, with minor modifications. The solidarity between the intimate members in the fighting unit is successively transferred to larger detachments. Uniforms, emblems and signs of rank combined with tough training and battlefield experience strengthen the coherence of the troops and raises fighting morale.

> The moral level of a disorganized mass is far lower then the mean of the individuals. A mob is capable of atrocities way beyond what anybody or at least very few of its constituents could contemplate. The morale of a body under discipline stands, on the other hand, far above what its separate members could accomplish. The history of war abounds with examples of how outnumbered but closely-knit units have defeated a demoralized or disorganized enemy.
>
> Modern nations have done everything within their power to project fundamental tribal loyalty on themselves. Flags and national anthems reinforce the feeling of community. History writing, education, language and culture are exploited for the indoctrination of the population. Regional differences have been systematically repressed in the name of national unity. Many big enterprises are using similar stratagems to cement the loyalty of their employees.
>
> In contrast to most European countries Finland still holds on to general conscription. A broadly based army not only vouches for the continuing existence of the nation, but it is also a societal education for young men (and a sprinkling of women). The enforced fellowship of youngsters from diverse backgrounds levels out differences in society and increases the social capital.

The manipulation of human morale has its limits, though. Despite desperate efforts, functional nation states are thin on the ground south of the Sahara – tribal identity still dominates. The disintegration of the Soviet Union and Yugoslavia shows that not even the total control of the state apparatus over several generations can create a genuine national identity. Nation building, not to speak of greater entities, requires moral evolution – a broadening, deepening and intensification of human togetherness.

It is natural, unavoidable and at bottom fitting that human solidarity is structured according to emotional distance. Generally, everybody is closest to him- or herself. Next come the family, relatives and friends, followed by the social networks, the local community and the nation, with all humanity in the distant rear.

> It is, at least for me, always disturbing to read news features of the type "20,000 dead in an earthquake (or massacre or epidemics...), no American (or British or German...) killed". In the eyes of the editors and the public one or two Americans are more important than 20,000 Chinese or Sudanese or Congolese. That is how we feel, but even so it is unseemly to trot out the lack of compassion so unashamedly.

The heroic efforts of missionaries and physicians in remote countries, exemplified by Albert Schweitzer (1875–1965) and *Médicines Sans Frontiéres*, deserve our respect. Alas, an abstract engagement for distant causes is all too often symptomatic of the evasion of personal responsibility. It is often an attempt at escaping forwards, away from more immediate but awkward and boring tasks at home. To quote Adam Smith's *The Theory of Moral Sentiments*: "The most sublime speculation of the contemplative philosopher can scarce compensate the neglect of the smallest active duty".[7]

Most of the eloquence squandered on universal human solidarity must be heavily discounted. Notwithstanding, a moral evolution is discernable in the longer perspective. It manifests itself not only in nation-building but, despite aberrations, also in the increasing empathy for the suffering of human beings (and animals). In *The Christian Tradition*, a huge work in five volumes, Jaroslav Pelikan has documented how the Christian message has been reinterpreted and re-formed from century to century.[8]

> The dogmatic power struggle was gradually supplanted by human-centered attitudes. The problems of the hereafter – hell, purgatory and heaven – yielded ground to worldly sufferings and hopefulness. When

the confrontation between reformation and counter-reformation was put on the back-burner, the religious idiom became more personalized, intimate and sincere. Pietism and Jansenism are the religious harbingers of The Enlightenment; the Nonconformists prepared the way for democratic reforms.

Humanistic values gained ascendance, and a partiality for the weak was emerging. The witch trials came to an end, slavery was drawn into the limelight, religious tolerance became a norm, freedom of expression an established fact. Freedom of thought was no more reserved for an inner circle of religious experts, but was democratized as a prelude to the political breakthrough. The short history of the democracies could, in turn, be illustrated by a long record of human-centered reforms, from correctional treatment to women's emancipation and social security.

Christian mission, The Red Cross, The Salvation Army and Alcoholics Anonymous are early examples of unselfish efforts outside government purview. The number of voluntary welfare initiatives has since been growing at an improbable pace. The coordination of the support, emanating through numerous channels, has become a problem when major disasters attract all too many Non Governmental Organizations (NGOs).

In step with rising prosperity, the democratic agenda has been extended with a long list of items which serve the common weal. Education for everybody, science and art, aid for developing countries, protection of the environment, all this and more is considered a public undertaking and places demands on the exchequer. Our wealth imparts both the possibility and the obligation to accept long-term moral responsibility.

The catalogue of good causes always grows faster than the available resources. Not least in protecting the environment, the best may once again be the enemy of the good. To restore a fictive state of nature is, in most cases, neither feasible nor morally defensible. References to health hazards are generally red herrings. In developed countries it is rather a legitimate question of aesthetics. Slimy water or foul air are distasteful while biodiversity is beautiful and a value in itself. It's nice that bears, wolves or lynx are roaming the woods.

Moral evolution during the last centuries is a Euro-American phenomenon. Corresponding developments did not take place on other continents. Even though the example of the Occident left some traces, nothing points to the imminence of a comparable societal change. Neither can colonialism be blamed for cutting short such a process – rather the other way round. Haiti, which liberated itself from France in 1804, bears sad evidence.

> Originally the colonies had been risky but lucrative investments, managed as profit-oriented enterprises. At the turn of the twentieth century, Belgian Congo was still a flagrant example of ruthless, commercial exploitation.[9] Yet the old colonial powers had in good time transferred administrative responsibility to government officials. British and French governance was certainly humane in comparison with putative local potentates.
>
> After the Second World War, the colonies became an economic, political and moral liability. The liberation of the colonies was rather a relief for the economies of the mother countries; unfortunately it was mostly too hasty with regard to the democratic preparedness of the newborn nations. Portugal, the poorest and weakest colonial power, was the last to cling to its possessions but it is certainly better off without them.

Europe was during the last century afflicted by a series of moral shipwrecks with concomitant political and social disasters. This trial was probably unavoidable. In the loyalty hierarchy, national allegiance came first and last, which opened the door for destructive minus-sum games. It is hard to see how the political self-importance of the Great Powers or the intellectual arrogance of the European intelligentsia could have been deconstructed without cataclysmic hardships. Europe has passed through a period of humiliating moral learning which has guided us to a new and better course.

More than anything else, the European Union is a moral challenge, a measure of our moral capital, of our ability to play plus-sum games. Under conditions of unprecedented complexity, religions and values must be reconciled, language barriers surmounted, old enmities and prejudices overcome. A clutch of nationalities with century-old traditions of hostility and bad will are forced to agree among themselves and on their relations with the surrounding world.[10]

> Today the Founding Fathers of the EU would have considered all their expectations fulfilled or surpassed. The Union has not only realized an open market economy, converted a couple of autocratic countries to democracy and established a high standard for human rights. It has also served as a model for corresponding endeavors on other continents.

A lot hangs on the success of the European Union and on the arrival of a new, strong and responsible actor on the world scene. The globalization of trade and finance is an encouraging signal of worldwide cooperation in the making, but we are in for a long wait before our moral evolution creates the preconditions for a political analogue.

5.4 Science – an exemplary plus-sum game

What is truth? That is the Pilatus question which science has taken on in fierce competition with myths, superstitions and sundry unfounded but all the stronger preconceived opinions. The internal competition is even harder, though. Every piece of research is scrupulously evaluated by experts in the field, and it can take decades before an adequate consensus has been reached. The balance of scientific accounts is always open to revision.

Cooperation is another pillar of scientific investigation. The results should be published in sufficient detail so that they can be reproduced by skeptical colleagues. Earlier research must be acknowledged, nobody should strut in borrowed plumes. Openness and honesty are self-evident values which, in the ideal case, maintain paradigmatic plus-sum play. Centuries of selfless, cumulative work have produced an unprecedented body of knowledge. The sciences are the present-day cathedrals, built by our best brains and an expression of our innermost strivings.

The scientific community is substantially self-organizing and therefore exemplary also in its social structure. The scientific interest is the pre-eminent uniting force. Transgressions are dealt with internally; ostracism is a sufficient sanction for foul play. Only scientific merit matters; the esteem of colleagues is the highest reward. Money is never unimportant, competition can be severe and foul play is not unknown.[11] Even so, the struggle centers on consistently insufficient grants and on professorial chairs with access to research facilities.

> In the beginning, science was a hobby, a self-contained pursuit by people of substance or enjoying the support of benevolent patrons. Contact with like-minded people was essential but difficult; publication was an even bigger problem. Accademia dei Lincei, the first scientific society, was founded in 1611 with Galileo Galilei (1564–1642) as a prominent member. Francis Bacon (1561–1626) was the first to develop a scientific methodology, and provided the impulse for scientific coteries which in 1660 led up to the founding of the Royal Society in London. Isaac Newton (1643–1727) served as chairman for almost a quarter of a century.

Nowadays the inexorable rise in expenditure and the potential gain has turned science into a public concern. The freedom of science is under pressure and scientists are struggling to preserve their innocence. They are also under attack from another direction. A radical school of sociology asserts that all science is conditioned by the social power structure, verging on well-paid commissioned work and necessarily lacking in objectivity. That was the case at least in Imperial China.

> The Chinese were excellent astronomers; in 1054 they (and the Arabs) observed a supernova which gave rise to the Crab nebula. Nonetheless, their calendar was out of joint. When twenty years later, the supreme astronomer Su Sung attempted to pay his respects to a barbarian prince during the winter solstice, he caused great scandal by arriving one day early. The chronicler adds a revealing commentary: "Because the astronomical and calendarian investigations of the barbarians were not [politically] restricted, their experts were better [than ours] in this field, their calendar was actually correct".[12]
>
> A new Emperor was inclined to proclaim his own personal calendar which supposedly increased his credibility as guarantor of the Harmony of the Heavens and correlated with good harvests and a content population. Under these circumstances, facts had to be massaged according to the political realities, and the astronomers had to bow to the dictates of power.

The natural sciences, not to mention mathematics and logic, are all but immune to accusations of lack of objectivity. Conversely, the social sciences such as economics, psychology, sociology and anthropology have been far from unprejudiced. The cumulative acquisition of knowledge has been disrupted by a lack of humility in relation to the enormously complex object of research. In the cultural sciences (or humanities), from jurisprudence and pedagogy to ethics, theology and aesthetics, the dependence on personal and cultural values is self-evident.

> In Conversation with Economists (1990), Arjo Klamer relates how eleven leading economists have been fettered to the political beliefs of their youth. A long life overflowing with scientific discussions had not upset the personal axiomatics. Neither are sociologists or ethicists inclined to change opinions when confronted with uncomfortable facts. The preferred procedure is to select data which fit the preconceived world view. As Jonathan Swift (1667–1745) says: "You cannot reason a person out of something he has not been reasoned into". Convictions and rational reasoning work on different levels of the psyche with little interaction.

Natural science is at core an empirical activity. Knowledge is acquired step by step through trial and error – conjectures and refutations – in analogy with biological evolution. This Darwinist principle is in harmony with Popperian fallibilism; our concern is only to make the unavoidable mistakes as quickly and cheaply as possible. Cultural science, on the other hand, implies the logical construction of a new, and at bottom subjective, reality. To be fruitful the work must build on an axiomatic value system. A split into competing schools is unavoidable, pluralism an absolute necessity. In contrast to the natural sciences, there is little pre-existing objective reality.[13]

In the social sciences, deep hypotheses can be tested only by extended human experience, and it takes even more time to certify the value of the intellectual constructs of the cultural sciences. To imply objectivity by imitating the methods of natural science is presumptuous and disingenuous. All practitioners of the 'soft' sciences should fly their own pendant and openly declare their basic assumptions and beliefs. This was first pointed out by Max Weber (1864–1920).[14]

> Marxism is the classical example of a scientific bluff. The dictum of Friedrich Nietzsche (1844-1900) "Every word is a prejudice" would for once be appropriate. In the end, Marxism could be falsified only by practical experience. Skepticism about the reach of scientific deduction was notable by its absence, and for that very reason many if not most social scientists jumped on the bandwagon. Marxism still has its faithful adherents. They cannot, and perhaps should not, be converted by rational arguments.
>
> Psychoanalysis and behaviorism are other depressing examples of scientific presumption during the early twentieth century. While the psychoanalyst assumed that childhood experiences predetermine adult life, the behaviorist was convinced of his ability to manipulate the human personality by early conditioning. Both neglected heredity and were equally incapable of realizing their narrow-mindedness. Even today the upbringing of children is the subject of confident 'scientific' recommendations, and we may have to wait a while for common sense to prevail.

In the shadow of self-deceiving mental edifices, the patient collection of fundamental data continues in the soft sciences, while fruitful interaction with the natural sciences is gaining ground. Neurobiological research, in combination with psychological insights, will in due course shed light upon the interaction between body and soul. While waiting for that to happen, laboratory experiments with people in artificial game situations have made some progress in the mapping of human morality.

In *Behavioral Game Theory* (2002), Colin Camerer reviews the progress in this area. By confronting volunteers in game situations of the 'prisoner's dilemma' type, the moral positions of the participants can be identified. To produce a realistic setting the winnings are paid out in hard cash. The research shows unequivocally that people possess a portion of good will, depending on a number of controllable variables. The variation between individuals is considerable and linked to the psychological profile. For the first time, an objective measure of morality is within reach.[15] Neural imaging is beginning to deliver similar insights from a different vantage point.[16]

Comparison along the time line and between peoples is quite interesting. For instance Henrich et al.[17] have established that commercially active tribes in Africa have a more developed sense of fair play in comparison with wholly self-sufficient societies. Contrary to current opinion, the market seems to provide moral tuition. It is also comforting that spontaneous plus-sum players seem to be in the majority. Moreover, an inclination to punish foul play at one's own expense is also prominent; our innate strong reciprocity can be empirically demonstrated.

The natural sciences have covered a lot of ground in describing the fundamental rules of the game in unambiguous, mathematical terms. We are capable of distinguishing the possible from the improbable or the outright impossible. Detailed insight into complex processes may be outside our reach but we can confidently survey the terrain. And as long as we dissect man like good veterinarians we are on the safe side. But the rules of the game are changing when we confront the genuine human factor.

The object of research must be significantly simpler and less complex than the investigating subject; otherwise it is not open to scientific understanding and explanation. The study of man is extremely cumbersome. The invariables are confined to our very individual genetic heritage. The reductionist researcher must be content with an amputated specimen (e.g. the rational *Homo economicus*). Or the observations are confined to a narrow aspect which, still, is hard to nail down (e.g. intelligence tests). Even so, identical twins open the possibility of separating genetic and environmental influences.

The credibility of the natural sciences rests on rendering a coherent, multifariously tested view of the world. Humans are an incomparably harder object for study, and the results are therefore fragmented, incommensurate and basically suspect. Extrapolation beyond the frame of the actual investigation is always doubtful due to the lack of a holistic overview. Even in the shape of a myriad researcher, man cannot ever understand himself. He remains enigmatic and unpredictable.

Art is the only legitimate science of man. Yet art is always implicit, it is information in immediate action, explaining nothing. Therefore the explicit, scientific quest for truth has its limitations. We must look elsewhere for evidence when we are dealing with ourselves, our life and the conjoining problems of social coexistence.

Despite the incapability of science to provide answers for our most important questions, it already serves as a common denominator for educated people all over the globe. Its principal values are impeccable and generally accepted. The basic insight of human fallibility should foil the exaggerated ambitions of science, while opening the way for freedom of thought, humanism and democracy.

5.5 The foundations of faith

What is truth? This question must be repeated. The mathematicians unanimously assert that no axiomatic language can describe or prove its own truth. The truth criteria must originate in a superordinate language which gains its relevance from an even richer idiom. A 'truth machine' cannot be constructed. Like faith, hope, love and morality, truth is a prospective concept which is basically indescribable and indefinable. The highest truth is always a question of faith.

Faith in science as the revealer of all truth is groundless, but science can uncover many untruths such as pernicious superstitions; truth is what remains when all untruths have been exposed. What then is a superstition in contrast to faith? It is a conviction which, at least in principle, can be falsified by observations, experiments or other scientific methods. Pseudo-sciences are the mirror-image of superstitions, entrenching themselves behind self-immunizing doctrines.

> Marxism like other theologies came within a whisker of immunizing itself. Whatsoever happens in the real world could be accommodated by experts in the formulas of orthodoxy. Psychoanalysis is another pseudo-religion where everything which has occurred finds its convenient explanation but the predictive power approaches zero.

Faith is the invaluable which remains when the dross has been sorted out. It is not falsifiable, except in the very long perspective. "By the fruit shall you know the tree", but the harvest can be long in waiting, not least in science. The relation between faith and science has been debated to the point of exhaustion. The judicious compromise is that they are complementary and should not intrude upon each others' domains. Even so I maintain that science builds on axiomatic, value-oriented rules of the game, in other words a faith.[18]

> Science is foremost a Western phenomenon. The ancient Greeks began the systematic search for truth. Islamic scholars enriched this heritage during the tenth and eleventh century but the effort came to a dead end, as did the sprouting of Chinese and Indian science.[19] Science gained momentum only in the Christian environment of Western Europe. Religion did not directly support science but both drew on the same sources.

Most religions become petrified over time, deteriorating into a ritual mumbo-jumbo, propped up by dogma and an often incomprehensible church language. The open message of Christianity was moving in the same direction; Church Latin and Old Church Slavonic created the obligatory distance to the sacred, which surpassed the comprehension of common folk. But the Reformation and the art of printing democratized the gospels; everyone could be their own priest. In due course, equality before God turned into equality before the law. Scientific research and political democracy follow similar articles of faith – the same elementary rules of the game.

All cultures are embedded in and derived from their religious backgrounds, which in turn seem to predestine social values and development. Obviously, during the progress a myriad of feedbacks are realized between the different levels of societal play. But it is a fundamental fallacy to perceive religious convictions as an afterthought, a product of economic and political power relations. Just as foolish is the division of humanity into the condemned and the redeemed, according to the observance of the detailed directives of holy writs.

> Religious fundamentalism and Marxism share a glaring self-contradiction. The future is predestined, yet we have to work with all our might for it to come true. When you believe in the laws of history or in the literal truth of the Scriptures, all means for the realization of the dimly discerned Utopia are legitimized in a logical somersault. If you are not fanatically committed, you have already distrusted the message, betrayed your faith, admitted a terrible mistake; all in all fallen from the heaven of firm convictions to the hell of existential uncertainty.

"The letter killeth but the spirit giveth life." Faith announces itself in our choice of values, the rules we try to apply in carrying out our everyday obligations. Faith is historical self-selection both in its personal and societal aspects. It implies a risky wager on a very distant future, impenetrable to any rational analysis. In the fullness of time the fruits of faith become manifest – the truths of tangible accomplishment as well as the falsity of delusions. Theology may, after all, be an empirical science.

> In their struggle with the concept of truth, the logicians have arrived at an ingenious definition, taking a leaf out of Darwin's book: "Truth is the provisionally winning strategy in an open and infinitely extended evolutionary game". The definition merely covers how to reach ever better and deeper truths, but that is as good as it gets.[20]
>
> The Old Testament renders the arduous understanding (or re-editing) of Jahveh's true character. Apostasy and the adoration of idols, with subsequent punishment and re-learning, is repeated time and again, while the chosen people achieves a successively deeper insight into the conditions of its existence – a question which is still in the balance.

Mircea Eliade (1907–86) has in *A History of Religious Ideas* identified the Sacred as a concept, shared by all religions. The Sacred stretches from Paleolithic cave paintings to the extreme abstractions of Teravada-Buddhism. The latest effort in this direction is Stuart Kaufmanns book *Reinventing the Sacred: A New View of Science, Reason and Religion* (2008). One is hard pressed to find a society without something they hold sacred.

> Indigenous people worship holy mountains, caves, animals, trees, groves or fountains as well as natural phenomena like thunder, lightning and storms – all nature is a mystery. Important human activities are circumscribed by a multitude of inviolable prescriptions, taboos and rites of initiation. The current fanatic advocates of animal and nature protection represent spiritual regression – they adore primitive idols. This holds even more for an abundance of modern superstitions. The inclination to introduce the supernatural at all times of the day extends back to the magical world view of our ancestors.
>
> The monotheistic religions have not been untouched by the worship of pictures and idols. Great Buddha sculptures testify to the attraction of concrete symbols for his followers. In the holy temple of Kaba in Mecca, a black cornerstone, probably a meteorite, is especially sacred despite damage caused by internal fighting in the tenth century. Wonderworking relics, icons and other paraphernalia abound in Orthodox

and Catholic churches and shrines. It is terribly difficult to live solely by faith.

For the ancient Greeks, the hometown was the most sacred; the gods served mainly as props. The native tribe has always been deified; alien people were barbarians, if not downright non-human. Later on, modern nations have become the object of idolization; my country, right or wrong. Excessive nationalism is an obvious throwback. The great religions all point at superordinate, transcendent realities. The sacred cannot and must not be tangible, its reality is of a higher dignity.

The alpha and omega of morality is the sanctity of our everyday rules of the game. Everything else is sanctimony without weight or value. But decent common people – the building blocks of democracy – can also fall into self-righteous smugness. The average man becomes the measure of everything; the majority has not only might but automatically also right on its side. The will of the people becomes an idol, the infallibility of the electorate a dogma, humble learning an impossibility. Hubris threatens each and everybody who blindly believes in himself.

> Martin Luther (1483–1546) recommended an infallible method for diagnosing enthusiastic sectarians, lacking in genuine conviction. Their faith was not up to much if they were not occasionally assailed by doubt.

The spiritual foundations of Christianity and democracy cannot be reduced to a few sentences. Nevertheless, I want to touch upon two aspects. The first one concerns the old Golden Rule of Reciprocity: Do unto others what you want others to do unto yourself. Kong Fuzi (Confucius 551–479 BC) dilutes the ethic by a negative formulation: "Do not do unto others what you would not have them do unto you". Jesus for his part elevates the reciprocity principle to a higher level by demanding a stronger commitment – "love your neighbor like yourself" – and to crown it all, includes adversaries and enemies.

> I was six year old in the first grade and had brought a cap pistol to school. Our strict schoolmistress did not approve of my shooting caps in class and took away the pistol. During the break I surreptitiously recovered it which was soon discovered. I was of course immediately under suspicion but blamed Mauri, a nice but not so quick-witted classmate. Under pressure I maintained my denunciation until one of the girls in the class revealed the truth. All my life I have felt ashamed

for this misdeed, but Mauri wanted to be my friend. He was prepared to love a person who had borne false witness against him.

I was twelve or thirteen, small but quick-witted and rather cheeky. A boy two grades above me took to bullying me. It became a small hell and, without being religiously inclined, I decided after mature deliberation to test the message of the New Testament – love your enemy and pray for him. It worked after a couple of weeks. Something had changed in my behavior. I did not arouse the same aggression and was not nettled any more. My adversary, too, went through a similar process. We became friends.

Two or three years later I witnessed how a bunch of younger boys made fun of a malformed classmate during the break. After a moments hesitation I told them to back off with immediate effect. I can still recall the strong revulsion I felt at the mocking, and remember the glance of gratitude which illuminated the deformed face of the victim.

The quest for truth is the other mainstay of our culture. The sanctity of truth goes back at least to Socrates and is also endorsed in the bible. "The truth shall make you free" says the Gospel according to St. John and this prediction has been amply fulfilled. But unconditional honesty collides with sacral inscrutability. Faith and doubt are inseparable; truth and deep conviction have a common root. Neither can be definitively described, they can only tentatively be realized in a long-term commitment.

"You shall not bear false witness" is the commandment which makes concrete the individual call for truth. It does not presuppose full insight but just unassuming good will. The Ten Commandments are prohibitions, in the first place. They structure the human plus-sum game, but leave ample room for the boundless quest for truth. We are spared all detailed instructions about food and drink, prayer routines, the eightfold way or the six perfections.

"You shall not have other gods besides me." God is what he is – what remains after all idols have been peeled away. Each and everyone is free to search for and to realize his or her personal relation to God. This sets the stage for the evaluation and rejection of values and the generation and regeneration of morality. Here in the hearts of individual humans, the struggle between right and wrong is decided – a struggle over the constant deficit in good will. Here in brief is the foundation of democracy.

Part II
The practice of democracy

The second part of the book comprises a critical examination of the practice of democracy, based on a sampling of contemporary issues.

*The problems of the political zero-sum game force the contenders to learn the art of compromise – nobody is ever quite satisfied.

*The value-creating metabolism of the market economy supports an expanding welfare state, which is politically justified by the call for equity.

*The judiciary, though, follows its own rules that do not always coincide with the people's sense of justice.

*The unofficial fourth estate is an essential, albeit often insufferable part of the power structure.

*The media participate in bolstering political correctness, which leads to a mendacious flight from reality.

*The democracies are on the point of losing themselves in a thicket of modern superstitions.

Chapter 6

Political zero-sum games

Political parties crystallize the divided opinions of the electorate into a number of intelligible alternatives. Hard competition tests the morale of politicians but the integrity of the administration is even more important. Corrupt civil servants are a drain on societal morality and the same holds for high taxation combined with extensive reallocation of resources. Extra-parliamentary extortion may also destabilize a democracy. Ultimately the people are in charge. Only if upright candidates attract the majority of votes can the political game uphold its plus-sum character. A democracy has the politicians it deserves.

6.1 The party system

To sketch out the high-minded ideals of democracy is easy compared with the hard work of reducing them to practice. Even apart from direct conflicts of interest, people disagree on most issues. In politics, the main question is not what is right but who benefits? The struggle for political power is basically a zero-sum game – one side's gain is the other's loss. Accordingly, the inherent logic involves secrecy and deception – no ideal background for long-term cooperation. Therefore, we should not be surprised by the dissension in democratic politics. Rather, the voluntary cooperation of hundreds of millions of citizens in fruitful plus-sum play is little less than miraculous.

Direct democracy may work in small communities when the majority is acquainted with the problems at hand. But executive decisions are only in the rarest cases taken by plebiscite as in classical Athens. In modern democracies, legislation too is normally the responsibility of the elected representatives of the people. Switzerland, though, provides ample scope for direct democracy, and most states in the United States have provisions for varying forms of citizens' initiatives, which become law if they are not declared unconstitutional.

> In California, the voters may have to decide on dozens of law proposals when electing political executives and sundry local civil servants. Small wonder then that the turnout is dropping as it is in Switzerland. In both places a clear self-selection of the voters can be observed. Po-

litical power is delegated to well-educated citizens, above middle age – a small step towards Aristotle's politeia, the rule of the judicious?

On the whole, participatory democracy is limited to local administration. Supported by sensible decentralization, it nevertheless constitutes a pillar of strength in many if not most democratic societies. The common affairs of the whole nation must, however, be entrusted to a small group of elected persons. Even for them it is a challenge to find a measure of agreement. The much decried political parties are indispensable tools in articulating conflicting values and reducing a plethora of individual opinions to a manageable number of alternatives. Parties usually try to maintain a façade of unity, but behind the neat exterior irreconcilable ambitions are seething.

> A senior member of the English Parliament is guiding a newly elected MP to the first session of the House of Commons. When they are entering the chamber, the agitated novice points at the benches of the opposing party and exclaims: "there is the enemy". The experienced colleague responds with a measured clarification: "there the adversaries are sitting; the enemies you will find on your own side". The political game is ruthless but, nevertheless, follows its own unwritten rules. A handshake can mean more than formal agreements, and political debts and claims are usually kept in reasonable balance. To avoid breakdown, political commerce too requires a certain trust capital – the more, the better.

The constitution and the electoral system have a decisive influence on the party pattern. Single-member constituencies are the traditional, Anglo-Saxon approach whereas continental Europe has preferred variants of proportional elections. As mentioned earlier, no optimal elective system can be defined. Basically, the efficiency and clear responsibility of government must be weighed against a balanced representation of the whole spectrum of political opinions in the parliament.

Single-member constituencies lead to a two-party system and one-party governments; the unavoidable compromises are worked out between and within the party fractions. Proportional elections usually result in party coalitions, and the political wheeling and dealing takes place in the glare of publicity. Populist posturing then becomes an acute temptation. Neither does a many-party system put the politicians on the spot for their actions and even less for their statements. The ensuing political squabbling is highly frustrating for the voters and contributes to the disrepute of politics.

For many reasons, full proportionality is problematic and, as a lesser evil, the freedom of the electorate is often curtailed, for example by introducing thresholds for small parties. But the two-party system has its own inherent shortcomings. For the party in power there is always the temptation to cling to its position by any means, fair or otherwise.

Besides Great Britain, the United States has the longest experience of a pure-bred two-party democracy. Gerrymandering is the art of fixing the boundaries of the constituencies in a manner favoring the dominant party. Both on the federal and state levels, the representatives of the people fight to the limit for the interests of their constituencies with little regard for the whole. The horse-trading is often intense before important votes, and occasionally the legislation is weighed down by the amassed pork.

The civil war was a catastrophic political failure and caused extended regional polarization. The after effects are still discernable even if the federal balance of power was re-established before long. Locally, single party dominance was and still is fairly common and can be cemented by corrupt 'machine' politics – the brazen manipulation of voters and voting procedures. Around the turn of the century the Tammany Hall machine was able to milk the city of New York for decades.[1]

Regardless of the political culture, power is abused in all political systems; the forms may vary but the symptoms are the same. Before elections the electorate is bribed by the government of the day with ample benefits. Party associates are placed in lucrative positions – sometimes pure sinecures – campaign financiers are well remembered and political important regions are favored.

The Japanese electoral system, like the Norwegian, blatantly favors the countryside at the expense of the cities, resembling England in the nineteenth century. The outcome is the most protectionist agricultural policy in the world (in hard competition with Switzerland and Norway) and senseless road building in the periphery. The building companies generously contribute to the election campaigns of the dominating liberal-democratic party which creates a perfect feedback circuit. It remains to be seen, if the reforms of Junichiro Koizumi have broken up the infamous political linkage.

In Japan, loyalty to the party and above all to its fractions is very strong, which simplifies the political calculations. But in many young democracies, party discipline is weak. The votes of the parliamentarians are up for sale, not necessarily for money but for ministerial positions or other benefits. Democracy loses its legitimacy if the parties do not act as dependable transmissions between electoral opinions and political decisions.

> Under Boris Jeltsin (1931–2007) Russian democracy took its first faltering steps. Professional criminals aspired for a seat in the Duma in order to enjoy immunity against prosecution; murder threats and bribes alternated in the political dialogue; diverse potentates became elected to local governorships to protect their economic interests. Jeltsin's successor Vladimir Putin has been severely criticized for his strong-arm measures, as in the case of the 'oligarch' Mikhail Khodorkovsky, who was aiming at political power by financing the parties as well as individual members of the Duma. In the absence of written and unwritten rules for political behavior, Putin applied the available means at his disposal to stop Khodorkovsky's influence peddling. Putin's regime is undoubtedly authoritarian. All the same, we can only hope that it leaves room for a gradual democratization of Russian society under his successor and bosom friend Dmitry Medvedev.

The Russian predicament is not unique; always and everywhere democracy is struggling with the rising tide of sneaking corruption. We are already acquainted with the lamentations of George Washington and John Adams regarding party fervor in the freshly amalgamated United States of America. Over the centuries, the political culture has not budged much.

Party rule can take on many, more or less legitimate disguises. In Finland people nowadays vote for individuals within a party frame, whereas in Sweden the ballot is cast on parties. In spite of some statutory window-dressing, the candidates are elected in the order of appearance on the party list which is decided by the bosses. The electorate are treated like cattle, incapable of electing the right persons in the hierarchy.

Party finance has always been a shady business and the source of major scandals. Many high-level politicians in Germany, Italy and France have been forced to resign and a number have been sentenced for illegal party financing. In the Nordic Countries, among others, parties are customarily supported by the state in relation to their strength in parliament. Members of parliament may also pay a portion of their salaries to the party. Companies are regularly pestered by requests for contributions to the campaigns of parties and individual candidates. The political process cannot function without money.

The United States, as usual, provides both the best and worst example of democratic politics. Staggering sums are spent on presidential campaigns. According to *The Economist*, two and a half billion dollars was spent on the campaigns of the two main candidates in the 2004 election, exclusive of the primaries and so called independent organizations which spent an additional half a billion – and the 2008 campaign will certainly beat that record. But USA has also the most sophisticated regulations concerning campaign financing. The McCain-Feingold Act favors small contributions (below $2000) and the money flow must be transparent and meticulously accounted for. A determined effort has been made to close all loopholes.[2]

There is an acute danger that the politicians become overly dependant on their financiers. But it cannot be illegitimate for organizations to actively participate in election campaigns. Unions for instance, routinely support left-wing parties whereas trade and industry assist more conservative candidates. Party and election finances mostly fall into a grey area bordering on impropriety, if not illegality.

The election struggle itself is usually a rather unattractive pageant. In the heat of the campaign, the sense of fair play is blunted. Unbiased, businesslike discussions are conspicuous by their absence, polemics and *ad hominem* arguments dominate. Only the negative reactions of the electorate can put a limit on the mudslinging and misrepresentation of facts.

6.2 Administration and bureaucracy

A democratic nation is dependent on its civil servants who should be honest, irreproachable, impartial, well-educated and well paid. The top civil servants should be as competent as chief executives of major companies. Even so, the public bureaucracy will never achieve the efficiency of the private sector. A public organization cannot learn from its mistakes because it cannot afford to make any. Every misstep can give rise to scandal, small or great. Furthermore, civil servants are normally irremovable and salaries are fixed; neither stick nor carrot is on hand. Worst of all, the public administration is not exposed to competition but enjoys considerable power along with security of employment.

The US congress instigated in the 1960s an inquiry in order to streamline the administration. The conclusion was that giant bureaucracies have an inbuilt capability to thwart any reforms. It is thus a waste of time to try to improve efficiency incrementally. The only way is to dissolve the whole organization and start again from scratch.

Crises and catastrophes can destroy established power structures, release shackled creativity and open the door for unprejudiced learning. Such effects are at least partly responsible for the fast rise of Japan and Germany after the Second World War; the victorious powers did not have the same incentive towards reinventing themselves. Despite the disintegration of the Soviet Union, most of the corrupt bureaucracy was left in place and today Russia seems to battle in vain with this suffocating hydra.

Power without transparency creates a moral hazard. State and local bureaucracies are always open to the temptations of corruption. Incorruptibility must be supported by high morale but this is far from enough. One rotten apple in a big organization spreads the contagion until it becomes a plague. Meticulous control of all transactions, decisions and reports is required. The division of responsibility and tasks are laid down to the letter, procedures are prescribed in minute detail; everything has to be documented, registered and filed away.

> In the United States, the Food and Drug Administration (FDA) carries responsibility for the safety of drugs and foodstuffs. Official decisions can signify not millions but billions in profit or loss, and the staff is under intense scrutiny. Every phone call from interested parties is immediately documented and filed. Two officials were always present when I made visits to the FDA in Washington; a private discussion was out of the question. It took a full ten years for us to get the final approval for the use of xylitol as a food ingredient; today it is widely used as a tasty and tooth-friendly substitute for common sugar.[3]
>
> Under such circumstances, the natural reaction is to postpone decisions, ask for additional information and clarification, resort to nitpicking; it cannot be a breach of duty. During the 1970s, FDA was grinding to a halt with its risk-minimizing internal procedures. The public was effectively protected from ground-breaking cures. The Reagan administration established a more business-friendly atmosphere but the turbulence continues. Damned if you do and damned if you don't.
>
> The Pentagon is another bureaucratic power centre which is subject to corruption. The difference is that decisions have to be made, preferably fast and right. A high-level office-holder was recently prosecuted for partiality. She had favored a giant order for the Boeing Corporation against the promise of a directorship in the company. In private enterprises too, the purchasing department is an Achilles heel. A half percent kickback to a private account in a Swiss bank is very difficult to expose.

Big corporations have similar problems with their bureaucracy. Staffs are usually mushrooming, centralization is like a force of nature – power without responsibility is an irresistible lure. You can always make the case for better coordination by central organs whereas the downside of impaired flexibility, muddled responsibility, escalating paper work and loss of motivation is hard to quantify. When organizational sclerosis eventually ensues, a comprehensive decentralization is high on the agenda if the company is still afloat. The burden of proof should always be carried by the advocates of centralization.

> For many years General Electric (GE) had the highest market value on the stock exchanges (it was recently surpassed by Exxon which soon lost out to PetroChina) It is the only really resilient conglomerate in the United States with 300,000 employees. When Jack Welch took over in 1981, the bureaucracy had expanded out of all proportion. He cut it down to size, deployed staff to the operating units and radically flattened the organization. He also introduced a tough personnel policy. An annual review of the managerial resources was mandatory in every unit. Twenty percent of staff were designated for additional training and a career in the company. The weakest ten percent had to be dismissed. Thus the drag of bureaucratic solidarity was nipped in the bud, and the supply of managerial talent was ensured while security was discounted.[4]

Public administration can uphold high professional standards and good morale but it cannot be made effective à la Jack Welch. The solution is to keep the central bureaucracy as small, competent and generously paid as possible. All operative activities should be transferred to self-contained units or be privatized whenever possible.

> The limits of the possible are farther out than is generally supposed. In the United States many prisons are privatized and a Swiss firm has specialized in training customs officers. It may also temporarily take over the operational responsibility.[*] A privatized customs authority can hardly be corrupted; that would threaten the whole business idea.

Structural decentralization has nothing to do with decisions concerning financing priorities, social policy etc. which unequivocally belong to the political realm. But without some kind of market discipline and competitive pressure, an operational organization cannot be kept in proper trim. The separation of responsibilities for public supervision

---

[*] The company I have in mind is SGS SA (Societé General Surveillance) with about 50,000 employees.

and actual operation is conducive of good governance, too. The crux is that the administration must acquire new competencies in order to manage the purchasing of services.

> In California the privatization of the market for electricity was a fiasco. Producers as well as consumers were under the impression that they had covered themselves, but the system broke down when neither supply nor demand followed the forecasts, and power shortages became acute. Incentives for new investment were lacking because prices in the retail market were strictly regulated. A mechanism for adjusting the rules of the game was also lacking. A market should above all be impartial and self-regulating within a wide span of unexpected fluctuations. The Californian regime was a jumble of myopic special interests, which was barely functioning in a static situation.[5]

The increasingly open economic race between the nations implies that governments, too, are feeling the pressure of competition. When capital can move without impediment and people can vote with their feet, politicians and civil servants have to reconsider taxation, income transfers and not least the efficiency of the administration. This holds even more at the local level, which is responsible for social infrastructure like schools, kindergartens and health care. The citizens are turning into customers who want the best possible service for their tax money.

Individual citizens often feel mistreated by overweening magistrates, without a fighting chance to assert their legitimate interests. To correct the balance of power, most democracies have introduced special agencies to take action against erring authorities (cf. chapter 8.2). Even more important is the transparency of the administration. The light of publicity leaves little room for bureaucratic arbitrariness. In a democracy an exposed abuse is a past abuse. Appropriate political procedures can also contribute to preventing misconduct, and maintain high standards among civil servants.

> In the United States, the integrity of top level civil servants is certified by rigorous FBI vetting; in addition they are mercilessly grilled in the Senate. I was present when the US Ambassador in Finland declined a rather modest farewell present from our Association of Trade and Industry. He was a candidate for a high position in the civil service and could not risk any suspicion of undue influence.

Civil servants have, like everybody else, their own agenda which unfortunately tends to bloat the bureaucracy. There is no lack of initiatives which motivate an increase of the budget or the personnel. The whole organization is wholeheartedly behind these goals, whereas cost reductions or efficiency improvements are resolutely resisted. Nevertheless, a high-quality corps of civil servants is a vital resource which can partly compensate for mediocre or even useless politicians. But if the administration is corrupt, a political Hercules is needed to clear the Augean stables.

Corruption is like cancer. Once established it spreads silently, sends forth metastases, and in the end becomes well-nigh ineradicable. When everybody participates, the extra income becomes an acquired right which can be relished with a clear conscience. Especially in a democracy, civil servants should form a select, impeccable elite.

6.3 Taxation and redistribution

"Nothing is sure except death and taxes" goes the old saying, even if the anarchists deny the inevitability of taxes. Small, self-sufficient communities can actually manage without taxes. Building, roadwork and other major undertakings are carried out by voluntary work, neighbors and relatives form a social safety net, the poor are cared for communally. Such collectives can survive only as isolated cocoons in a larger, benevolent realm.

> The Hutterites of South Dakota are followers of Jacob Hutter, an anabaptist preacher who suffered a martyr's death in Innsbruck in 1536. They still live in communistic solidarity and are an example of the resilience of small groups of religious dissenters.

Local taxation is rarely a problem. The taxpayers have reasonable insight into the utility of the expenditures and can ascertain that they participate in a plus-sum game. Taxes which are payable to distant, anonymous authorities are less acceptable and are often felt to be a burden. We have already noticed that every administration tends to maximize taxation, regardless of the form of government. The democracies have developed this art to perfection. An abundance of deserving causes is always competing for public funds.

The private sector generally takes care of productive investments but lack of capital or risk aversion can force the government to make big investments in, say, infrastructure. Debt financing is appropriate if the beneficiaries pay for interest, amortization and other accrued costs, for example as road tolls or gasoline taxes. Basic education, art and science fall into a different category. Their profitability is difficult or impossible to calculate; rather it is a matter of beliefs, based on fundamental values.

> In the democracies, the tax-financed investments in human capital have paid themselves back many times over and in addition yielded immensely valuable immaterial benefits. The willingness to budget for education and research is far from self-evident, keeping in mind the short perspective of party politics. Here the popular striving for advancement through learning forms a remarkable synthesis with the elite's Faustian quest for truth.

In every society, external and internal security is a top priority in order to safeguard the societal plus-sum game. Besides the military and the police, a number of other indispensable expenditures can be listed. Even so, the minimum requirement for tax revenues on the national level should not exceed 10% of BNP, except in wartime or during other serious crises. At the local level, perhaps another 10% should be set aside for basic education etc. But then we have not accounted for the politically motivated redistribution of the national income. It represents a zero-sum game, or rather minus-sum play, due to the considerable administrative costs.

Income transfers have long been the main battle ground for democratic politics.[6] Soaring tax revenues, due to techno-economic growth, have only increased the appetite for spending among politicians. The competition with the Soviet Union certainly softened the resistance of the taxpayers, uncomfortable with the prospect of a rebellious proletariat. The upshot has been surreptitious socialization which has advanced in all democracies with Sweden in the van. The reliance on public support stretches through all sectors of the economy.

> -Agricultural subsidies are the dominating item in the EU-budget, but most democracies support their farmers, one way or another.
> -Industrial activities receive sizeable regional and investment support. In addition, product development is backed directly and indirectly.
> - Underdeveloped regions enjoy tax relief, 'unjustified' infrastructure and political relocations.
> -High-level education is free or highly subsidized.
> -Health care is heavily subsidized everywhere. In different disguises it builds up to a massive expenditure at the national level.
> -A substantial part of pensions are state-financed which is causing major headaches all over the West.
> -The unemployed receive generous support which often becomes permanent.

-Lastly we have social support, the original poor relief, which in the end is a fairly small item accounting for, at most, a few percent of BNP.

-To round it off we pay for help to developing countries which is equivalent to international poor relief.

Interference with the market should always be met with skepticism, regardless of real or presumptive concern for justice, equality, human care or economic growth. Such expenditures generally have eloquent advocates who presume that people, enterprises or regions cannot or would not assume full responsibility for their own future. Emergency relief and transitional support is often justified, but entitlements without time limit should give pause for thought.

In a welfare society the state has taken over the responsibility for all and everybody – not only for dropouts and those in need of emergency support, but for ordinary, steadfast citizens as well. Excepting the ministry of finance, every department from the minister down to the humblest civil servant has an interest in finding new ways to please the electorate by increasing its budget.

The Public Choice school emphasizes the evident self-interest of politicians and officials.[7] Every request for additional money is a partisan plea in an attractive package, labeled the common weal – happiness by legislation. A gullible electorate for long bought this message but in 1978 the tax revolution started in California. Proposition 13 was approved and put a ceiling on local property taxes. The centralization of education became the unintended effect, and Californian taxation has since then been in a state of turmoil.

In the budget all income transfers should be accounted for under a separate heading. The situation is complicated by the intricacies of dedicated taxes and municipal taxation. The tax code in most countries is a jumble of different revenue sources, special rules and politically motivated exemptions which are incomprehensible for the ordinary citizen. Except for experts, these documents are currently almost impenetrable which suits politicians, civil servants and diverse pressure groups just fine.

For that very reason we should insist upon transparency in national and local budgets to facilitate an informed political discourse. To avoid welfare losses, taxation should also be neutral vis-à-vis resource allocation. Inconsistencies abound, not least in the taxation of capital income.

All income from capital should in the name of consistency be taxed according to the same rate, excluding basic deductions for small incomes. But for limited liability companies (corporations) double taxation is, nonetheless, international practice. The logic of the taxman is always the same. The limited company is an exceptionally effective mode of operation, and it could and should be taxed accordingly.

Taxes on consumption are increasingly popular and they encourage saving, which remains a good cause. The European version (the added value tax) is neutral all along the value chain. Political aims can be incorporated by grading the tax; necessities may enjoy cut rates whereas luxuries and vices such as tobacco and alcohol can be severely taxed. Even so, prostitution and narcotics have so far, with minor exceptions, avoided the clutches of the tax-collector.

Luxury taxes have a long ancestry. Salt was for a long time on important object for taxation whereas coffee, another presumptive extravagance, was a later source of internal revenue. Today, communication by mobile phone is taxed as a luxury in many African countries. The European taxman still views private motoring as self-indulgence, even if fiscal income is not the only objective. Gasoline taxes cover road expenditures, and can be justified by environmental concerns and the conservation of scarce resources.

The long-term availability of oil is or should be a major concern above all for the United States. The problem has caused much agony but a rise of the gasoline tax is scrupulously avoided. Such a market-friendly solution would deliver badly-needed cash for the exchequer but is said to entail political suicide for its advocates. Instead a set of clumsy and ineffectual laws has been introduced to put a lid on average gas consumption. The Americans will in the future have to confront each and every one of the problems they now so resolutely put on the back burner. (Originally I wrote these lines in 2006. In the summer of 2008 as I am redrafting them, it appears that the future has already arrived.)

The exemption from taxes for the nobility and the clergy was probably the strongest incentive behind the French revolution. Now we have tax privileges in the low income bracket. Progressive taxation has for long been a mantra but now it is being questioned. The discussion was initiated in 1985 by Robert Hall and Alvin Rabuschka with *The Flat Tax* which was inspired by the monstrous tax code of the United States. Russia, Ukraine, Estonia, Latvia and Slovakia already apply a flat income tax, and it is discussed in many of the core countries of the European Union. Iceland has recently introduced a flat tax and the whole taxation system has been deemed exemplary.[8] On the other hand, a negative income tax is also on the political agenda. It would endorse the right of the citizens to live at the expense of the state, that is, off other people.

> The wantok system in Papua-New Guinea exemplifies the streamlined social security of a tribal society, as well as its shortcomings in an imposed national state. Wantok is Pidgin English for "one talk" viz. the same language. A wantok is a kinsman who is obliged to help a poor relative after "one talk" – a complementary interpretation of wantok. A civil servant is not only bound to give preference to his wantoks; he is also expected to steal or embezzle to supply their needs. On payday a wage earner is pestered by work-shy relatives who insist on their share.[9]

Finally, some of the main tenets of the public choice school deserve to be recapitulated:
-Permanent income transfers are always dubious.
-Decentralize taxation, responsibility and decision making to the limit.
-Introduce competitive market conditions wherever feasible
-Trust the market mechanism in preference to political intervention
In brief: economize on love.

6.4 Extra-parliamentary power games

To listen and to consider all points of view is part and parcel of the democratic tradition. The parliamentary process is backed up by surveys, reports and analyses, first in the ministerial departments and then in committees where experts and vested interests can vent their views. But democracies also accept extra-parliamentary expressions of opinion such as public demonstrations and assorted delegations, frankly speaking their mind before the responsible politicians.

A forcefully presented opinion stays within the bounds of democratic argumentation, but violence of any kind breaks the rules of the game. The street parliament is often romanticized as democracy in direct action. In established democracies it rather represents a loud and ruthless minority, attempting to impose its will on the law-abiding majority. If the police intervene, they are tainted as the lackeys of the powers that be.

> Violent demonstrations are often seized on as popular entertainment. In the embrace of a mass of people, individual responsibility evaporates and you feel an intoxicating affinity with those similarly minded.

Furthermore, you are self-evidently on the side of justice, good conscience is for sale at a bargain price. Recent mass demonstrations, for
instance against globalization, are relatively innocuous happenings
centered around a nucleus of itinerant professional demonstrators and
trouble-makers. But they elicit unpleasant associations with a time
when black-, brown- and red-shirts came to blows with the police in
European cities.* Contrary to their modern successors, they knew exactly what they wanted – to get rid of democracy.

Activists readily refer to important democratic reforms which alleg-
edly were instigated at the behest of extra-parliamentary action, such
as virulent agitation, strikes and street violence. This is a misunder-
standing. Strikes may produce a short-term wage increase for delimited groups, but in the long-term the standard of living depends on the
added value of the nationwide economic plus-sum game. Riots may
speed up legislation but they poison the political atmosphere, weaken
democracy and provoke adversaries to use similar stratagems.

To replace the art of compromise with mutual dictates is an invitation to catastrophic minus-sum games. A succession of democracies
have suffered shipwreck at the cross purposes of ruthless group interests. After World War II, Latin America particularly was affected
by political turbulence of this type. Revolutions and military coups
alternated, leaving no openings for democracy.

> Chile could pride itself of its democratic traditions until 1973 when
> Salvador Allende (1908-73), the President in office, was removed by
> a military coup and committed suicide. The prelude is a cautionary
> tale. Despite the manipulations of the United States, Allende received
> 36.3% of the votes in the 1970 presidential elections. The conservative
> candidate got 35.7% while a moderate got the remaining 27%. Despite
> strong doubts the Congress followed precedent and appointed to Presi-
> dent the candidate with the plurality of votes. But it forced Allende to
> accept a declaration that he would not undermine the constitution.
>
> All the same, Allende at once began to introduce socialism. In his
> first speech to Congress, half a year after inauguration, he presented a
> radical program and intimated that he would proceed with or without
> the approval of Congress. When the legislators objected, Allende gov-
> erned by decrees. In 1973, economic and political chaos reigned. Con-
> gress requested the army to restore law and order which brought about
> the resignation of the commander in chief. Allende appointed Augusto
> Pinochet to command the army; two weeks later Pinochet pulled off a
> military coup, supported by the navy and the air force.[10]

---

* The Italian fascists wore black shirts, the Nazis brown and the communists red.

Allende had stretched his weak mandate to a point which conflicted with the spirit and the letter of the constitution. Instead of imposing socialism by hook and by crook he could have been content with a less ambitious program. And when society was breaking down he should have had sense enough to resign. But Allende was no democrat and neither was Pinochet, who established draconian order at a heavy price in human lives. In 1990, Chile could return to a stable, democratic regime and comparative prosperity. Politicians on the right and the left had assimilated the dearly-bought experience.

After numerous twists and turns, democracy has gained a footing in South America but many countries still live under the threat of relapses into authoritarian rule or revolutionary follies. For example in Venezuela, President Hugo Chávez pursues a dangerous balancing act, bordering on populist dictatorship. But there is a fair chance for democracy all over Latin America.[11] Every country has to pass through its own painful learning process (cf. chapter 11.4).

Peaceable mass demonstrations and strikes have sometimes moved autocratic regimes towards democracy. In 1905, a general strike forced the Russian tsar to constitute a parliament (the duma), but the concessions were soon revoked. In Portugal however, the carnation revolution swept away the tottering one-party rule for good in 1974. In 2004, persistent demonstrations in Kiev against rampant election fraud managed to give Ukrainian politics a democratic turn and Georgia has passed a similar process. But noisy mass manifestations do not serve established democracies well, much less riot and rebellion. Legitimate ways to voice a divergent opinion are always available.

> The suffragettes of Great Britain were notorious for their violent demonstrations, but it is hard to tell if their intemperate actions expedited the reform. After all, the women of New Zeeland and Finland had been peacefully franchised much earlier. Switzerland, on the other hand, procrastinated until 1971; even so it was hardly deficient in democracy.

Established special interests can pursue their aims by lobbying. Politicians and civil servants in key positions are under intense courting from executives, union leaders and diverse organizations. It is difficult to draw the line between valuable exchanges of opinion and devious string-pulling.

> The United States is making valiant efforts to curb undue influence.[12] Washington lobbyists have to register and twice annually they have to deliver a report which divulges clients, lobbying objects and expendi-

tures among other things. Lobbying cannot be restricted, because the first amendment to the constitution guarantees freedom of expression and the right of the citizens to present petitions to the magistrates. But by making lobbying public, the worst misconduct can hopefully be checked. After the Abramoff scandal the rules will be tightened again, though to what effect remains to be seen.

My only experience of lobbying in the USA is positive. We had introduced crystalline fruit sugar in the US-market and tried to attain legal equality with common sugar. Our lawyers contacted a congressman and a ten line law amendment sailed through the house and the senate to be signed into law by President Jimmy Carter a few months later.

In most democracies, the tide of lobbying is ever rising due to the propensity of the state to interfere in the market mechanisms instead of confining itself to defining the rules. Besides, ideologically motivated pressure groups plead loudly for their narrow-minded views. Furthermore, petitions abound from an untold number of non-profit organizations looking for public support. The noise level in the corridors of power can be high indeed.

Indirect lobbying by the media has become routine. A major part of domestic media material can be attributed to the manipulations of interest groups. Usually, money is the core issue, either as an appeal for direct support or as concealed advertising. It can be hard to separate legitimate opinion from political wangling, but for the trained eye the self-interest shines through the veil of spurious public interest. We will come back to the role of the media in chapter 9.

Extra-parliamentary blackmail can work at the local level, too. Illegal squatting has in many places come in handy to put pressure on local government. Students have over the ages noisily presented their inalienable views about professors, the curriculum, accommodation and provisions. The international repercussions made the disturbances of 1968 exceptional. The students were dissatisfied, not only with the universities and their education, but with society and the ways of the world in general.

The hippie movement was an indication of a youth rebellion which in 1964-66 attained political expression in Berkeley, University of California. But it was Columbia University in New York which in 1968 became the scene for the first student tumults. The protest was linked to the Vietnam War but was quickly radicalized and soon shrank to a core of amateur terrorists, who called themselves the Weather Underground.[13]

In France the student rebellion had more serious consequences. In

May 1968, clashes with the police initiated widespread strikes which paralyzed the country and set off a political crisis. The Parliament was dissolved by President de Gaulle (1890-1970) who won strong support in the subsequent election. The disturbances ebbed out, teaching and tuition were renewed (not necessarily for the better), but society mostly reverted to the old ways. Still, de Gaulle retired the next year, after losing a referendum he had called.

The student rebellion of 1968 may signify a generation change, but there is no reason to romanticize the bumptious self-assertion of privileged youngsters. The strongly expanding university system was breaking at its seams under the pressure of the baby-boom generation. Young men have an inherent need to assert themselves which sometimes spreads like an epidemic. During 1968, the common denominator included an even more primitive element, the sexual drive. The decisive reform was that the universities refrained from maintaining a conservative sexual morale on the campuses. After that the enthusiasm waned.

> Mark Rudd, the leader of the Columbia upheavals, went underground and eventually became a teacher of mathematics in a New Mexico school. Referring to an earlier interview, he says that "it was difficult for me to speak about my moral dilemma – which actually really is a euphemism for shame".[14] Daniel Cohn-Bendit, the spokesman for the rebellious Paris students, was expelled from France, but in 1994 he was elected to the European Parliament, representing the German green party. He repeated the feat in 1999 as a leader of the French environmental party. Today Cohn-Bendit is the leader of the green parliamentary group in Brussels.

The life stories of these prominent actors can serve as a brief abstract of the student rebellion. After all the sound and fury, the great majority of the rebels were assimilated in the democratic society they had vehemently criticized. They made their mark, but it is hard to say of what kind; they also exerted an influence, but it is hard to say how big. In a democracy, sincere initiatives rarely disappear without a trace, and the outcome is often better than the intention. But one should not forget that the rebellion of 1968 also prepared the ground for the murderous attacks of the Red Brigades and The Red Army Fraction.

6.5 The people in charge

In a democracy, the sovereign people have the power and the responsibility. We may tell off our politicians as much as we like but the parties must sell their message to the electorate in fierce competition. The product is always adapted to the preferences of the consumer. If lies and slander, demagoguery and populism are strong sales points, the quality awareness of the customer is wanting. The people can only blame themselves when, for instance, public expenditures run amok.[15]

Political apathy is, with some justification, touted as a major problem for modern democracies. In times of affluent peace, only spectacular crimes, accidents or scandals arouse political passions. Then the field is open for political lightweights to invoke radical legislation in fast order. Fortunately, precipitate action is usually prevented by the frustrating slowness of democratic decision-making.

It cannot be denied that nowadays the common voter is rather uninterested in politics. An old business slogan presents a partial solution to the problem: Keep it simple stupid! The electorate can follow and understand only a limited set of important legislation. Complex acts and regulations often reflect muddled compromises or undue influence; in any case they alienate the electorate.

> Mancur Olson shows in *The Rise and Decline of Nations* (1969) how government failure ensues when small, closely knit interest groups, whom he calls distributive coalitions, achieve disproportionate influence, not least on taxation. In many countries the tax code produces a veritable science which serves as a base for sophisticated tax planning. In the United States the assumed loss to the national economy is hundreds of billions of dollars when compared with a straightforward flat tax with basic deductions.
>
> Specially constructed loopholes for the super-rich pass ever so often below the radar of publicity with little discussion. For instance in equality-fixated Sweden, the tax planning of the really wealthy is facilitated by tailor-made rules. Within the European Union, the Commission has for years tried to eliminate the scandalous tax-havens in Luxemburg, Liechtenstein, Monaco, the Isle of Man, Gibraltar and the Channel Islands – to little avail. Some progress has been made but public opinion in the EU-countries could not care less.

Democracy goes wrong when egotistic politicians are given a free hand by a listless electorate. The diffuse public interest falls prey to the manipulations of a small number of highly motivated actors. Decision-making easily slips into the hands of well-organized interest groups, which in the end will reach an agreement at the expense of the taxpayer. The whole of society can be engulfed in a morass of endless negotiations and proliferating zero-sum play.

It bears repeating. Leave to the market what belongs to the market and let the people and its elected representatives concentrate on the essentials. An overgrown public sector is a thieves' paradise, a haven for foul play. The itch of politicians to splash favors around aggravates the societal elephantiasis. Shrewd patronage is applied to reward important supporters and to pacify influential adversaries. Broad voter categories can be bribed by introducing tax-financed benefits, frequently mortgaging future tax revenues. A reaction is often delayed until the till is empty, despite heavy taxation and maximum indebtedness.

Slimming the national budget is as difficult as personal weight reduction. By heroic efforts temporary results can be achieved, but the appropriations are back at the very instant our collective self-control fails. In the political debate, the inherent human instinct to secure attained benefits assumes the character of a constitutional right.

> The market is a superior method for the allocation of economic gains and losses. First and foremost, the market is an effective (but not necessarily an optimal) plus-sum game. Furthermore, the losers have to acquiesce; to cry over spilled milk does not bring any profit. In contrast, a political allocation is equal to a zero-sum game; it rarely creates added value. What is worse, the losers do not give in but persist in whining, and clamor for reconsideration and revision. The merited tire and lose out, the winners are usually the most brazen with the best contacts.

A democracy refrains from riding roughshod even over small minorities; the politicians would like to please everybody. This can lead to Navajo-democracy; the palaver continues until everyone is content. In any case, each and everyone have to be heard. Frequently, the outcome is a sequence of appeals and exorbitant delays. Individual rights form the foundation of democracy, but they can be abused and lead to a tyranny of the minority. Good manners should imply the acceptance of defeat when it is inevitable, eschewing the waste of public resources on pointless self-conceit.

> The same holds for the political game. Ever so often you have to be a good loser, concede defeat and give up the prerogatives of power. In a democracy, all is not lost in opposition. In the same vein everything is not gained by one election victory. For authoritarian rulers, resigning or retiring is a much harder choice. They might face the same treatment that was meted out to their antagonists.

Public opinion is a mighty force in a democratic society. It is notoriously fickle but represents a political reality which is impossible to ignore when feelings run high. Public opinion does not ignite on factual arguments or strategic considerations but its response is all the stronger to dramatic incidents, large or small.

> When in the early 1990s Slobodan Milosevic started his Greater Serbia campaign with war and ethnic persecution, the international reaction was muted and irresolute. The efforts of the United Nations ended in scandal when in July 1995 a Dutch UN-force helplessly witnessed the slaughter of thousands of Bosnians in Srebrenica. The massacre precipitated a limited NATO-operation and a settlement was reached by the end of 1995. Milosevic had to withdraw into Serbia but clashes with militant Albanians in Kosovo escalated to systematic persecution and ethnic cleansing.
>
> The European Union lacked both the will and the strength to intervene whereas the United States viewed the Balkans as a European rat-hole, lacking strategic importance. Only when footage of the masses of fleeing Albanians reached the TV-watchers in 1999, did the public opinion in the US insist on decisive action. President Clinton was under pressure to do something but did not want to risk American lives. The outcome was an USA-lead NATO-operation without the sanction of the United Nations. The capitulation of Milosevic was enforced by the massive bombing of Kosovo and later of Belgrade.

Already de Tocqueville noticed how spontaneously people affiliate to opinions which are perceived as the majority view. For good or for worse, this bandwagon-effect is not only a display of political opportunism but an age-old democratic reflex. To side with a widespread opinion is risk-free and emotionally satisfying – you can comfortably assume a self-righteous stance. The outcome is belief conformity, also called political correctness, a morally disquieting phenomenon which we will return to in chapter 9.4.

The people's sense of fair play is put to the test in many other contexts. Equal opportunity is a widely accepted principle but in practice it leads to unexpected and unacceptable differences in individual outcomes. Does it suffice that everybody starts at the same line or should society see to it that each and everyone is adequately positioned at the finish? Political freedom and equality inevitably ends up in economic inequality, whereas economic equality with the same certainty eliminates liberty. Therefore an unequal distribution of income is inescapable, but it is and will remain the source of political conflict. One way or another, positive discrimination will be a feature of every democratic society.

The political process may, in a narrow perspective, look like a zero-sum game but its mission is, or should be, to secure and promote the fruitful cooperation and the personal self-realization of the citizens. Political institutions and political decisions form the indispensable frame for the multitude of societal plus-sum games.

In the last instance the citizens are responsible and in charge. The sovereign people is free to make mistakes. But if the people fails to learn, the rebuff will be repeated. The political game can sustain a plus-sum character only if a majority of votes fall to upright candidates. A democracy has the politicians and the policies it deserves.

Chapter 7
The economic plus-sum game

A good national economy is founded on sufficient capital formation and vigorous entrepreneurship within a sensible institutional frame. Preferably company profits should reflect the added societal value and free-riding must be discouraged, not least in biological reproduction. Externalities such as environmental impact and changes in human capital should be accounted for in the assessment of national income and wealth. The globalization of trade is the best development aid, despite the loud complaints of the losers when the market demolishes their privileged positions.

7.1 The national economy

Bypassing whole libraries of national economic writings, the same rules should apply to a country as to a household – in the long term expenditures must not exceed income. But the state has a few cards up its sleeve which can be used in the event of foul play. The classic card is inflation which is useful in reducing the indebtedness of the state (and other debtors). Furthermore, employment is sustained, at least according to the Keynesian post-war economists. What they got in the 1970s was stagflation – recession, unemployment and inflation.

The suppression of inflation in the 1980s must be counted as a major political success, but other financial self-deceptions have come to the fore. The biggest problems are entitlements which are voted through in a spirit of resolute, wishful thinking. Pensions especially are devious instruments. There is no charge when the decisions are made, but the burden becomes crushing if the population base dwindles.

Most countries have state pensions organized on the principle 'pay as you go'. Around 2020, the rising pension costs will begin to overwhelm taxpayers in a number of countries. The same holds for health care and other social costs. The retirement age must be raised and the benefits reduced. Measures have been taken but it might be too little, too late. Corporations like General Motors, with a brilliant past but a gloomy future, are in for a similar crunch. Generous retirement agreements can, in the worst case, drive companies and the affiliated pension funds into bankruptcy.[1]

Democracies habitually postpone unpleasant decisions. As a rule, the electorate and thus the politicians give precedence to short-term interests. The national debt reflects this mindset; many countries are heavily in hock. In the early nineties, interest payments amounted to around 20% of the national budget in Belgium, Italy and Canada. Decreasing interest rates eased the burden for a while but indebtedness increased. In 2006, Japan held the top slot with 150% of the annual BNP; Italy and Belgium occupied the other medal positions. Many democracies have rashly mortgaged their future.

> Walter Wriston (1920-2005), legendary chief for Citicorp, once let out that "countries do not go bankrupt". He was right but their central banks could do the trick and his company lost a lot of money on Latin American public debt. The United States currently produces government bonds in a steady stream and they are still considered rock solid investments. A major part is taken up by Southeast Asian central banks which have all but tied their currencies to the dollar. We are witnessing the absurd state of affairs that the Chinese poor are financing American over-consumption, an unsustainable situation.
>
> The rise of Western Germany after the war was based on frugality, not least in the public domain; the constitution stipulates that public debt is allowed only for new investment. However, economic success led to imprudent political commitments and Germany now struggles with a stubborn budget deficit; the constitutional statutes have quietly been set to one side.

In poor countries a high rate of savings is the best indication of future economic upturn. In the early 1970s, private capital formation in Japan was around 25% of BNP, while South Korea saved more than 30% in 1988. According to the International Monetary Fund (IMF), the rate of saving in China was 50% in 2005. In Latin America only Chile has exceeded 10%, if oil revenues are excluded.

In the developed countries the figures are much lower; in 2007 Japanese savings had dropped to 3% of BNP. This is in part due to the rise in depreciations which increasingly finance the investments. The economists have a habit of castigating exaggerated thrift because it strangles consumption. But most experts agree that the consumption craze in the United States was out of hand when the savings rate fell to close to zero in 2005. In 2007 it was still a measly 0.4%.[2]

Unearned riches can be sugar-coated poison pills. They distort the perception of reality and are equal to a giant subsidy, compromising the competitiveness of the nation. Political and economic decision-making goes awry, frugality is thrown to the wind and featherbedding becomes the name of the game.

> After the Second World War, Argentina and Uruguay rode high on an export boom of agricultural produce. They swiftly erected an inflated welfare state which became a crushing burden when the boom turned to bust. In the oil-rich countries in the Near East, foreign workers perform most of the manual tasks and taxes are an unknown concept for the natives. The limitless acquisitiveness of princes and sheiks can continue as long as the money suffices to keep the people content. In Nigeria the oil money has thoroughly degraded the morals of politicians and civil servants. The anti-corruption minister recently triumphantly declared that the share of embezzled oil income had decreased from 70% to 40%![3] Even in Norway, many sectors of trade and industry are struggling despite brave efforts to neutralize the surplus oil revenue.

The prerequisites for an economic plus-sum game are sound public finances and a capable administration. A coherent set of regulations for the business sector is essential. In addition, the government has to build and maintain the infrastructure which cannot readily be handed over to the market. The lodestar should be fair competitive play, with the implied objective that profits should be proportional to the accrued benefits to society.

> In 1985, I served as the representative of trade and industry in a committee which prepared a new competition law for Finland. During the first session I proposed, tongue in cheek, that agriculture and the labor market should be covered by the legislation. That came to naught, but in 1988 our unanimous proposal became law with only minor modifications. It has stiffened competition in the industrial sector and thanks to the European Union and globalization the farmers and the unions, too, have faced increased competition.

Market failure is a condition which should trigger government action. It is often caused by so-called natural monopolies like electric power distribution where special regulations are called for to uphold fair play. Dominant market positions are always suspect and must not be abused; cartels are outright criminal. Consumers and the labor force are protected by specific laws. They are intended to anticipate a delayed 'natural' market response because the immediate consequences are deemed unacceptable.

Milton Friedman (1912–2006), the dominant figure of the Chicago school and the standard bearer of neo-liberalism, consistently pleaded for a deregulation of the market. For instance, the authorization of physicians, apothecaries, engineers, lawyers, bankers etc. etc. is considered superfluous, because the customers eventually will separate the wheat from the chaff.[4] This may work in a small-scale society, but the prescription will probably not be tried out in modern democracies for very good reasons.

Administering the market medicine is not always straightforward and many markets, not least the financial ones, require constant supervision by competent authorities. Just the same, we suffer from overregulation. Any misdeed, misfortune or social evil releases calls for more detailed regulations. Politicians, experts and civil servants readily enter the merry-go-round of stricter directives, lower tolerance and firmer control. Nobody has an interest in opening the floor to advocates of deregulation.

When the government tries to intervene in lopsided market conditions, for instance unemployment, it may just make matters worse. The underlying causes are usually the lack of flexibility and market adaptation. Retraining and flextime for working hours are thus sensible steps, whereas the security of employment and compulsory cuts in working hours are counterproductive measures. In the long term, it is no good trying to fight the market.

Widespread and extended unemployment is a serious market disturbance; the economy has not adapted to the swift changes of trade and industry. The ultimate cause is the detailed regulation of working life which impairs the adjustment of supply and demand by the price mechanism. A safety net for the less fortunate is quite legitimate, but the costs of unemployment insurance should fall on the unions. Their members are, to be sure, the beneficiaries of monopolized wage-fixing.

The endemic unemployment in many West European countries indicates that something has gone wrong. In Germany, one half of the unemployed are long-term, whereas in the United States the corresponding proportion is one out of ten. The safety nets have become hammocks; unemployment benefits, supplemented by incidental untaxed income successfully compete with wage earnings. A rising proportion of the registered unemployed are dropouts, unable or unwilling to work; their claims on societal solidarity, if any, derive from their unemployability. But in many countries, the eighteen year olds are steered directly towards the support system and early on learn to consume without working.

In modern democracies, the aspirations of governments are rising unrelentingly. This is reflected in the taxation level and in public expenditures as a proportion of BNP. In peacetime, one half should be the ultimate limit but Sweden reached 73% of BNP in 1993, a world record. In 2006 the country had retreated to 52% but was still the global leader. A serious consequence is political inbreeding. Civil servants, government employees, pensioners, students and the unemployed constitute a majority of the electorate, which is reflected in the parliament. When society has socialized itself beyond a certain point it may be difficult or even impossible to break out of the vicious circle. The situation is getting worse as the number of the elderly is increasing.

> A survey of the Swedish parliament in 2005 showed that 61% of the members were directly dependant on the public sector. Only 20% were close to business, the rest (19%) were indefinable. Among the women (45%) more then 70% had public connections.[6]

The main task of government is to establish a safe and predictable frame for value-creating plus-sum games, providing adequate scope for free enterprise.[6a] To quote James Buchanan: "Government should lay down the rules but not interfere in the game" Petty supervision spiced with envy and distrust erodes societal creativity. After all, the government participates, via the taxman, up to a level of 50% in every private company.

7.2 Business economics

Business and politics should be kept apart as far as possible. A developed economy hardly needs an active industrial policy, except a judicious financing of research and development. Government action may be induced by the lack of risk capital but, on the whole, industrial policy smacks of a planned economy. The global outcome is mixed, to say the least, with Singapore as an interesting exception.

> In Singapore, a moralizing Confucian administration has kept the small city-state on a tight rein and has successfully implemented an economic master plan. The rather forced political stability has facilitated long-term strategic thinking, so far with little backlash. Grossly simplifying, one could maintain that China is emulating Singapore after its depressing experience with a socialistic planned economy.
>
> METI (earlier MITI), the Japanese ministry for the economy, trade and industry, has also done its best to guide business, but the good advice has often fallen on deaf ears. In the early 1950s, MITI tried to

discourage a tiny company named Sony from entering electronics. A decade later MITI aimed at a consolidation of the car industry around one or at most two companies; for instance the entry of Honda into this line of business was shockingly self-willed.

Government planning used to leave a trail of so-called called white elephants – giant political investments, uncompetitive by any measure. The value destruction has been monumental in many developing countries. The Soviet Union was one of the worst offenders; I once had a hand in selling an industrial plant to Bishkek in Kyrgyzstan which was delivered and installed by my company but never commissioned by the buyer.

In a competitive market, a sound corporate strategy must be adjusted to the specific situation of the company. Save for trivial statements, valid guidelines for strategic thinking in business are therefore few and far between. The most pervasive is to try to minimize competitive pressure. Surprisingly, this egoistic precept provides guidance for long-term plus-sum play by promoting the sensible division of labor far into the future. The invisible hand of Adam Smith is quite instructive in a strategic context, too.

The governing strategic principle should be that an enterprise must be different, representing a unique business idea within its market area.[8] Otherwise it does not participate constructively in the plus-sum game of the market. Thus it will not provide any added value and cannot be successful in the long term. Learning from competitors is commendable, but all-out copying is futile in the absence of a clear-cut cost advantage. During the daily grind, zero-sum games are prevalent but strategic competition requires a more creative approach in order to achieve sustainable profitability.[9]

I have already (in chapter 2.4) referred to Gause's law which can be applied to business as well as to biology. In the long term, companies pursuing the same business strategies cannot coexist in the same market; only one of them will survive, barring artificial restrictions on competition. Current business dynamics, if not the law, sooner or later cuts short any all too cozy cohabitation. Genuine, value-creating cooperation can be realized only between diverging organizations. Collaboration between similar companies always smells of conspiracy; mergers and acquisitions are the obvious alternative.

As a business executive, my best strategic initiatives were based on a readiness to turn away from the beaten track, strengthened by a feeling of mission (cf. chapter 4, ref. 15). The outcome often surpassed the most optimistic expectations and amply exceeded the return on 'normal' investments. The moves were risky but not foolhardy, because the expansion could soon be financed by the new cash-flow – learning by earning. I have observed corresponding patterns of behavior in successful entrepreneurs and executives close by and far-away. The right values serve as a shortcut to good decisions. Superior profitability is often tied to an urge to create, the will to improve the world.

An innovative strategic approach always implies risk-taking, but exaggerated risk-avoidance buries a company for sure. The company must contribute by defining, developing and implementing a distinctive business idea with the potential to create added value for existing and presumptive customers. A new market can only be built over time but the trust of the customer can be lost in one, short moment. In marketing, morality is at least as important as in internal company relations. Contemporary corporations can be as particular about their reputation as medieval knights.

Creative collaboration is being extended from customers to the suppliers of goods, services and capital – even to competitors. Such networks have proved competitive and are surfacing in most branches of trade and industry.[10]

> Toyota was the first company to systematically establish an open relationship with its sub-contractors. In the ensuing network the different organizations cooperate symbiotically. The Toyota system has become standard in the car industry.

Network organizations call for a substantial degree of trust between the parties and thus a corresponding amount of moral capital. The same holds for joint ventures where the owners all too easily fall out about issues, great and small. I have participated in many, mostly successful joint ventures. Openness and honesty is the only admissible currency. Distrust and mutual recrimination disrupts a joint business in no time.

> The theory of business administration always lags behind the practice. The divisional management model appeared in the textbooks only after considerable delay and the same holds for project organization and outsourcing. All these measures aim at increasing the return on scarce moral capital, one way or another. The matrix organization, on the other hand, calls for a larger input of moral capital and therefore it is an uphill battle. Morality is coming into its own as the critical success factor (cf. chapter 4.5)

Moderate socialists readily admit that free enterprises are superior in the production of goods and many services, but in the same breath they exclude education and health care. It is, perforce, unacceptable to allow anybody to profit from teaching and healing. Health care and medical treatment is widely socialized in most democracies, and the typical symptoms are easily recognized: queues, bureaucracy, inferior customer service, frustrated personnel, lack of innovation and high cost despite low wages. The problems are complex but therefore an open market is just the right medicine.

> Skeptics refer to the United States which has the highest medical costs in the world, both absolutely and as a percentage of BNP. The comparison is flawed. The Americans are prepared to pay heavily for first-class treatment which is not generally available elsewhere. Moreover, legal processes are an omnipresent hazard which drives insurance costs through the roof and leads to superfluous diagnostics and medication. Fundamental market failure is, however, the deepest cause for the spiraling costs. The customers, providers and paymasters of health care are largely decoupled; businesses, insurance companies and the tax-payers are footing the bill without much grumbling. Market feedback stalls when demand does not depend on price and neither the customer nor the provider are exposed to the forces of competition.[11] (cf. 13.3)

Despite the political resistance, privatization on the quiet is making progress in many countries.[12] The better off are turning to private institutions and thus relieve the congestion of public care. Standardized operations such as bypass, cataracts and hip junctions are subcontracted to specialized private clinics, whereas geriatric care is transferred from public to privately managed but tax-financed establishments. Obsolete principles are slowly yielding to a pragmatic health care policy.

Higher education is another sacred cow for left wing politicians and the same socialistic syndrome is evident in this sector. Publicly financed universities generally charge very low fees and are usually underfinanced. Overcrowding is the norm and educational efficiency and quality leave much to be desired. James Buchanan has presented a typical public choice solution to this problem.[13]

> Buchanan's reasoning starts from the assumption that income transfers are dubious especially when the wealthy middle class is the beneficiary. Accordingly, academic studies should be self-financed and preferably privatized. The students would pay market prices for their studies, sup-

ported by long-term, government-guaranteed loans. The future earning capacity should cover interest and amortization.

The American top universities actually work along these lines, albeit
with substantial modifications. Over the years they have, by donations,
amassed huge funds which make possible high academic standards
with affordable fees and many free openings. But in Europe, a new approach to salaries and taxation will be required besides the soft loans.

A well-working educational market is not yet on the cards. Today academic degrees are overvalued as well as over-invested. Practice is still
in many ways the most efficient education, not least in entrepreneurship. Entrepreneurs rarely boast academic merits; self-made men and
women are heavily overrepresented among successful entrepreneurs.
In *Managers not MBA:s* Henry Mintzberg berates the business schools
in the United States for trying to make executives out of immature
youths.

Broad areas of the economy still linger out of the reach of creative
entrepreneurship and an open market. Without competition, organizations eventually petrify and even the best intentions come to naught.
It is depressing that the publicly employed generally seem to resist the
unavoidable reforms.

In virtually all democracies, the schoolteachers' unions fight any
changes in the status quo tooth and nail. Merit-linked promotion and
salaries are unacceptable; only examination certificates and seniority
should be counted. Vouchers too are inadmissible. They would, after
all, allow parents a free choice among schools in the neighborhood.
The unions want to hang on to their cuddled, bureaucratic nest – competition is anathema.

On every level, public administration must be transformed from a big,
clumsy employer to the clever purchaser of qualified services, supervising a diverse bunch of providers. This calls for new competencies
which even in the best case will require a lot of time and toil to develop. But this process would introduce much-needed dynamics and
release immense human resources.

In health care and education the societal responsibility of private
enterprises is called into question, ignoring the plain fact that it is in
concord with their self-interest. Furthermore, the public authorities are
relieved of the duty to supervise themselves, and are free to intervene
against any transgressions of the norms. The fear that greedy businessmen will line their pockets at public expense is naive and narrow-minded. In a competitive market, superior performance is rewarded but in

the long run the surplus flows to the consumers; the profit has to be earned again and again. Companies live up to their purpose by playing a fruitful plus-sum game; serving their customers, paying wages and taxes, getting a return on the capital – in short by making money.

7.3 Natural resources and the environment

In 1972, the Club of Rome predicted (in *The Limits to Growth*) a global breakdown due to overpopulation, famine, scarcity of raw-materials and pollution of the environment. Since then the warning bells have tolled ever harder and there is a danger that we turn a deaf ear when the alarm sounds in dead earnest. We will go deeper into these matters in part III. At this point I will only take up some glaring misconceptions.

Supplies of ores and minerals will not become a bottleneck in the foreseeable future. Better technology, reuse and substitution (for instance of copper wiring by aluminum and glass-fiber) is the market response to scarcity and price increases. In the last analysis it is a question of energy resources. With unlimited access to energy, all other bottlenecks can in principle be eliminated. Only technical prowess and capital are required to turn the trick.

The use of fossil fuels is doubtless a stumbling block for economic development, but not primarily due to the exhaustion of supplies. Coal, oil sands and methane hydrates will suffice for several centuries, albeit at an elevated cost level. The actual problem, as we all know by now, is the increase in the carbon dioxide content of the atmosphere, which can have catastrophic consequences.

> Despite a massive deployment of computer power, all future projections are plagued by persistent uncertainties. Suffice to say that the greatest caution is in order. Escalating changes in the atmospheric and oceanic circulation are possible though not very probable, to be sure. But in the worst case, the situation can spiral out of human control. It takes a long time to change the prevailing energy regime, and corrective action should thus be initiated without delay.

Taxation is the obvious, market-oriented reaction to onerous greenhouse gases. A universal tax on the release of carbon dioxide would be easy to administrate and would be a support for government finances without any economic distortions. The developing countries could be given time-limited exemptions and rule breakers could be checked by punitive custom duties. But for obscure reasons, the international community committed itself to the Kyoto agreement, a bureaucratic nightmare. In the European Union it started with individual quotas for 12,000 enterprises – a full-blown equivalent to the milk-quotas of European dairy farmers.[14]

> In Europe and United States, the release of sulfur dioxide was successfully curbed in the 1970s. This became a model for the Kyoto agreement despite a serious flaw in the analogy. In comparison, separation and storage of carbon dioxide is very expensive. Sulfur dioxide emissions are also a regional, not a global problem. In many developing countries sulfur dioxide pollution is still rampant, which hurts only themselves.

The European Union has the laudable ambition to establish a global leadership in environmental care, and the Kyoto agreement is seen as a symbol for responsible action. This is a wrong departure as will be seen, at the very latest, when the developing countries ought to be part of the process. Taxation is the superior method when an indispensable but polluting activity must be regulated. It is the height of folly not to apply it to fossil fuels.

> The Kyoto agreement is better than nothing but it is for this very reason an obstacle to a sensible international settlement. Carbon dioxide trading introduces a market element in the regulations. Even so, the regulations are arbitrary; they distort the competition and are heavily politicized. Every time when a change should be imposed – say stricter norms introduced or developing countries brought into the fold – a new hullabaloo breaks out when countries and industries fight for their interests with all the means available.[15]
>
> A switch from the cap-and-trade ideology of the Kyoto agreement to a clearly superior carbon-tax regime is difficult. In game-theoretic terms, the key actors are stuck in a Nash equilibrium which is far from optimal. But the optimum is hard to reach because unilateral step-by-step moves are unrewarding. The great majority of players must make a joint decision to achieve a change which benefits everybody.
>
> It does not help that taxation is a loaded word which implies an additional burden. It is easily forgotten that the customer (or the taxpayer) is always the final paymaster. Revenues from a carbon tax would enable the reduction of, say, other indirect taxes. If carbon dioxide allowances are auctioned off in a consistent manner, a carbon tax will be applied in a roundabout way, but it would apply only to power generation and heavy industry. At best, the system will be clumsy and very hard to put on a global footing.

Nuclear power has in many countries caused even more confusion. In Austria, an almost finished nuclear power plant in Zwentendorf was never commissioned when 50.5 % of the population voted against it. Germany has decided to abolish all nuclear power by 2021, but is still subsidizing coal mining in the Ruhr area (this is now set to be discontinued in 2018). The greatest policy disarray is found in Sweden, even though about half of Sweden's electricity production is nuclear.

> A referendum in 1980 in the shadow of the Three Mile Island incident produced a majority for shutting down nuclear power around 2010. Since then public opinion has turned around. Opinion polls are consistently showing a substantial majority for the continued use of existing nuclear plants; an expansion too has considerable support. Just the same, the government pushed through the shutdown of a plant (Barsebäck 1) in 1999. Barsebäck 2 was decommissioned in 2005.

Alternative energy sources are still all the rage in the media even if they will have little impact on the release of carbon dioxide in the foreseeable future. Nuclear power has been subject to a shameless smear campaign and political horse-trading based on misinformed voter opinion. All means have been permissible to mislead and to frighten the common man about nuclear perils which are blown out of all proportion.

The reactor trouble in Three Mile Island in 1979 did not hurt anyone and the radioactive emission was insignificant, but the jitters were all the worse.[16] At the close of extensive investigations only one strong argument against nuclear power remained on the table – people were afraid of it. After the Chernobyl accident in 1986, the rabid opponents could gloat over a notable increase in mortality in the United States during the following months. If the correlation is at all relevant, the blame can squarely be put on the media uproar – physical causation is out of the question. But the root cause was probably a prolonged heat-wave.[17]

> Chernobyl was a calamity which could occur only in the Soviet Union; no graphite moderated reactors were built elsewhere. The accident claimed 56 casualties, less than in a medium-sized coal mining accident. The radioactive leakage was massive, but according to WHO (World Health Organization) the clinical effects on the population at large was limited to thyroid cancer among children in the adjacent area (99 % of those hospitalized survived). This could have been avoided by the prompt distribution of iodine pills. In theory, a small increase of the cancer incidence can be calculated over time, all in all about 4000 deaths[18]. Even that number is doubtful (cf. chapter 10.1). In Chinese

coal mines, around 20,000 workers die every year according to a recent estimate.[19]

France was for long the only European country with a consistent pronuclear policy. In Finland the construction of a fifth nuclear reactor of 1600 MW capacity started in 2005. A thorough appraisal showed that a nuclear power plant was the best alternative from all points of view. The parliament refused a permit in 1993 but since then opinions have shifted among the citizens and politicians. Now the talk is about additional reactors and the international mindset, too, is changing apace.

Environmental research has become a whole industry with intense competition for available financing. Any reduction of risk assessment will be fiercely resisted by people who get their livelihood from chasing negative health effects from all imaginable sources. For many media, hyping health foods has become a source of income, and ecological products pride themselves on the absence of additives.

In *The Sceptical Environmentalist* (2001), Björn Lomborg presents a tough rejoinder to the scare-mongers, in effect an optimistic counterpart to the doom and gloom of the Rome Club. Lomborg, formerly a Greenpeace activist, point by point refutes the exaggerated views of the environmental movement. His analysis is biased but not easily disproved (there are web sites devoted to this purpose). That's why his adversaries have tried to dismiss him *in toto* as an exponent of wrongheaded opinions. But the fact remains that the developed world in general and the Nordic countries especially exhibit positive trends for the environment and the quality of life. Nevertheless, serious problems remain in the region.

> The Baltic is considered the most polluted sea in the world. Excessive nitrogen and phosphorus effluents have caused considerable eutrophication. While the discharge of industry and communities has been brought under control, the diffuse pollution from agriculture has been harder to check. The recovery of the Baltic will be slow, because the accumulated phosphorus in the bottom sediments periodically dissolves, with the sea continually fertilizing itself.

Danger alerts can be unjustified. The dioxin content of the Baltic herring has temporarily exceeded the EU-norms, which created hysterical consumer reaction; everybody knows that dioxin is one of worst super-poisons. This misconception lays behind a tragicomic incident, when the Ukrainian presidential candidate (and later president) Viktor Yushchenko was the target of a homicide attempt with a massive dose of dioxin. He suffered from the typical chloracne lesions in the face but survived and finished his election campaign.

The assassins did not know that the toxicity is tested on rabbits, which, like most mammals, are extremely sensitive to dioxin. Man is different, probably due to an ancient adaptation to dioxins from camp fires. A substantial dioxin release in Seveso in 1976 did not cause chronic symptoms or an increase in human mortality but thousands of animals died from acute poisoning.[20]

The environment is under constant pressure, especially in the developing countries, but encouraging signs are appearing on all continents. New areas are set aside as natural reserves and reforestation is initiated at a grand scale, especially in China where reportedly up to 100 000 km^2 are planted annually.[21] The Montreal Protocol on Substances that Deplete the Ozone Layer is a good example of successful global cooperation.

Chlorine and fluorine containing substances (CFCs or freons) are ideal components in cooling systems and air-spray products and became widespread after World War II. In 1974 the first suspicion of adverse effects surfaced, but only in 1985 were they confirmed by satellite observation. CFCs are quite stable, with a half-life in the atmosphere of more than a hundred years. But high in the stratosphere chlorine atoms are dissociated, which catalyzes the decomposition of ozone. The upshot is a potentially dangerous increase of ultraviolet radiation at high latitudes.

In 1987 the international Montreal Protocol was approved which gradually curbed and later prohibited the production and use of freons, first in the developed counties and subsequently (by 2010) in the developing ones. Adequate substitutes were developed and the consumers were never at a disadvantage. In 1994 the CFC content of the atmosphere started to drop by about one per cent annually.[22]

Constructive, fact-based collaboration can go a long way in combating environmental threats. Regrettably the debate has been marred by self-righteous posturing, which has only been detrimental to the good cause. The quality of the environment is basically a technical and economic problem which should be amenable to a rational approach. As long as facts about, for instance, nuclear power are systematically misconstrued, the public debate cannot serve as dependable guide for the politicians. General confusion and ill-advised decisions are the outcome when irrational aims justify any means and unrestrained polemics prevail.

7.4 Human Capital

Human reproduction has pivotal environmental and economic consequences and should take centre stage in any economic analysis. First
let us take a look at the reproductive strategies of man in primitive
societies.

> Birth control has from time immemorial been a common practice. If
> abortion did not work, the newborn was abandoned to die of expo-
> sure. (This praxis was applied in many high cultures, too.) The Austra-
> lian Aborigines used a more sophisticated method. During an initiation
> ceremony the spermatic duct of the young men was slit open so that
> sperm would not enter the vagina during ejaculation. If insemination
> was intended, the leak was closed with a finger.[23] Populations close to
> the natural state do not multiply recklessly.

The autonomous smallholder has been an icon for a long line of idealistic Utopians. A self-sustaining family homestead is independent of
market forces or the money economy and has been the resting place
for romantic escapism. Somewhat incongruously, economic logic appears unadulterated in such circumstances. The conflict between work
and capital is eliminated and *Homo economicus* has a free rein.

The marginal cost of an additional child is low because the mother
lacks alternative occupation and the needs of the children are slight.
In the longer term, the family gains additional laborers and social security because the children are obliged to care for their infirm parents.
But high mortality means that the number of children must be disproportionate to be on the safe side. The upshot is excessive nativity even
if every family makes a rational, statistical calculation.

> In the early fourteenth century, the population pressure in Western
> Europe had led to the cultivation of nearly all suitable land, save what
> kings and grandees could reserve as hunting grounds. In Northern Eu-
> rope the clearing of new fields and pastures continued into the eighteen
> hundreds. For us it is difficult to imagine the unforgiving circumstances
> which drove our forebears to break new stony ground for cultivation
> in extremely unfavorable conditions. Small wonder that emigration to
> the United States became an attractive alternative.

Emigration aside, the major part of the population surplus was eliminated by famine and disease up to the industrial revolution. Only then
could useful work for significant numbers be found outside agriculture. But concurrently mortality was dropping due to improvements

in nutrition, hygiene and health care. People still multiplied faster than they could be employed and wages were kept close to the minimum for survival. The scarce resources were capital and raw materials, whereas the supply of unqualified manpower usually surpassed demand. The marginal cost for an additional laborer was low and child labor was even cheaper.

Accordingly the founding fathers of economics placed common people in the same category as air, water and sunlight. They were essential production factors, but without economic value since they were abundant. The industries of the developing countries still work according to this logic but in the developed world it is out of date. The quality of the workforce lies behind the enormous differences in productivity. Accordingly, investments in education and professional skills are duly included in the BNP. But man as such still resides outside the calculations of the economists even though he and she is becoming a scarce resource in the developed world.

> Children are not assigned any value in assessing the national wealth. Rather, they are an economic burden because they reduce the female labor pool. People should be part and parcel of the national book-keeping, on a par with material resources – infrastructure, real estate, shares on the stock exchange, forests and arable land. Skilled, industrious and honest people are without doubt the most important resource of the nation. And the value chain starts from birth (actually from fertilization) with proper care, upbringing and teaching – all in all a substantial investment already before the entry to higher education. If changes in this biological capital were accounted for, the BNP growth of many countries would turn negative.

In our post-industrial society *Homo economicus* is still thinking rationally, only that the economic incentives are turned topsy-turvy. Children have become an economic liability. For a couple, the standard of living is clearly maximized over their life span if they refrain from procreation, heedlessly consuming the capital invested in them. Their livelihood in retirement is produced by somebody else's progeny. Except for the dirt poor, children are driving down the economic well-being of the family in comparison with a childless peer group.

> Child support has little impact except for the low income bracket. Taxation should be the vehicle for compensating, at least in part, the added costs of raising a family. Such systems exist but are generally insufficient. To become effective they must be combined with a tax increase for the childless. A straightforward way would be to differ-

entiate pension payments; study debts could be abrogated on similar grounds. Thus parenthood would be recognized as an investment in the future of society.

Economic considerations are not all-pervasive as children are still born in our societies. But the disastrously low fertility across Europe (and Japan) shows that the domestic economy matters. Adequate human reproduction has literally become a question of life and death for the developed world.

The biological capital has lately been sorely neglected in rich societies but we have made amends by concentrating on quality. General education was a particularly far-sighted reform which was introduced during a period of high nativity. Today lifelong tuition is a generally accepted doctrine, putting ever increasing demands on the public purse. The relevance and productivity of our educational efforts has become a pivotal issue.

> The transfer of knowledge from the teacher to the pupil still takes place in a medieval manner – the teacher lectures and the pupils listen, rehearse and exercise. This might be the best available method for basic skills such as reading and writing but teenagers are easily frustrated and/or passivated by the straightjacket of ordinary class teaching. Computer-fluent youngsters should be capable of self-sufficient learning instead of revolting against the teacher's authority; the acquisition of self-discipline would come as a bonus.

The concept of education implies that pupils are processed according to a prescribed scheme. Despite many attempts at differentiation, our centralized school systems generally cast everybody in the same mould. Standardized examinations facilitate certification and employment in public administration.

> The history of China vividly illustrates the pros and cons of extreme centralization. From the Tang period (618–907) onwards the Chinese administration was dependant on a complex bureaucracy, manned by well-educated mandarins. This Chinese version of a gentleman combined scholarship with loyalty to the authorities in the Confucian spirit. Competition for admission to the schools was vicious, especially on the higher levels which guaranteed an entry to the most lucrative positions. Eventually the studies were refined so that in the Ming period (1368–1644) they focused entirely on classical literature.

Our educational system has not suffered from lack of criticism. All the fore-mentioned and much more has been repeated *ad nauseam*. Education was one of the more deserving targets for the student rebellion of 1968. Some changes materialized but it was mostly old, sour wine in new bottles with a spicing of women's science and ethnic folklore. Socialistic planning with all its flaws still dominates education at least in Europe. That the taxpayer is the main paymaster is not at issue. The contest is about the creation of more space for private initiative by partial de-socialization.

> It was something of a surprise when a short-lived right-wing government in Sweden provided room for so-called independent schools. They receive the same support as publicly operated schools but are producing better quality at the same cost; some of them are very innovative.[24] Close to ten percent of the pupils now go to independent schools. About half of the independent schools are organized as limited companies, but the main driving force for new establishments is parental concern. Finland is lagging behind its Nordic neighbor. Perhaps the international success in the Pisa comparisons has led to inordinate self-admiration.[25]

The opponents of privatization fret about plummeting standards of education but they are even more afraid of a marked improvement. Equality is trumping liberty, and it has to be conceded that deplorable segregation cannot be ruled out. In any case, appropriate regulations are necessary to minimize drawbacks. But the advantages of open competition predominate. A market constantly produces new ideas. The failures are the price of progress and are weeded out, whereas the successes are copied in no time. We feel at ease with the market turbulence in goods and many services but it is obviously less acceptable when the education of the next generation is at stake.

> Practice has however outdistanced theory. Despite all attempts at centralization, universities as well as colleges and high schools are subject to an incontestable differentiation by reputation which determines the market value of the examinations. Friedmannian self-regulation is at work.

Modern societies are committed to joint responsibility for all their citizens – a projection of Christian humanism into practical politics. This strong solidarity has, however, produced an expanding crowd of free-riders. They enjoy full insurance cover but eschew the trouble and cost of biological reproduction. The resulting distorted age structure has produced a temporary surplus of labor and an artificially enhanced standard of living. The next generations will face the immense challenge to rebalance the deformed population pyramid.

7.5 The global economy

As an international invective, globalization has succeeded capitalism with equally scant justification. Both practical experience and economic theory indicate that the global liberation of trade stimulates the plus-sum game and increases added value. In *Why Globalization Works* Martin Wolf has systematically refuted current myths about the iniquities of globalization.[26] The Nobel laureate Joseph Stiglitz has become a kind of spokesman for the opponents even though he mainly criticizes the high-handed policies of the International Monetary Fund in his *Globalization and its Discontents*.

> The IMF has conceded some mistakes but certainly learned by its errors. Stiglitz recommends a democratization of the International Monetary Fund. Electoral reform has recently been instigated but banks are by their nature undemocratic; power must be tied to the capital at risk. The IMF is the lender of last resort for countries with insurmountable currency problems. It also serves as a scapegoat for unpopular measures and the painful repercussions of a credit squeeze. If the IMF causes more harm than benefit, as asserted by opponents, it is easy to shut it down and return the capital to the original sources in the rich countries.
>
> The contention that globalization restricts the sovereignty of independent states is nonsense even if cornered ministers of finance like to hide behind this argument. To refute the allegation it is not necessary to refer to extremes like North Korea or Myanmar. Argentina has for years defied the IMF and a host of other banks; there are no means to enforce the demands of the aggrieved creditors. Whether this is good policy is another question but Argentina has so far ridden it out. The IMF temporarily lost its market when Turkey was the only major debtor, but once again the fund has more than enough on its plate.

The international financial community has become a popular target for the opponents of globalization. They proclaim that uncontrolled currency movements precipitate the occasional balance of payments crises of developing countries. Here cause and consequence are inverted. A run on the currency is not the root case of the evil but a symptom of mismanagement of the economy. The so-called Tobin tax would be an empty gesture. The only road to economic development and financial stability is a responsible long-term policy, which is always a hard sell domestically.

It is also maintained that globalization exacerbates the shocking income differences in the world. This may be true, but without globalization the poor would be much worse off, unfortunately they rarely have an opportunity to speak up. I do not want to belittle the misery in many developing countries, but the widely spread talk of an income level below one dollar a day is disingenuous.

> A self-sufficient household or hamlet can manage without any money and in a wider context barter often dominates the marketplace. The grey economy, too, falls outside the preview of the economists. It does not register or pay taxes but is a substantial factor even in developed countries. (The grey economy in the Mediterranean countries of the European Union is assessed to be about 30% of the official BNP). Finally, the price parity must be considered which reflects differences in the price level. One dollar buys a lot more in Calcutta than in New York.

The grey economy predominates in the shanty towns of Latin America and Africa which are a fixture of the major population centers. Local entrepreneurship is flourishing but the enterprises cannot or do not want to grow. Growth would increase the risk of exposure to arbitrary taxation and extortion. Private property often lacks the protection of the law.

> In *The Other Path* (1989), Hernando de Soto describes the thorny trail of the law-abiding entrepreneur in Peru in the 1980s. Registering a company required visiting a dozen different government departments. In a test, bribes were requested in most places; twice it was impossible to proceed without paying up. To procure a building permit for barren government land required a seven year struggle with the bureaucracy, scattered between 48 points of entry. (Peru has since tried to deconstruct its bureaucracy.)
>
> In *The Mystery of Capital* (2000), de Soto has expanded his view to developing countries in general. The subtitle of the book is: *Why Capitalism Triumphs in the West and Fails Everywhere Else*. Traps abound for honest businessmen. The "Doing Business" report of the World Bank goes into illuminating detail about the efforts of many underdeveloped countries to strangle all legal economic activity. The bureaucracy has been stunning but the trend is encouraging; many African countries are mending their ways.

Without legal title to property there is no credit, which further restricts the growth opportunities of small business entities. No wonder that capital formation is weak, the real interest rate dizzying, income differences outrageous and the economy in tatters. In underdeveloped countries, success in business all too often builds on political contacts, crony capitalism. For mavericks, legal protection has much to be desired and the same holds for foreign investors, who enjoy an official welcome but often become the victims of harassment, if not worse.

> In the context of a Nordic business venture in Russia, Ukraine and the Baltic countries (see chapter 4.5) the management wanted to enter Belorussia too, but as chairman of the board I was against it. With President Lukashenka at the helm there was, in my view, no chance for an honest enterprise to succeed. Later on however, an investment was done through our Russian daughter company, which putatively had the right contacts. A binding contract was signed and the necessary reconstruction was immediately started with funds we lent to the company. Everything went down the drain when Lukashenka appeared on the scene with new demands. The money was finally returned after years of litigation in an international court of arbitration, threatening the seizure of Belorussian property abroad.
>
> The majority of developing countries, especially in Africa, have not been fertile ground for foreign investment with the exception of high margin extractive industries (oil, gas and minerals). Uncertainty discourages any long-term investment without the participation of influential politicians – even so the probability of a coup d'état must also be taken into consideration. It is no longer fashionable to take over the whole state behind the scenes as was done by big American business in the so-called banana republics of the 1920s.

Countries with an old ingrained culture have found it easier to introduce western technology and to create their own capital base without development aid. Even communist China has discarded its socialist prejudices and adopted the principles of the market economy. Many new nations have, however, met with great economic difficulties despite big doses of good advice, subsidized loans and outright financial aid. Corruption, political instability and civil war are not the right preconditions for sound business activities. Under such circumstances no help will be effective. Yet if the investment climate is right no help is needed because capital from abroad will be available for all sensible purposes.

It is doubtful if the financial support of developing countries makes sense. To donate from a surplus is all right but most donating countries are deeply indebted despite high taxes. Helping by diving into ever deeper debt sounds irresponsible; we should concurrently reduce our own consumption. Ultimately, the middle class of the rich nations is supporting the corrupt elite in the poor countries. For these people solidarity with their compatriots does not stretch to the payment of taxes even if the length of the limousines holds its own in international competition; capital flight often exceeds the development aid. But the solidarity of the poor emigrants to their kin is impressive. During 2005, approximately 250 billion dollars were transferred to relatives in the developing countries which many times exceeds the official development aid.[27]

The economic problems of the developing countries can be solved only by themselves, but the richer parts of the world cannot close their eyes to the acute emergency needs. One of the problems is that the population density often exceeds the limits of sustainable agriculture. The devastation of forests by slash-and-burn cultivation exacerbates the effects of climate fluctuations, which then immediately precipitate famine.

In the Sahel excessive grazing is common, even if nature seems to recuperate after the dry periods. The situation is worse in Ethiopia where the forest cover is less than three percent today, down from about forty percent in the early nineteen hundreds. In Indonesia, illegal clearing of the rain forest cause widespread peat and forest fires, which produce suffocating smog covering whole regions. The population dynamics creates a vicious circle when the common land is ruthlessly exploited in an extended minus-sum game. The fish catch too is suffering in many developing countries in contrast to the successful application of fishing quotas and no-fishing areas in Iceland and Chile.

The worst predicament is when the emergency aid prolongs the agony by interfering with a sensible accommodation. The generous stream of food and other necessities rarely reaches its target before corrupt authorities, hungry soldiers or roving bandits have taken their ample share. North Korea is the most flagrant example of the distortions of emergency aid. A substantial part of the population is dependent on food aid from the United Nations and South Korea while the vile dictator constructs more nuclear weapons.

It should be obvious that a global economic plus-sum game offers the only opportunity for the developing countries to escape their vicious circle. From this point of view there is a globalization deficit, because the developed countries are breaking the rules by trade restrictions and subsidies. Losers can be found in all countries, loudly protesting when the free market robs them of their privileged positions. But the great majority of consumers benefit, even if they are mostly mute, and the process moves on with the indisputable logic of plus-sum play.

Nevertheless we must be wary of a rash optimism. The First World War showed how irrational forces can in an instant destroy fruitful international cooperation. But I believe we have learnt from our mistakes. Commerce requires reciprocity, but for that very reason it creates mutual respect and self-respect. Trade depends on trust and generates trust; it needs peace and strengthens the peace. Finally, trade creates wealth and is the best development aid.

Chapter 8

Law and justice

We insist on safety for life, limb and property but tend to shackle the police as they try to do their job. Nevertheless our sense of justice is violated when the judicial system over-emphasizes the rights of criminals at the expense of law-abiding citizens. Further contradictions abound when the calls for absolute 'cosmic' justice become strident. We have to be content with the amelioration of injustices, assisting disadvantaged groups in helping themselves. A global solidarity is emerging but it has yet to find a suitable frame of reference.

8.1 The price of security

Beside the legislative and executive power structures, an independent judiciary is indispensable in order to maintain the respect for the rules of the game we have agreed upon. In peacetime the police have a monopoly on violent suppression; all other violence is banned with a few, specific exceptions.

The police are part of the executive structure, but a serious infringement of civic rights always requires the decision of a judge. Police work is demanding and often dangerous, but the pay is generally mediocre and the status of the profession is open to question. The temptation to supplement income can be overwhelming. A corrupt police force is an abomination which corrodes the foundations of society. Attempts to supervise the supervisors just move the focus of corruption to the next level. The best way to improve morale is to strengthen the reputation of the police as the impeccable servants of society.

> In times of old, an unwritten rule of honor protected the unarmed London Bobbies on duty; violent resistance was not fair play. Today the authority and inviolability of the police must be further strengthened by law. Nowadays in many a big city, resisting the police can be just a popular pastime. Threats or violent behavior against police officers should be an extremely aggravating circumstance; a special riot police should not be necessary. On the other hand, the police ought to be irreproachable and any abuse must be severely punished.

These ideas imply a departure from the principle of equality before the law. The police would be raised on a pedestal with a strengthened personal integrity but would also suffer more severe sanctions for breach of duty. This may sound radical but even old, well-worn principles should be questioned if they work against the original purpose.

Among the public and consequently among legislators, a profound wariness or even distrust of the guardians of the law is apparent. Detailed instructions abound to protect the legal position of the suspects, and the means and scope of police investigations are curbed in many ways. The intention is to guard the citizens against a prying and ruthless police force. This is fine, but the outcome is that the safety of the law-abiding majority takes second place.

> Instead of harassing honest policemen, we have to accept that some misconduct is unavoidable in all human activities. A suspect police force cannot be held in check by preventive directives but only by strict selection, satisfactory pay, good training and sufficient sanctions for abuse of power. Today a high morale and quick results are demanded in an atmosphere of basic distrust – a very demoralizing combination.

Anxiety regarding high-handed and arbitrary action by the authorities is in itself a healthy reflex, but the fear of a police state is far-fetched. On the contrary, the reluctance of democratic states to take action against its enemies can be devastating. For malevolent forces planning to take full control of the levers of society, breaking a few additional statutes is neither here nor there. The defense of democracy must be thoroughly entrenched so that a coup is unthinkable.

Organized crime is a real threat against society in many countries. The southern parts of Italy are still economically depressed due to the paralyzing presence of the mafia, the camorra and the 'ndrangheta. In Russia, the criminal gangs became a plague after the fall of communism but their influence has gradually diminished. Japan is famous for its law-abidance but the local yakuza leagues are said to count about 100,000 members, even if they do avoid provoking the police. And in the United States the Federal Bureau of Investigation has for decades been fighting organized crime in the major cities.

> Successful criminal organizations have a strong internal morale, often based on ethnicity and long traditions. They are hard to penetrate; there are few witnesses and those at hand tend to disappear before the trial. Supported by high-class lawyers, the leaders could usually escape a conviction. In 1970, the U.S. congress passed the Racketeering Influenced and Corrupt Organizations Act (RICO) which was di-

rectly aimed at the mafia. Leadership is criminalized and carries heavy penalties. Money laundering by legal activities is included in the crime classification and triple damages can be imposed.

Many democracies are threatened by increasingly effective organized crime; in developing countries it is sometimes difficult to discriminate between politicians and criminals. New born democracies, too, may be vulnerable. In Mexico the rule of law is still very weak, despite reforms, and most violent crimes remain unsolved.[1] International drug trafficking and terrorist organizations globalize criminality and call for an appropriate response. A further intensification of police cooperation at the European Union level and through Interpol is needed. Not even the Nordic countries are impervious to the new threats.

Formerly, Finland was regarded as a calm corner despite the relatively high incidence of violent crime. But in general, the crimes were spontaneous, alcohol-influenced and very unorganized; in 2004, 86.3% of the serious assault and murder cases could be solved.[2] The following year, parliament nevertheless deemed it necessary to pass a law making membership of criminal gangs (narrowly defined) a punishable offence. Likewise the wearing of a facemask in public was criminalized (but only if illegal activities were intended).

A few years ago, a close acquaintance of mine was murdered by professionals paid by his drug-addicted son. The crime was solved but the professional killers are here to stay. Recently, three men were convicted for the murder of an informer though no corpse could be produced; the Swedish paymaster got the same life sentence. Hollywood movies have invaded real life in tranquil Helsinki.

In spite of the obvious hazards, every imagined or real intrusion into privacy evokes howls of indignation. Comprehensive registration of the citizens, which is uncontroversial in many parts of Europe, induces a storm of protests in the Anglo-Saxon countries. The prospect of detailed surveillance in a thoroughly computerized society conjures up unpleasant feelings everywhere.

Personally I find this anxiety hard to understand. Granted that information from video-cameras, credit-cards and phone connections etc. presents new opportunities for scanning the whereabouts of citizens. But there is scant motive for the different arms of the administration to extend their surveillance beyond suspect or illegal activities. A considerable conspiratorial imagination is required to perceive the appearance of a Big Brother society in the computer revolution.

But, say the critics, already the possibility of monitoring is an intrusion into our private life. Hardly, if we are not caught involved in some shameful activity, and in our societies this threshold is rather high. At worse we might take a short step towards the norms of a small village which, according to credible authority, is required to lick our children into shape. In the good old times, all new data of human interest were daily delivered by the gossip mill. An additional dose of social control would hurt neither children nor adults in our post-modern society.

A more pragmatic attitude to privacy violations is called for. Instead of conjuring up imaginary terrors it would be advisable to accept a few inconveniences to reduce the risk of bloody terrorist attacks and the spread of drug-addiction. Laws and regulations can always be corrected if the powers of the police are deemed excessive. A practical question of pros and cons should not be misrepresented as a matter of principle.

> In the United States it has not been easy to accept even a moderate tightening of public control, but so far this seems to have worked wonderfully. After 9.11.2001, new attacks have been averted despite blood-curdling threats from terrorist quarters. Unfortunately renewed terrorist outrages are still on the cards both in the United States and in Europe.

The efficacy of the police force is wholly dependent on the support of the citizens. The old tradition of police deputies could be one way to reinforce the public spirit and reduce the need for private security guards. After all, it is only natural that the residents are responsible for neighborhood security. Minor misdemeanors like littering, damage to property and harassment could be checked by local deputies, thus satisfying the craving for public security. (The United Kingdom has a voluntary force of 15,000 'special constables').

Security has its price even in democracies which try to combine the safety of citizens with a maximum of personal liberty. Complete anonymity is not achievable any more if one does not want to open the door to the enemies of ordered society; neither is it morally legitimate. The rights of the criminal offender must also be weighed against protection of the honest citizen. No magistrate is ever held responsible for the murders and rapes, not to mention burglaries and frauds, which are committed by well-known criminals on the loose. There are strong reasons to keep professional criminals and habitual malefactors under continuous surveillance, for instance by electronic monitoring. The intention is not to mete out an additional penalty but to protect the innocent.

8.2 The legal system

Every country has its own historically conditioned legislation which varies a lot even between democracies. Laws are made to establish rights but often create new wrongs. Thus the citizens cannot be protected against all injustices. That would require a superhuman wisdom which is not obtainable. But we can try to guarantee the predictability of the legal system. Then each and everyone should know when he or she is breaking the law.

If a crime is uncovered or controversies arise, the legal machinery springs into action. Integrity and objectivity are essential, as moral weakness cripples law and justice. The previous section pointed at exaggerated caution which can be counterproductive in regulating the police. The judicial process has similar problems. Many guilty people are never caught or are acquitted but, in return, very few innocents are convicted.[3]

The Nordics and Continental Europe follow Roman legal tradition of written law whereas the Anglo-Saxon common law relies more on legal precedent and the jury institution. Today Nordic courts have no jury proper, although Scandinavian tradition goes back to pre-Christian times. The old provincial laws consistently stipulated that "twelve good men" should decide in criminal cases.

> Trespassing justified self-defensive action but manslaughter was legal only if the intruder had actually entered your home. The adjudication became problematic when the slain fell over the threshold. The fourteenth century law of Magnus Eriksson lives up to the challenge. If the feet of the deceased were inside the threshold the home had been violated and the perpetrator was acquitted. If the feet were outside the threshold, manslaughter was in evidence and heavy fines were imposed.

The jury is a sort of people's court. Its aim was, and is still, to represent the common sense of justice as a counterweight to the power of the judge and his occasional corruptibility. The lords of lore, too, preferred to be judged by their peers, not by a court which probably would be the king's puppet. Elected parliaments were primarily supreme courts. In Great Britain the House of Lords (actually the law lords) is still the highest court in the land. Historically, parliament and the jury institution have functioned as a bulwark against the might of a power-hungry central authority. The abrogation or neglect of these institutions imperiled any emerging democratic traditions which can be hard to revive later on.

In the 1860s, Alexander II initiated a great reform comprising local self-government (*semstvo*) and jury in criminal cases. (Feodor Dostoevsky (1821–81) has immortalized such a trial in *The Brothers Karamazov*). The juries were cleaned out during the Bolshevik revolution together with all other manifestations of incipient democracy. Boris Jeltsin reintroduced the jury system for serious crime cases.

All democracies have a hierarchy of at least three judicial levels and flawed verdicts can be repealed or modified by a higher court. For instance the enormous damages, which are occasionally meted out by the juries in the United States, are usually adjusted after appeal. Inbuilt inconsistency is the great weakness of the jury institution. The verdicts vary exceedingly, depending on the venue and on the domicile and ethnicity of the parties, to say nothing of the emotional manipulations of the lawyers.

Then again, a court-dominated judiciary can lead to excessive solidarity between the police, the prosecutor and the court. In Russia, 99% of the indicted are sentenced in criminal cases, and in Japan the situation is similar – in practice the accused are already convicted when they arrive before the judge.[4] In Japan a system of mixed courts with laymen members is under consideration. The jury is still out regarding the pros and cons of different court procedures.

The administration of justice implies a continuous conflict between form and content, between abstract legislation and personal judgment, between the letter of the law and mitigating or aggravating circumstances. A minor technicality can upset a watertight argumentation. To exclude relevant evidence is contrary to the layman's conception of justice, if the procedural error is not of material significance.

> Democratic judiciaries tend to provide some leeway for the defense because the prosecutor is deemed to have the upper hand due to superior, state-financed resources. This is fine on principle, but if the defense can mobilize even greater funds the balance may be reversed. O.J. Simpson was in 1995 acquitted by an almost all-black jury of the murder of his Caucasian ex-wife and her boyfriend. Later on, a civil court sentenced him to pay 33 million dollars as compensation for a crime which he, after all, had committed.

For the defense everything is permitted. It is contrary to our sense of justice that the accused and his or her lawyers can resort to all kinds of deception and dissimulation without any sanction. To lie and deceive in court is an unalienable legal right which does not conform to prevalent morality. Easier to understand is the principle that nobody should be obliged to prove his or her innocence; the burden of proof lies unequivocally on the prosecution. But laudable principles are often impractical in confrontation with hardened criminals. In tax fraud prosecution, a reversed burden of proof is not unusual; the suspect must present a credible source for his income or wealth. At least it was the only way to nail the notorious gangster Al Capone in 1931.

In civil cases the antagonists should be on an equal footing but inequities appear once again due to the differences in resources and influence. A giant corporation can draw out the trial, exhausting the weaker party especially if the loser is not ordered to pay legal expenses. Big business is, on the other hand, vulnerable to deep-pocketed lawyers working on a provision basis. Once the best business idea in the computing field was to sue IBM, the dominant company.

> The United States is the most litigious country in the world. If an accident has occurred, somebody must be at fault – preferably somebody well-heeled. The law commands respect which is reflected in the imposing court architecture. Damages can be astronomical and even major companies may be driven into bankruptcy. The asbestos trials, based on tort law, have to date caused about seventy bankruptcies.
>
> Historically, Japan never had recourse to impartial courts, which has created a business culture built on personal relations. A young Japanese engineer once appeared out of the blue in our head office. He was well received and guided around our modern sugar refinery. The contact was maintained and he became our adviser and representative in Japan. We never wrote a contract but became business partners and friends for life.
>
> In East-Asia, business relationships are directed by an unwritten code of honor which is often more binding than a detailed contract. To approach a court is almost scandalous because the defeated party would inevitable lose face. Although the figures are not strictly comparable, the United States has twenty-five times more lawyers per capita than Japan; the output of law-schools is now increasing all over East Asia.[5]

Courts of arbitration are a significant advance for the rule of law in civil cases. Since 1923, The International Chamber of Commerce (ICC) maintains a network of arbitration courts, encompassing 130 countries. This facilitates the speedy and relatively cheap resolution of contractual disputes. Nowadays, a clause on arbitration is routine in international business agreements. Considerable damages can be levied and executed by the ICC.

The worst shortcoming of the judiciaries is an almost criminal tardiness in contrast to the courts of arbitration. In a number of countries, the suspects are held without trial for extended periods and in many quarters, wealthy or powerful malefactors can extend the judicial process without limit. In most places it is very difficult for the common citizen to prevail if public servants have encroached upon his rights.

> The Ombudsman institution is a Swedish innovation which aims to empower the individual against an overbearing administration, bypassing the lengthy judicial process. The European Union has its ombudsman and the institution is spreading around the world. Ombudsmen are in vogue and now abound for gender equality, children, data protection, the media etc. In any case, ombudsmen are reducing the imbalance between the common man and a judiciary which is inexorably growing in complexity.

Improving the predictability of verdicts would be a great boon to the legal system; in America, close to 90% of criminal cases are decided out of court. In civil law too, assisted mediation is gaining ground in many countries.[6] The most quarrelsome cannot be shut out of the courtroom but reasonable people could avoid lawsuits, agree amicably and save a lot of time and money – after all litigation is a glaring minus-sum game.

A functional and impartial judiciary is indispensable for any sustainable societal plus-sum game. It is easy to criticize discrete failings and to underestimate the value of ethical norms which for generations have maintained satisfactory law and order in the democratic countries. But the citizens are after all customers. In the long term, their views cannot go unheeded. Spotless procedures do not exclude unjust sentences, while judicial perfectionism may prevent tackling nascent terrorism and organized or habitual crime; the means must not trump the aims in absurdum. As Adam Smith says "mercy for the guilty is cruelty to the innocent". In summary, the best can be the enemy of the good.

8.3 Crime and punishment

"An eye for an eye, a tooth for a tooth" prescribed King Hammurabi of Babylonia who reigned c.1792–1750 B.C. The principle of a life for a life goes even further back, though there were people and people. A grandee could without much ado kill off common folk but his own death often called for ample human sacrifice. In Sweden, common manslaughter was expiated by a suitable indemnity but the old provincial law from the 13th century prescribed hanging for theft. In those times, material wealth was more valuable than life.

The classification of crime has changed since the times when crime and sin were conflated. Fornication (sexual intercourse outside marriage) was criminalized in Massachusetts in the seventeenth century and it is still on the statute books in several states in the USA, although lawbreakers are not pursued any more. The penalties were dissimilar too. People were not jailed except for the duration of the trial. If the death penalty was not applied, physical punishment – the whip or the pillory – was meted out. Public shaming was considered the most effective preventive measure.

> In *Law in America,* L.M. Friedman tells us how the law in the United States has developed from the local justice of colonial times to a tangle of immense complexity. For the settlers, the social and religious community was sacred; deportation was only a milder form of the death sentence. Friedman takes note of the ups and downs of support for capital punishment but cannot explain why the Americans are clinging to it, contrary to other democratic nations.
>
> During their ascendancy, the Dutch were almost as puritanical as the New England settlers, but they had to deal with sin on a bigger scale. In 1595, the magistrates of Amsterdam felt a need to build a house of correction for youthful delinquents. Instead of execution or mutilation, hard discipline and moral indoctrination were applied to produce improved human beings. The chronically work-shy were placed in a contraption where water was streaming in. The culprit had continuously to work a pump to avoid drowning.[7]

With some justification it was thought that not only the victim but all society suffered from a criminal act. In modern terms, every disturbance of the fine-tuned social plus-sum game has been considered an evil to be eradicated. Today we are less strict even if fornication still spreads venereal diseases, causes unwanted pregnancies and breaks up marriages, all at the expense of society. But when drugs are in play we use the same arguments as the puritans of old.

> Singapore is, as far as I know, the only country which has been successful in maintaining a consistent drug policy. The death penalty is pronounced for the possession of more than 25 grams of heroin, 30 grams of cocaine or 500 grams of cannabis. Anybody can be tested and drug addicts are forcibly interned for rehabilitation for at least six months.[8] Still, a small local market is supplied by smuggling from adjacent Malaysia.
>
> In most countries we encounter typically democratic compromises. Drugs cannot be legalized but neither is there the will to make a determined effort to enforce the ban. The United States has strict legisla-

tion and the prisons are overflowing but, all the same, drug trafficking seems to be an attractive business.

The drug policies in Europe are more or less a façade. In the west we generally practice what Friedman calls the Victorian compromise. Many laws are not intended to be rigorously applied but serve to prop up public morality. Flagrant crimes are brought to trial but a strict supervision would be too expensive, too intrusive and politically inexpedient. The official norms can be flouted, provided there is no scandal. Antiquated laws are simply forgotten and are annulled only after a long delay.

Drug addiction is a crime where the culprit is the only victim, and it should accordingly be neglected in line with our attitude towards moral laxity in general. Concerning addictions of any kind, we are instead assuming an expanded social responsibility, which is not so far removed from the ideology of puritan regimentation. The difference is that sin has been converted into sickness and priests have given way to psychiatrists – both probably equally ineffective. Individual responsibility and thus personal liberty are again called into question.

> In *A Clockwork Orange* (1962), Anthony Burgess defends the freedom of man to choose evil in contrast to an inflicted medicalized harmlessness. Genuine good can only be the outcome of a voluntary choice. The confrontation with evil is indispensable for our spiritual growth; our inbuilt evil tendencies cannot and should perhaps not be surgically removed.

Busybody know-alls are about to define away crime and guilt from this world. We are just at the beginning of this sea change but the logic seems irrefutable. All deviations from the social norms must have an underlying cause. The delinquent has been exposed to bad upbringing, bad company or bad genes. He (less often she) is not to be blamed for his transgressions. Every misdemeanor – serious crime in particular – is the result of unhappy circumstances and on a level with mental derangement. A sound human being does not commit crimes; a criminal is consequently always sick.

> In the former Soviet Union criminals were jailed as in other places, but honest opponents of the regime remained a puzzling problem. The only explanation was mental derangement because resistance against the Soviet state was obviously irrational. Such cases were consequently interned in a mental hospital; the most notorious was the Serbski Institute for forensic medicine in Moscow. Its director Georgi Morozow

diagnosed slow schizophrenia, a condition hitherto unknown. The patients persistently went against their own, personal interests in order to promote abstract illusions such as human rights, freedom and democracy.[9]

From a judicial perspective the whole voluminous discussion about the causes of deviant behavior is irrelevant. In a game of soccer, the players get yellow or red cards on equal grounds; there is no recourse to a hot temperament. The rules are there to be followed, and most transgressions in soccer as in life are due to an effort to achieve an unfair advantage. This temptation is ever-present and must have a sufficient counterweight.

> The duration and kind of punishments are constantly debated. The police are frustrated by the repeated pursuit of the same habitual offenders who are released almost as fast as they are jailed. At least in the Nordic countries, the police and the prosecutors have few means to put pressure on hardened criminals. According to common horse sense (but not to legal convention) lack of cooperation, for instance concerning accomplices or stolen property, should be an aggravating circumstance. But in judicial practice, cooperation is seen as exceptional and produces lighter sentences.
>
> The so-called zero tolerance against minor misdemeanors has had a salutory effect in American cities. In Europe too, littering should be a punishable offence on the Californian model.[10] Many liberals profess that harder sentences do not act as a deterrent. Then lighter sentencing would not increase criminality either and we could get rid of prisons for good. In any case, inmates rarely commit crimes except when they are on leave or at large.

The respect for the rules of the game must be maintained to preserve the plus-sum game. Punishment has primarily a preventive purpose; crime must not be profitable. Recurrent relapses indicate that the disincentives are insufficient. Alternatively, the culprit is not capable of controlling his impulses and should anyhow be excluded from free intercourse with other people. The old argument that hunger and distress drives the indigent onto the path of crime does not hold up today.

The persistence of criminality in our welfare societies has been a disappointment for the spokesmen of socialism. Independent of the political system, the law-breakers seem to form a permanent underclass and constitute a major challenge for scientists, as well as for well-wishers of all categories. The lack of insight is reflected in the dearth of dependable methods for rehabilitation. Prison sentences could, at best, act as a kind of conditioning therapy, but more often it is the first step on the path to professional crime.

> At the inception of the prison system in the first half of the eighteenth century, a thoroughly planned corrective regime was applied with solitary cells, silence during meals and the bible as sole literature. The idea was that contemplation supported by the word of God would bring the delinquent on the road of moral recovery. But the outcome was not as intended. Mental disorders and suicides ran rampant. Costs were high and eventually the makeover was made to the present-day, chronically overpopulated penitentiaries and corrective institutions. In many countries, the liberalization of the prison regime has reached a point where it is no deterrent for habitual criminals.
>
> As a treatment for offenders, the normal prison regime is a capital failure. Voluntary organizations have fared better. In the care of the Salvation Army, first-time youthful offenders in Florida show dramatically improved rehabilitation compared with the corresponding prison population.[11] KRIS is a Swedish voluntary initiative aiming at recidivists with a background in alcohol and drug abuse.[12] For hardened criminals, time is the only remedy. Delinquency decreases after the age of 35 and in the fifties the crime propensity drops to a very low level.

It would be fine if we could empty the prisons like the mental institutions of yore. The problem is that we have no access to magic pills which would protect the criminally inclined from the temptations of freedom. Many investigations point to a criminal personality which emerges in childhood.[13] A genetic variation has been found which predestines the bearers for risk-taking, restlessness and weariness. Depending on the genetic and social environment, the hereditary deviation can give rise either to creative entrepreneurship or criminal activity.[14]

> John Laub and Robert Sampson have in *Shared Beginnings, Divergent Lives* analyzed the lives of 500 juvenile offenders during a sixty year period. The divergences are explained, less by the psychological profiles than by the social relations after leaving the different types of reform schools. A suitable employer, often the military, and good marriages were decisive for reintegration into society.
>
> The incidence of criminality can vary a lot depending on seemingly unrelated circumstances. John Donahue and Steven Lewitt aroused considerable interest with their study *The Impact of Legalized Abortion on Crime*. They contend that the major part of the decrease in criminality during the 1990s is due to the legalization of abortion twenty years earlier. According to their theory, unwanted children are badly treated and therefore more often get into trouble with the law.

A criminal course is rarely predestined but is largely dependant on external conditions, in particular the efficacy of the judicial system. A strict and highly probable punishment deters rationally thinking people from breaking the law, whereas the mentally underprivileged have a harder time understanding that crime does not pay. They live in the present and can be discouraged only by continuous supervision combined with quick and unpleasant consequences. Soon medical remedies will be available for this type of criminality. It remains to be seen if we want to apply them.

8.4 Social injustice

The ancient Greeks stated that those who are loved by the gods die young – and thus avoid the unfair blows of fate. Sophocles (496–406 BC) reached ripe old age but may for that reason have let Oedipus exclaim "Not to be born, is past prizing". Life is unjust from beginning to end, something we just have to accept.

People have in religious terms sought explanations and consolation for the misfortunes and injustices of life. The faith in a just and almighty celestial being compensates for temporal inequities; debts and credits in the hereafter balanced the books. Fatalism is the logical endpoint of a suchlike logic, which alleviates the pain of injustice.

In parallel with the breakthrough of democracy, celestial assets have been heavily discounted. The expectations of the citizens are concentrated on worldly matters and injustices have thus become insufferable, on principle. The claims on redistribution of the earthly good have grown even faster than the economic resources. Thomas Sowell has in *The Quest for Cosmic Justice* (1999) analyzed this frame of reference and its political consequences.

> Cosmic justice insists on the modification of the rules of the game for the benefit of all underprivileged groups. Thus it can be manifestly unfair if the best wins or the most qualified advances. Statistical differences in any outcome are deemed an unfailing sign of gross injustice which has to be rectified by positive discrimination. Destructive side-effects do not concern the stalwarts of cosmic justice. They rest assured of their moral superiority.

> Sowell shows that positive discrimination not only creates new injustices, but that it hurts the people it alleges to help. To fight the odds is, in the long run, more salutary than getting an unfair advantage. Frederick Douglass (1817–95) was a runaway slave and a famous champion for the abolishment of slavery. He reacted negatively to the philanthropists of his time and did not want to deliver an alibi to the

Negros for lack of performance: "… if the Negro cannot stand on his own legs, let him fall … All I ask is, give him a chance to stand on his own legs! Let him alone!"

Sowell sees the radical call for equality as a threat to the judicial system, to the freedom of the individual and in the last instance to the constitution of the United States. Although Europeans have mostly avoided overt positive discrimination, we have advanced further along other avenues. In its redistribution policies, Sweden has gone farthest in the pernickety administration of social justice. But even social democratic governments have found it expedient to deviate from cherished egalitarian principles.

> In Sweden the wealth tax and the inheritance tax have been abolished. The left has traditionally held that such taxation is an important tool for social equalization. But the proceeds had been hollowed out by special statutes and astute tax planning; finally the tax only applied to the average Swede. Superrich sports stars of all nationalities regularly have their domicile in tax havens without any loss of popularity on their home turf.

"Skin the rich" is a catchword which has lost some of its allure on the political market in the west. Jealousy, our most enduring natural resource, cannot have diminished. But an increasing number of citizens have after all accumulated possessions, which they would like to pass on to their descendants. Moreover, a dawning insight is gaining ground. Wealth may be based not on theft, but on genuine added value which has benefited society at large.

Instead of tying people down in poverty by permanent, means-tested support, the aim should be to make the indigent productive. That would restore their self-respect and open the door to advancement up the social scale. In Europe, the landless crofters could in a few generations establish themselves as relatively well-to-do townspeople. In America, wave after wave of poor immigrants have advanced from the slums to a comfortable middle-class existence. Poverty is not an unsolvable problem.

> This is a provocation for people who have betted their political future on a permanent underclass. Propping up their position, they have turned to qualified deceit by statistics. In the European Union, poverty is defined as an income which is less than 60% of the median – a semantic hocus-pocus. Previously, the figure was 50% which obviously did not produce the desirable outcome. In any case, one arrives at a

number of between 10 and 20% 'poor' in society, which is virtually unshakable and is 'scientific' evidence of the prevailing injustice.

The statistics are based on taxable income. Students as well as wealthy individuals with irregular earnings are unashamedly included among the poor; untaxed income is completely disregarded. Sowell cites a study by Greg Duncan et al., *Years of Poverty, Years of Plenty*, which shows that only three percent of the US population was permanently below the official poverty line. Most of the 'poor' are youngsters or persons who are temporarily out of work.

A big income or wealth is hardly morally despicable as such. Alternatively, differences in consumption between social groups could be the target for criticism. But the relevant statistics are plainly of less political utility. For example, in the United States the total expenditures of the officially poor exceed their official income by more than 100%! Almost half of the poor have title to their homes.[15]

Poverty cannot be scientifically defined, but we know that in the democracies by and large about ten percent of the population is dependent on government support. To wean people from dependence on charity is extremely difficult. The beneficiary is deprived of motivation to provide for himself while the provider is frustrated by the lack of initiative of the recipient. Both parties are caught in a vicious circle of disrespect.

In Sweden and Great Britain whole blocks of subsidized apartment dwellings are razed; they have become uninhabitable in a few decades. The inhabitants ought to be responsible for their surroundings, but in a collective with no ownership interest the hooligans often take over. The City of New York, the bulwark of capitalism, excels in rent regulation; almost half of the flats are isolated from the free market. At least the lawyer Mary Ann Hallenborg is making money out of the inherent contradictions. She has written *New York Tenant's Rights* as well as the *New York Landlord's Law Book*.

During Bill Clinton's presidency, a federal ordinance was promulgated which prescribed eight hours monthly social service (with many exceptions) for the inhabitants of federally subsidized apartment blocks in New York. The implementation was delayed by local New York politicians and as late as in April 2004 agitated tenants were demonstrating against the 'racist' directive.[16] In Stockholm however, the owners of valuable tenancy rights are keeping mum. They have qualified for subsidized housing as impecunious youngsters and can retain undivided possession as wealthy grown ups.

Health care is an even more sensitive matter touching on cosmic justice. Nobody is hurt by adequate health treatment, and a better investment than preventive baby care is hard to come by. The only problem is that the demand for health care tends to grow without limit, especially if psychological pains are included.

Good care for the sick is a self-evident aim in all democracies even if the affluent usually have access to better services. Even so, free treatment of self-inflicted ills may evoke feelings of unfairness. In high-tax countries, surcharges on alcohol and tobacco should cover additional health care costs, though. Besides, the early demise of the abusers will reduce retirement expenditures. In any case, we cannot leave any member of society to suffer and die, earlier misbehaviors notwithstanding. Here too justice falls short of perfection.

Society cannot and should not guarantee absolute justice for its citizens, no more than their happiness or success. But we can try to alleviate obvious injustices without creating undue restrictions on the opportunities for personal self-realization. As customary in a democracy it is a matter of a reasonable compromise, a social-psychological plus-sum game. Freedom in all its aspects is the precious joint heritage which should be optimized.

8.5 Global security and justice.

Genuine democracies do not make war against each other despite occasional conflicts of interest. But beyond the bounds of democracy the law of the jungle prevails, which has exacted extensive investment in military preparedness. This historical reality is now changing, albeit slowly, due to the rise of democracy. Totalitarian enclaves are under constant pressure and it has become more dangerous for disturbers of the peace to pursue national interest by violent means. A credible international judiciary is, however, still a pie in the sky.

Besides the courts of justice, an efficient police force is indispensable to maintain law and order. The United Nations has neither democratic legitimacy nor executive power to live up to this role. Even a unanimous Security Council hesitates to apply coercion to enforce its resolutions, which might be as well. UN-soldiers have fulfilled their mission in peace-keeping when the warring parties have acquiesced, at least tacitly. But when the situation calls for real warfare (euphemistically peace-enforcing operations), the United Nations has failed miserably.

After the Second World War, the United States provided the only protection against totalitarian aggression. The first clash of arms took place 1950–53 in Korea under the UN flag. In Vietnam the mission was similar but the support of the other democracies was not forthcoming; in the 1960s, the Europeans were not equally concerned about the advance of communism. After the implosion of the Soviet Union, the United States has taken on the role as a world police, with or without the sanction of the United Nations. The terrorist attack on the World Trade Center on 9.11.2001 was an incitement to make the world safe, once and for all, for democracies in general and for the United States in particular.

> The invasion of Afghanistan was reluctantly accepted by world opinion. But when President George Bush set about to depose Saddam Hussein, arguably the worst tyrant in the world, President Jacques Chirac of France did his best to sabotage the operation. Tony Blair, the British premier, lined up in support of the United States but the Western Europeans by and large dissociated themselves from the 'warmongers' Bush and Blair – an echo from the irresponsible pacifism and appeasement of the 1930s. The lack of approval of the United Nations caused a great stir, despite Saddam's persistent refusal to comply with the resolutions of the Security Council. The hypocrisy of this argument was quickly exposed when the European Union unanimously agreed that the fast deployment forces being established could act without the UN approval.
>
> Most observers were surprised when it became clear that Saddam was not sitting on a secret store of weapons of mass destruction; that would have been the only sensible explanation for his posturing. His well-documented will and capability to produce and to use such weapons is highly relevant. Saddam Hussein swimming in oil money and brooding on revenge, joining up with sundry terrorists, is a nightmare we have been spared. But it is too early to judge the feasibility of a democratic government in an Islamic context.

Bellicose dictators are today running considerable risks, and brutality against the domestic population can also cause embarrassment. Neither terrorists nor deposed tyrants can find a really safe haven anymore. National sovereignty is being chipped away piecemeal – contrary to the principles of the UN-charter but in accordance with the demand for global security and justice. Democracies around the world are today relieved of the fear of aggression or a totalitarian world revolution. Poor, undemocratic regimes are nevertheless locking horns all too often – Ethiopia and Eritrea is just one example. But in such cases economic sanctions can be effective.

Much more problematic are genocides, as in Ruanda, and civil wars in completely failed states like Liberia and Somalia. The civil war in Sudan continued on and off for twenty years and has been succeeded by the massacres in Darfur. The call for help sounds ever higher from countries where the government has to be rebuilt from the ground up, with or without democracy. The European Union is developing its capability to project 'soft power' by preventive action. How this will work out is an open question; at the time of writing the outcome of interventions in Lebanon and Congo is pending. In general, the actual application of force still falls to the United States, which is becoming increasingly reluctant to engage itself in unpopular international policing.

With few exceptions, the world has in any case become secure enough for international trade. Globalization has gathered all significant nations into a gigantic plus-sum game, contributing to peaceful relations. At all times there are relative winners and losers but the great majority has shared in the increased prosperity. All the same, the prevailing differences in living standards are no longer taken for granted but are slowly transforming into glaring injustices. We are far from a working global order but we are feeling the pangs of an emerging global conscience.

These public sentiments have been exploited by equality enthusiasts, who are facing a decline in their national markets. Here within reach are new, unlimited opportunities to encumber the middle class of the democracies with guilt, and to create an outlet for a diffuse zeal to improve the world – as always at the expense of the taxpayer. It is truly tragic to see so much money and good will wasted on fundamentally flawed policies, which do not abet self-help but rather confirm dependence on the donor.

The United Nations has settled on a figure of 0.7 % of BNP as a general target for the support to underdeveloped countries. Although only a few small nations attain this level, with oil-rich Norway to the fore, it is rarely questioned in the media. Development aid has become an excellent business for a highly paid and often tax-exempt establishment, which acts in symbiosis with uncritical media and with the usually corrupt politicians in the target countries. Ever more vociferous international conferences and resolutions are turning a blind eye to abuses and inefficiencies. The aims are becoming increasingly unrealistic; nonetheless the money claims grow incessantly. The futility of increased spending should eventually be dawning. Not even the hundreds of billions of Nigerian oil money has produced a basis for sustainable development.

Good governance has been introduced as a condition for outside support, but it is not consistently applied. The developing countries are playing off the donors against each other and have developed considerable expertise in misrepresentation. Since 1978, when Daniel Arap Moi rose to power in Kenya, corruption has been rampant. But the 'cooperation' with the providers has continued, accompanied by the empty threats of shutting off the gravy train.[18] The examples can easily be multiplied; the donors obviously want to get rid of their money at any price!

The prestige of the United Nations was not exactly underpinned by the spectacle of Mohammed Gaddafi as chairman for the UN commission for human rights; a recent reform did not shore up the non-existent legitimacy of the commission. Neither is Zimbabwe as a newly-fledged chairman for the UN commission for sustainable development a cause for celebration. Many of the independent UN-organizations have, nevertheless, done a good job. The great success of the World Health Organization (WHO) was the eradication of smallpox. The promotion of culture (UNESCO), children's health (UNICEF) and refugee subsistence (UNHCR) have also been effective, although UNRWA (United Nations Relief and Works Agency for Palestine Refugees) has indirectly contributed to the Palestinian refugee problem by financing temporary 'camps' for generations of Palestine refugees. It has provided an attractive pretext to impede integration into the surrounding societies.

The Arab recipient countries, Jordan excepted, have done their utmost to prevent the assimilation of the refugees. According to Amnesty International, Lebanon is systematically discriminating against the Palestinians. They are not allowed to enter any qualified trade and cannot own real estate.[19] Saudi Arabia employs millions of foreign workers but does not accept any Palestinians. Everything is done to keep the trauma of the displaced alive.

The Palestinians provide a good example of ingrained and, so to speak, self-inflicted injustices. The denial of realities is a sure method for remaining in offside. Wailing in injustice becomes an occupation and a livelihood; in the end it turns into an addictive dependence on self-deception. The developing countries tend to perceive themselves as the victims of colonial exploitation. It is high time for them to face the facts, revise their world-view and tackle their own faults. Then outside support could achieve a sorely needed lever effect.

The perniciousness of colonialism is a myth ready to be buried. If it were to be the source of all evil, then Ethiopia, Liberia, Haiti and Afghanistan should be problem-free.[20] South-Africa, on the other hand, was the most thoroughly colonialized country on the continent. But under the enlightened guidance of Nelson Mandela it opened a new chapter in its history by resolutely turning away from its past and facing the future challenges.

China blocked any outside influences for centuries, totally convinced of its own superiority, but was eventually forced to reconsider. Japan too isolated itself in 1639 but abruptly changed course through the Meiji restoration in 1868. After 1945 the Japanese once more had to change their frame of mind, which swiftly produced spectacular results.

The demands for cosmic justice have transferred from the national to the global level where they are misconceived in the extreme. The systematic amelioration of injustices requires a strong political structure and a mutual solidarity which we can only dream about. Extensive redistribution would merely create a gigantic minus-sum game – monstrous waste and expanding corruption. Besides, such an aim stands in ironic contrast with the condemnation of western values, poured out by post-modern critics of our culture. Why should we expose innocent people, happily living in harmony with nature, to an unhealthy western life-style – hard work, stress and competitive pressure?

Professional world-improvers habitually occupy an elevated moral platform, swinging their scourge over us common mortals. Pragmatic solutions are denounced as half-measures and the present, provisional security system – Pax Americana – is offhand condemned as imperialism and neo-colonialism. The current situation is, after all, quite acceptable in a historical perspective. But even a superpower will not act as lone world policeman in perpetuity.

Chapter 9
The fourth estate

The media are an inalienable and inescapable part of modern existence. They stand for transparency and insight but also for duplicity and scandal mongering. Nobody controls the fourth estate, except the readers and watchers, who get what they deserve. The media-conditioned public opinion is a mighty but capricious power, usually shining in political correctness. Occasionally, the regimentation degenerates into outright suppression of opinions. All the same, electronic communication is already enabling people to establish contact on a global scale. This means that the media are no longer the sole makers of public opinion.

9.1 Good, bad and ugly

The mass media is the nervous system of the democracies. They expand the classic agora, the scene for commerce, gossip and politics to include every home in a nation. News is conveyed almost in real time; information, comments and above all entertainment is delivered in greater quantity than anybody could digest. Without the media, we would live in virtual isolation with few means to arrive at an enlightened opinion.

The media have achieved the rank of a fourth estate by virtue of their key role in the political process, which is played out in the newspaper columns, on the television screen and in radio programs. The role of watchdog fits the media hand in glove. The exploits of the high and mighty, in intimate detail, have always and everywhere been the hottest news. The scolding of politicians is an ingrained habit, and sometimes degenerates into a chase when the wretched prey is hunted down by a temporarily concordant pack. But most of the time the yelping is rather ineffectual; the dogs may bark but the caravan proceeds.

When Alexis de Tocqueville opened a newspaper on his arrival in New York in 1831, the first thing that caught his eye was a diatribe against the sitting president Andrew Jackson. "Ambition is his crime, and it will be his punishment, too: intrigue is his native element, and intrigue will confound his tricks, and deprive him of his power. He governs by means of corruption, and his immoral practices will rebound to his shame and confusion. His conduct in the political arena has been that of a shameless and lawless gamester. He succeeded at the time; but the hour of retribution approaches, and he will be obliged to disgorge his winnings, to throw aside his false dice, and to end his days in some retirement, where he may curse his madness at his leisure; for repentance is a virtue with which his heart is likely to remain forever unacquainted." The writer did not pull his punches but President Jackson was re-elected with a comfortable margin and he would certainly have been at home in the re-election campaign of George W. Bush in 2004.

Not much has changed in politics during two hundred years, but fortunately the same holds for the role of the media, particularly as conduits for individual grievances. Sometimes the oppressed citizen has no other recourse than to seek publicity for his case and shame his adversary; a scandal-hungry press is usually keen to oblige. In the words of de Tocqueville: "the newspapers are a powerful weapon within reach for the common man, even the weakest and loneliest".

In Imperial China the wronged had no recourse to impartial courts of law and least of all a free press. The only way to make a case against a mighty oppressor was to commit suicide at his doorstep. This brought shame on him to his dying days.

For politicians, artists and celebrities of all kinds it is imperative to be visible in the media, preferably in a positive light. At a pinch, bad publicity will do; the worst case is no publicity at all. All participants aim at maximum visibility and try to attract the broadest possible public; hence the vulgar tone and the mediocre quality of the mass media. In a market economy, the average customer is king. His or her preferences are decisive and the relatively few members of the elite must look elsewhere for complementary channels of information.

The standardizing impact of the dominating newspapers and television channels is a frequent cause for complaint. Totalitarian regimes have exploited these opportunities to the hilt. Political indoctrination works optimally as a coordinated effort using all available media; no room is given to deviating opinions. But, like commercial promotion, the propaganda is at its most efficient when it amplifies the prevailing attitudes. When trust in the product or the ideology is failing, no amount of media power will help. Credibility is further eroded when outworn clichés are repeated over and over again.

During the Brezhnev-era, the Soviet Union was declining materially and ideologically. I recall a television program from the middle 1980s. Before their departure abroad, a party functionary was indoctrinating the players of a basketball team against the corrupting influence of the west. The facial expressions of the youthful team members were quite telling when the female lecturer went through her exhaustively repeated phraseology. It crossed my mind that the days of communism may be numbered. When Mikhail Gorbachev later on tried to reform the system, the total media control did not strengthen a weak hand.

During the 1990s in the 'freedom era' under President Boris Jeltsin, the television channels were quickly bought up by the newly rich oligarchs. The combination of financial and media power gave them disproportionate political influence. President Vladimir Putin chose to put an end to the political ambitions of the oligarchs. All significant television channels are now directly or indirectly controlled by the state, but traffic on the internet is unrestricted. The press is still free and rather outspoken, despite the numerous killings of journalists. Authoritarian regimes have generally been satisfied with a partial control of the media. Publications which 'the people' generally neglect actually preserve considerable freedom.

In the democracies, relations between the media and the government are rarely frictionless. More often than not, whole sectors of the media are at war with the powers that be. The leaders, in particular, can evoke strong emotions. In the United States, President Bush was resisted by a unanimous liberal establishment, whereas the tabloid press in Great Britain inexplicably sank their teeth into Prime Minister and Mrs. Tony Blair. In Italy, Prime Minister Silvio Berlusconi controls a substantial part of the media, which has caused much commotion.

Through Fininvest and Mediaset Berlusconi reaches about half of the television watchers. The state-owned RAI is the only serious competition and would hardly go against the Prime Minister. In addition, Fininvest has considerable interests in newspapers and journals as well as in book publishers. This is however less important because for 80% of Italians, television is the only source of news. The criticism has been boosted by Berlusconi's murky business affairs which have been scrutinized in several trials. A sentence for bribery handed down by an Italian court never gained legal force because of the statute of limitations.

Political success does not show a clear correlation with media attitudes. Neither their sympathy nor their antipathy has necessarily sufficient political impact. The voters generally distrust the politicians but they are equally wary of media manipulation. A strong politician can be more credible than rancorous media which have their own axes to grind.

When a democracy is under threat, the media stand by the government, almost to a man. Critical voices become almost inaudible; the patriotic public would deem diverging views treasonable. When the pressure is off, the argument starts again and the opposition applies all available means to undermine the government. If the swings of opinion are strong enough, tried and tested statesmen are swept away regardless of the media.

> Great Britain held parliamentary elections on the fifth of July 1945 though the Second World War was still going on in the Far East. Clement Attlee (1883–1967), the Labour leader, swept the floor and replaced Winston Churchill at the conference table in Potsdam on the 17th of July. Stalin was the only extant victorious leader remaining since Harry Truman had just succeeded the deceased President Roosevelt. Stalin certainly had good reason to ponder the advantages of the communist system.

The media can, on the other hand, be thoroughly manipulated by a single-minded government which uses experts to steer public opinion. Every decision, measure or piece of news is presented according to a meticulous plan as an attractive package at the right moment and in the right context – with the appropriate spin. Meanwhile, the opposition parties enjoy the latent support of the press, which is always looking for bad news. The government message that everything is in good hands rarely produces smashing headlines. Sensational journalism is a big seller but occasionally it backfires.

> In the autumn of 2003, Tony Blair received a thorough scolding when the assumed caches of mass destructive weapons did not materialize in Iraq. The BBC joined the pack with a biased interview that lead to the suicide of the interviewee. The brouhaha was great but when an impartial investigation established that the program had been disingenuous, top BBC-chiefs had to resign.

Joseph Göbbels (1897–1945) was a superb media strategist in charge of Hitler's propaganda department. He was a master of linguistic foul play and used to say that if a lie is repeated often enough it becomes true. In America it is assumed that some of the mud will stick after a bout of mudslinging. Ronald Reagan was an exception in this respect and accordingly he was called the Teflon President. But Tony Blair suffered from the accusations; the majority of the people still think that he acted in bad faith when he misinformed the public about the Iraqi weapons of mass destruction.

Our attitude vis-à-vis the media is ambivalent. One is shocked by the exposition of the violence, disgusted by the pornography, worried by the ignorance, enraged by the stupidity. Nevertheless the press, the radio and television have turned into a drug we cannot dispense with. What is more, "[the press] constitutes a singular power, so strangely composed of mingled good and evil that liberty could not live without it" (de Tocqueville). Despite all their faults, the media embody openness in our society. We must ourselves stand for honesty, the other pillar of the plus-sum game.

9.2 Control and self-control

The media supervise the politicians and other powers brokers, and above all their abuses. Much will escape their attention but ever so often they make a lot of fuss about nothing. Even worse are the hidden agendas and the murky influences. Who holds an eye on the watchmen and how are they held to account? How to guarantee a versatile and unbiased flow of information? These questions impose themselves in every democracy but there are no clear-cut answers.

He who pays the piper calls the tune. The proprietor inevitably exerts an influence on the content and the general slant of a media channel. Thus governments have consistently been very interested in this trade. Today, democratic states do not control the media, but until quite recently, radio and television were state monopolies in many countries. A pluralistic owner structure and fierce competition can be considered the best guarantee for the versatility of information. But if publicly financed media are isolated from political interference, they can appear as paragons of objectivity.

The British Broadcasting Corporation (BBC) has since the start in 1922 been an exemplar of public information service. The legendary Lord Reith (1889–1971), who left the helm in 1938, created an independent and responsible organization with high professional standards and an active mission of adult education. During the war, the BBC was perceived as the most dependable news channel in the world, and contributed to the consolidation of democratic ideals. When commercial television was later permitted, the program policy gradually shifted towards lighter entertainment to hold on to a broad audience. By January 1st 2007, a reorganized BBC received a renewed mandate for ten years, but it has to refrain from direct competition with the commercial channels.

Private ownership does not in itself solve the media problem; rather the reverse. The media channels can become mighty instruments of power and the dependence on advertising revenues does not improve the situation. Competition can drive down quality; if the consumer pays little or nothing for his information, the market feedback will be absent or distorted.

Gossip makes for big sales, hence well-known personalities are under constant surveillance, which often leads to transgressions. The law prescribes punishment and compensation for libel but is of little avail against the tabloid press and the ubiquitous paparazzi. Court procedures amplify the negative publicity and even a conviction seldom clears the libeled party in the public eye.

> For many celebrities the heaven of publicity can turn into its opposite when the media show their unpleasant side. To protect their privacy has become a supreme challenge for prominent persons. It is almost comical that the anonymity of people without publicity value is rigorously protected whereas influential persons, who have much more to loose, can be exposed, even if their guilt is still an open question.
>
> In a high-brow journal, a good friend of mine cited Friedrich von Hayek, who in *Constitution of Liberty* intimated that persons wholly dependent on the state (i.a. retirees) perhaps should be bereft of the right to vote. A tabloid picked it up which caused a minor media incident and very unpleasant phone calls from enraged senior citizens. I wrote a comment to bring back the discussion onto a sensible course. But my friend thought that it just would pour oil on the fire and my small contribution was shelved – probably a wise decision.

On the whole it does not pay to tackle the press. The newspaper always has the last word and if a clarification or even a retraction can be extracted it is usually a Pyrrhic victory. Politicians who disrespect media representatives will sooner or later pay for their insolence, irrespective of their party allegiance. Slights against the fourth estate do not go unpunished.

It is unquestionable that press magnates like Randolph Hearst (1863–1951) in the United States and Lord Beaverbrook (1879–1964) in Great Britain exerted undue influence on the policies of their respective countries. Today Robert Murdoch is the mightiest media magnate with a manifold of interests mainly in the Anglo-Saxon nations.

Murdoch's starting point was News Corporation, a small Australian company which he inherited and expanded with impressive effectiveness. In liaison with Margaret Thatcher, he crushed the flagrant abuses of the printer's union in London. Later on he established BSkyB as the dominating satellite television network in Great Britain. In the United States, Fox cable television has surpassed CNN, the former market leader. To increase market share, Murdoch gives the public what it desires, but he does not hesitate to impose a common political stance on the whole corporation; all his newspapers, numbering 175, supported the latest war in Iraq.

The concentration of media power is not commendable of course, but market dominance has a bright side. Arm-twisting, political or otherwise, is less effective and strong newspapers are very particular about their reputation. They are also less inclined to dig in the bottom mud of sensational journalism to improve their competitive position.

Neue Zürcher Zeitung first appeared in 1780 and is today considered the most dependable newspaper in Europe, and possibly in the world. NZZ has consistently pursued a policy of strict factuality in a conservative perspective. From 1934 it was prohibited in Nazi Germany because it reported that the Nazis were behind the burning of the parliament building which facilitated their bid for power. If one is interested only in following the ways of the world in so many words, then NZZ is the right source.

Helsingin Sanomat is the only countrywide newspaper in Finland. I was the chairman of the supervisory board at Uusi Suomi, the number two daily paper, when it had to throw in the towel in 1991. The circulation and thus the advertising revenues had irrevocably fallen into a death spiral. Helsingin Sanomat became sole king of the castle, but it has not abused its dominant position. The liberal, EU- and NATO-friendly editorial line diverges in many ways from the views of the main proprietor.

Fierce competition can lure even quality newspapers and especially their journalists to resort to shady practices or outright fraud. Among many others, the *Boston Globe*, *New York Times* and *Washington Post* have met with this calamity, though rarely against their better knowledge.[1]

In democracies, control of the media is possible only within the widest limits, which was perfectly understood already by de Tocqueville. Self-control by trade associations may check the worst misconduct but has no legal force. Browbeaten editors-in-chief can tie the whole staff to the expressed or expected wishes of the owner. Self-censorship sometimes assumes semi-official forms, more faithfully obeyed than any directive.

> Urho Kaleva Kekkonen (1900–86) exerted during his long presidency (1956–81) a growing influence on the Finnish media. Throughout the war years, censorship had suppressed defeatist and anti-German opinions. Now no expressions of an anti-Soviet sentiment were allowed in the media. Transgressions created diplomatic controversy and were often arraigned by the president in person.

We are left with the journalist's ethic, the ultimate bastion of self-control, which is stronger than is generally believed. There are of course reporters of many kinds, but self-respecting journalists see themselves as qualified policemen, prosecutors and judges, all in one person. The editors of quality organs sometimes assume an elevated moral position, which can be trying for the reader but is acceptable in a pluralistic context.

Good journalists play by generally accepted rules of the game. A news story, for instance, keeps facts and analysis apart, to avoid undue influence on the reader. Sensational news from obscure sources is double-checked; denounced people, companies or institutions are given a chance to rejoin; off the record information does not get into print, etcetera. Protection of the sources is a question of principle, which touches on the problem of confession. The person who wants to relieve his or her bad conscience must not face the dangers of exposure, but the journalist can also become a tool for shady interests.

The profile of a publicist reaches from the personal brand of the syndicated columnist to the total anonymity of the beginner. The praxis varies for the editorials which mark the political line of the paper. *The Economist* for example is completely collegial; the name of the contributor appears only exceptionally. Despite the fierce competition, journalists as a guild exhibit a strong cohesion, which sometimes goes too far. "One raven does not savage another" says a Finnish proverb in so many words.

> As vice-chairman of The Finnish Confederation of Industry in 1987 I was travelling to China as a member of a delegation of business leaders, headed by our Prime Minister Kalevi Sorsa (1930–2004). We met prominent Chinese leaders, chief party secretary Zhao Ziyang (1918–2005) among others. Several notable reporters were participating in the trip. One of them, who represented the state owned television-company, was constantly drunk but fortunately mostly absent. I felt it was scandalous and expected a public denouncement on our return.

But – not one word in the media in spite of the blatant misbehavior of a well known personality.

Incisive self-criticism is naturally rare, but hopefully journalists could be induced to keep a check on each other. After all, there is nobody else around to raise a hackle at their offences. Abuses cannot be that uncommon, considering the temptations of the trade. Publicity is very valuable, not only for politicians and commercial actors but for sundry organizations and artists as well; indeed a veritable symbiosis has arisen between pop-artists and the popular press.

The quality of the media correlates with the level of democracy – the dependence is strong and mutual. Beyond the magic circle of the democracies, independent media channels are thin on the ground. Most are on a tight leash or their pages are cynically up for sale. In our democratic countries we are fully occupied with keeping such abuses in check. While maintaining a minimum of fair play, we have to put up with many bad habits as a reflection of our own vices and limitations. Do not blame the mirror if the countenance is ugly.

9.3 Public opinion

During election times, the will of the people is gauged and the legislative and executive powers are delegated for the period to the elected representatives of the citizens. However, this does not mean that the opinions and emotions of the electorate are put on hold. Though the shrinking turnout and the lack of political interest are widely lamented, the public influence on day to day politics has seldom been higher. Party activity may be waning but the politicians are following voter reactions with hawk-eyed interest. Public opinion is powerful and this is the fault and the merit of the mass media.

Politicians are professional newspaper-readers and the letters to the editor are not passed by. Television and radio are beyond continuous monitoring, but all sensational items are reflected in the papers. The recurrent opinion polls produce the most dependable data on the public mood, broken down by party allegiance, age group, gender, geographical region and so on. The constant polling implies that the parliamentarians are political weather-wanes, which could convert the constitution to a 'gallupocracy'.

Dr George Gallup (1901–84) originally developed his technique to improve the dependability of market research, and business is still the biggest customer segment of the trade. Gallup got his public breakthrough when he, against all odds, predicted the victory of Franklin Roosevelt in the 1936 presidential elections. In spite of occasional setbacks, the methodology has been refined over the years. It has even been suggested that the expensive and complicated elections should be replaced by Gallup polls.

Opinion polls lend themselves to issues where the presented alternatives are simple and unambiguous. Measuring the strength and the persistence of the opinion is a major problem, though some progress has been made. In any case, the politicians are pretty well informed about the fluctuations of the public mood. But their task is not to go along with the flips and the flops of the public opinion, but to lead the electorate in the desired direction and act responsibly. It redounds to the credit of the electorate that weather-wane politicians are sidelined when things get tough.

The political infighting takes place on the newspaper pages and television screens. All actors fight for publicity; demonstrations, for example, have minuscule impact without mass-medial attention. Tiny pressure groups can exert disproportionate influence by using the media as a lever. A television crew is usually in position when the police arrive to curb the illegal action. If all goes well, catching pictures of police brutality will appear on the evening news.

> Greenpeace is good at producing sensational publicity stunts. The organization is an example of how an idealistic movement over time transforms into a business, which provides its leaders with a lucrative living. Nonetheless, the media opens its pages and screens for everything with a Greenpeace imprimatur. The factual arguments of business enterprises carry little weight when trying to fend off such attacks.
>
> Brent Spar was a discarded oil platform which Shell planned to sink in the Atlantic with the permission of the British authorities. Greenpeace occupied the desolate platform under great publicity and stated that the disposal was a serious threat to the environment. It was alleged that the platform contained 5000 ton of oil which was an outright lie. But the media attacks were savage, company products were boycotted and violence broke out at service stations in Germany. Shell gave in against its better knowledge and the platform was scrapped in a Norwegian fjord. Costs were ten times higher and the environmental impact was much worse.[2]

Trade and industry are under increasing critical surveillance and have generally adopted a proactive strategy. PR (Public Relations) is quite an industry today and every self-respecting company has a director for public or community relations with the mission to influence the administration and the public opinion – often two sides of the same coin. This raises another challenge for the media who are guarding the access to the public. In the Brent Spar case the guardians were obviously not up to their task.

The number of Non-Governmental Organizations (NGOs) has increased exponentially. According to The Union of International Associations, 28, 223 international NGOs were active in 2006.[3] Most of them are small, for sure, and may not be long-lived. But together they form a mighty opinion. The majority is certainly driven by a will to help, not a political or ideological agenda.

> Amnesty International is a good exponent for the latest humanitarian trend. Amnesty was founded by the Englishman Peter Benenson (1921–2005) Even at school in Eton he supported unfairly victimized pupils and at the age of forty he was prompted to found Amnesty International. After a few years, his relations to the organization became strained and he resigned. But Amnesty has not diverged from its original aim of working, mainly by negative publicity, against torture and injustice all over the world. Amnesty has retained its credibility, although the striving for objectivity has resulted in misdirected fault-finding in democracies of good repute.[4]

Less appealing are local and obviously partial interest groups of the NIMBY-type (Not In My Backyard). By using appeals left and right, they can overturn or at least seriously delay local and even nationally important projects.

> The NIMBY-phenomenon shows how small determined groups can get a hearing for their views, which as such is an appealing feature of our democracy. If the authorities plan a waste disposal site close to a residential area we do not react with barely hidden Schadenfreude. On the contrary we feel a spontaneous solidarity with the wronged group. Everything which can be interpreted as administrative arbitrariness gets our hackles up against the local or national bureaucracy.[4a] Just the same, the abuse of the right of appeal is a plague which should be curtailed one way or the other.

In a similar way, single-purpose movements have an astonishing capability to engage the media for their cause. An old trick is to personify the argument by introducing a human interest perspective. Contrary to impersonal statistics, the pitiable individual arouses our sympathy which may force the authorities to diverge from a well-conceived policy 'for humanitarian reasons'.

Deviations from agreed rules of the game are always suspect. To let a capricious public opinion influence the authorities contradicts fundamental democratic principles. The whims of today are usually forgotten tomorrow, if not wholly reversed. The adequately expressed opinions of the people emerge in the election process. Democratic leaders are elected to carry responsibility and take the right decisions, not necessarily the most popular ones. Such personalities are the main theme in *Profiles in Courage* by John F. Kennedy (1917–63). Kennedy's heroes do not compromise their convictions but rather sacrifice their political carrier.

> The art of politics is to sell the right decisions to the public; by definition, successful political leaders have consistently had public opinion on their side. Like Churchill and Roosevelt, sundry dictators have also had the knack of producing a good show, tailored to the preferences of the audience. Every people tends to get the leaders it deserves, even if there is no free choice.

A democracy is always looking ahead; old merits do not count. Brilliant leadership is acknowledged by decorations and speechifying, may be a sinecure, but not necessarily by a renewed political mandate. Public opinion moves in waves. During a prolonged stay in power, the problems mount for the governing party; internal conflicts, the dearth of new ideas and general weariness take their toll. Sooner or later the public tires of their old favorites and clamors for new faces. A new government may be granted a short honeymoon but soon the sniping starts again. Trivial mishaps are blown up to scandals and the impression of massive incompetence grows when the inevitable blunders start to surface, one by one.

Stepping down from political leadership does not exclude a comeback. Thus it is important to be a good loser. Surly looks and limping excuses do not go down well with the electorate and it is obligatory to congratulate the winner and to wish him all the best. Many renowned politicians make a second career in international organizations. Then they can strive to alleviate the prejudices of domestic opinion and to improve the understanding between different countries, cultures and religions.

9.4 Political correctness

People have an inherent tendency to build a majority around a core of highly motivated individuals. This aptitude has been a competitive advantage on the tribal level and facilitates the stability of modern large-scale democracies. It has, however, a less desirable side-effect called political correctness. The quasi-official, loosely grounded frame of reference has then become normative and the whole community has assumed a taint of conceited self-righteousness.

The dividing line between political correctness and a democratic value community is a matter of taste. All the same, political correctness implies a compulsory behavioral pattern spiced with a measure of hypocrisy. Beyond a restricted circle of friends one does not dare or want to speak one's mind. This phenomenon goes to extremes in totalitarian countries, but we have all met with such self-censorship close to home. Political correctness becomes a burden on society whenever a majority of citizens are forced to live a lie. The situation is not much better if only a minority feel that they are muzzled.

Presently, political correctness amounts to creating support for political decisions, aiming at the assistance of the suppressed, wronged, neglected or otherwise mistreated. For this good purpose, openness, objectivity and respect for facts are sacrificed. Diverging opinions are immediately denounced as ingrained prejudice or manifestations of self-interest which makes a serious discussion impossible. The upshot is entanglement in diverse illusions which blocks sensible policies and works against humanitarian goals, at least in the long run.

> Slavery is supposed to be abolished but it is still widespread particularly in Central Africa – in Niger the number of slaves is put at 43,000. Recently 7000 slaves were to be publicly released but the government changed its mind and frankly declared that there are no slaves in Niger. In Chad, Mali and Mauretania there are many slaves, too. No sanctions are contemplated by the international community; on the contrary, the slave countries enjoy considerable development aid. World opinion does not react because it would mark out dark-skinned people as slave-drivers and increase prejudices. Meanwhile slavery goes on and nobody lifts a finger.[5]

The common theme in this manipulation is a sort of conspiracy between intellectuals, activists and media people, seated together on a platform of moral supremacy. The politicians willingly ride on the ascending opinion wave, which obviously serves an admirable cause. When the attractive ideas become sacrosanct and beyond questioning, we are entering dangerous territory. Incitement to hatred against specific groups is criminalized in many countries, which opens the door for official opinion control. Typically, politically correctitude has rarely been endorsed by the electorate. A self-appointed elite has taken command.

> Freedom of expression is curtailed even without legislation; religious bigotry has been replaced by fashionable hypocrisy. The self-censorship of the media takes care of the suppression of adverse utterances about minorities of any kind. It is always the majority population which is in the wrong and carries the burden of guilt. Relevant statistics are concealed or must not be compiled. A sympathetic attitude towards minorities is appropriate but the suppression of facts, for instance in crime reporting, only causes rumor-mongering and militates against its purpose.

Voluntary emigrants usually get on rather well in their adopted country, if they get a chance. Regrettably, European policies on immigration and refugees have become stumbling blocks for the integration of the newcomers. They are isolated from the surrounding society and are not even allowed to work. There is no room for personal initiative which is strangled by overprotective authorities in the name of humanity. No demands are made on the new arrivals, in stark contrast to the successful American immigration policy – swim or sink.

> An unholy alliance of the unions, the media and the administration maintains the stalemate position of the immigrants. They must not compete with lower wages, the only way for them in the beginning. Small-scale business – small shops and eateries, newsstands and sweet stalls – is the only venue where their industry is rewarded as it falls outside union control. The media do their very best in rubbing up maladjusted immigrants the right way and the main task of the authorities is to administrate demoralizing social security. I want to stress that the refugees and immigrants cannot be blamed. It is the system which inflicts passivity. To make demands on people who have landed here and live here at our expense would be politically very incorrect.

The immigration policies of the democracies suffer from a serious lack of consistency. Real refugee problems are by and large restricted to the developing countries. The great mass of immigrants to Europe and the United States are simply in pursuit of a better life. (Japan does not accept any immigrants.) The problem is that legislation (in Europe) and border controls (in USA) allow for a stream of illegal or half-legal newcomers with an unclear position in society. The politicians have, in a typical democratic manner, sidestepped the problem instead of clarifying the legislation or enforcing restrictions on immigration. Meanwhile, radical measures are called for by a swelling public opinion.

A stricter immigration policy is on the way and not only in the United States. Great Britain and Denmark have tightened their legislation and other countries their praxis. The call for the expulsion of all illegal immigrants is becoming louder and an unreasonable aversion against aliens is spreading in Europe. A major part of the responsibility for the potential violence falls on people who consistently have delivered doctored facts, if not outright lies. They have with the best intentions duped themselves and their public.

The attitudes toward the immigrants have a clear coupling to racism. Dark-skinned persons with a deviating cultural background create the strongest antipathy. The root causes of racist prejudices have been elucidated in the first chapter. They are not diminished by being denied or concealed. A certain distrust is natural and unfortunately it is often justified. The politically correct apply an inverted prejudice by positive medial discrimination. The outcome is hypocrisy in the manner of Victorian sexual morality, which only entrenches the suspicions of the really prejudiced.

Rabid anti-racists are mendacious when they time and again assure that there are no scientifically valid racial differences. It is true that the variation within a racial group in most cases is much bigger than between the groups. Nevertheless, a number of genetic divergences correlate with the conventional racial divisions, with repercussions for clinical research and medication. Racial differences have been tremendously exaggerated but they are real. This fact does not violate the fundamental equality of human beings or the citizens.

We ought to strive for an open mind which recognizes the behavior of the individual instead of the group identity. But the reputation of a group can, with a certain delay, be improved only by members who live up to higher standards, one by one. A linguistic redefinition is a cheap and condescending way to attempt to raise the status of a group which is discriminated against, with or without cause. It is also ineffective. "The name does not soil the man if the man does not soil the name" says a Finnish proverb.

Originally "Quaker" and "Methodist" were derogative nicknames which were tolerated with equanimity and transformed into their opposite. "Mongol" and "Jew" have for a long time been used as insults without interfering with the self-esteem of the afflicted groups. But to achieve respectability, the Negroes obviously have to be transmuted into Afro-Americans, blacks, colored, dark-skinned and what not, while the mulattos have made a complete disappearance. A person with a substantial Caucasian background is still considered pitch black according to modern parole.

The prerogative of the people has always been to define the common usage, disregarding the objections of academic busybodies. Finding faults with this democratic right is reminiscent of the 'Sprachrege-lung' of the Nazis. This was a directive for the regulation of wordings and expressions in the media, with the intention of streamlining the ideological message.[6] The ultimate goal for suchlike intrusions is the prevention of the expression and even the formulation of heretical thought.

An analogous reasoning wants to enforce an artificial balance of the pronouns he/she in order to eliminate a source of gender discrimination. The Finnish language, however, has only a neutral pronoun 'hän' which covers both genders. This has not influenced the position of women in the Finnish society, one way or another. Many other languages, such as Chinese, Japanese, Persian and Turkish, share this gender neutrality.

It is only too easy to find additional examples of ridiculous, annoying and even injurious cases of opinion censorship. To revile Nazism, fascism and right-wing extremism generally is politically correct. On similar grounds the late remnants and new manifestations of communism ought to be a free for all in the political witch hunt – but that is not the case. The asymmetry reveals a resurrected quest for cosmic justice which arrogantly prescribes the politically correct. The obliging simpletons of the Soviet-supported peace movement are now fighting poverty in a way which secures the position of sundry corrupt potentates, if nothing else. A last example demonstrates how good intentions in a tragicomic manner mix with political cynicism.

On the war fields of the developing countries, thousand of children are annually mutilated by landmines, indiscriminately dispersed in the terrain. Years of patient and dangerous mine removal are needed to solve this problem. The world community concentrated instead on a grand resolution, which banned production, trade, stocking and deployment of infantry mines. The Montreal protocol was signed in 1997 with great fanfare by a number of countries at a cost which did not exceed the ink on the paper. But the United States, Russia and China among others did not sign on.

Finland has a long and hard-to-defend border with Russia. No Finnish mine has ever hurt a civilian. Nevertheless, the Finnish president Tarja Halonen forced through the adherence to the Montreal tractate, referring to the international reputation of the country. It will cost about €200m extra to maintain the defense capability. This input will not save a single life, while the United Nations (UNMAS), the Quakers, the Methodists and other NGOs suffer from a chronic lack of resources in their field work. When political correctness is at stake, appearances are invariably more important than the realities on the ground.[7]

A narrow political elite is steering important segments of the public opinion by remote control, according to its own ideology and visions. As such this is not illegitimate. The task of the elite is to show the way and to sell its views to the public, to the best of its abilities. The whole EU-project is an example of fortunate elitist advance planning. Even so, loud bad-mouthing of the European Union is a privilege which is made the most of. But nothing negative about underprivileged groups must appear in public. Political correctness implies a blackout on reposting, a deviation from the openness and honesty which weakens our plus-sum game. In the end it is more a hindrance than a help.

9.5 Electronic communication

The telegraph, the telephone, radio and television have in turn enriched our information environment. Equipped with mobile phones we are now open for worldwide contact in real time. The Internet with the World Wide Web has created direct communication between the members of self-selected global communities and now provides access to an avalanche of new information. Soon it will comprise also in-depth knowledge of science, art and literature. In due course, all the historical information of public libraries, pictures and movies included, will be available on the web.

We have passed the threshold to a media revolution with far-reaching consequences for the future of democracy. Already, it is impossible for authoritarian regimes to uphold a monopoly on information, and the opposition can quickly organize itself by mobile phones and the internet, regardless of the countermeasures of the government. Without these devices, the peaceful upheavals in Ukraine and Georgia would have come to naught. In this respect too, the remaining dictatorships

are kicking against the pricks. China is groping for a third way between democratic freedom and totalitarian control.

> China has introduced special legislation for the regulation of the web.
> Google, for instance, acquiesced in modifying its search engine to
> conform to the local directives. The goals and the effectiveness of the
> censorship vary, but tens of thousands of international sites (i.a. Wiki-
> pedia) have been blocked, at least temporarily. The censors also try
> to filter specific search phrases for example democracy and freedom,
> Tibet and Tiananmen, but with rather poor results. Such an ineffec-
> tive censorship does not serve any sensible purpose and seems to be a
> political end in itself; the authorities have to do something to preserve
> the appearance of control. But the forbidden fruit is all the more ap-
> petizing.[8]

The stock exchange crash of IT-companies in 2001 showed that making money on the net is not that easy, but instead there is ample room
for civic activities. Whosoever can today present himself or herself on
the web for all the world, and likeminded persons can converge on
chat sites for a qualified exchange of information or just for gossip.
Blogging has transformed the web into an everyman's news medium.[9]
It has become an important forum for the free expression of opinion
and a weapon in the political struggle. A blog may be closed or open
for comments with or without editorial control; some of the blogs are
served by well-respected editors. Others are offering advertising space
and are increasingly resembling newspapers.[10]

The number of blogs is rising exponentially and has probably passed
the hundred million mark; a few count up to a hundred thousand daily
hits. All interests and opinions are represented but editorial responsibility is usually in short supply. The anarchy on the net has some less
desirable consequences. Mass-distributed e-mail (spam) is a serious
nuisance and the web is overflowing with worthless, idiosyncratic ego-
trips.

> Early search-engines tended to drown the net surfer in meaningless
> information, and a lot of experience was needed to navigate in the
> jumble. In the late 1990s, Google developed a new search paradigm
> which ordered the information according to its relevance and the com-
> pany is now the clear market leader. Economic success was a given
> when Google introduced an innovative advertising approach which
> served the interests of the surfers as well as the marketers. The intelli-
> gence level of the search engines is still low and there is ample room for

further innovation. The search program could, for instance, be tuned to the individual profile of the surfer.

After the initial bankruptcies, commerce on the net has now found its format; Amazon, the pioneering company, has achieved sustained profitability not least due to the worldwide parcel service. But the net comes really into its own as an open marketplace and in trading with immaterial goods. In addition, the consumer has easy access to the supply and price level of an increasing number of goods and services. No more does the buyer need to suffer from asymmetric information. He or she can be more knowledgeable than the seller about the market for, say, used cars or tourist destinations. Search engines will find the best offers on the net, according to given specifications. The salesman's hyperbole loses its grip on the consumer and competition can be fair and square. Transparent information once again contributes to the efficacy of the plus-sum game.

Every good opens the door for something bad. The net is an ideal medium for irresponsible extremists, subversive elements and perversions of every kind. Malevolent persons publish recipes for producing explosives, poison gases and even nuclear bombs. Pornography is said to be the biggest business on the net and pedophilic material is easily accessible, despite occasional police raids. As an emblem of virtuosity, hackers enjoy creating havoc in susceptible data systems. But less destructive sub-cultures are also roaming the net.

> In his doctoral thesis *Electronic Potlatch* (2001), Alf Rehn describes a net community which excels in getting hold of interesting material, mainly software, for open dissemination on the web. The number and the quality of the published programs define status within the group which leads to acid commentaries and heated arguments. The activity is completely self-organized and is regulated by unwritten rules which have emerged en route. It is a serious hobby but also an anti-commercial manifestation.

There are plenty of young enthusiasts who are willing and capable of contributing to the future electronic society on a voluntary basis. Linus Torvalds is their hero and the Linux software a focus for their efforts. The upshot is a serious competitor to Microsoft. On the other hand, ill-intentioned or merely mischievous talents find satisfaction in constructing viruses or worms which can cause trouble no end. They have called forth a whole industry for the protection of computer integrity. The marauders may actually fulfill a function by contributing to computer security. Without the continuing attacks, the whole system would be very vulnerable and prone to unexpected disasters.

> The biological analogy is striking. Parasitic micro-organisms and the animal immune system are involved in an extended arms race, an inexhaustible series of moves and countermoves. Most parasites are highly specialized and can exploit only one or a few species. But a population lacking an adequate immune defense can be wiped out by alien or newfangled pathogens.
>
> The spread of computer viruses conforms to the same mathematical laws as human epidemics. If a patient on average infects more than one person before recovering (or dying) the disease will spread exponentially, otherwise it fades away. Quarantine is the equivalent to a computer fire wall and vaccinations correspond to special protective programs which identify and eliminate known computer viruses. But dormant viruses are very difficult to detect before symptoms are in evidence.

Every breakthrough in electronic communications has evoked a flood of predictions of the decline and fall of the printed word. So far the apocalyptic visions have come to naught. Newspapers may loose some ground but influential news media are floating net versions of their publications which are generally financed by subscriptions and/or advertising. Only letter-writing has succumbed to the onslaught of the telephone, e-mail and text messages.

Despite the superiority of electronic means of communication, people are clinging to the printed word. A successful newspaper or journal succeeds by profiling itself according to the preferences of the readership. It is like a cherished relative, arriving at regular intervals to strengthen the family identity and coherence. Professional journals however may fall on harder times.

> Research in the natural sciences is increasingly published on-line. Conventional publishing implies a delay of at least several months which has become unacceptable. On the web, the impact is instantaneous and priority is established at the earliest date. Nevertheless, ambitious research will normally appear in print after a thorough peer review. This amounts to a quality guarantee which is related to the reputation of the journal; *Nature* and *Science* are at the top of the hierarchy. The journals are also important for reliable documentation, even if the release of publicly financed research on the net will probably become mandatory.

Books are better entrenched, though electronic books will have an impact as complementary devices. Literature as belles-lettres has a lasting, self-evident value but pure entertainment also holds its own in competition with the deluge of computer games and television soap. The book is still the dominating conduit of structured knowledge, even if computer-based teaching is gaining ground.[11] Data bases such as maps, charts, encyclopedias, dictionaries and thesauri are eminently suitable for on-line presentation. Easy updating, cross-referencing and handling are decisive advantages. For the producer, the problem is to collect adequate payment for the service.

Electronic communication, including the videophone and video-conferencing, will never supplant personal contacts. Presence, body language and the actual staging of the meeting are essential attributes, particularly when new trust capital has to be generated. Moreover, the investment in time and effort is a tangible proof of honest intentions. The plus-sum game can be maintained electronically, but its preconditions can be created only by being and talking together in the old-fashioned way – face to face.

Chapter 10
Democratic fallacies

Democracies are groping ahead in the unknown and frequently go astray. Novel technologies give rise to phobias, and all kinds of hypochondria are rampant. Modern superstitions are propagating and mesh with a facile mysticism. The permanent trust deficit foments all kinds of conspiracy theories. The most virulent is a gender ideology which persuades itself that the suppression of women still persists in our societies. Spiritual disorientation extends from fanatical fundamentalism to intellectual self-conceit. Meanwhile a new breed of intrepid truthseekers is coming forth. They may make less of a splash but will find a real purpose in life.

10.1 Phobias and hypochondria

New technology has always frightened but also fascinated people. Conservatism usually has the upper hand, particularly when the establishment is entrenched and regards every change as a threat to its privileges. A notorious example is the Emperor Ch'ien-lung's (1711-99) snub to Lord Macartney, who at the head of a British embassy had arrived in China in 1793 to broaden trade relations.

> "Our dynasty's majestic virtues have penetrated unto every country under heaven, and kings of all nations have offered their costly tribute by land and sea. As your ambassador can see for himself, we possess all things. I set no value on objects strange and ingenious, and have no use for your country's manufactures...There was therefore no need to import the manufactures of outside barbarians in exchange for our own produce. But as the tea, silk and porcelain which the Celestial Empire produces are absolute necessities to European nations and to yourselves, we have permitted...that your wants might be supplied and your country thus participate in our beneficence."[1]

Under Ch'ien-lung China reached its greatest extension, which may have contributed to the Emperor's feeling of superiority. According to an old Chinese tradition, all other countries were in principle considered inferior and inhabited by tribute-paying barbarians. In Europe,

Chinese technology had for centuries been copied but xenophobic self-complacency blocked all traffic in the other direction.

In the West, the intense competition between countries and companies was pushing technological innovation. Since the enlightenment, progress optimism had been the prevailing attitude and new technology was enthusiastically received by the public, even if it caused dislocation and occasional upheavals among the workers. Symptoms of technophobia were virtually unknown among the educated until the second half of the twentieth century. Electro-sensitivity appeared one century after the breakthrough of electricity, but the cancer alarm for mobile phone users went off with little delay. Nanotechnology has already set off a proactive negative reaction although novel products are yet to appear in the marketplace.[2]

No scientific evidence exists for the dangers of electric appliances or mobile phones. A few alarmist reports have never been corroborated and their purpose is probably to beget more research money. But a round trip on the web shows that there are scores of people who are convinced that their ills are due to the influence of electromagnetic waves. The fear of radioactivity is an even worse affliction, widely spread in our democracies. Public opinion has swung from complete naivety to hyper-allergic reactions.

> Radium was discovered 1898 by Marie Curie (1867-1934) and was deemed a wonder drug, not least by herself. Soon radium was also used for all kinds of self-illuminating objects, from seating numbers in movie theatres to glittering on dolls and toy animals. The most important application, however, was self-illuminating watches. In the factories the radium-containing color was applied with a brush which frequently had to be pointed with the lips. The outcome was serious poisoning and a few deaths which in the 1920s led to litigation and eventually to improved work processes.
>
> Marie Curie died probably due to extended exposure to radium, but only in extreme cases did the widespread carelessness lead to health problems, even if long-term effects cannot be excluded. For the consumers, the health risk was negligible and the sorry fate of the 'radium girls' did not touch the popularity of radium-based products. Radium continued to be used by industry into the 1950s.[3]

Today radioactive radiation elicits anxieties which are easily amplified. The toxicologists have embraced a hyper-cautious approach, assuming that even a minor increase in exposure is injurious and causes an increase in mortality. But this conjecture is contradicted by the available facts.

The survivors of the nuclear bomb in Hiroshima are less at risk for cancer than the population at large. After the Soviet hydrogen bomb testing in Novaja Semlja in 1957, the Finnish Laplanders ingested considerable amounts of radioactive strontium but no increase in the cancer incidence has been established to this day. Extensive studies have shown that the correlation between the cancer incidence and the strongly fluctuating natural background radiation is on the negative side.[4]

The toxicologists are now re-thinking the matter. Many poisonous substances seem to possess salubrious properties at sufficiently low concentrations. This appears to hold for radioactive radiation, too.[5] So far our anxiety over environmental influences has increased in step with the sensitivity of the analytical methods. In the future we will hopefully assume a less hypochondriac stance towards the risks. Despite the extant scientific evidence, time will pass before the researchers arrive at a new consensus. Even more time is needed for a change in public opinion, which is steeped in artificial horror scenarios.

The overblown fear of radioactivity is just at the head of a list of irrational phobias. Synthetic chemicals, 'chemical substances' are a good runner-up. Of course, caution is in order. The first generation of pesticides did not affect humans, but animal life was damaged by the accumulation of chlorinated hydrocarbons. In the developed part of the world, DDT has therefore been replaced by degradable substances which are more selective, too. Up-to-date pesticides and herbicides do not, to our best knowledge, constitute a danger for our health or for the environment.[6]

When our food intake is in focus, hypochondria reaches new heights. Impurity phobias are nothing new in the world history; the Jews, the Muslims and Indian Brahmins were early adherents to painstaking rules regarding nutritional intake. The oversensitive consumers of today, too, would have every reason to be shocked by the skepticism of Jesus Christ at the Jewish kosher rules: "Do ye not yet understand, that whatsoever entereth in at the mouth goeth into the belly, and is cast out into the draught? But those things which proceed out of the mouth come forth from the heart; and they defile the man."[7]

Nothing is more thoroughly investigated than food additives, which must pass meticulous testing with wide safety margins. Even so, the sale of mould-resistant bread meets resistance because it implies the 'unnatural' addition of 'chemical' substances. The additive is benzoic acid which is abundant in cranberries for instance, and is the cause of their remarkable preserving qualities.

On the other hand, many vegetables do produce poisons in quantities which by present standards would disqualify them as a foodstuff. Rhubarb and spinach, for example, contain sizable amounts of oxalic acid, which can cause kidney stones; the lethal dose is about 25g. Bitter cucumbers contain a poison (cucurbitasin) which occasionally has caused sickness.[8]

The European Union has recently stiffened its directives for the supervision of chemicals. Industrially produced 'chemical' substances have to be proved innocuous. This reverted burden of proof does not apply to 'natural' substances, save for exceptional cases (for instance aflatoxins in nuts, almonds etc.). Many natural products are probably as guilty (or as innocent) of causing cancer as the suspected industrial chemicals.

Our excessive hygiene is probably the root cause of the steep increase in allergies, which does not correlate with pollution or poverty but with high living standards. Small children must be confronted with micro-organisms to condition their immune system and avoid over-reaction when facing harmless irritants.[9]

Gene technology is the latest source of hysterical reaction, particularly in Europe. It has been fomented by clever agricultural lobbyists who welcome any obstruction to trade. Pundits of every extraction expatiate in the media on the disastrous risks to our health and environment. The explications of real experts are to no avail; folks know better.

Every expert knows that the consumption of genetically modified foods carries virtually no risk. Therefore the adversaries have been targeting putative environmental problems. The modified variants or their genes may inadvertently spread in nature and influence the ecological balance. This is improbable in theory and extensive testing has not revealed any adverse effects. The relevance of such an enquiry is also questionable. Agriculture has always had inescapable ecological consequences.

Europeans are like the princess and the pea in Andersen's fairy tale. Striving for an unreasonable maximum of security and emotional comfort, we are casting about for every imaginable risk factor, one thing becoming more labored than the next. But the steady growth of genetically modified products in other parts of the world conveys the incontestable facts in the plainest possible terms. The enormous potential of gene technology will be realized, even if risk-averse Europeans think they can do without its blessings.

An open debate illuminates the potential problems of novel technologies from all imaginable points of view and contributes to minimizing the risks, though they can never be completely eliminated. Every change implies an element of risk-taking, but in the long run stagnation entails greater risks, which the Chinese Emperors had to face in the fullness of time. Our aversion to technical innovations breaks out in irrational phobias; the resulting hypochondria have become a serious drag on the techno-economical plus-sum game. All due deference to the precautionary principle, but we are reacting like spoiled princesses to key technological challenges. *Homo sapiens* is, after all, a rather robust survival artist.

10.2 Modern superstitions

Since times of yore, notable natural objects have been the subject of adoration around the world. Sacred mountains and groves, animals and plants were singled out; the bear, the oak and the mistletoe were especially popular. Nature was unpredictable and intimidating but also venerable and sometimes even generous. By various sacrifices it had to be pacified or preferably persuaded to assume a benevolent stance.

The adoration of an original mother is a more advanced form of religion. In agricultural societies, motherhood was linked to the annual crop which was secured by appropriate fertility rites. This ancient cult has recently been resurrected in new quasi-scientific disguise. Gaia, the earth goddess of Old Greece, has become the symbol for our globe as an autonomous, living organism. The basic idea is that life on earth symbiotically maintains its own conditions for survival.

> The Gaia hypothesis was introduced by James Lovelock in 1979. It has never won scientific respectability but has earned all the more approval from environmental enthusiasts. They are not disturbed by the convulsions of nature – ice ages which 600 million years ago covered the earth or giant lava flows and gas eruptions with even worse consequences for the climate. Time and again, the major part of life forms have been driven to extinction. The latest ice ages are modest sequels to these primeval cataclysms.
>
> Besides the self-stabilizing, negative feedback, the life processes can also undermine the very preconditions for their existence. Oxygen was a poisonous by-product of carbon dioxide assimilation, before it became the point of departure for new evolutionary gambits. Eventually most of the life-sustaining carbon dioxide was withdrawn from the atmosphere, which contributed to the recent ice ages. Our globe is no doubt an exceptionally hospitable planet. Nevertheless, the earth

provides just the background for the fabulous creativity and resilience exhibited by life itself.

Green ideologists tend to furnish nature with an unlimited intrinsic value. Any interference becomes a sacrilege, every change an incalculable loss. To the most radical, nature is an idol which deserves any sacrifice, and humanity an affliction which should be wiped off the face of the earth. A primitive cult of nature, trying to manipulate natural forces for human benefit, has transformed into its diametrical opposite.

> Now and again, the protection of endangered animals goes too far. Hunting of any kind is considered contemptuous even if, for instance, many seal species have propagated so that some degree of culling would be advisable. And when the increasing population of elephants in the nature reserves of South Africa is threatening the ecological balance, culling is resorted to only in extremis. Instead a preventive pill is recommended to curb over-elephantization. The delicate sensibility has no bounds.[9a]

We have every reason to strive to understand, preserve and care for perishable natural resources, but man is after all one actor in the dynamics of nature. Furthermore, he has a unique perspective, an overview of the ways of the world, and can show consideration for his environment. That's why he is the measure of all things. The superstitious adoration of the state of nature and its putative status quo must be included among modern delusions. It has a common root with the artificial division between natural and unnatural substances.

Our attitude towards the so called indigenous people is marked by the same distorted sense of reality. They are put on a par with endangered animal species, and thus ought to enjoy protection or special treatment in separate reserves. The presumed respect for their peculiar characteristics is patronizing; at least it does not facilitate adaptation to the contemporary world. Once in a while, obsequious legislation can have absurd consequences.

> In 1996, a 9000 years old skeleton was unearthed close to Kennewick in Washington, USA. Local Indian tribes soon demanded the release of the remains for burial, referring to The Native American Graves Protection and Repatriation Act (NAGPRA). After a four year investigation, the Department for the Interior decided that the remains should be assigned to five Indian tribes, but the scientists appealed and two years later a higher court judged them in the right. (Meanwhile a group

of Polynesians, among many others, had claimed possession of the Kennewick man). In 2004 an Appeal Court confirmed the verdict.[10]

It is understandable that there is a will to accommodate indigenous populations to make some remedy for old sins. But we should also live up to our own values. Seeking the scientific truth benefits the whole world and should not be curtailed on flimsy grounds. As late as the 18th century, old superstitions still obstructed autopsies in Europe and impeded medical research. Strong prejudices can still create problems for modern health care.

> If people refrain from a blood transfusion for themselves or their dependants it must be deemed their own business. But the refusal to participate in a vaccination program may jeopardize the health of others as well. By avoiding a minimal risk exposure, those concerned in effect become free-riders, provided that the majority is inoculated. Then epidemics are precluded and the unvaccinated are indirectly protected. But if only a minority does get vaccinated…

Matters which are susceptible to our understanding, at least in principle, need not and should not be subject to an unshakable conviction. The superstitions of primitive peoples can be excused because they lack better knowledge. But in the name of a preposterous cultural relativism the equality of beliefs, howsoever absurd, has become mandatory in the West. Paganism, Wicca, shamanism, occultism, astrology, etc. etc. – all these expressions of the New Age movement (which is not so new anymore) are on par with the balderdash of shamans and medicine men. Sadly, people do not really want to know better; they stuff themselves with superstition.

> Lafcadio Hearn (1850–1904) was probably the first to use the term 'modern superstition' in the headline of a newspaper article, in which he agonizes over everyday superstition in America.[11] It was the golden age of spiritism and many prominent personalities fell prey to its temptations. Among the gullible were Darwin's colleague, the evolutionary biologist A.R. Wallace (1823–1913), the chemist and physicist William Crookes (1832–1919), the Nobel laureate Charles Richet (1850–1935) and to top it off Conan Doyle (1859–1930), the spiritual father of the master detective.[12]
>
> Today, movies and television entertainment are flooded with paranormal phenomena. For many people it is just an exciting spice but, unfortunately, many watchers take it at least half-seriously. Opinion polls consistently report that a majority of Americans believe in UFOs

(Unidentified Flying Objects). This world view has become a surrogate religion, which conflicts with genuine religiosity.

The creationists, who deny evolution, represent a more serious variant of superstition with surprisingly broad support, above all in the United States. A fundamentalist literalism induces many believers to take the basic incompatibility of Darwinism and Christianity for granted. Nothing in Darwinist evolutionary doctrine contradicts the message of Jesus Christ. On the contrary, science in general and evolution theory especially can be seen as a vindication of the quest for truth of the New Testament. Its spirit has led us on the right path. The truth is rarely obvious; it must be sought and doubted, divined and ascertained from one generation to the next.

A generally applicable scientific method for finding the truth does not and cannot exist. Faith in science as an infallible truth machine is clearly a fallacy, even if it is less common among first rate scientists than in other quarters. Such a belief is a form of superstition, too. It is scientifically barren, but in combination with our techno-culture it can call forth strong allergic reactions.

> In *Life is a Miracle: An Essay Against Modern Superstition*, Wendell Berry has taken aim at science and zeroes in on the usual whipping boy – scientific reductionism. Edward Wilson gets a well deserved hiding for his latest book *Consilience* (1998), where he pleads for a total synthesis of all human knowledge into an interconnected, coherent network. Most scientists perceive this effort as an interesting but wholly unrealistic thought experiment. With increasing complexity, molecules, cells and individuals become ever more independent and unpredictable. If nothing else, unsolvable mathematical and computational problems will stand in the way.

While Wilson's faith in science verges on the irrational, Berry is skeptical towards all scientific progress, discharging the baby with the bath water. He represents the most widespread fallacy: the idealization of times past and mindless anxiety in the face of an insecure future. In his quest for a fictive homeostasis, Berry wants to stop all change. This is an age-old theme rooted in antiquity. The fear of innovation has always carried religious overtones. The unprecedented touches deeply ingrained taboos, disturbs a hallowed order and releases a superstitious terror of the unknown.

10.3 Conspiracies everywhere

In a small and static community the qualities of every member are common knowledge. Expansion of the group dilutes the trust capital and the predictability of behavior is weakened. When power is transferred to remote political structures, the authorities are increasingly distrusted. Democracies do not escape this effect. Distant centers of power are usually blamed for real or imagined wrongs.

> In the United States, the federal capital early on became a symbol of shady manipulation to the detriment of the public, notwithstanding the severity of corruption in many states compared to Washington. In Europe, Brussels has become a spittoon for trivial malcontent. Fictitious stories about absurd directives gain credibility and circulate as urban legends despite repeated denials. We readily believe the worst about the power brokers, especially if they are far away.

The general mistrust is a fertile soil for diverse conspiracy theories. Every evening they confront us on the television screen as rather trivial entertainment. All imaginable and many unimaginable conspiracies are presented with the police, criminal syndicates, intelligence services, chief executives, business tycoons, foreign powers, politicians and the press involved in fanciful combinations. This can be dismissed as an innocuous pastime, but the fictive plots nevertheless have links to reality and may thus distort the judgment of the watchers.

> The UFO superstition is mainly the product of media sensationalism. The belief that the American secret services are suppressing material proof of the existence of UFOs has become widespread. The persistence of these rumors attests to the infatuation of common Americans with conspiratorial thinking.
>
> The creationists still perceive the theory of evolution as a devilish machination against the biblical message. More understandable are the doubts that many Americans have about the assassinations of the Kennedy brothers. On the surface, any conspiracy looks more plausible than the string of improbable coincidences of the official Warren commission. But reality is usually less coherent than fiction.[12a]

The most effective conspiracy is to accuse the adversary of conspiratorial activities; the absence of a plot is almost impossible to prove. The Jews have since times immemorial been the victims of slander and persecution which culminated during the last century. Widespread anti-Semitism had prepared the ground for the most fantastic accusations.

The Protocols of the Elders of Zion is the main source for the allegation that the Jews are concocting a world-wide conspiracy. The book is pure fiction with a checkered past. In 1864 Maurice Joly, a Frenchman, wrote a pamphlet against Napoleon III, which was recast into an anti-Semitic manifest by the German Hermann Gödsche. The book was translated into Russian and finally revised by the secret police. After the wave of democratization 1904–05, it found its first application in the hands of Russian reactionaries.

In due course the book became required reading for inveterate anti-Semites, with Adolf Hitler in the van. The fabrication is discredited in the West but in the Islamic countries its popularity is undiminished. Saudi-Arabian textbooks feature a summary of the putative program for Jewish world domination. A small light in the dark tunnel: The Arabian translation of *The Protocols* was removed from the web site of the Palestinian Administration on May 19, 2005.[13]

The Bolsheviks were not to be overtaken by the Nazis in conspiratorial tactics. They referred ceaselessly to the evil designs of the capitalists and the imperialists while attempting to undermine the democratic societies by every means at their disposal. Devious disinformation was systematically disseminated by friendly channels and was readily soaked up by the western media. The Kennedy assassinations were exploited to the hilt by the Russian secret service.

In less developed countries with weak communications, sensational rumors spread like wildfire. In Africa it is widely believed that the HIV-virus was developed in the United States in order to decimate the black population. (This allegation is apparently taken seriously by some prominent Afro-Americans, too.) Many Arabs maintain that the attack on the World Trade Center on 9.11.2001 was staged by the Americans (alternatively the Israelis) to create a pretext for an assault on the Arab states.

There seems to be no bounds to imputing every evil in the world to the United States. The tsunami of 12.24.2004 produced wild speculations around the Arab world, that American weapon tests were the cause of the disaster. A Saudi-Arabian professor asserted that Allah's punishment of the Christians was appropriately imposed during Christmas, callously disregarding the overwhelming Muslim majority among the victims.[14]

The inhabitants of less developed countries project their frustrations on the surrounding world. This practice is not alien to democracies, albeit in more moderate terms. Nowadays the debasing of neighbors in the European Union is beyond the pale and therefore the United States has become a bugbear, responsible for most of the wrongs in the world.

> The battle for oil has been a favorite for conspiracy mongers; it has a sufficient basis in reality to provide credibility in many situations. It is widely assumed, that the selfish oil interests of the United States dominate its policies in the Middle East. But only 6.7% of the US oil consumption came from this area in 2005.[15] Other importers, particularly the EU, Japan, China and India are much more reliant on oil from the Middle East.

Conspiratorial allegations are symptomatic of a trust deficit in society. In half-baked democracies, like Russia, official proclamations are a priori perceived as unreliable and disingenuous. In the core democracies, too, it is a popular pastime to look for hidden motives behind government announcements. There are good reasons for taking the statements of politicians with a pinch of salt; more or less obvious hidden agendas are often telling. This does not necessarily imply malicious intent. Each and everyone is just trying to hold his or her own in the political marketplace.

Appealing to the dread of conspiracies makes for cheap political points. Every proposal to utilize existing data-bases to achieve improvements in policing, administration, banking, health care or scientific research is fiercely resisted with reference to the threat of an all-pervasive, big brother society. The whole population appears to be suffering from chronic paranoia.

We should be more concerned about the looming presence of a big brother in matters of health and nutrition. High-ranking experts always act with the best of intentions when they do their utmost to touch off the bad conscience of the consumers of sugar and salt, animal fats or 'empty' calories in general – for some reason the intake of alcoholic drinks usually falls outside the exhortations.

> Following public recommendations does not hurt, for sure, but they are saddled with a couple of problems. They address mainly those already converted and do not get through to the intended target groups. Nor do the directives take account of personal differences. When combined with ample safety margins, an over-cautious approach leads to widespread skepticism, and even reasonable guidelines lose their bite. More harmful may be the stress, which is the upshot of a compulsory diet fixation due to personal idiosyncrasies as well as to official enjoinders.

Like prominent politicians, big multinational companies are vulnerable to public mishaps which the media like to blow up into major scandals. In such cases good advice is thin on the ground. The same mistakes are made again and again even if the involved parties should know better.

> When Coca Cola met with quality problems in Belgium in 1999, the inclination of the top management was to play down the incident, but it soon engulfed the company. All Belgian production had to be stopped and the products recalled. The giant factory in Dunkirk was closed and products had to be recalled in France, too. Coca Cola systematically tried to escape the blame but was continuously overrun by events. The scandal contributed to the dismissal of Douglas Ivester, chief executive since 1997; Warren Buffett, a major stockholder and member of the board, called him "tone deaf".
>
> Over the years I have had repeated contact with the top management of Coca Cola (except Ivester). My diagnosis is that the company fell into a success trap and suffered from the concomitant arrogance, which culminated under Ivester. Arrogance is a bad adviser, particularly in dealing with customers and the mass media. Humility is the best approach but ever so hard to employ. Under Neville Isdell, Coca Cola has rediscovered its values and regained its vitality.

Openness is the only way for companies as well as for politicians to preserve or regain the trust of the public and to puncture malicious rumors. It is not enough to eschew lies; correct information must immediately be made public and mistakes should be admitted in so many words, preferably erring on the safe side. Most destructive is a series of exposures, which are dragged out piecemeal by the trumpeting media.

Transparency and honesty are the only remedies for the exaggerated suspiciousness of common people. Concealment of facts, not to mention mendacity, undermines the democratic plus-sum game and arouses justified anger. The unelected representatives of the people in the media world could, for their part, retreat from their self-righteousness and openly reflect on their own shortcomings. This would increase public trust and benefit democracy.

10.4 Gender ideology

The twentieth century marked a comprehensive change in the praxis of democracy when the feminine half of the population gained full civic rights. Women's liberation went from strength to strength and gender discrimination has become a criminal offence in the majority of democracies. In principle, and very far in practice, women now have equal opportunities to establish themselves in society. So far the outcome has not been parity in all areas, which is perceived as decisive proof for the persisting repression of women. This is muddled thinking.

The original motto of women's liberation was equivalence, not similarity with men. The radical feminists, however, insist on complete equality in all respects; they do not accept any differences except obvious physical characteristics. All behavioral differences between boys and girls are passed off as cultural ballast which should be heaved overboard without delay. Here the demand for absolute 'cosmic' justice reaches absurd proportions.

Both genders display great variations regarding spiritual and physical aptitudes and there can be no question about the rights of everybody to realize him- or herself within the bounds of their personal qualifications, irrespective of gender. But on average the differences are so conspicuous that one must be purblind not to perceive them.

> Convinced developmental optimists have undertaken to let chimpanzee young grow up together with their children in the vain hope that they would learn to talk. Similarly, efforts have been made to enforce unisexual behavior on small boys and girls – in vain. At the outset, the Israeli kibbutzim were radically socialist. Both genders were raised according to strictly egalitarian principles and the work assignments for the adults rotated irrespective of traditional gender roles. But later on, when people could make their own choices, the gender distribution between trades by and large reverted to the pattern of the surrounding society.[16]

Upbringing certainly plays a part in reinforcing the gender roles, but the endocrine system does – fortunately – steer boys and girls in different directions. The great variations in behavior and aptitude within the same gender thus depend on individual differences in the hormonal balance. More research in this area would facilitate a dispassionate debate. All the same, gender does not inform about the competence of an applicant. But the rather spontaneous segregation into male and female occupations does, at least in part, depend on differences in average aptitudes and should not be seen as a problem. Quota thinking is at bottom an undemocratic plague which only precipitates new injustices.

> One has to admit that the stratification was blatant only a few decades ago. In the 1980s, I was a member of the supervisory board of the biggest commercial bank in Finland. When lecturing about personnel

policy, the director for human resources routinely divided the personnel into three groups: top management, middle management and the women (actually a few women had made it into middle management). Nowadays, no bars exist for ambitious women to make a carrier within Finnish trade and industry. To discriminate against gifted people would simply be unprofitable.

The capability of women to restrict their reproduction, irrespective of sexual activity, is a revolutionary change. Of course, birth control is nothing new in itself but, together with access to legal abortion, the pill has become a symbol of women's liberation. The so called morning-after pill is further increasing the safety margin against unwanted pregnancies. The whole of society has been sucked into the torrent of women's emancipation without a clue about the final consequences.

> The precautionary principle is a rationalization of our inbuilt conservatism and is strictly applied in medicine, biotechnology and nuclear power. But when deliberating on social structures, say gender relationships or the upbringing of children, we proceed with the unwitting self-confidence of an ignoramus. The damage, if any, caused by nuclear waste in a distant future evokes more anxiety than the influences of abortions and the preventive pills on the psyche of women and the stability of families. (The adverse influence of the pill's pseudo-hormones in sewage effluents seems to be more cause for concern.)[16a] We are now beginning to see the upshot of the widespread sexual license, but advance heedlessly with an experiment which could severely affect our long-term future.

In the 1960s and 70s the most rabid feminists were not content with the pill but underwent hysterectomy, removing the putative cause of their repressed position in society. This protest against the perceived patriarchal dominance was a bizarre maneuver in the power struggle between the genders – equality was attempted at any price. Nietzsche's power ideology became the improbable loadstar for fundamental feminism, which senses masculine abuse of power and oppression of women at every corner. Extreme feminists still spout about women's power and the elimination of the male chauvinist pigs, not least in Sweden, which recently was bestowed with the first purebred women's party in the world.

> The notorious SCUM-manifest (Society for Cutting Up Men) from the 1960s was latterly translated into Swedish and got an enthusiastic reception. "...the most brilliant feminist book which has appeared in

Swedish in this time"; "one of the most important feminist tracts in the West"; "the book should be placed as a Bible in all hotel rooms of the world". The volume could be properly prosecuted for inciting hatred against an ethnic group: Men are animals, machines and a biological disaster.[17]

Extremism aside, mainstream feminism is still encumbered by many quirks and fads. The demand for positive discrimination is becoming ever louder. In the Nordic countries gender parity at the ministerial level has been achieved which has wetted the appetite for government intervention. In Sweden the minister for equality threatened punitive legislation if company boards were understaffed with women. In Norway such a law is already enforced. Every deviation from parity produces outbursts of accusations and demands for immediate corrections.

In the United States Larry Summers, the president of Harvard University became the target for furious attacks. At an academic seminar he had intimated that the female under-representation at the science faculties may have other causes than discrimination. He could continue in his office only after repeated apologies (later on he resigned). In gender as well as in race discrimination, the burden of proof in practice rests on the defendant; you have to prove that you are innocent.

The feminists grudgingly concede that men are physically stronger on average. Consequentially, the genders are separated for example at the Olympic Games, which has led to a rather dismal doubling in virtually all the competitions (riding is the only unisex exception I can recall). Nowadays we can also enjoy the sight of female boxers and weightlifters. Ski-jumping is, as far as I know, the only significant sport which is male only. Even American football has recently been appropriated by women.

Military service has traditionally been a male prerogative, though women's battalions existed in the Red Army and Israel features conscription for both genders. When the barriers were broken in other countries many exceptional women could make a career in the armed forces, but the number of modern amazons has not grown inordinately. Generally the use of women on the frontline is avoided; they are more useful at other tasks. Such conclusions evoke immediate rebuttals, and it is true that there are brave women around as well as a lot of cowardly men. But male comradeship strengthens the courage of men while a female presence disrupts the fellowship.

Chess and bridge should be perfect arenas for a fair competition irrespective of gender. Even so, no objections are raised against the division into an open class and a ladies class in these games. Men seem to be too superior in the top echelon, despite a few exceptions like Judith Polgar and Pia Carling in chess. The explanation could be that the variation in intelligence is greater among men, with more extremely gifted and more blockheads. (This was Larry Summers' hypothesis which earned him a thrashing.) A complementary hypothesis could be that the female intelligence is not bent on sharp logic but favors empathic human insight. Moreover, to win is not always the overwhelming goal for women, while men instinctively want to come out on top.

Women apologists try to compensate for former under-exposure by presenting early female mathematicians, scientists and artists in a glorifying light, but such market-sensitive research has no future. In the long run, there is no reason to harp on a misdirected inferiority complex. Self-evidently, the differences between men and women are riches to be treasured. If anything, gender relations make for a fruitful plus-sum game. It is idiotic to place the genders at opposite sides in some kind of power game, or insist on amends for the real or putative wrongs of times past.

Future generations will be flabbergasted when their historians report on the ideological absurdities of our time. Even today it is extraordinary difficult to understand why our elected representatives waste their time on discussing state-subsidized artificial insemination for lesbian couples. That the most extreme ultra-feminists descend into grotesque incongruities is up to them. But we can only blame ourselves if our legislators squander their energy on futilities instead of concentrating on essential matters.

10.5 In the doldrums

Despite the recent political and material successes, the democracies seem to be afflicted by an internal hollowness. The threat of terrorism has not been a substitute for the struggle with communism; there is a dearth of good enemies. Without falling into pseudo-profound pessimism, I want to point out symptoms for a widespread malaise, the feeling of vacuity and disillusion which on our continent is called eurosclerosis.

The low and falling nativity is a cause as well as the consequence of the despondency. The surplus of infirm oldies is bound to be depressing, despite all the slogans about a golden old age. Without children there is no future, a fact we have learned to ignore despite, or rather because of our sexual fixation. One does not need to be puritan to feel disgust at the torrents of irresponsible sex which are pouring out of all media. Like overfed baboons in their cages we try to kill time and boredom with insolently public but basically unsatisfying sexual intercourse.

> The bonobo is a chimpanzee subspecies. Sexual contacts are promiscuous, disconnected from reproduction and commonplace for both genders in all combinations. This behavior has probably evolved as a way to reduce internal conflicts, particularly during food intake. Deviating from the chimpanzees, the bonobos lack a patriarchal social structure, another reason for their adoption as a mascot for ultra-feminists.[18]

The dissolution of the family institution is a serious warning sign for our societies. Singularly unsettling is the trend that sees women losing their virtues and eagerly adopting male vices like foul language, smoking, abusing alcohol and sleeping around. Remarkably, this goes hand in hand with a general feminization of norms and views; security, care and other soft values are in the ascendant.

> We have reached a point where soldiers must not to be killed in war. They are permitted to expire in traffic accidents or diseases like civilians, but death through enemy action is becoming scandalous and precipitates indignant calls for immediate evacuation from the life-threatening area.

In modern societies the male is desperately looking for a role. Morally he is by nature the weaker vessel. Therefore he should by hook or by crook be held accountable for the sustenance of the next generation. The fully emancipated female has, however, lost her interest in keeping her mate in check. And nothing suits the young male better than easily accessible women who at any moment can be left to their own devices.

> Single mothers supported by the public purse have become the hallmark of modern morality. Male deceit receives its reward; no trouble, no burdens but the genes are propagated at the taxpayer's expense. Disregarding other drawbacks we can conclude that moral evolution goes into reverse gear when free-riders are favored.
> The infidelity of women is increasing, too, in step with the sexual liberation. It may be promoted by a hypothetical process, rooted in evolutionary psychology. When a woman in a partner relationship has used prevention for a long time, she eventually gets the message that her mate is sterile. Her intellect explains the causal connection but her

emotions transmit an age-old endocrine message – it is high time to look out for another male.

Post-coital depression is spreading in the West when sexuality has lost its sacral dimension and sexual intercourse has become a parlor game. Youngsters become used to the satisfaction of all wants without any exertion or sacrifice. The citizens begin to resemble spoiled children, loudly airing their discontent at any adversity. Despite the best available care, mental insecurity and disorientation are on the increase; psychiatrists are enjoying halcyon days.

> No news about a serious accident is complete without an officious comment that the shocked victims and/or their relatives had received psychiatric help. Who would want to withhold the best available relief from extremely vulnerable human beings? Nevertheless the question remains: how could people in the old days cope with crushing disasters without recourse to expert support? Would not close friends and relatives or perhaps priests be more suitable to alleviate the inescapable grieving process? Moreover, follow-up research indicates that the results of these psychiatric interventions are mixed; efforts at professional compassion may even worsen the condition.[19]

It is an illusion that an improvement in living standards automatically enhances happiness (although a decreased standard is definitely unpleasant). Even so it is shocking that our mental health seems to have suffered total shipwreck. An authoritative American study maintains that one fifth of the population are vulnerable to mood disorders including depression and bipolar psychosis, one fourth suffer from impaired self-control and almost one third are affected by various anxiety symptoms.[20] When the list is extended to alcoholism, drug addiction and a number of less common syndromes, the conclusion must be that most of us are afflicted by one or more neuroses, if nothing worse. This is confirmed by the increase in pill consumption with Prozac as the market leader.

> Nevertheless, wide-ranging surveys show that people, despite everything, are rather content with their lot; happiness is surprisingly independent of circumstances. In *Happiness: Has Social Science A Clue?*, Richard Layard has made an effort to quantify happiness.[21] The answer to his question is hardly affirmative, but this study confirms that happiness is decoupled from living standards. In the 1990s, the happiness index in Brazil, Ghana, Colombia, Canada, Japan and France was almost the same. The situation was worst in the countries of the former Soviet Union and former Yugoslavia. In a later book (*Hap-*

piness: Lessons from a New Science) Layard arrives at the less than original conclusion, that envy is the bane of happiness. More surprising is the hereditability of happiness; investigations of twins show that about one half of the feelings of happiness are due to an inherited disposition.

The collective hypochondria is not credible. We have, rather, become unaccustomed to the worries and pains which are an unavoidable and an unalienable part of the human condition. The major part of our mental maladies is rooted in egocentric self-obsession. It is a matter of welfare afflictions which would be swept away by a serious crisis – for real. Stress and burnout have become fashionable concepts but they have only very vague medical relevance.

> A considerable part of the mental problems are simply due to our life in democratic societies where lack of success cannot anymore be blamed on the social setting. To comfort the pupils, many modern school systems have tried to abolish all visible marks of differences in industry or talent – in vain. The truth will transpire, not only in the classroom but on the sport grounds and in relations with the opposite gender. An increasing number of youths, especially teen-age boys, cannot live with this insight and commit suicide.[22]

Waiting for the really serious crisis, the new generation has to accept its shortcomings and grow up to adults like their forefathers and -mothers. The parents should not encumber the process by indulgence and lack of commitment. Loving guidance should be mitigated by consistent demands. We leave our children in the lurch by insisting on loose upbringing and norm-free school surroundings.

> Corporal punishment of children is prohibited in many democracies. The intention is good, no doubt, but the legislative intrusion into the citizen's nurseries can be questioned. The letter of the law hardly restricts real abuse of children, which remains a challenge for the relevant authorities. But conscientious parents may become insecure and loose control of their offspring. Children can be terribly infuriating, self-willed or just naughty. A spontaneous outbreak of anger may be necessary to draw the line and restore parental authority. It is striking how a child, after a period of willfulness, regains its mental balance only when the provoked reaction is sufficiently clear-cut and a sincere reconciliation becomes possible.

Youthful idealism is steadily looking out for new directions which intimate the winds of change. When the most talented are manning the barricades, something is in the offing, even if the majority sooner or later will be integrated into society. At present, the caliber of the dissidents is not very impressive. They form a B-team and have learned nothing and forgotten nothing.[23] No fresh suggestions or strong convictions are offered, only a hotchpotch of discarded ideas and fuzzy concepts which are adequately expressed in the incoherence of the anti-globalization movement.

> The massive gatherings which often shadow major international conferences could be an effective way to present alternatives to the prevailing policies. Sad to say, the resolutions usually end up in pious wish-lists and simplistic criticism of the responsible leadership. Yet, a stronger solidarity with the developing countries is in the air and has elicited loan concessions for the poorest countries. Whether this will have the intended effect remains to be seen.

The least common denominator is a nostalgic yearning for the bright illusions of socialism. The tyranny of the market, the greed of capitalists and the imperialist lust for power are reiterated in a resurrection of the worn-out catchphrases of communism. But this pseudo-commitment must comply with the outspoken individualism and hedonism of the participants. The world reformers do not put strenuous demands on themselves – although the noise level is high, striking power is wanting.

Nowadays political differences of opinion rarely erupt into violence. But single-cause movements can be all the more ferocious in our democracies. Violations of the rights of animals and embryos evoke the strongest passions, accompanied by arson and homicide. Yet, large-scale assaults on humans in distant countries do not invoke similar emotion. On the contrary, using violence to stop the torture and murder is considered highly questionable.

The so-called post-modernistic school represents a more sophisticated version of a reluctant Marxist disillusion. Philosophers like Paul de Man (1919–83), Michael Foucault (1926–84), Jean-François Lyotard (1924–98) and Jacques Derrida (1930–2004) did their best to baffle an already bewildered public with putatively profound post-modern tracts.

> The common point of departure was the negation of objective knowledge. Truth then becomes highly relative, a sort of fiction. All state-

ments are only a play with words; not even the insights of natural science possess a unique purport. They are calmly interpreted as just the emanations of the prevailing power structure and social order.[24]

These gentlemen can be designated scientists manqué. Instead of delivering their share of patient work, they entered a shortcut to fame or at least notoriety. By arbitrarily projecting their own disorientation on every quest for truth they sought a *revanche* for personal frustrations. The bluff succeeded, not least in America. Apparently lots of students preferred incomprehensible twaddle to logical stringency.

Although post-modernism is already passé, the meaningless self-assertion and fashionable flight from reality illustrates the desperate chase for any purpose in the doldrums of contemporary society. *Bonjour tristesse* (1954), a novel by François Sagan (1934–2004), mirrors the weariness and boredom of a lost generation. *The Golden Notebook* (1962) by the Nobel Laureate Doris Lessing is an audit of all the dead ends of her erotic and political exploits. And Elfriede Jelinek, another Laureate, renders the total breakdown of human and particularly gender relations in *Die Klavierspielerin* *(1997) and *Gier*** (2000). In the frenetic struggle against disillusion, old-fangled modernisms are strenuously re-circulated but there is no escape from the vicious circle.

Art is the science of man. Thanks to art we have some insight in the turmoil of the human mind; facing the facts is the first step in healing. We must leave behind us the petty preoccupation with our transient emotional discomforts – happiness is not a fundamental human right. To secure a virtuous circle, it is high time for a new breed of intrepid truth-seekers to come forth and explore the future. They may make less of a splash but will find real content in life.

---

*   In English *The Piano Teacher*
** In English *Greed*

Part III

The Future of Democracy

The third part of the book discusses the evolving threats and the preconditions for democratic success.

New technology will in the foreseeable future solve most of our environmental problems and help us to ward off other predictable dangers.

The rectification of the distorted population structure is up to ourselves; a democracy is always in the wrong but, like the market, it is constantly correcting itself.

A sensible world order can be erected through trustful cooperation between major democratic powers, while a sovereign global government would be a disaster.

The expansion of democracy must not lead to conceited passivity; the democratic mission implies continuous value generation and regeneration.

The future of humanity depends on our response to these challenges and the accumulation of the relevant moral capital.

Chapter 11

The Lessons of history

Historically, high cultures have paid for their stability by stagnation and suppression. The cultural evolution is mainly driven by communication between people and peoples; the plus-sum game builds on the exchange, borrowing, copying and hybridization of ideas. Democratic learning is an extended process and every new generation has to pass the political manhood test. The road to collective self-control is lined with temptations; democracy cannot be handed over as a gift. The price to be paid is respect for the overriding rules of the game at the expense of personal advantage and immediate satisfaction. Our future cannot be foreseen but for that very reason it depends on us, ourselves.

11.1 The rise and fall of cultures

Edward Gibbon (1737–94) is the classic representative for cultural criticism in a historical perspective. In his *Decline and Fall of the Roman Empire* he presents the protracted disaster with perceptive bitterness. Later historians have supplied a wealth of new facts and nuances, yet the basic problem remains refractory.

> Some historians deny, in the name of value relativism, the reality of the cultural decay. Since history has no direction, ups and downs must be illusory. But military defeats, the decreasing population, increasing lawlessness and inflation, the dissolution of government and loss of quality consciousness bear clear witness of a persistent decline long before the final disintegration of the western part of the empire in the fifth century. The death throes of Byzantium were much longer and lasted more than a millennium.

When one tries to follow the chain of cause and effect which leads to the breakdown of the plus-sum game, it is all too easy to get stuck on the proximate causes of the decay. Useless emperors, internal power struggles, a corrupt administration, excessive centralization and suffocating taxation, environmental destruction, barbarian incursions, unruly mercenaries and an unemployed, state-supported proletariat is just the beginning of a list of weaknesses in the societal structure.

Deeper down one encounters shortcomings pertaining to the moral capital – a serious deficit in civic virtues and faith in the future.

According to Gibbon, Christianity undermined the original Roman virtues and in Byzantium ended up in a fixation over theological quibbles with accompanying destructive sectarian conflicts. But the decay had begun before the birth of Christ. The Romans themselves understood that the failure of republican self-government was the crucial point. Imperial rule was an emergency expedient which carried the seeds of its own destruction (cf. chapter 3.1).

> Perhaps we should not ask why the Roman Empire fell, but how it could achieve such an expansion and survive for so long with aggressive enemies on many sides. The staying power of the Byzantines is particularly impressive, with several revivals after crushing defeats.

The rise of Rome was built mainly on military power, and military defeats marked in due course the breakdown of both parts of the empire. In contrast to the Republic, which fought to the last man against intruders, the subjects of the late emperors had little worth protecting. Whole provinces fell like skittles before barbarian conquerors; the new tyrants could not be much worse than the old ones. The administration of the empire simply did not produce any added value, but rather was bent on maximizing extortion.

The study of Roman history, east and west, is exceptionally well endowed with documentary and archaeological material. Nevertheless, it is very difficult to get to the bottom of cause and effect. Rome became the victim of its own success and its concomitants – spiritual shallowness and escalating foul play. Honest and loyal citizens were sidelined; the cultural and perhaps the genetic selection favored freeriders, bent on shortsighted self-interest. Half-hearted reforms could not stop the vicious spiral of decay.

> Roman citizenship was gradually extended until in 212 the Emperor Caracalla made all free inhabitants of the empire Roman citizens – at that point a status without much substance. In Byzantium, the Orthodox Church was linked to the bureaucratic structure of the empire, and proceeded to waste its inspiration on theological disputes.

Decline comes slowly, on the sly. The long perspective disappears, like changes in climate in the abrupt meteorological fluctuations of human life. Already under the Emperor Augustus, Rome had adopted a defensive stance and under Hadrian (Emperor 117–138) it became official policy. The feeling of a civilizing mission had evaporated. No more had the Empire anything to give or to gain; the Romans just wished to be left in peace. Such self-sufficiency always and everywhere signals a slackening of vitality which invites aggression. But in the fullness of time, Christian evangelists of varying shades spread the good message among the heathens and prepared the ground for a new civilization.

Archaeological excavations have uncovered a range of other high cultures. The first cities were established at the lower Euphrates and Tigris (Uruk was founded before 4000 BC). About 2350 BC, the Sumerian city states were succeeded by the Akkadians which were replaced by a sequence of rather unstable power structures. The Assyrians and the Babylonians long fought for hegemony in Mesopotamia until Cyrus (died 529 BC) incorporated the land into the Persian Empire in 539 BC. The conquests of Alexander the Great (356– 323 BC) marked the end of the multi-millennial Sumerian cultural tradition and the first written language in the world.

> The great ecological disaster struck, however, only after the Islamic invasion in the seventh century. By the twelfth century, the inhabited area in Mesopotamia had decreased to 6% of its former extension and the population reached its lowest level in 5000 years. Baghdad and its surroundings excepted, the country was taken over by wandering nomads beyond the control of any central power.[2]

In Northwest India, The Harappa culture (c.2500–1800) was flourishing and in Minor Asia the Hittites created the first Indo-European high culture (c.1800–1200 BC) which was destroyed by other Arian immigrants. In pre-Colombian America, successive city cultures have been uncovered in today's Peru and Mexico. The oldest known is the Norte Chico-complex which prospered on the dry pacific coast of Peru between 2900 and 1800 BC.[3]

> The Norte Chico culture was based on a symbiotic exploitation of the rich coastal fishing grounds and the limited area under culture in the river valleys. The most important crop was cotton for clothing and above all for fishing nets. The archaeological findings are scarce because Norte Chico lacked pottery. The sacred places were built with a peculiar technology; the walls were erected by layering stone-filled bags like bricks.
>   The Maya culture in Southeast Mexico, Guatemala and Honduras was the only one in America to develop a proper written language.[4] The first well-documented kings were installed around AD 250 but the

roots of Maya culture go back at least to the seventh century BC. The rivaling city states reached their apogee in the eighth century AD, but around AD 1000 most of the cities with their monumental temples had been abandoned. A few outlying areas managed to hold out; Chichén Itzá, in Northern Yucatan, went down only around 1250.[5]

In America, a multiplicity of city cultures followed each other for millennia without crossing the threshold to cumulative advances in technology, communication or social structure. The Inca and Aztec realms were socially stratified and militarily organized empires, which happened to dominate their region when the Europeans landed, armed with microbes and superior weapons. But there is no indication of cultural innovation which would have changed the established pattern of rise and fall. In Asia, the Khmer empire (c.800–1400), centering on Angkor in Cambodia, exhibits a similar concatenation although its end was less abrupt.[6] The causes of the recurring collapses were certainly diverse but some common features can be perceived.

> Everywhere, cultural advance was based on intensive agriculture. In most places, water management was the main challenge. Forest devastation or soil salination in dry areas tended to disturb the ecological balance, undermining agricultural productivity. An adverse climate change could then trigger an irreversible decline. A healthy society should, nevertheless, be capable of coping with such exigencies. But the elite regularly focused on prestigious projects such as monumental buildings and military conquest. Overpopulation and recurring warfare would have exacerbated the disruption of social relations. When the upper classes cease to deliver any added value for the population at large, the people revolt and opt for a primitive life in small self-sufficient units.

The sweeping generalizations of Oswald Spengler (1880–1936) and Arnold Toynbee (1889–1975) are not fashionable any moore[7], but during the last decades the literature of decline and fall of cultures has revived. Joseph Tainter launched the new wave with *The Collapse of Complex Societies* (1988), followed by *The Collapse of Ancient States and Civilizations*, edited by Norman Yoffee and George Cowgill. While Tainter traces back the decay to the increasing complexity of high cultures, Jared Diamond has in *Collapse* (2005) abjured any societal or ecological determinism, which is reflected in the subtitle: *How Societies Choose to Fail or Survive*. He does not myopically ascribe cultural collapses to overwhelming external circumstances or social mechanisms. Instead, an inadequacy in human response is seen as the main culprit.

> Diamond refers to human shortsightedness and lack of adaptability which is not very illuminating. Lack of solidarity and 'unsuitable' values are plausible explanations but do not bring us much closer to the core of the problem. The cultural collapse of small communities like Easter Island, Pitcairn and the Vikings of Greenland may have little in common with high cultures of the Maya type. Anyhow, Diamond identifies two complementary mechanisms for the rectification of ecological destruction. Grassroots activities can create environmental stability (cf. the Subak system, chapter 4.2) and so can decisive measures by a central government. The forestation program of the Tokugawa regime in 18th century Japan is referred to as an encouraging example.

Obdurate historicism is obviously on the retreat and more nuanced attitudes are gaining ground. The quest for generally applicable laws is certainly in vain. Cultural evolution is, like its biological counterpart, tied to historical happenstance; in scientific jargon it is called 'path dependence'. We are dealing with chaotic systems – very weak impulses can beget incalculable consequences. This insight does not imply resigned value relativism. Despite the fundamental unpredictability, history is developing according to its own rules and may express hidden invariances. Predictability is weak, but for this very reason the future is open and malleable.

11.2 Stagnated high cultures

Most high cultures have fallen prey to destructive internal dynamics combined with the attacks from 'barbarian' neighbors. The exceptions from this pattern are instructive. Long-term stability has been achieved at the price of stagnation. A secure homeostasis has always been a tempting alternative for the upper classes, which in most cases had more to loose than to gain by the perpetuation of a creative plus-sum game.

Egypt is the classic example of untouchable durability, symbolized by the sphinx and pyramids at Giza. Every dynasty represents a political discontinuity but after the pyramid-building Pharaohs of the Old Kingdom (2920–2152 BC), no major development is discernible. The 18th dynasty Pharaohs deftly reconnected the New Kingdom (1539–800 BC) to the old traditions, even if the burials became less ostentatious and the temples correspondingly grander. The turbulence of the Middle Kingdom, which lasted for centuries and was interspersed with invasions and social disturbances, had not upset the continuity of Egyptian culture. Pharaoh Akhenaton (ruled 1353–1336 BC) was the only one to attempt radical change during the New Kingdom but all political, artistic and religious renewals were cancelled after his death.

> Akhenaton (originally Amenhotep IV) introduced near-total monotheism by prescribing the exclusive adoration of Aton, the sun god. He also built a new capital at present el-Amarna to make a break with the past. The establishment certainly resisted the changes but Pharaoh was obeyed. His word stood for more than any law. It was the expression of divine wisdom and power. In Egypt, the deification of the ruler was driven to its extreme, which guaranteed stability but pre-empted lasting reforms.

In military terms, the New Kingdom was a major power which aggressively asserted its interests against the Nubians in the south and in the conflicts with sundry Anatolian, Assyrian and Babylonian rulers. Around 1200 BC, Egypt could also hold its own against the attacks of the so-called sea peoples, which ravaged the Eastern Mediterranean and caused great commotion in the region.

> The history of the sea peoples is more a matter of speculation than facts. The sea peoples probably reflect an extensive Indo-European migration, a chain reaction where the defeated people gladly joined the plunder. (The pillages of later violent migrations probably followed a similar pattern; it is well documented for the Mongol incursions in the 13th century.) The downfall of the Mycenaean culture seems in any case to be due to the sea peoples. At this time all Greece, including Crete and the archipelago, went through a period of catastrophic decline. To be sure, Crete had been conquered by mainland Greeks two centuries earlier, which marked the end of Minoan culture. Greek became the administrative language but otherwise the upheaval was moderate compared with the later destruction.

Subsequently Egyptian culture could in relative peace devote itself to ardent self-perpetuation, temporarily disturbed by Cambyses, son of Cyrus, who invaded the country 525 BC. After the appearance of Alexander the great 332 BC, the Ptolemies embarked on the hellenization of Egypt and Alexandria became a superior cultural center. Later on the Egyptians compliantly adjusted to the rule of Rome and the conversion to Christianity under Byzantium. When the Caliph Omar conquered the country in 642 and the people were converted to Islam the linguistic continuity, too, was finally broken – Egypt became a part of the Arab world.

In contrast to Egypt, Japan and China as well as India have clung to their ancient core values, despite serious reverses and periodically debilitating stagnation. Japan's stability is the most easily explained. The realm has been protected by geography; the county was never invaded before the defeat in the Second World War. In 1274 and 1281, the invasion fleets of Kublai Khan, the Mongolian emperor of China, were routed by a determined effort but even more by sheer luck. The population is ethnically and linguistically homogenous, excepting a small remnant of Ainu people, the original inhabitants, in the north.

Japanese values are an eclectic mix of Confucian and Buddhist imports from China, spiced with group loyalty and samurai morale of domestic provenance. Japan has endured its allotted share of civil war, but the country has enjoyed internal peace since the middle of the 17th century. Japanese organizations are committed to consensus and the team spirit is very strong, which makes the competition between competing corporations all the more vicious. Still, a strong national solidarity guarantees social stability.

The young generation is not so stringently programmed. Lifelong employment is, for instance, not a matter of course any more, and women are increasingly active in the labor market. The Japanese are masters at adaptation and learning. The Meiji-revolution of 1868 and the forced democratization after 1945 were traumatic processes which, despite the radical changes, could be handled without renouncing basic traditional values.

In *Bonds of Civility* Eiko Ikegami uncovers the historical roots of Japanese culture. During the Tokugawa shogunate (1603–1867) Japan was unified but the rigid regime did not permit any political activity. The energies of the upper classes and eventually the middle class, too, were focused on etiquette and aesthetic refinement. A universal everyday culture became the unifying link between people from different parts of the country. In Japan, social capital acquired a national dimension; society was connected by a collective sense of good manners. The daily observances – mutual respect and politeness, personal cleanliness and neatness, the emphasis on quality and frugality – are manifestations of a concordant aesthetic sensibility.

Before the establishment of the first Empire 221 BC, many aspects of Chinese history resemble the development of modern Europe. Sovereign kingdoms fought each other in a glorious muddle of political and military maneuvers. Concurrently, material and spiritual culture was flourishing. In China, Confucianism eventually gained the upper hand in the fierce competition between differing philosophical schools. Eventually, it came to determine social norms and political legitimacy. Respect for parents, the powers that be and authority in general pervades Chinese culture. The ruler is, on the other hand, obliged to serve the welfare of the people – otherwise he has forfeited the mandate of 'heaven'.

> The first Emperor Shi Huangdi (ruled 221–210) was a severe tyrant. As well as uniting China, he imposed totalitarian order in the country. Objectionable books were burned and objecting persons were subject to similar treatment. The history of the Empire is a long fluctuation of rise-and-fall periods. After a run of competent statesmanship, every dynasty faced its demise through peasant uprisings and/or barbarian invasions. The Huns (Huang Su) were an early and recurrent plague. Later on the Mongol and the Manchu invaders could wrest political power and take over the country, which soon led to their sinicization. Mao Zedong can be perceived as the founder of a new dynasty, as ruthless as Shi Huangdi.

In the meantime the population growth continued, interrupted only by minor downturns due to particularly disastrous collapses. But technical progress stagnated in the 15th century and artists restricted themselves to the refinement of classical models. Science as a pure quest for truth was never a part of Chinese culture.[8]

The Chinese written language, which is based on pictograms, stems from the Shang period (ca 1600–1050 BC) and provided a base for countrywide mutual understanding. People could communicate by letter even if the vernacular was incomprehensible. The common cultural heritage remained accessible, irrespective of place, time and local dialect. The political unity of China has time and again been restored, whereas Chinese entrepreneurship has come into its own only outside the realm when the innate frugality, industry and individual initiative have been released.[9]

Contrary to the experience of Japan and China, India has been divided or repressed for most of its history. The linguistic and cultural multiplicity has contributed to this unhappy condition. The incursion of Alexander the Great in North-Western India 327 BC sparked the rise of the domestic Maurya dynasty 321 BC; the domains of King Asoka (ruled 273–232 BC) extended over most of India. The Maurya kingdom collapsed in 185 BC and although foreign invaders from the

Northwest periodically dominated the country, only Britain was able to unify all the states of the subcontinent under its colonial rule.

Religious continuity partly compensated for the political disorder. While the Japanese and the Chinese are next to agnostics, in India life and religion have been woven together even if the ruler never was deemed divine, as in Japan and China. Hinduism is a syncretistic religion which defies all description – multifarious, adaptable and tolerant but extremely resilient.[10] Buddhism is a magnificent attempt at refining the central ideas of Hinduism, above all the doctrine of transmigration of the souls, and it became the state religion under Asoka. It did not last in India but emigrated to neighboring countries such as Tibet, Ceylon (Sri Lanka) and Burma (Myanmar). China and Japan, too, have been strongly influenced by Buddhist thought.

> During the eighth century, Islam was catapulted to India by trade and conquest. Muslim conquerors and rulers dominated the political scene for extensive periods but Islam remained a minority faith. Despite the sharp religious divides, the life style and general attitudes are surprisingly homogenous all over the subcontinent, irrespective of religion and citizenship. The caste system is a Hindu institution, for sure, but conservatism and a resigned fatalism are the hallmarks of existence throughout. Therefore the success of the Indian Diaspora, almost on a level with the Chinese, is all the more remarkable.

Islam provides its own examples of triumphant but slowly stagnating and disintegrating political entities. In the 11th and 12th century, the Caliphates of Bagdad and Seville represented the apex of civilization, and the Ottoman Empire was a major power until the late 17th century. Religious indoctrination did not succeed in maintaining political stability, whereas cultural stagnation seems to have been the inevitable outcome of the curtailed spiritual freedom.

The ruling stratum generally perceives economic, political and religious freedom as a source of instability and a threat to its position. The concentration of power may offer short-term benefits but also implies the unlearning of civic virtues and capabilities. Spontaneous initiatives melt away, individual responsibility evaporates, reforms become ever harder to implement and ultimately impossible when the ratchet of centralization has run its course. The government has by then wedged itself into a dead end and a new regime can be introduced only at the price of a societal collapse. The French revolution (cf. chapter 3.2) and the collapse of the Soviet Union serve as instructive examples. The susceptibility of giant corporations to a similar syndrome was discussed in chapter 6.2.

Our occidental culture is erected upon the ruins of past civilizations; we have built on the heritage of our predecessors. Furthermore, we have borrowed ideas and technologies from all over the world – inventions, materials and cultivated plants. By increased insights in alien and totally disappeared cultures we can also deepen our understanding of human coexistence. This should be helpful in our quest for dynamic stability, but to learn from the experience of other people is a great intellectual and moral challenge.

11.3 Aborted cultures

We have repeatedly noted that cultural evolution in many ways mirrors its biological counterpart. The vast majority of new species have died out without direct successors and, similarly, most efforts to establish a high culture have certainly met a harsh and unheralded end. Archaeological excavations usually cannot resolve the causes of collapse but in a few cases the available material is quite illuminating.

The Chaco culture in Northwest New Mexico (900-1150) covered about 100,000 km^2 but never achieved the rank of a fully developed city culture. The main settlement (Chaco Canyon) was distinguished by multi-storied 'big houses' holding up to 650 rooms. They were not permanent dwellings and probably used mainly for festivities linked to religious ceremonies. A network of roads, measuring several hundred kilometers, connected Chaco Canyon with the outlaying settlements. The roads give an impression of 'over-engineering' – up to nine meters in breadth with a straight, uneconomic layout – and obviously served a ceremonial purpose. Long-distance trade was limited to a few luxury products.

At the beginning of the 11th century, the population may have risen to about 5000 persons. The water supply was a critical input for agriculture and fluctuated heavily. In such circumstances, societal integration would enable the subsistence of a larger population by providing insurance against local starvation. The political plus-sum game was evidently stabilized by a religious ceremonial which was maintained by a privileged upper class. The big houses and the imposing roads were built to project power and authority.

Around 1100 a period of low precipitation commenced which must have contributed to the collapse of the Chaco culture. The society had repeatedly made it through similar dry spells, but the exaggerated investments in monumental buildings and an inflexible societal structure certainly aggravated the situation. The upper class lost its legitimacy when it failed to guarantee a subsistence minimum for the people. The end phase of the Chaco culture is marked by warfare, including massacres, conflagration and cannibalism. Starvation and administrative breakdown brought on a surge of mutual hostility. The surviving Anasazi Indians returned to their original way of life in widely dispersed independent settlements.[11]

The Chaco culture mirrors a universal pattern; its history can be seen as a miniature of the Maya. The Mississippi culture in North America and recently identified agricultural communities in tropical South America went through analogous development stages, albeit in a more benign climate[12]. A few centuries of successful cooperation and concomitant population increase are followed by political collapse, whereupon the survivors return to a more primitive way of life.

> Cahokia in present day Illinois was the main center of the Mississippi culture and during its height around 1100 it counted about 20,000 inhabitants. Scores of mounds up to thirty meters high are the equivalents of the big houses and monumental roads of Chaco Canyon. Like Chaco Canyon, Cahokia dominated a network of satellites but the city was also engaged in long distance trade. The decline started around 1250 and the city was depopulated before 1400.

Similar developments can be discerned in South-Saharan Africa despite the unfriendliness of the environment. Communication and transports are hampered by the scarcity of harbors and navigable waterways. In vast areas, the tsetse fly excludes livestock-keeping and curtails husbandry; trade relied exclusively on porters. Diseases laid (and still lay) a heavy burden on tropical Africa. Chronic infections and the climate put a damper on human activities.

> All the same, major kingdoms arose like Ghana (c.900–1240), Mali (c.1200–1450), Monomotapa (c.1450–1629) and its mythic forerunner Great Zimbabwe. Their success was built on military might coupled to distant trade in gold, ivory and slaves. The transport difficulties facilitated monopolization and big profits which propped up the kingdoms and the ruling elite. In the 19th century, the Europeans encountered well-organized societies, for instance the Ashanti, Uganda and Dahomey (which mustered terrifying amazons), but they did not match the power of the earlier states.

In Africa, only Ethiopia features a continuous history which goes back to the beginning of our common era. The country was converted to Christianity in the fourth century and has conserved the external attributes of the Coptic Church. In the eighth century, Ethiopia was a major power and battled with Islamic conquerors for the control of the Red Sea. The societal dynamic fizzled out but tokens of the cultural heritage were preserved to modern times, despite a temporary breakdown in the 18th century.[13]

In Eurasia, competing high cultures absorbed preceding cultural impulses early on, though many tribal people persisted on the periphery. An interesting exception is the Mongol expansion which started in the beginning of the 13th century. In no time, the uncivilized nomads created the largest Empire in world history. Without flinching, they slaughtered hecatombs of humans to strike terror into the next state to be conquered. By around 1400 the Mongol storm had abated. The open trade routes stimulated cultural contacts between East and West, but the only lasting influence of the Mongols was a genetic imprint on the population.[14]

In Australia people did not surpass the hunting and gathering stage, while their racial relatives in New Guinea developed horticulture – small scale gardening of tubers combined with pig and poultry breeding.

> The highlands of New Guinea have been and still are an Eldorado for anthropologists. In the 1960s, many natives still lived in isolated valleys and could be observed as in a time machine which stopped 5000 years ago. Every tribe was a world unto itself under constant threat from skull-hunting neighbors.

The islands of the Pacific Ocean present a sampling of societies in varying stages of development. Tiny societies on the smallest islands balanced on the verge of extinction, while the cultural level generally tended to rise with the size of the territory and the population (cf. chapter 2.4). But no attempts at a city culture can be discerned even in New Zealand; perhaps the Maoris did not have enough time to develop their cultural potential?

When looking for universal causes for the miscarriage of 'natural' development the relative isolation stands out. Close contacts with other societies – near by or far away – increases the relevant population and expedites the plus-sum game. The exchange of goods, ideas, genes and beliefs enhances the richness of variety, intensifies competition and augments the cultural capital. Traditional policies and practices are opened up to falsification while economic and political entrepreneurship are invigorated.

Religious conceptions have in many, if not most cases exerted a predestining influence on societal development.[15] We may postulate that the aborted cultures generally submitted to a very ethnocentric world view which fortified the inherent conservatism. Embryonic states cannot afford such extravagancies, contrary to stagnating high cultures which can draw on a sizeable cultural capital.

The prevailing values often imply a ban on any alteration in the indigent natural state. Perhaps the Papuans of New Guinea did not want to change their life style. (Perhaps they still do not want to?) For centuries the Romany of Europe, too, preferred a roaming life to the amenities and worries of the surrounding high culture. Today the Romany have largely settled down but the cultural heritage still exerts its grip.

> The Romany are a unique remnant of nomadic forbears. The constant discrimination has certainly contributed to their isolation, but it also depended on their self-selected cultural autonomy. Regular work was not attractive. The vagrant way of life did not produce tangible value and alienated the settled inhabitants. Resulting prejudices were mutually reinforced by the ensuing vicious circle.[16]

Why does the cultural response vary so much between different populations? What prevents a society from realizing its inherent development potential? The value relativists have the simplest answer to these questions. There is no problem, there are no more or less developed, better or worse societies, super- or subordinate stages in the cultural evolution (or in biological evolution for that matter). The whole idea of evolution is an empty construct, a manifestation of human or more precisely western, self-centered arrogance. Everybody lives happily by his own devices!

In *The Spirit of the Game* I have delved deeper into this peculiar mindset. I find the conclusions absurd even though they give food for thought. We are touching deep existential problems which at bottom are questions of faith. Here I just want to submit a pragmatic approach. Give the people the liberty of choice! All our experience shows that the overwhelming majority will, given a chance, opt for a free, rich, developed and thus preferable society. The traffic in the opposite direction is negligible. People are not cultural relativists.

11.4 Democratic learning

While the holy alliance kept Continental Europe in an iron grip, the Spanish colonies in Latin America severed the ties with the mother country and embraced democracy modeled on the United States. (In 1822 Brazil, too, declared its independence from Portugal under a Portuguese emperor.) Visionary leaders like Simon Bolivar (1783–1830) and José de San Martin (1778–1850) envisaged super-ordinate federalist structures, but such initiatives were soon foiled by narrow-minded provincial interests (a Middle American confederation survived until 1838).[17]

In the new-fashioned nation-states, democracy was promptly set aside as the political hurly-burly opened the door for a long line of military dictators. The meticulously worded constitutions were revealed as paper barriers which could be swept away by any opportunistic coup-monger; caudillismo became the dominant form of government in Latin America. But the democratic values never lost their appeal and were often paid lavish lip service.

> The career of Antonio López de Santa Anna (1794–1876) illustrates the instability and the shaky political rules of the game in Latin-American societies. First he fought for Spain against the Mexican insurgents. Then he changed sides and 1822 lent a hand in placing Agustin I on the throne as Emperor of Mexico. Despite several setbacks, Santa Anna dominated Mexican politics between 1823 and 1855 (President 1833–36, dictator 1839 and 1841–45, President 1846–47 and 1853–55). During this period, Mexico went through thirty-six changes of government.[18]

During the past decades, democracy in Latin America has been in ascendance. Nowadays the military juntas and dictators are conspicuous by their absence, even if only a few countries can be accepted as stable democracies. The history of Latin America reflects the difficulty of engaging conceited politicians in a long-term plus-sum game. Usually the short egoistic perspective gets the upper hand and the logic of zero-sum play reigns supreme. The deficit in bad conscience, inherent in Catholicism, had unfortunate political consequences.

> Plainly, the peoples were not prepared to underpin a democratic regime. Poverty, the lack of education as well as class conflicts made them into easy prey for demagogues and populists. Dictatorial order often felt better than an equally corrupt democratic disorder. The elite and the Catholic Church, for their part, were not prepared to forgo their old colonial privileges. The outcome was a condition of latent civil war where far-sighted and constructive efforts regularly ran into the ground. Bolivia and Ecuador are still balancing on the verge of credible democracy. Despite its oil billions Venezuela is going downhill, while Colombia is laboriously climbing out of the narco-political swamp.

Centuries of centralized colonial rule precluded local democratic learning; neither were the democratic traditions of the mother countries anything to brag about. Latin America had to start in the kindergarten of democracy, guided only by distant models. After almost two-hundred years of internal and external conflicts, economic misery and general misrule, people are beginning to recognize that democracy, after all, is the least bad way of government. The collapse of reality socialism has certainly contributed to this insight. Cuba in the end became a discouraging example, except for reborn populists like Hugo Chavez of Venezuela and Evo Morales of Bolivia. Unexpectedly Brazil has become the standard bearer of Latin American democracy and prosperity.

India received its independence from Great Britain in 1947. The secession of Islamic Pakistan caused large population movements and led to terrible bloodshed. Yet India could establish an adequate democracy. The administration and the judiciary had long been manned mainly by Indians and the power transfer was conducted in good faith. India has preserved political stability despite social tensions and a swift population increase. The actual changeover to an independent democracy was conducted without birth pangs – a next to unique performance.

> In contrast, the economic development has been disappointing, particularly in comparison with Japan and the South-East Asian tigers; in the last decades China too has outperformed India. From the very beginning, a socialist doctrine diverted the economy on the wrong track. The outcome was exaggerated state intervention, subventions, trade barriers and an incredible bureaucracy. Market forces were subjugated and domestic enterprises were sheltered against foreign competition. Political wangling and outright corruption became the chief competitive means. A cautious liberalization has already brought positive results but the resistance to change is fierce and the caste system is still a drag.

The long British rule laid the foundation for Indian democracy.[19] Nevertheless it is astounding how painlessly more than a billion people, most of them very poor, can manage their common affairs under proper democratic law and order, excepting sporadic violence triggered by tensions with religious minorities – Muslims and Sikhs. Even the poorest Indian shares an old cultural heritage, an identity that obligates; cultural norms keep violence under control. All in all, India is an encouraging example of the viability of democracy in less developed countries.

In contrast, the situation in sub-Saharan Africa is hardly reassuring, even if decolonization opened the door for formal democracy. In 1956, Ghana became the first entrant. Kwame Nkrumah (1909–72), the charismatic President, was met with considerable expectations. The British were in a position to transfer a rather flourishing country with a well-functioning administration and a prospering but fragile economy. All the same, the problems started to pile up.[20]

> Nkrumah rule of his one-party state became increasingly arbitrary; in 1960, a change in the constitution gave him autocratic powers. Nepotism and corruption spread like wildfire in politics and the state-governed economy; ministers routinely charged a commission of ten percent on government purchases. Nkrumah's agricultural policy impoverished the farmers while the available capital was spent on silly industrial investments. Education and health care had got a promising start but soon deteriorated for lack of resources; a substantial part of the trained personnel emigrated. Nkrumah's grandiose foreign initiatives came to nothing. As a sideshow he supported rebellions in neighboring countries.

In 1965, Nkrumah was deposed by a junta of generals and new military coupes followed in tight succession, interspersed with short-aged attempts at civilian rule. In 1992 Jerry Rawlings seized power for the third time and managed, against the odds, to initiate a democratic political tradition.

Elsewhere in black Africa, the situation is bleaker. Instead of rather well-meaning personalities like Nkrumah and Rawlings we are in many places faced with ruthless extortionists, vying with each other in brutality, venality and incompetence. Well-educated idealists, like Kenneth Kaunda in Zambia and Hastings Banda (1896–1997) in Malawi, were also corrupted by their unlimited power; ultimately they presided over poorhouses. Only Julius Nyerere in Tanzania was sensible enough to retire when his utopian socialism had failed.

Besides South-Africa, few African countries of any significance carry conviction as democracies. Botswana and Senegal, where the legendary Léopold Senghor (1906–2001) laid the foundations for his nation, stand out while the Ivory Coast, which was long held up as another bright spot, has been engulfed in an extended civil conflict. A democratic power shift is difficult to imagine in most countries. In one-party states, succession is always a problem; presidential insistence on a life-long mandate does not make it any easier. It is tempting to write off Africa politically and economically, but Latin America did not look much better after the first half-century of independence. Democratic learning is a slow process.

The surprising and bloodless dissolution of the Soviet Empire left in its wake a sundry lot of states with very varying democratic potential. The political future of Russia is particularly interesting, not least due to the energy resources and the nuclear arsenal of the country. It is also fascinating to follow how Russia is trying to find its own way out of the old totalitarian structure towards a modicum of democratic stability.

> In 1991, Boris Jeltsin, as the first President of Russia, took over a state apparatus which did not fit the new democratic frame of reference. The economy was close to collapse in the critical transition between disintegrating central planning and chaotic market forces. Due to the lack of experience and relevant rules of the game, the hasty privatization turned into a scramble, not dissimilar to the exploits of the financial robber barons in the United States at the close of the 19th century.[21]
>
> Vladimir Putin (President 2000–2008) strengthened the central power and has ruled almost like an autocrat, with due respect for democratic niceties. He has kept illegitimate power centers at bay and in the eyes of the Russian people he stands for stability and prosperity. The state finances and the economy are in good shape thanks to the sky-high oil price. Legislation has been modernized but Putin has not made much progress in his self-proclaimed struggle against corruption and bureaucracy.[22] Moreover, nostalgia for the Soviet Union is taking hold and an ugly, nationalistic streak is reappearing. The European Union might gain in cohesion by the bully at its border; as for Russia it will only hurt itself by these antics.

The greatest challenge for Russians is unlearning. The dependence on superior directives must be overcome and the glorious past as a great power forgotten. A genuine democratic succession at the top is also on the list of desiderata. The present situation is suggestive of Mexico during the PRI-regime, when the sitting President single-handedly appointed his successor. Finally, the grim accounts of the murderous Soviet state must be settled. On the credit side, the absence of bloodshed during the traumatic transition should be noted. The cohabitation of Putin (as Prime Minister) and his protégée Dmitry Medvedev (as President) could facilitate the implementation of democratic principles, already enshrined in law. All in all, Russia's progress after the fall of the Soviet Union has so far been better than could be expected.

Lastly I want to refer to the forced democratization of Germany and Japan after the Second World War. Rarely has a victorious power managed to introduce its ideology as effectively as the United States. The deep discredit of the former regimes and their war adventures simplified the task. The defeat was total and unambiguous. The unlearning was similarly complete and an earlier, albeit underdeveloped, democratic tradition could be evoked. Most importantly, the victor was generous and not bent on suppression or plunder. The United States consistently displayed its good will and the outcome was a resounding success. In Iraq or Afghanistan, this is a hard act to follow.

11.5 The lessons of history

In the foregoing I have tried to sketch a mini-panorama of the development or introduction of democratic rule against a background of disparate historical dead ends. The limited selection of data does not allow far-reaching generalizations, but I doubt that an extensive review would be more conclusive. One thing is certain: the advance of history is conditioned by our collective experience as reflected in cultural values and the tacit rules of the game.

In principle, race related differences in democratic aptitudes should not be excluded. The genetic setup is not irrelevant (cf. chapter 1.4), but it cannot be decisive. Long ago, all our ancestors solved their common problems in the same way – by democratic deliberations headed by senior persons with limited authority. And not so long ago many leading democracies were populated by primitive barbarians, despised by the civilized Greeks and Romans. We can safely start with the assumption that, irrespective of the present situation, all human groups have similar potential in the global democratic plus-sum game under development.

In the preceding chapter we have tried to discern the factors which by their absence are precipitating cultural stagnation and decay. But what initiates the cultural plus-sum game in the first place? Our data base is very scant in this area which leaves the field open for a range of hypothetical scenarios.

According to Arnold Toynbee, environmental challenges bring forth a creative cultural response if the conditions are right. If the challenge is overwhelming, the population lives close to the subsistence level and cannot accumulate the necessary start-up capital. (The Inuit were Toynbee's favorite example, but the Anasazi Indians also fit the bill.) But if life is too easy, you don't have to care for the future. The challenge is not forthcoming and long-term efforts are not rewarded. Toynbee felt that the so-called hydraulic cultures – Mesopotamia, Egypt, Harappa – provided a reasonable balance between the existential challenge and the possibility of controlling the environment.

Robert Carneiro has presented a competing model which actually is complementary to Toynbee's thinking.[23] Carneiro contrasts the relative cultural poverty of the Amazon area with the isolated river valleys of the Peruvian coast, where prehistoric states are the rule rather than the exception. If emigration is practically excluded, as in Peru, the unavoidable warfare drives political integration. Taxation and forced labor provides resources for irrigation systems and the construction of monumental buildings. But if the geography does not limit emigration, no substantial states will arise. During internal conflicts, due for example to population pressure, the weaker party can always evade confrontation and look for subsistence in the limitless wilderness.

Norman Yoffee has discarded all theories and tries to avoid drawing any conclusions from his detailed analysis of the origin of the Sumerian culture.[24] Here the rich archaeological material, including a wealth of cuneiform tablets, provides unique opportunities for the falsification of rash speculation. On close inspection, a sudden change dissolves into a concatenation of small adaptations, just as in biological evolution. The Sumerian breakthrough – a city culture and a written language – was prepared during millennia of gradual cultural development at the village level.

Cultural evolution is driven by the interaction of divergent communities or groups. The contacts may be peaceful or conflicting but in any case they will create new stimulating information and a better division of labor. The cross-fertilization of different cultural spheres has, time and again, accelerated societal dynamics. Even if isolated societies can exhibit admirable inventiveness, the size of the population sets an upper limit for collective creativity and for the complexity of the cultural web. Human plus-sum play builds on exchange, borrowing or plain copying, but also on the hybridization of fruitful yet unfulfilled ideas.

The size of the relevant interactive population is thus a decisive variable in the evolution of culture. The isolation of the Peruvian coast valleys, which was the impetus for state building, set a ceiling for the expansion of the culture and thus also for its vitality. For an advanced culture, too, isolation due to blinded self-satisfaction is the beginning of the end. Strict separation from the neighbors, whether enforced or deliberate, will obstruct learning as well as unlearning. Such cultural inbreeding is devastating for cultural creativity.

As far as we can understand, our modern democracy is the form of government most worthy of man. But it is also the most demanding and requires societal cooperation on a grand scale. Democratic learning is indeed a long and difficult process with many reverses. Every new generation must pass the political manhood test, whether it wants to or not. The road to collective self-control is lined with temptations, which must be rejected, development traps which must be avoided and difficulties which must be overcome.

> It is ironic that present-day South Africa is building on the democratic legacy taken over from the internationally condemned apartheid regime. The truth commission has come to terms with the past and laid the foundation for racial reconciliation. Despite the high criminality, the judicial system is working right up to the superior court and the media are free. Among the blacks land hunger is strong but arbitrary measures, model Zimbabwe, are not on the agenda. The income differences are big but so far the white minority has not been harassed. The emigration of skilled people is on the increase and South African companies are diversifying abroad but international capital is moving in. The moderate Africanization of ownership and management has not yet affected productivity. The weakness of the opposition is a problem. South Africa is in practice a one party state and has yet to face the political maturity test – a genuine change of government.

Democracy cannot be handed down as a gift. It has a price which must be paid in the shape of the respect for superordinate rules of the game, and at the expense of personal advantage and immediate satisfaction. Rarely does it demand heroic sacrifices, but instead an everyday tribute of ordinary morality. Africa has abundant social capital but this is not sufficient. The new overarching plus-sum game must be built from the ground in the family, in the school, in the congregation.

> Christian mission is widely considered old-fashioned and is accused of undermining local cultures, among other things. The religious enthusiasm may at times have been excessive but the quest for better education and health care has certainly not been in vain. Gibbon took to blaming Christianity for the downfall of the Roman Empire but in the final analysis, evangelization was the key to a better plus-sum game. Africa's local traditions, too, must be supplemented at the grass roots level to create a chance for democracy. There are worse alternatives than Christian learning and indoctrination.

A revealed religion or an established philosophy has in all high cultures acted as a plea for the long term view. The associate values lend structure to the culture-specific plus-sum game, providing a guarantee for social stability. It is hardly pure coincidence that modern democracy developed against a backdrop of protestant Christianity. The American founding fathers strived, on the other hand, for religious neutrality. It was decided to separate state and church to avoid the poisoning of the political atmosphere by confessional strife. Democracy is not tied to any specific religion but it depends on the associated funds of moral capital.

Modern democracies aim at an open society where people are free to communicate and realize themselves in fruitful plus-sum play. The richness of variety through human contacts grows exponentially in comparison with authoritarian societies. It is not population size as such but the number of meaningful interactions which sets the stage for joint creativity and prefigures the added value of the plus-sum game.

Democracy in its modern shape has a short history. Many things can and will go wrong during the next decades, centuries and millennia. But a lot speaks in favor of democracy as a robust platform for sustainable human cooperation. The preconditions exist for breaking the historical pattern of rise and fall. In the next chapters an effort will be made to identify the success factors as well as risks and threats, and to get a glimpse of what lies ahead. Our future cannot be foreseen but for that very reason it depends on us, ourselves.

Chapter 12
Future perspectives

The lifeblood of democracy is free self-organization with power and responsibility decentralized to the lowest feasible level; democracies convert complexity to an asset. Energy is a key resource which will not be in short supply even if the price may rise. The democratization of information is the most significant outcome of the computer revolution – knowledge cannot be monopolized any more. Space research is the ultimate scientific and technical challenge; it is a focus for human ingenuity, perseverance and faith in the future. When, and if, our genetic set-up can be systematically modified by biotechnology, humanity will face its greatest ethical challenge ever.

12.1 Complexity and self-organization

Research about complex phenomena has recently made substantial advances but has not improved the predictability of complex systems.[1] Futurology is the science of the future course of events in our extraordinarily complex society, clearly a self-falsifying program. Every genuine and public forecast will enrich our database. This changes the basis of the prediction and will necessarily falsify the original forecast. In practice, the task of futurology is restricted to the construction of scenarios, in other words to the systematization of our limited foresight.[2] These virtual futures often act as early warning signals but they can be abused.

> The first report of the Club of Rome in 1972 was a loud alarm call, but it was soon discredited when the prognosis turned out to be all too pessimistic. Yet the real weakness of the report is the biased mathematical structure. The population and the energy consumption, for example, are schematically supposed to grow exponentially. The mathematically inclined will immediately perceive that such a model inevitably leads to disaster; the conclusions of the report are inherent in the model. The underlying agenda was to present arguments for a strictly centralized society which applies a zero-growth ideology and thus guarantees the survival of humanity by ecologically enforced socialism.
>
> Open exchanges for stocks, raw materials, futures etc. represent the

other extreme in the practice of futurology. An exchange is an ongoing Delphi questionnaire. The opinions of all the participants are registered and a floating consensus view emerges through the interaction of putative 'experts' in the marketplace. Everybody has a belief but nobody is in the know. The output of an exchange obviously has an influence on its own input which opens the door for the well-known, chaotic instabilities. Exchanges are, nevertheless, the best available indicators for the economic development in the middle term. The market is always in the wrong but is incessantly correcting itself.

A Club of Rome one hundred, a thousand or ten thousand years ago could confidently have predicted that the game would be over in the near future, all based on solid evidence. It is presumptuous to casually rule out any unpredictable responses to the upcoming ordeals. Our forbears did not throw in the towel and we have much better cause for optimism. That is not to say that disasters, predicted or unexpected, are excluded. Rather the other way around, but the successes, not the setbacks, will be decisive.

By now it should be obvious that the complexities of human interaction severely limit our capability to understand, to predict or to control societal processes.[3] Even so we have retained the capability to consciously organize human cooperation, groping our way towards a future more fit for human beings. Every plus-sum game calls for a set of rules, written or tacit, to avoid the temptation of short-sighted self-interest. It is a matter of finding those self-regulating feedbacks, which create a balance between individual freedom and the interests of the community.

> An age-old problem is to divide a cake, real or figurative, in two equally valuable parts. The simplest solution is to let one of the parties divide the cake and let the other one pick the preferred piece. (The divider is in a slightly inferior position and should be selected by casting lots.) The process is self-controlling; neither morality nor a referee are required. Conventional morality comes up short if the cake pieces are of unequal size. Anna coolly picks the bigger piece. Bert reacts angrily "How could you be so forward!? Anna: "What would you have done? Bert: "Taken the smaller piece of course! Anna: "Then it's all the same!"

Democratic self-organization faces more complex problems but the rules of the game can still be transparent and simple when the aim is to make the most of the scarce, pooled resources. Co-operatives are good examples of the self-organization of independent economic actors. Then again, the democratic decision mechanism hampers risk-taking, decision making and the access to capital. Flexibility suffers and a strategic reorientation is virtually impossible. Therefore, joint-stock companies have become the dominant form of enterprise in the market economies.

> At the beginning of the 19th century, far-sighted legislation in the industrial countries paved the way for the fruitful cooperation of investors, bankers, entrepreneurs, inventors, skilled workers and unqualified laborers. The crucial change was that the owners of stock in a limited company did not carry any responsibility beyond the investment in shares. This facilitated the procurement of capital for risky but profitable ventures. The profit motive and the threat of bankruptcy mobilized human energies and inventiveness; in favorable circumstances the surplus could be utilized for aggressive expansion.

Joint-stock companies have been a pivotal dynamic element in the economic plus-sum game. They act vigorously on the rewards and sanctions of the marketplace – the profit and loss account is a mighty steering mechanism. The profit incentive is still under-utilized in our societies due to political blockage.

> Today, the national economies are burdened by significant costs due to more or less self-inflicted diseases. The health authorities have met with little success in campaigning against alcoholism, obesity and unhealthy lifestyles in general. It would be sensible to outsource the care of these people to a health insurance company which would have a strong incentive to change the self-destructive behavior pattern of its customers. This company strategy is already applied in the United States with considerable success.*

The aim of the politicians should be to promote the self-organization of the citizens and minimize the need for political interference. Yet, this is contrary to their self-interest. The upshot is a continuous surge of political encroachment and bureaucratic structures in all democracies. Within the flexible framework of democratic institutions, we have preferred to transfer a substantial part of our personal responsibilities to a set of impersonal public organizations. de Tocqueville's somber prediction (cf. chapter 4.3) is about to be fulfilled – the voters have disfranchised themselves.[4]

Nothing prevents the electorate from clawing back part of the responsibility handed over to the government; such a trend is already

---

* Healthways Inc. is the pioneer in the area.

discernable in Europe. Left-wingers are lamenting the reduction in the scope of political decision making but the citizens now get more latitude for their personal preferences. A retreat to bygone times is not on the cards; the welfare state is here to stay. The aim should be to make it more efficient and equitable, and above all to encourage people to assume responsibility for themselves.

Charities and NGOs, rooted in the local communities, are better suited than any public administration to handle social problems and public support. After all, every human being is unique and calls for committed, personal guidance. Particularly in the United States, the involvement of the NGOs on a semi-official basis is being tried out, but the right procedures for such a privatization are still unclear.

In Great Britain, the National Health Service is increasingly falling back on competing subcontractors, without regard for the ownership background. Moreover, the long-term goal is that the patients should have a free choice of physician and hospital. Only such a reform would create a genuine market in health care. In basic education, too, the aim is to increase parental choice to the horror of the teacher's unions and the lunatic left. Whether these Blairian policies will ever be realized is still an open question.

In Continental Europe, particularly in the Nordic countries, a national accord has traditionally been achieved by agreement between mighty unions and employer confederations with the government as a third party. But such corporative self-organization takes place above the heads of the common citizen; it brushes aside the rules of the open market as well as democratic decision making. The door is opened for an exploitative zero-sum game where strong, monopolistic groups grab more than their fair share at the expense of the weak and meek.

Syndicalism is the name for the organized extortion by unions in key positions such as stevedores, electricians, air traffic controllers or even nurses and physicians. These practices are now backfiring. The public opinion is turning against arbitrary union action, which triggers political reactions. For example in Norway, compulsory mediation has been introduced for oil platform workers, policemen and other key groups on strike. The Japanese system with company-oriented unions is paving the way for a constructive relationship.

Complexity obstructs authoritarian control. Therefore the authorities have always strived to standardize the societal structure. The subsequent amputation of creativity was often regarded as a beneficial side effect. Tyrannical regimentation can assume quite surprising guises. In the 19th century, a French minister of education boasted about his real-time control of the proceedings in every single classroom in France.

In democracies, equity and equality are habitually paraded as a justification for the quest for uniformity. If nothing worse, the outcome is a succession of never ending inquiries and negotiations. Democracies are also prone to opposite pressures from special interest groups who apply the fairness argument when trying to secure exceptions from the prevailing rules of the game. This protracted conflict of interests can eventually end up in political and administrative immobilization. Everybody is terribly busy, nothing is ever finished and the plus-sum slowly evaporates during the extended bargaining.

> Joseph Tainter is on the right track when he maintains that increasing societal complexity has been a major cause for the collapse of ancient societies; the authorities have lost control of the convoluted interplay. Always provided that an omnipotent power center tries to be in charge of everything. The bureaucratic paralysis which led to the demise of the Soviet Union is an illuminating case in point; for the present, the Chinese leaders struggle to keep their heads above water.
>
> The Internet validates the trust in liberty as the only way to manage increasing complexity. The Internet is a rapidly growing and changing network (actually a network of networks) of computers, servers and routers which automatically channels the myriad message along the most favorable route. The net is robust, flexible and practically self-organizing. The minimal administration is in the hands of ICANN (Internet Corporation of Assigned Names and Numbers), a community of experts which mainly supervises the allocation of internet addresses. Recently an Internet Governance Forum was organized in order to expand the basis for consultation.[5]

Free self-organization with power and responsibility delegated to the lowest feasible level is the lifeblood of democracy and an antidote to excessive politicizing. The democracies possess all the necessary qualities to convert the burden of complexity into an invigorating asset. Complexity strengthens cohesion because the mutual interdependence becomes obvious for all the participants. Society cannot any more be dangerously polarized by escalating conflicts of interest. Instead people organize and reorganize themselves all the time depending on circumstances. The enormous diversity may be the bureaucrat's nightmare but the great advantage is that the daily grind takes care of itself and, equally important, people can blame only themselves.

We still live in the youth of democracy and it is difficult to understand what we are really trying to accomplish. I believe this to be a permanent condition; democracy is highly emergent. It is no ideology but an open value frame which does not impose any superordinate goals. Democracy only imparts means and mechanisms for common decision making, preserving maximal scope for human freedom.

12.2 Energy supplies

New sources of energy have always been the key to a better life. Beasts of burden replaced slaves and were in due course superseded by machines driven by wind or water power, and lately mainly by fossil fuels. With access to sufficient energy resources we are in the long term capable of achieving practically whatever we want; a shortage of energy correspondingly curtails our freedom of action.

> The only halfway admissible argument against nuclear power reads as follows. A virtually unlimited source of energy would increase our capability to damage the environment and ourselves to a disquieting degree. Better then to place a taboo on nuclear power and thus reduce the scope for our blundering. This attitude is patronizing as well as undemocratic. Moreover, the putative logic is derailed by the fact that we are already saddled with the destructive scenario. We are bound to live with the risk of nuclear warfare or at least nuclear terrorism. The genie cannot be squeezed back into the bottle anymore and we should just as well put it to work.

The production and recycling of metals and other raw materials can always be secured by employing sufficient amounts of energy. The same holds for extracting potable water from the oceans, for pollution control and even for food production. By hydroponic methods, agriculture can be transformed into a fully controlled industrial process, should the need arise.

> In hydroponics, all plant nutrients are delivered in solution; the growth bed can be for instance moist mineral wool. The water consumption drops to a fraction of the normal and the environment is not disturbed because the system is practically closed. The productivity can be further increased by artificial lighting, by the delivery of carbon dioxide from adjacent sources and of course by plant genetics. Israel is pioneering this technology, which so far has been applied mainly for the production of tomatoes and other vegetables.

Presently the consumption of fossil fuels covers 80% of our energy demand but it has to be reduced on account of the greenhouse effect. The storage of carbon dioxide in geological structures or deep in the oceans is expensive and can only be a partial and temporary solution. Oil and gas will anyhow soon be in short supply.

The so called renewable energy sources utilize solar radiation, either directly by solar cells or indirectly by exploiting water, wind or wave power. Plant material is counted as renewable and can of course supplant fossil fuels in conventional power stations; solar heat can be focused and applied in the same way. Geothermal energy and tidal power do not stem from the sun but will play only a marginal role.

> Wind power is today the most popular kind of 'pure' energy but it is everywhere dependant on subsidies and has its own environmental problems. Restricted accessibility is the main drawback of wind power. An extended high pressure with slight winds can interrupt electricity production over vast areas. Unfortunately, high pressures are tied to low temperatures (in winter) or hot weather (in summer) when energy consumption is at its peak. A sizeable expansion of wind power basically requires a similar wattage of reserve power to maintain the security of supply. Long-distance transfer of electricity can ameliorate but cannot eliminate this problem. In an open market, the value of wind power drops with any substantial increase in capacity.

Wind power will certainly expand but it can only work in combination with other, more reliable energy sources. Water power is an ideal complement. It is easily adjustable and highly valuable but there is little scope for expansion in the developed countries and it can have dire environmental repercussions.

> Giant dams usually have a major impact on the surroundings. The local population has to be relocated and the environment is radically altered. Two million people had to leave their homes when the huge reservoir at the three gorges in the Chong River (Yang Tse Kiang) was recently filled. A notable upside effect is the control of the devastating floods which have claimed untold numbers of victims in the past.
>
> In the future, the checks on dam building projects will become ever stricter (cf. chapter 14.4). Dam construction increases sedimentation and the seasonal variations are supplanted by an unnatural daily regulation. Fish suffer despite fish ladders, and vulnerable species may die out. In the United States many small dams have been demolished to restore the environment.

Silicon-based solar cells can convert 15–20 % of the solar radiation to electric energy in field conditions. That may seem inefficient but it is much better than the conversion rate achieved by vegetation.[6] Solar cells are already competitive in niche applications. A sizable contribution to the global energy supply must await further innovations and price reductions. An interesting alternative is the direct utilization of solar radiation for the catalytic splitting of water into hydrogen and oxygen.[7]

The use of food crops for the production of liquid fuels can only bring temporary relief. Any major expansion would cause a major disruption of the food supply; the first tremors are already in evidence. The systematic cultivation of specific energy crops is still in the research stage but has considerable potential if marginal drought-ridden or salt-compromised areas can be exploited by growing suitable, genetically modified plants. Agricultural and forestry waste may also serve as a cheap raw material.[8]

> In the late 1980s, I was as the chief executive of Cultor Ltd. involved in pioneering the large scale production enzymes that break down cellulose and hemicellulose to glucose and other digestible sugars. These biocatalysts are key to the conversion of organic wastes to liquid fuels. Given the present oil price, this can become profitable but high-temperature chemical processes might be more competitive when the chips are down.
>
> Micro-organisms as a group boast a very versatile metabolism; they can for instance generate hydrogen in sunlight or electric power from organic sludge. In principle the possibilities are limitless but the practical applications are not yet around the corner; biologically based production of methane has only local significance. However, the research effort is in full swing.[9]

Fission-based nuclear power is today and tomorrow the only technically and commercially proven, virtually pollution-free energy source with sufficient expansion potential. I have already (in chapter 7.3) enlarged upon the misinformed public opinion in the West. Encouragingly, attitudes are now shifting and nuclear power is becoming acceptable once again.

> The limited supply of fissile uranium 235 is not a serious problem. The common isotope uranium 238 comprises 99.7 % of the mined ore, and can be converted to nuclear fuel in breeder reactors, when and if this becomes profitable. Thorium can also be used as a fuel in such

advanced reactors. Fission power can keep us afloat for centuries if fusion power or solar cells prove impractical.[10]

Conventional nuclear power is not problem-free. The disposal of nuclear waste evokes strong emotions even if satisfactory technical solutions are on the table. Neither is the link to nuclear weaponry desirable. Nuclear power plants can be a disguise for secret weapon projects, currently an urgent issue in North Korea and Iran. Fusion power would, however, be the ideal technology for large-scale energy production. There is neither a waste problem nor any link to nuclear weapons. Best of all, the fuel is water or more precisely the deuterium isotope of hydrogen, a practically inexhaustible energy source. Without doubt, fusion power is the energy of the future – if it pans out.

> A half-scale, tokomak-type pilot reactor (ITER) is under construction in Cadarache in France. It is financed by the major industrial countries, including China and India. ITER is supposed to start operations in 2015 and cost five billion euro. (The cost has recently been upped to about 6.5 billion.) The reactor will produce power continuously so that the technical problems can be studied and the design optimized. The first commercial prototype may be working around 2030 and in the 2050s a significant supply of fusion power can be foreseen, barring unexpected problems.[11] A laser-based alternative HIPER (European High Power Laser Energy Research) is in the early project stage.

The ITER project is unique. Not only are costs high and the time span unprecedented; the risk of failure is very real. This clarified the minds of the leading actors and, despite occasionally trying rivalries, all the prominent nations in the world are now cooperating in laying the foundation for our future energy supply.

Oil products are easy to handle and provide energy in a concentrated form but they have to be replaced one way or another. The production of liquid or gaseous substitutes from a range of raw materials is rather straightforward. The problem is to find a primary energy source which does not release carbon dioxide or compete with vital human needs. The much touted hydrogen economy is just so much hot air without a robust supply side. Hydrogen has definite drawbacks of its own and there are many other potential energy carriers.

> The energy density of hydrogen is low, even if compressed. This creates logistical difficulties at every point. It is very flammable and prone to leakage; a synthetic hydrocarbon could be a better choice. Anyhow, the cost of production (and distribution) has to be brought down to an

acceptable level. An attractive symbiosis can be envisaged. Electric energy is very difficult to store. Temporary surpluses from nuclear, wind and solar power plants could be utilized for producing hydrogen or suitable hydrocarbons from water by electrolysis. The energy carrier would be an offshoot of electricity production and would avoid the fixed costs of producing the primary energy.

In power generation, change ensues at a snail's pace. Due to the slow rate of capital turnover (about 40 years), swift moves would lead to a massive destruction of capital. My vision for the energy supply of the world up to 2100 is as follows. Electricity production is dominated by huge fusion power plants. They are complemented by a multiplicity of smaller units, which utilize solar radiation, directly or indirectly. In the population centers, the district heating and cooling facilities are coupled to electricity generation. Cars are mainly driven by electric batteries and/or capacitors. Liquid or gaseous fuels are based on biomass and cheap surplus electricity; efficient fuel cells take care of pollution-free combustion. Global taxation of carbon dioxide (and other greenhouse gases) keeps the old-fashioned use of fossil fuels within desirable bounds, as long as need be.

We are at the end of a short period of cheap energy based on a half-baked technology. It is high time to change our ways and put our hard-won scientific insights to good use. Virtually limitless energy sources are within reach and awaiting exploitation. The price may be rising and thus call for economy but the supply of energy will not interfere with our long-term ambitions.

12.3 Information and communication

Energy and information are interrelated in a strange way. Intense energy flows spontaneously create complex but very transient information like lightning and thunder. Between three and four billion years ago, self-reproducing structures started to incorporate meaningful information about survival and reproduction by utilizing accessible sources of energy. Since the very beginning, relentless competition for energy resources has promoted cumulative learning, driving the development of life on earth. Finally the steep increase in the oxygen content of the atmosphere about one billion years ago facilitated effective metabolism and the rise of complex multicellular organisms.

Richard Dawkins has come up with the idea that Darwinist learning by trial and error is the only way to create genuinely new information.[12] The scientific quest for truth can be understood as systematized

Darwinism; old theories are falsified and are superseded in an unpredictable succession of ever more competitive information.

Communication is a goal driven transfer of information between a sender and a receiver. Bacteria communicate and multicellular organisms are totally dependent on the internal exchange of information. For a social animal, contacts between members of the same species are essential. Contemporary man is well equipped in this respect. Language, writing and printed material are complemented by electronic aids which already provide instant communication worldwide. Soon we will enjoy free access to the major part of accumulated information.

> In 1948, Claude Shannon (1916–2001) published *A Mathematical Theory of Communication*. In the next year, the title was for good reason changed to *The Mathematical Theory of Communication*. Shannon had succeeded in catching the very essence of digital communication in simple mathematical terms. He went on to develop encryption from an art to a science. Only quanta-based information transfer has called for an expanded frame of reference.[13]
>
> Information as a concept is much harder to nail down because it relates to the meaning of the message, its practical relevance. A string of bits, perfectly transmitted, can be completely meaningless while a distorted message can be meaningful if it has enough redundancy, that is surplus or repetitive information.[14]

Very well, but it remains for us to use the information, to refine it to knowledge and to a basis for decisions. The extraction of wisdom and general truths is even more challenging. We are easily suffocated by the present torrent of information and the overview can be lost. Fortunately, evolution has equipped us with mechanisms to select relevant information.

> Our senses transmit in every conscious moment an abundance of information which must be sorted out. The faculty of vision, for instance, selects at an early stage literally eye-catching peculiarities such as movement and contrast. Superordinate brain structures then rearrange the primary input into meaningful patterns, forms and shapes. Abstract thought builds on similar mechanisms, equivalent to an internal beholding. Mnemonists are exceptional individuals with an almost unfailing memory. They can perform on the circus stage but their intellect is on the weak side because of an inability to concentrate on the essentials – they cannot forget anything.[15]

A good thought economy calls for apposite selection criteria. Our common sense will in the future be supported by sophisticated software which can select, sort and organize the information according to our preferences. In other words, we can get sensible answers to well-formulated questions. In the future, we can also rely on ever brighter robots which will take over most of the tasks in production and some of the chores of everyday life, from cleaning to home delivery. But the intelligence level of the robots must be radically increased.

> Artificial intelligence probably tops the ranking list for over-optimistic expectations. The chess computers may have reached grandmaster level but they are not relevant to our daily duties. Another type of intelligence is called for when acting as an empathetic assistant nurse in a home for senior citizens. The solution may be to develop super-flexible software programs which are trained for specific tasks and then can continue learning on the job. The necessary mechanical and cognitive aptitudes – the sense organs and fine-tuned motion – will present comparable difficulties.
>
> The realization of such visions presupposes considerable progress in computing and robotics. The optimists confer to Moore's law which says that the performance of microprocessors is doubling every eighteen months; it has so far been empirically verified. In the not too distant future, molecule-size components will probably be produced by nanotechnology; ordered DNA-sequences are good candidates. Computers may start to compete with the central nerve system of insects regarding size, energy consumption, robustness and flexibility. Software will be the bottleneck assuming the validity of Moore's law. Quanta-based data-processing is the joker in the pack, and can have quite unforeseen consequences.

Over-intelligent robots may never cross the threshold to reality but our descendants will in any case be supported by advanced automation in performing heavy, boring or dangerous work. This may in the most favorable (or is it the worst) case include the guardians of law and order as well as military missions. But robots as power-wielding masters belong to science fiction. They remain our obedient servants but can of course be misdirected, as can every kind of technology.

The democratization of information is the most important upshot of the computer revolution. Knowledge cannot be monopolized or serve as a power base any more; subjects as well as citizens will be capable of creating their own world view. Tyrannical regimes will be shaken up and must, willy-nilly, take account of public opinion inside and beyond the borders of their country. In the established democracies, where the individual citizen is empowered, abuse of authority can be checked and arbitrary practices restrained (cf. chapter 9.5).

> Hundreds of pay-free satellite channels are already enveloping the greater part of our globe together with a profusion of pay-TV and radio transmissions. The ongoing digitalization will further multiply the supply of TV- and radio channels. More important is the information exchange at the grass-root level which facilitates participatory democracy. Every individual has access to a large network which can make him or her part of public opinion. By switching to dedicated screen-saver programs, computer-smart citizens can even participate in distributed computing projects and thus contribute to cutting-edge science.

These beautiful visions presuppose a minimum of computer literacy which has been seen as augmenting social divides. This is nonsense. Elderly people may have difficulties but children and youngsters have no problems; computer competence is more easily acquired than language literacy. Moreover, the machines are becoming not only cheaper but more user-friendly as well. As in a modern car, we do not need to know what is going on under the slick surface. In the future, following the road or the route will become redundant in both cars and computers; we just set the right destination.

The computer revolution is already providing marginal or marginalized populations new opportunities for advancement. Today the mobile or cell phone helps many smallholders in Africa and India to post up on market conditions and to hold their own against avaricious go-betweens. The next step in the civic emancipation is to influence social development by creating political networks which transcend the traditional dividing lines between tribes and castes.

What remains is to overcome the Babylonian confusion of languages and thus to democratize international communication. The English language has with some success succeeded Latin as a worldwide lingua franca but leaves the majority of humans at a linguistic disadvantage. Artificial languages like Esperanto are literally stillborn; they lack roots in live culture. Chinese characters could perhaps work as an international written language but in any case we lack a common vernacular for oral contacts. Hopefully, radically improved translation automata will soon bring a remedy.[16] But the human touch is indispensable in advanced communication. The translation of demanding content calls for highly committed individuals endowed with an adequate frame of reference.

Belles lettres, drama and poetry especially, are almost untranslatable and must be literally re-created; the Bible and Shakespeare have, thanks to inspired translations, become well-known to all the peoples of the world. Movies, theatre, dance, architecture, sculpture, paintings, music can each and all transmit elusive information through their own idioms. But the recipient must find the right wavelength which can be a challenge. In The Spirit of the Game, I have gone into greater detail in contemplating art as communication.

Great works of art articulate our innermost emotions and values. They speak straight to us, bypassing the diversions and detours of intellectual processes. Beauty creates trust in the message. It is the hallmark of truth while beauty criteria are a measure of the spiritual level of the beholder. Art conveys knowledge about man; it can reflect all humanity as well as individual peculiarities in their limitless variety. Popular music is already spreading around the globe. Perhaps it is preparing the ground for more profound messages which can build durable bridges over the cultural divides.

12.4 The biotechnological revolution

There is no doubt that the twenty-first century will see the breakthrough of biotechnology. Most of the announced medicinal and health benefits are yet to be realized, but they will arrive, slowly but surely. Compared to information technology, biotechnology calls for more time and more money. The outcome will be all the more revolutionary.

These self-confident predictions are underpinned by the recently acquired insights into the basic mechanisms of the life processes. It is a very complicated jigsaw puzzle, and many pieces are still lacking, but the edge pieces are falling into place, so to speak. The frame of the picture is in evidence and so are the fundamental rules for joining the pieces. A lot of work remains to be done but it is proceeding apace.

To understand the interplay between the discrete compartments and components of the living cell is a major problem. In eukaryotic cells, the dynamic interaction between the 'legislative' DNA in the nucleus and the 'executive' proteins is exceedingly complex, particularly during the development of the embryo. The introns of the genes and a lot of other non-coding, 'junk' DNA has turned out to be crucial for when, where and how the genes are expressed (cf. chapter 1, ref. 1).

Gene technology is making tremendous progress and the detailed mechanisms of protein machinery are being elucidated in detail. The latest advances in very fast, as well as distributed computation, support the research programs of molecular biology which opens up dizzying perspectives. Organic and inorganic nanotechnology may enter into a highly productive symbiosis. The transhumanists, for example, believe that life can be extended without limit.[17] Here we will however keep our feet on the ground. Those who are interested in fanciful future visions are referred to other authors.[18]

Fermentative microbiological processes have ancient roots. The baker's and the brewer's professions are among the oldest in the world, while wine and vinegar are biotechnical products, too. The enzyme directed life processes are very economical and usually feature excellent selectivity and yield. Therefore a 'green' or 'soft' production technology, based on biocatalysts, is quite attractive; in many cases there are no alternatives.

> The conversion of bland glucose sugar to the sweeter fructose moiety is an important step in the production of starch-based sweeteners. In the early 1980s, we in Cultor decided to produce an enzyme for this process. The breakthrough came only when we got hold of a genetically modified *Streptomycetes* strain offering tenfold productivity. In a single stroke the production cost was reduced to one tenth – a small demonstration of the power of biotechnology.

In future, more and more pharmaceuticals and fine chemicals will be produced by parsimonious and pollution-free enzymatic processes; the production of liquid fuels is on the horizon, too. The micro-organisms themselves can be transformed into complex but hyper-effective production platforms. Genetic engineering has pushed plant and animal breeding into a new era of vast opportunities. Commercialization is already in full swing but we are only seeing the first modest samples of what the future will bring. Resilient plants will thrive under adverse conditions in marginal areas producing fuel, fiber and forage. Algae can be grown for food as well as for energy. Moreover, high technology agriculture can provide for the forecasted global population with an ample margin.

> By the 1950s, the biological insights already sufficed for a major breakthrough in plant breeding. With the Rockefeller and Ford foundations as financial backers, superior short-straw varieties of wheat, corn and rice were developed within two decades; Norman Borlaug was the leading personality and received the Nobel peace award in 1970. The

so called green revolution was based on new seeds combined with irrigation and adequate fertilization. According to FAO (Food and Agriculture Organization, a UN agency), harvests in developing countries have multiplied and the endemic famines, for instance in India, are a thing of the past.[19]

Today, military and political conflicts are the main cause of hunger and they cannot be ruled out in future scenarios. But food supplies will not face any technical problems concerning quantity or quality. For example, soy protein can replace meat or fish in the diet. Only our old-fashioned eating habits and perverse agricultural policies apply a brake on the transition to vegetable raw materials. In the future, the taste and palatability of the food will be fully adjustable regardless of the sourcing. Personally I believe that animal products will eventually loose market share, not least due to the growing aversion to animal rearing conditions.

I will bypass the biotechnical applications for animal breeding and focus on *Homo sapiens*, the main object of our interest. Despite great research efforts, new rationally designed medicines are still few and far between; progress ensues in short, cautious steps. Anyway, the utilization of newly-won insights will strain our medical resources and budgets. Extended self-care in combination with individualized health plans would help in solving the problem.

In the foreseeable future people will have access to a personal gene map with an attached expert opinion which will spell out the inherited medical risk profile. It will also provide some guidance when pondering different lifestyles or careers. Thus informed, the individual can take better care of his or her life and health. Regular blood tests will sound the alarm bell if any serious disease is in the offing. Up-to-date expert systems on the web will provide a diagnosis and give medical and medicinal advice. Personal consultation with physicians could be limited to exceptional cases and optional health checks. Hospital visits will be necessary only for severe treatments such as surgery or irradiation. Health insurance companies could be the driving force behind the systemic change (cf. chapter 12.1; 13.3).

Cancer exemplifies the dilemma of the present health care system. Every case of cancer is unique and should get individual treatment. We need exclusive medication (probably based on monoclonal antibodies) to optimally exploit the small deviations from the genome of the mother organism. This goal is within reach, considering the impending automation of genetic diagnoses and miniaturized production processes.[20] In geriatric care, the prolongation of life should not be a goal in itself.

Instead we should aim at taking part in the plus-sum game to the very end. Here too, biotechnology offers encouraging perspectives.

> Stem cells are the body's all-round reserves which, in their most flexible totipotent form, have retained the embryonic capability to convert into all the different cell types of the specialized body organs. In principle, the stem cells are thus capable of repairing all extant physiological damage and wear. It is 'only' a question of releasing the correct dormant gene program in the right place and in the right way.[21] The greatest expectations focus on spinal marrow repair and cures for juvenile diabetes. Degenerative diseases of the heart and the brain (Alzheimer's and Parkinson's) are also among the targets.
>
> Gene therapy is already tested on humans but the marksmanship leaves much to be desired; the new gene may land at the wrong address with unpleasant consequences. Even so the future prospects are breathtaking. Many, perhaps most of our inherited defects could be corrected. The immune defense could be rearmed by a kind of super-vaccination which would render possible custom-made cancer prevention. The immune system could also be fine-tuned to parry allergies and auto-immune diseases. Cattle could be made resistant to the tsetse fly and malaria could be eradicated by developing mosquito strains which are resistant to the *Plasmodium* parasite. And so on.

In the United States as well as in Europe, excessive caution and a diffuse regard for human rights has restricted the progress of stem cell research. Even so, the American Constitution has made it possible for California and several other states to disregard the federal guidelines by financing their own research. In the European Union, too, local restrictions keep many projects on the back-burner. The lame and the crippled are sacrificed on the altar of political irresolution.

The stem cell and gene therapies offer real cures for our common diseases, replacing the present costly, protracted and often only palliative care. Inheritable illnesses could be cured, root and branch. If genetic intervention is extended to the germline, the offspring is transformed as well. Then we will cross the border to a new, perhaps braver world where intelligence, health and life span transcend the present frontiers. If and when this becomes possible, humanity is faced with its greatest ethical challenge ever.[22] To cope with it we must position ourselves in a multidimensional value universe. What we need is a heightened moral awareness, in other words a modern theology which I will touch upon in the last chapter.

In the midst of our future visions we should not forget the ordinary problems of health care. To be sure, the common infections are under control thanks to improved hygiene, vaccination and antibiotics. But the development of resistant bacteria is a reminder of our vulnerability and there is a severe shortage of virus medicines (cf. chapter 13.3). Biotechnology will probably ascertain progress on these fronts, too.

12.5 Exploring the universe

Like biology, astronomy has during the last decades achieved substantial breaktroughs.[22a] The origin of the universe is beginning to look like a solvable problem and the theory of everything is under construction. The aim is to combine the quantum mechanical sub-microscopic rules of the game with the laws of general relativity which describe the interaction of mass, energy, space and time. The major advances, however, have occurred on the empirical side. Thanks to bigger and better telescopes on the ground and in space, the dynamics of the universe have been elucidated. The starting point – the Big Bang – has been nailed down to 13.7 billion years from date. The greatest surprise was that the rate of expansion of the universe is not decreasing anymore; on the contrary, it began to increase about seven billion years ago.

> The total energy content of the universe can be approximately calculated. The actual building blocks of matter – protons, neutrons, electrons – stand for only 4–5 % of the total. About 25 % consists of so called dark matter. It reveals itself only by the gravitational effect which keeps the stars in the galaxies together. The remaining 70 % constitutes the even more enigmatic dark energy which is believed to be the cause of the accelerating expansion of the universe. Dark energy is somehow tied to the energy of the vacuum, one of hardest problems of physics.[23]

Neil Armstrong's first steps on the moon were a gigantic stride for humanity but only an inch on the way out into space which comprises hundreds of billions of galaxies. The diameter of our own Milky Way, with its hundreds of billions of stars, is about a hundred thousand light years. The mean distance to the moon is only 385,000 km, a round light second. The spacecraft Voyager 1 was launched in 1977 and recently reached the heliopause, where the solar wind meets the interstellar medium; the distance covered was 17 light minutes. The gap to the closest star, Proxima Centauri, is 4.4 light years and inhabitable planets are probably much farther away. While our own extraterrestrial planets are rather unfriendly, the colonization of space seems out of the question.

This conclusion may be too hasty. Mars, for example, could perhaps be made habitable by ingenious 'terraforming'. This will take time of course, but the greatest optimists reckon on only a few centuries.[24] Much bolder plans have been aired. In the *Anthropic Cosmological Principle*, John Barrow and Frank Tipler envisage the colonization of the Milky Way in 300 million years, using today's rocket propulsion technology. The idea is that the human genome or the equivalent information would be transported to suitable planets together with sophisticated automatons. The robots would incubate a new human population which would continue the project and initiate an exponential expansion.

Such speculations may appear out of this world, even if they are based on well-known technological principles. The sun wind can be utilized for 'sailing' around in the planetary system; robots can be both self-repairing and self-reproducing and thus become virtually immortal; nanotechnology renders possible the construction of super-flexible micro-machines which can shape their surroundings on the molecular level.[25]

Granted all this, the laws of nature still seem to set intolerable limits on our space travel. According to Einstein's theory of relativity, neither material nor information can travel faster than the velocity of light in vacuum – about 300,000 km/s. Theoretical calculations show that enormous energy flows beyond any human capability are needed to create shortcuts in the four-dimensional structure of space-time. Even if we could colonize the Milky Way, the impossibility of communication with the colonies would be immensely frustrating.

> Einstein's theories of relativity may be firmly grounded but they are certainly not the last word in the quest for the truth about our universe. A number of question marks remain to be straightened out and many surprises will emerge; radically novel energy sources could become accessible. Elusive but undisputable quantum effects such as entanglement and action at a distance may offer an opportunity for the immediate transmission of restricted amounts of information over cosmic distances, even if the velocity of light puts an upper limit for actual communication.[26]

We may already be touching at the uttermost limits of the technologically possible. Such has been the sentiment during most of human history – and it has been fallacious. Perhaps our descendants will find new doors to open, unforeseen roads to roam, unknown forces to exploit. Perhaps we still live in the technological Stone Age. Science fiction is beholden to excessive hyperbole but sometimes the far-flung visions turn into reality, though rarely in the way envisaged.

Whatever the odds for visionary space travel, the utility of space research can still be questioned. Truly, there is no lack of down-to-earth objects for government largesse. Valuable spin-offs such as weather and communication satellites have materialized but this is wisdom after the event. The first expensive steps in the conquest of space were prompted by military competition and great power prestige. Only later did the scientific interest become a driving force. Presently, most rocket launches are commercially motivated and even space tourism is in the offing.

> At the moment, an estimated 3000 operative satellites are circling our globe. The Global Positioning System (GPS) has a military background but also serves civilian navigation. Diverse imaging satellites support weather prognostication and surveillance of the environment. The largest commercial impact is in global communication. The slight delay between questions and answers in many actuality programs is due to the fact that it takes a few tenths of a second for the electromagnetic radiation to travel back and forth to the geostationary satellite, 35,800 km up in space.

Despite the commercialization of space, new exploits will be dependent on the good will of the taxpayer. The basic motivation is the thirst for knowledge, a need for explanation and clarification, a will to test the limits of the possible and impossible. In other words, a passionate quest which does not take 'no' for an answer. Space has to be investigated simply because it is there – inaccessible, enigmatic, promising.

> Are we alone in our galaxy or perhaps in the whole universe? What forms can life assume in other solar systems? These questions may never be answered but still insist on an answer. An encounter with an alien civilization would be the most exciting thing imaginable. The search is on for signals from distant worlds, even if the probability of achieving contact is diminishingly small.
>
> Conventional wisdom says that we cannot be unique; already our Milky Way should in all probability teem with life. So far, no extraterrestrials have been observed (*pace* all UFO enthusiasts) and the depressing conclusion is that long-distance communication is impossible in this universe of ours. That may be so, but there is another explanation. Even if primitive life forms would be common, civilizations may still be a rarity.

On earth it took almost four billion years to create the first multicellular organisms. Elsewhere the local sun could well be finished before intelligent beings could develop. Neither the evolution of life nor of human high culture is a natural necessity but the outcome of a succession of fortunate circumstances. Moreover, advanced civilizations seem to be constitutionally unstable; they tend to self-destruct by decay or stagnation. A sustained plus-sum game is more difficult than it appears – it could be extremely rare.

Space research is the ultimate scientific and technological challenge. It can be perceived as a focus for our collective creativity, for human ingenuity, perseverance and faith in the future. Due to its extreme long-term nature, space research is vulnerable to budget cuts. Propitiously, the United States and the European Union have not yielded to this temptation. Russia, too, is still in the race. Japan nurtures an expanding space program while China and India are preparing to join the contest. A common ambition to proceed is prevalent.

In space, at least some of the swords have been transformed into ploughshares. Sophisticated technology serves peaceful purposes and may be sorely needed in defense against threats from outer space (see next chapter). In future, space research should be the concern of all humanity. Setting aside other arguments, we need an ambitious common cause to avoid the descent into minus-sum play. Lacking an outlet for creative energies, it is difficult to visualize any kind of long-term stability, except dismal self-repetition. Our mission is to bring forth life as we know it out in the universe. Perhaps our descendants will some time encounter kindred spirits out there.[27]

Chapter 13
Threats galore

When the comet comes, we must be prepared to take our destiny in our own hands. Only global challenges such as threats from space and the release of greenhouse gases imply stringent international coordination. Virus-induced pandemics may also require strict quarantine and extensive vaccination. The global population increase is slackening, and it should level out at about ten billion people, but the developed countries are threatened by a demographic implosion. Destructive cultural collisions constitute the main threat to our common future. Time and again, constructive plus-sum play has fallen prey to discouraging historical experience and deep-rooted prejudices.

13.1 The comet cometh!

In the beginning, about 4.5 billion years ago, earth was bombarded by asteroids; the biggest was Mars-sized and gave rise to our moon. The bombardment has continued at lengthening intervals and devastating meteoric impacts have repeatedly extinguished major parts of the biosphere. The latest cataclysm took place 65 million years ago when the dinosaurs were wiped out.[1] The threat is not over by any means. The Tunguska comet struck Siberia in 1908 with an assessed power of half a dozen hydrogen bombs according to the latest estimates. Such impacts can be expected several times in a millennium.

A half-kilometer size rock will hit us once every hundred thousand years and has the destructive power of 10,000 million tons TNT (a 'customary' hydrogen bomb corresponds to one million tons). The diameter of the dino-killer was about ten kilometers and it weighed more than a trillion (10^{12}) tons. They appear perhaps once in 150 million years.[2] Most celestial objects are small meteorites which are annihilated as shooting stars, all in all about one hundred tons per day. Meteors of between a few kilograms and a few tons reach the earth's surface without causing much damage. Only when the diameter approaches 50 meters and the weight 200,000 tons does the meteor become a menace which creates a kilometer-wide crater. Statistically, such impacts happen once in every millennium.

NASA (National Aeronautics and Space Administration) is funding a surveillance system (NEAT, Near-Earth Asteroid Tracking) which can identify close-to-earth asteroids bigger than about one kilometer. An improved but less than watertight system should be in place by 2009. It will detect objects bigger than 140 meters which still leaves a fatal gap in the in the relatively frequent range between 50 and 150 meters. Outside the United States, there has been scant interest in asteroid tracking.

> The public has occasionally been scared by the prospects of immediate disaster. Therefore the textual part of the Torino impact hazard scale, which gauges the risk for a collision by numbers between 0 and 10, was recently made more intelligible. The asteroid 2004 MN4, later dubbed Anophis, attained level 4, the highest reading so far. "Level four indicates a close encounter, meriting attention by astronomers. Current calculations give a 1% or greater chance of a collision, capable of regional devastation. Most likely, new telescopic observations will lead to re-assignment to Level 0. Attention by the public and by public officials is merited if the encounter is less than a decade away." Later observations reduced the collision risk to zero but Anophis is calculated to pass earth in April 2029 at a distance of only 30,000 km. And Anophis will be back in 2036.[3]

There is also a risk that unexpected meteorite impacts can be interpreted as a nuclear attack and cause devastating retaliation. The southern hemisphere, particularly, has glaring observational gaps. A close surveillance calls for a network of small dedicated satellites which eventually are reaching the planning stage.[4]

Countermeasure capability is at least as important as an adequate early warning; we cannot be content with a passive policy of civil defense. In the United States voluntary organizations act as pressure groups. The most visible is the B612 foundation chaired by the astronaut Russell Schweickart. He recommends the expansion of NASA's Prometheus project to include the active defense against the asteroid threat.[5]

> In his testimony to the Senate subcommittee for science, technology and space research in November 2007, Schweickart reiterated the goal of the foundation: "To significantly alter the orbit of an asteroid, in a controlled manner, by 2015." The planned Prometheus spaceship would land on the asteroid and carefully alter its course, applying its nuclear powered rocket engines. The consistence and cohesion of the asteroid material is still a source of considerable uncertainty.

Our knowledge about the near-earth objects is increasing step by step. In 2005 Deep Impact, a NASA space probe, investigated the structure of the comet Tempel 1 with a massive copper missile which penetrated to a depth of thirty meters. ESA's Don Quijote project is contemplating a similar mission. JAXA's (Japan Aerospace Exploration Agency) space ship reached the asteroid Itokawa in 2005. It did not accomplish its main task to bring back samples from the asteroid but, nevertheless, produced valuable data.[6]

If the threat is detected well in advance of the potential impact, very gentle deflection methods can be effective. The course of an asteroid could, for instance, be changed by a gigantic sun sail which would exploit the sun wind to produce the necessary momentum. The same effect could be achieved with a gravitational 'tractor', a spaceship placed in front of or behind the asteroid. The job could also be left to nuclear-armed missiles but the explosion could create a multitude of dangerous fragments which have to be dealt with separately. When a comet is threatening, nuclear warheads may be the only expedient because the loose comet material does not provide any anchorage.

In any case, international coordination is imperative to optimize the available resources and create readiness for sufficient countermeasures. Now or never, we all sit in the same boat. The simplest way ahead is to consolidate the present ad hoc cooperation. The financial base should be broadened; the greater part of the human race should contribute according to its wealth and means. One flinches from a new UN-organ, but for instance the G8 countries (see the following chapter) could constitute the hard core for the development of our space defenses.

Threats from space are easily neglected. In general, people have a propensity to disregard infrequent hazards. The survivors of devastating earthquakes and floods soon return to business as usual, often without any intention to invest in protective measures. In the developed countries, the cities at risk such as Tokyo and Los Angeles are reasonably prepared. Nevertheless, great human suffering and huge material loss can be foreseen when the big quake strikes. Most poor countries have so far preferred to accept the inevitable, despite very distressing experiences.

The Boxing Day tsunami in 2004 is still in fresh memory. The strength of the earthquake reached 9.15 on the Richter scale and it caused up to 200,000 deaths; the relatively few tourist deaths multiplied international awareness and aid. At least the same number perished in the

Tangshan earthquake in China 1976 without a flicker of an eyebrow from world opinion. Sudden volcanic eruptions are also life-threatening. The notorious Krakatau explosion of 1883 and the associated tsunami killed around 100,000 people. In 1815, atmospheric dust from the much stronger Tambora eruption, also in Indonesia, caused a global temperature drop of two degree Celsius and famine in many places.

The Laki eruption on Iceland 1783–84 was particularly disruptive. Iceland lost 25 % of its population and more than 50 % of its livestock to famine and fluorine poisoning (eight million tons of fluorine and 120 million tons of sulfur dioxide was emitted). The eruption created an atmospheric haze (a 'dry fog') which caused abnormal weather conditions all over Europe and parts of the United States. Mortality increased markedly and the succeeding winters were the severest ever recorded. The concomitant food shortages may have contributed to the outbreak of the French Revolution.

Volcanism can be a destructive force on level with an asteroid impact. The biggest eco-disaster ever recorded took place in the boundary between the Perm and the Triassic geological periods 251.4 million years ago. It coincided with gigantic lava flows and pyroclastic formations in Siberia (the Siberian traps). They still cover two million km² and the original area was much larger.[6a] The Deccan traps in India were produced by repeated lava eruptions between 60 and 68 million ago. They cover half a million km² up to a depth of two kilometers. About 75,000 years ago the Toba volcano on Sumatra emitted around 3,000 km³ of debris which covered India and influenced the global climate for many years.

In contrast to the cosmic threats, the convulsions of our own planet are beyond our control.[7] The movements of the tectonic plates and the rising magma in 'hot' spots have unavoidable consequences such as earthquakes, volcanic eruptions and tsunamis. We can prepare ourselves only by appropriate building codes in the areas under threat. Dependable forecasts would be a great help and a lot of effort has been exerted on that score but with meager results. Tsunami warning systems are practicable though and are installed around the Pacific and (after the 2004 disaster) in the Indian oceans.

Tsunamis occur in the around the Atlantic Ocean, too; after all the Lisbon earthquake of 1755 took 100,000 lives, most of them tsunami casualties. But the tsunamis are not ocean wide[7a] and an advance warning would usually come too late. Nevertheless, the United States is now launching a warning system which will cover the Caribbean as well.

Extraterrestrial as well as subterranean threats should strengthen our feeling of a common destiny on this planet of ours. We already exhibit a will and a capability to support earthquake victims around the globe, regardless of race or nationality. This good will should in the near future be channeled into joint efforts to ward off avoidable disasters. When the comet arrives we must be prepared to take our destiny into our own hands – otherwise we have only ourselves to blame.

13.2 The climate and the environment

Our sun is a comparatively stable star which arose together with the planets about 4.5 billion years ago. After the initial warming phase, the sun has kept its energy production fairly constant; during the eleven year sunspot period, the radiation varies only 0.1 %. During the so called Little Ice Age in Europe (1650-1715), the sun spots virtually disappeared which indicates a causal connection. The average global temperature presumably dropped by approximately one degree Celsius. In the very long term, solar radiation will slowly increase and at the very end, when the hydrogen is depleted, the sun enters a violent heating phase. We have a respite of a couple of billion years before life on earth becomes impossible.

> The earth has passed through many dramatic climate changes. In the beginning, the relatively weak solar radiation was probably compensated for by the very high concentration (perhaps 80%) of carbon dioxide in the atmosphere. The disastrous glaciations 600–700 million years ago may be connected with a precipitous drop in atmospheric carbon dioxide content.[8] Yet the interaction between climate and carbon dioxide is somewhat obscure; several other mechanisms are obviously involved.
>
> Anyhow, a balmy climate around twenty degrees Celsius has been the rule during the last 500 million years. But the greenhouse climate has been interspersed with ice ages which caused fluctuations of up to ten degrees in the mean temperature and lasted tens of million of years. About 25 million years ago the climate once more entered a cooler phase. The present ice age commenced 2.2 million years ago and is characterized by extended (50,000–150,000 years) cool periods and much shorter warm interglacials. These variations can partly be explained by astronomical changes in the elliptic orbit of the earth around the sun and the inclination of the earth's axis against the ecliptica. Presently the average temperature on earth is close to 15° C.

Our own interglacial begun about 14,700 years ago and is already rather extended compared to the preceding ones. The climate has been atypically stable after a short cold spell (the younger dryas) which abruptly came to a close 11,700 years ago. The temperature seems to have risen seven degrees in a few years; the sea level rose by twenty meters in 500 years. All in all, the sea level has risen 120 meters over the last 20,000 years. It is now close to the previous interglacial.

> During the last 3,000 years, the sea level has been almost constant but around 1900 it begun to rise by two mm pro annum. The Intergovernmental Panel on Climate Change (IPCC) reckons with an accelerating trend. The forecast for 2100 lies in the wide range 110–880 mm compared with the 2006 value. The thermal expansion of the water in the oceans is the main cause for the rise. The melt from the shrinking ice cover and glaciers is partly compensated for by increases in snowfall over the Antarctic and by water basins on land.[9]

New and better simulation models for climate change are emerging all the time. The only way to test them is by historic comparisons. The climate fluctuations during the last 800,000 years have been mapped out in considerable detail, thanks to the information available from ice core samples obtained by drilling in the Arctic and the Antarctic. Indirect research methods give an approximate picture of climate variation which goes back 650 million years. Certain qualitative relationships have been verified but by and large the models have not been capable of predicting the past. The problem is the vast range of variables and above all their non-linear interactions which lead to chaotically unpredictable outcomes.[10]

> The interaction between cloudiness and climate illustrates the complexity of the problem. An increase in cloudiness has a cooling effect because sunlight is reflected, but the clouds also have a warming effect due to the reflection of the infrared radiation from the surface. The wind speed over the oceans is coupled to the production of aerosols, microscopic particles which promote drop nucleation and thus the formation of clouds. Water vapor is a potent greenhouse gas but its impact depends on the atmospheric circulation. Finely dispersed particles produced by volcanic eruptions, car exhaust and industrial processes have a cooling effect. And so on and on.
>
> A warmer climate and a higher carbon dioxide content increases the capture of carbon in vegetation at high latitudes but the risk of methane release in the melting tundra regions is also increased. Methane is a potent greenhouse gas and vast quantities are stored on the deep sea floor, coupled to water as so called clathrates. An increase in water temperature could release the methane and unleash a chain reaction. This is conjectured to be the mechanism behind the swift warming at

the boundary between the Paleocene and the Eocen periods 55 million years ago. Over long time spans, the continental drift, too, must be taken into account because its influence on the atmospheric and oceanic circulation. Moreover, the reflectivity of the earth is dependent on the distribution of the continental land mass.

A warming of around 0.7 degrees during the last century and a recent acceleration in the temperature rise are generally accepted as facts. The atmospheric carbon dioxide increase is smaller than expected because the oceans and the land vegetation seem to absorb more than the calculated amount. Still at issue is the degree of culpability of the greenhouse gases. A change in solar radiation is the obvious alternative and its impact could be enhanced in surprising ways.

> Danish researchers have argued for an indirect influence due to variations in the intensity of the solar sun-spot cycle. The magnetic shielding of the earth varies accordingly and affects the influx of cosmic radiation. That in turn alters the ionization of the upper atmosphere, the nucleation of water drops and finally cloud formation. The authors have been accused of fraudulent massaging of the data but the argument continues.[11]

The common if not consensual view is that the sun answers for only a minor portion of the recent increase in global temperature. The latest IPCC report of 2007 presents the exceedingly wide range 1,1–6,4°C as a forecast for the global warming up to 2100, but the high value is based on unrealistic assumptions for the future release of carbon dioxide.[12]

If we take the climate change seriously, the main point is the necessity for action, irrespective of the causal connections. Overall, there is a strong case for curbing the release of greenhouse gases. Here, if ever, the application of the precautionary principle is justified. It is much better to be too early than too late. The risk of setting off a tipping point of run-away climate change may not be that big. But if it happens it could cause irreversible havoc and turn into a worldwide disaster. Thus the control of the global climate is one of our key challenges.

> The reduction of greenhouse gases has dominated the debate but there are other ways to influence the climate.[13] Cloudiness could be increased by the release of aerosols in the stratosphere.Another possibility is to stimulate the primary production of the oceans by the addition of iron which in vast areas is the bottleneck for plankton growth.[14] The most

straightforward method is to position a huge parasol between the sun and the earth. At the Lagrange point L_1 four times the distance to the moon, the parasol would remain in place and reduce the insolation.[15]

On the other hand, a new ice age may be just around the corner. Then a dependable heating system would be welcome. William Ruddiman maintains in *Plows, Plagues and Petroleum: How Humans Took Control of Climate* that slash-and-burn agriculture, rice cultivation and husbandry began to influence the climate thousands of years ago by the release of carbon dioxide and methane. He asserts that the next glaciation has already been postponed by human intervention. James Lovelock takes the contrary position in *The Revenge of Gaia* (2006). He foresees disastrous desertification and mass migration, and sees nuclear power as the only short term solution to the climate problem.

The climate hazard has become the great battle field in the international debate while other environmental problems have got less publicity. Deforestation in the tropics threatens the ecological balance and water supply. The biodiversity is diminishing and many animals and plants are close to extinction. Logging in conjunction with industrial projects is often presented as the main malefactor, but in reality the slash-and-burn cultivation is the biggest villain.

Slash-and-burn can be a sustainable form of agriculture and husbandry, especially at high latitudes where the climate and the soil is conducive of regrowth. In the tropics, the population increase in countries like Brazil and Indonesia is causing extensive environmental damage; slash-and-burn affects a much bigger area than commercial logging.[16]

Even so, a global trend reversal seems to be on the way. P. Kauppi et al. (2006)[17] certify that the deforestation in a number of poor countries, with Indonesia in the lead, is compensated by the forestation efforts in other regions. Particularly encouraging is the progress in China and India. Around the Mediterranean, too, the tree planting is restoring regions which were laid waste in antiquity, while the situation in the Sahel and in Ethiopia is only getting worse. And the remaining rain forests of the Far East are still in the danger zone.

Poverty and population pressure are the root causes of the problems. The solution is thus an improvement in living standards coupled to a reduction of nativity – easier said than done. In many areas, the involvement of the local population in tourism-related business has produced good results. The inhabitants have become responsible owners of their natural resources.[18]

The list of environmental problems could easily be prolonged but the worries are generally local or regional. In most cases we are faced with the 'tragedy of the commons' (cf. 4.2) which can be resolved by establishing responsible ownership for the vulnerable resources. International coordination is called for only when we are confronted with global challenges like atmospheric emissions or deep-sea fishing. In general we should accept that the utilization of natural resources, the environment included, has to be taxed and/or priced by a market; the taxation of carbon dioxide emissions is a case in point. Only through adequate market processes can scarce resources be allocated in a sensible way.

13.3 The menace of micro-organisms

Like all life forms, man is threatened by a horde of parasitic organisms. In the tropics millions are plagued by sundry spongers, worms and grubs which wind their way into the human body with unpleasant consequences. Even more dangerous are a multitude of pathogens – unicellular protozoa, bacteria and viruses – which are transmitted by bloodsucking insects. In the developed world, improved hygiene and health care has finished off the troublesome macro-parasites. Vaccination and antibiotics are keeping virus and bacterial infection in check although aids and tuberculosis are latent threats in countries with shaky health administration.

This explains the fact that during the last decades medical research has prioritized welfare-related inflictions which correlate with a long life span and a western life style. Widespread tropical diseases like malaria are difficult to cure and do not present lucrative markets. A substantial part of the world's population still struggles with devastating illness and high child mortality.

The lack of medicines and money is not the only and perhaps not even the main problem for health care in the least developed countries. Often political turmoil and ubiquitous corruption hamper or nullify medical efforts. All the more remarkable is the complete eradication of smallpox which was achieved in the 1970s under the aegis of the WHO, despite very feeble support from the governments concerned. Neither did the sister organization UNICEF warm to the project.[19]

The campaign against the polio virus, which started in 1988, has repeatedly been sabotaged by local authorities. During 2004, the global polio incidence had already been reduced from around 350,000 to 1,255 cases annually when local imams in Nigeria denounced the vaccinations as an American conspiracy. The polio spread again to Chad and further on to Egypt, Saudi Arabia, Yemen and as far as Indonesia.[20] In 2007, the number of cases had once again subsided to 1181.

Most diseases have to be fought by conventional methods because only a few pathogens can be completely eradicated. Mosquito nets, impregnated with insecticides, protect against malaria, and better medicines for many tropical inflictions are in the pipeline. Special pricing for the less developed countries (LDCs) makes for improved affordability and many NGOs are tirelessly extending their operations. A tolerable health care system could be within reach even in the least developed countries, always provided a minimum of political stability. The exception is aids despite the huge amounts of publicity and cash expended. Yet aids is easily avoidable.

> HIV (Human Immunodeficiency Virus) is an extremely variable retrovirus which by its propensity for mutations can dupe the immune defenses and straightforward medication. After the infection, the virus transcribes its RNA-genome to double stringed DNA which is incorporated in the nucleus of the infected cell and directs the production of virus-specific proteins. HIV attacks mainly the so-called T-helper cells which are key players in the immune defense. Aids ensues when the number of T-cells falls beyond a critical limit, opening the door for deadly infections and cancer. HIV adapts swiftly to single medicines but can be checked by combination therapy, utilizing three or more different medicaments But the virus cannot be eliminated; neither is vaccination within sight.
>
> HIV is spread predominantly by sexual contacts. In the worst afflicted areas the authorities and the inhabitants have been equally determined to hush up the matter, despite the fact that condoms provide adequate protection. The inability to face unpalatable realities is the cause of unnecessary suffering and premature death. In Sub-Saharan Africa, many countries are still in deep trouble despite the extensive international support. Outside Africa the aids threat is less acute due to different sexual mores.[21]

The HIV-virus demonstrates a dilemma of medical research. In general, the pathogens have a capability to develop resistance against new medicines. This adaptability is the result of fierce selection. For eons the pathogens have lived in a hostile environment and learnt to hoodwink the manifold countermeasures of the immune defense. This game of life and death has singled out sophisticated parasites that usually are a step ahead of their hosts due to their short generation cycle. The host specificity of the pathogens is attributable to this evolutionary history; a successful invasion requires a high degree of specialization. Sexual bifurcation was an early countermove of complex organisms and dramatically improved the odds for the emergence of resilient immune systems.[22]

> Since the 1970s, resistant bacteria have been a problem which has called for a stream of novel and more expensive antibiotics. The general population has not been that exposed; the victims of the super resistant bacteria strains are mostly elderly patients with a reduced immune defense. Nevertheless we are involved in an extended fight, where the spread of resistance can be surprisingly fast and benign bacteria suddenly acquire pathogenicity. Specific genes for resistance, toxicity or virulence can, surprisingly, be exchanged between bacteria. This traffic goes on even across species barriers.
>
> The fast buildup of microbial resistance is largely our own fault. Indiscriminate application and sloppy practices have blunted the efficacy of most antibiotics.[22a] Moreover, pharmaceutical companies lack incentives to develop new antimicrobials. This market failure could be corrected if big health providers, private or public, commissioned the development of new antibiotics. A successful drug would produce great savings in their own operations and turn a profit when licensed to outside parties.

The pathogenic bacteria, protozoa and fungi, are formidable foes but they should be no match for modern biotechnology. The development of new medicines will become ever more efficient with deeper insights in the mechanisms of virulence and resistance. Every life form has its Achilles' heel and, contrary to the bacteria, we can increase the pace and keep a few steps ahead.

Pathogenic viruses are more menacing. A combination of infectious influenza and incurable HIV-viruses would be devastating. Influenza in itself is an annually returning scourge because the virus regularly modifies its protein shield and thus maintains its infectivity. Sometimes mutational leaps occur and can cause worldwide pandemics. The Spanish flu swept over a war-weary world in 1918 and in two years killed around fifty million people, much more than the Great War. In India alone the death toll was 17 million, five percent of the population.

> Pandemics usually arise when the virus takes the leap from an animal species to man by a recombination of DNA or RNA. Enough people then lack resistance to the virus which spreads avalanche-like. About one third were susceptible to the Spanish flu which was more than enough for global coverage. An unusual feature was the high morbidity of the 20–40 years old. High mortality was also atypical and often

amounted to between 20 and 30 percent – among indigenous populations sometimes even higher. Death could follow in a couple of days after the first symptoms.

Recently the virus in question has been reconstructed from frozen flu victims in Alaska. A detailed investigation of the unique characteristics of the Spanish flu thus became possible. The basic type (H_1N_1) points at the hybridization of animal and human viruses but deviates from the notorious bird flu (H_5N_1) which does not yet spread between people. The reconstruction project could open the door for would-be terrorists, but on balance the scientific community, after consultation with the relevant authorities, came to the conclusion that normal scientific publication practice was warranted.[23]

A multitude of afflictions are virus-related, beginning with the common cold and herpes. Unfortunately, the list of remedies is much shorter. Dengue fever, yellow fever, hepatitis, measles, mumps and rabies exemplify life-threatening virus diseases; vaccines are not yet available for dengue or hepatitis C. The Marburg and Ebola viruses have been widely publicized due to the dramatic course of the illness – the short incubation time and the high mortality, above 50 %. For that very reason they can be stopped by quarantine and do not constitute a serious threat. The same holds for prions, which are devious protein poisons affecting the brain. The most prominent malady is mad cow disease which has been practically eradicated.

Viruses may be the root cause of many, perhaps most, autoimmune diseases. Insignificant or entirely unnoticed infections can cause havoc when the body sometimes starts to attack its own cells and tissues with serious consequences. Strong evidence exists for the involvement of viruses in, for example, juvenile diabetes, rheumatism and multiple sclerosis.[24] Virus-dependent autoimmunity can also be at least a partial cause of brain diseases like Parkinson's and Alzheimer's. Fetal damage due to virus infections is well-documented and mild, virus-related disturbances in brain development may be behind many psychic afflictions.

Viruses are difficult to cultivate in the laboratory. They are extremely small and can propagate only in specific living cells. The smallest viroid genome so far detected counts only 359 RNA bases (it attacks potatoes). Not long ago, the enormous prevalence of viruses in the oceans was recognized. One milliliter of sea water contains hundreds of millions of viral particles and bacteria in the oceans are heavily virus infected.[25] In a recent investigation of small children, a high incidence of unknown viruses was established; they eventually disappear.[26] The virus community will be capable of many nasty surprises.

The viral DNA can fuse to the cell genome and erupt at a later stage. Alternatively it can cause mutations and an increased risk for malign processes; many cancers are clearly virus-related. The Epstein-Barr virus is an interesting case. Most people are asymptomatically infected though symptoms can appear in the form of mononucleosis (kissing disease). But the virus can also give raise to non-Hodgkin lymphoma, a cancer which requires chemotherapy or radiation treatment. Moreover, the virus is suspected of complicity in the development of leukemia, sarcoma and multiple sclerosis. Human cytomegalovirus (HCMV) has recently come under suspicion for involvement in atherosclerosis and strokes.[27]

Only a small fraction of the bacteria and viruses have been characterized so far. In the worst case, we must reckon with new pandemics which for want of vaccines call for a stringent international quarantine regime. The value of international cooperation cannot be overrated if and when we have to nip sinister pandemics in the bud. But the permanent threat should not bring about a microbe fright. Most of the time, we live in peaceful coexistence with the myriad micro-organisms on our skin and in our digestive tract. Too strict a hygiene regime is probably the primary cause of the advance of allergic disorders.

Many yeasts, molds and bacteria have in the past served us well in preparing food, drink and nowadays in producing modern antibiotics. Our deepened insights allow the employment of viruses for sophisticated medicine. Gene therapy depends on suitable viruses to introduce genetic material into the nucleus of the cell. Tailor-made viruses, which selectively attack cancerous cells, are under investigation in animal tests.[28] In the future, the menace of micro-organisms may be turned on its head.

13.4 Too many people?

Every species seeks to propagate and fill its ecological niche. When all emigration options are exhausted, the population either stagnates or enters a sequence of violent fluctuations. Man is no exception. Territorial or technological breakthroughs have always been accompanied by unbounded propagation until the new lebensraum has been filled to the brim. In most cases, hunger and disease have done the duty of population control.

Famine and population explosion do not tally. Africa cannot be as wretched as the slanted media reporting indicates. Africans, too, complain about the one-sided news coverage of their continent. Still, when the resources exceed the subsistence level the surplus is literally eaten up by the population increase.

In a primitive society, the children provide cheap labor and serve as retirement insurance. To top it off, the group solidarity of the tribe and the extended family make for collective responsibility. Childcare is a kind of commons. Curtailing your own reproduction just pushes you into caring for your neighbor's offspring. The suppressed position of the women acts as a shackle on social development. She carries all the burdens but has scant alternatives.

Close to nature, high status persons, men in particular, produce a lot more offspring than the mean. In a class society the roles are reversed. A host of children is dispersing the accumulated wealth and high status women shun childbirth. This trend was discernable in antiquity and was taken up by upper class Europeans (except in England cf. chapter 1.4). The industrial revolution brought on a steep population increase in Europe which abated during the first half of the twentieth century. The aftermath of the Second World War brought an unexpected baby boom which was soon succeeded by a baby crash in all developed countries. The average fertility has in most quarters dropped far beneath the sustainable number of 2.1–2.2 births per woman.

> Already in the 1970s, the ominous trend was clearly visible but any attempt to raise the question met a wall of silence. The whole subject was taboo and is still weighed down by political incorrectness despite the looming demographic disaster. In the European Union, the fertility varies around 1.5; Italy and Spain are at rock bottom with 1.3. The population of Russia, Ukraine and Japan is already dropping whereas the United States features a fertility of 2.1. The poor immigrants probably compensate for the fertility deficit of the well off. A similar relation certainly holds in Europe too, but no data has come to my knowledge.[29]

Is then the anomalous relation between income and reproduction a problem? Many people routinely shake off this question by referring to the looming overpopulation of our planet. Every unborn child would thus improve the deteriorating ecological balance. But the division of mankind into an expanding poor majority and a shrinking wealthy minority is a prescription for conflict and instability. If the present trends prevail, the rich democratic countries will come up against very serious political, economic, social and – inevitably – military problems.

For destitute people, propagation is irresponsible whereas the rich are shirking their responsibility when they abstain from procreation.

> The national economies of the developed countries are drifting into an absurd dead end. Most of the inexorably rising health care expenditures is spent on the elderly and the dying while reproduction is neglected. The West is sinking into senility. As early as 1980, Günter Grass published a book *Kopfgeburten oder die Deutschen sterben aus*[*] The warning cry of the title did not call forth any reaction. In 2005 Udo Di Fabio is again chiming the alarm bells in *Kultur der Freiheit*.[**] The constitutional judge and father of four pleads among other things for a thorough renewal of family life. Meanwhile the German fertility dropped to around 1.3 although a slight rise is apparent in 2008.

The good news is that the world population increase is abating and the statisticians calculate that it will level off at approximately ten billion.[30] But such forecasts are notoriously undependable and they cover up the actual problem. The earth could well make room for say fifteen billion humans who individually and in groups take responsibility for themselves, their offspring and their environment. A much smaller number could, however, cause permanent misery if the indigent continue to procreate irresponsibly within an obsolete political, economic and social structure.

> Immigration is proffered as a universal remedy to cure the imbalance. A certain movement of people stands to reason if the immigrants can be integrated in the new surroundings. Even the best intentions can come unstuck. The Netherlands is well known for its liberal immigration policy but now the wind is veering. "Holland is full" goes the saying and the population density is in fact the highest in Europe, Malta excepted. The proportion of non-European residents has risen above ten percent.
>
> Manuel Barroso, the Chairman of the European Commission, recently announced that up to 2050 the number of retirees (above 65 years) will increase by 58 millions while the active population (15-64 years) will decrease by 48 millions.[31] No response has so far been elicited by this distress call. The imbalances cannot be solved by immigration without the risk of a dangerous discontinuity in the societal development.

---

[*] Head Births or the Germans are dying out. Refers to Pallas Athena who was born from the head of Zeus.
[**] The Culture of Freedom

The successful immigration policy in the United States depends on the incessant pressure on the newcomers to pull their weight from the very beginning. The second generation immigrants have usually embraced the American way of life and the corresponding values. This has not worked in Europe. Considering the high nativity of Muslim settlers in particular, a creeping Islamization of Europe cannot be excluded.

Many less developed countries have understood that unchecked procreation is aggravating their situation. On the other hand, a rise in living standards generally leads to a drop in fertility, albeit with a certain delay. To escape the vicious circle of propagation and poverty, India and China resorted to compulsive birth control.

> India fell back on compulsory sterilization of the poor which brought the whole family planning campaign into disrepute. Nevertheless, in 1994 the fertility had dropped to 3.34 and the 2008 estimate is 2.76 (the Muslims exhibit a higher fertility than the Hindu majority). Pakistan lingers on 3.58 but in Islamic Bangladesh the forecast for the fertility in 2025 is 2.1 – a steep drop from the present level 3.08 and spot on the sustainable level.[32]
>
> In China the rules were gradually tightened up until the one-child system was introduced in 1979. It applies both a carrot and a stick. One child families are favored while the next children have serious economic consequences. The Chinese have succeeded in reducing fertility to 1.77, and are already concerned about the demographic structure. The tough policy has had an unintended side-effect, well known in other countries with similar values. Due to the widespread preference for boys, baby girls are often terminated, before or after birth. In China the girl deficit is above ten percent.

In vast regions, such as South East Asia and Latin America, the population increase is subsiding. The exceptions are many Islamic countries and Sub-Saharan Africa; Mali and Niger are at the top of the fertility league, featuring an average of over seven children for every fertile woman. Some populous countries too, like Nigeria and Ethiopia, have a high nativity only partly compensated by the high mortality. But in South Africa, the population is decreasing due to the Aids epidemic; a round twenty percent of the fertile population is infected.

On the whole, economic growth seems to diminish the population pressure in the less developed countries. This trend is obviously supported by the ongoing democratization, urbanization and the emancipation of women. The Islamic countries are somewhat exceptional. By and large, the negative correlation between income and fertility is holding in this category, too. The fertility in Tunisia and Algeria is already below two, but rich countries like Saudi Arabia and Libya exhibit high figures. Perhaps we have to wait for the strict orthodoxy to be undermined by covert secularization, as has happened in Catholic Southern Europe.

The demographic imbalances in the democratic core countries, with the exception of the United States, may be a more refractory problem than the uncontrolled propagation in the LDCs. The increasing life span exacerbates the dilemma. In Europe we are on our way to a geriatric society, a unicum in world history. We could and we should remove the economic obstacles to reproduction – voluntary childlessness must not be too attractive. This may not be enough. We are dealing with a complex network of human motivation, centered on the family institution. To carry forward a new generation is the most demanding long-term mission ever undertaken by ordinary people.

> Marriage is instituted to create a safe environment for the rising generation. If the woman realizes that she can be left unsupported at any moment, her lack of commitment to family building is understandable. A deep trust between the parties is imperative. It excludes wanton affairs, which does not tally with the hedonistic individualism of our time. The core family deserves all the support it can get by legislation and by societal values. The survival of our societies is at stake.[33]

Ultimately it is a question of self-confidence and trust in the future. All too often one can overhear utterances about the futility of bringing up children into this miserable world; a rather odd interpretation of the present, in comparison with the exertions of our forefathers and -mothers. Those blessed with children understand that they are worth all our pains and worries, an insight which often arrives only after the fact. In former times, large families were a sign of poverty and stupidity. It is encouraging that fertility in the high income bracket nowadays seems to be above average. Like a slender waist, a large family is becoming a status symbol. Perhaps a break in the trend is approaching when more and more people cross the line to economic independence.

Are there too many people on our earth? In any case there is always a deficit of good citizens, the only guarantors of the survival and the sustenance of our societies and our values. A sustainable population structure is a question of life and death for the democracies. People are not interchangeable; our personal offspring are always closest to our heart and best at managing our long-term plus-sum game. In an extended perspective, a shrinking population becomes disastrously unstable – with a grain of dramatization you could call it collective suicide. Much more resources, money, time and care, must be set aside to maintain our biological capital. Otherwise the future if not the very existence of our children and grandchildren is in doubt.

13.5 Clashes of culture

Under this heading, one cannot pass over Samuel P. Huntington's *The Clash of Civilizations and the Remaking of World Order* (1997). Huntington presents a rather gloomy picture of future international relations, which by and large are envisioned as extrapolations of historic conflicts. He predicts that the influence and staying power of the Western democracies eventually will be undermined by demographic inferiority and economic regress. Huntington does not believe in the democratization of alien civilizations but sees international politics in terms of a zero-sum game, marked by ferocious competition and violent conflicts occasionally interrupted by relatively brief peaceful periods – Pax Romana, Pax Britannica and Pax Americana.

> Huntington is provocatively ringing the alarm bells and his presentation is underpinned by a thorough exposition of modern history. The reasoning sometimes gets rather strained when he tries to squeeze disparate phenomena into a preconceived pattern. Neither have recent events confirmed his views in all respects. For instance Japan is more and more looking like a Western democracy.
>
> Huntington is not wholly attuned to confrontation and keeps the door ajar for other, less probable scenarios as he sees it. But for him as for many others, a reconciliation of the separate civilizations and their values is difficult to imagine. Islam is singled out as the leading potential troublemaker. In too many countries, poverty and the demographic imbalance as well as the severe sexual discipline is producing a surplus of frustrated young men – a suitable soil for unbridled expansive ventures.

The early history of Islam is a conquering expedition, comparable only to the Mongolian one under Genghis Khan (1162–1227) and his successors. Religion was from the very start amalgamated with the traditional nomad culture of profitable plunder. When internal strife was proscribed, the aggression and the rapacity were turned against the surrounding people which were lawful prey. Islam has an inbuilt superiority complex. The infidels can, on principle, be tolerated only if they submit; apostates incur the death penalty. This is the hotbed of

Muslim terrorism which, however, in a number of important points clashes with the teachings of the Koran.[34]

> Core values are changing very slowly and the old religious divides have not lost their relevance; there Huntington is right. A historical community of values facilitates cooperation, and spontaneous solidarity with distant fellow-believers is a well known phenomenon. But Islam has since times immemorial failed as a politically unifying force just like Christianity, Buddhism or Confucianism. Discord in the Muslim world is very much in evidence.

A large-scale religious war is not in sight. But there are other, less dramatic expressions of cultural collisions. Suppressed, ill-treated or injured groups, feeling powerless or slighted, easily embrace an ideology of violence with terrorism as the logical outcome. So far we have escaped rather lightly in the West but in the future we must, despite the countermeasures, take into account the probability of terrorist access to weapons of mass destruction. The political and psychological preparations for such a calamity leave much to be desired. Lacking correct information, plain horror of the unknown can cause mass hysteria and manifest, psychosomatic symptoms which imitate the expected symptoms, for instance nausea, vomiting and rashes.[35]

Another kind of cultural collision occurs when the well-heeled West is confronted with the poverty and wretchedness of the LDCs. In emergency situations, the impulse to help is strong and usually reaches its target despite the rather chaotic circumstances. Long-term help is more problematic. A continuous resource flow tends to increase corruption and creates an unsound dependence on the donors; for the middlemen the aid often turns into just a profitable business.

> Michael Maren tells us in *The Road to Hell* (1997) about the adverse side of development aid. The subtitle *The Ravaging Effects of Foreign Aid and International Charity* says it all. Somalia is Maren's foremost example. In the 1980s, the dictator Siyaad Barre vied with diverse clan chiefs for the exploitation of the inpouring goodies. The development projects increased the internal tensions and a substantial part of the imported food was used for financing domestic warfare.
>
> In the absence of humanitarian aid, bleak necessity would long ago have forced the warring parties into a meager compromise in Somalia. As it is, all sides are relatively satisfied with the situation. But the underlying logic is hard to accept for Christian people, and aid keeps pouring in though nobody can see an end to the misery. A UN-organ,

SACB (Somalia Aid Coordination Body), sits in Nairobi and coordinates the efforts of some 120 aid organizations as best it can.[36]

Obviously the development aid has by and large missed its target; only a minor proportion of the input reaches the needy. The donors have learned by their mistakes. Today the World Bank emphasizes the importance of good governance and corrupt regimes are moved down to the end of the grant line. But reputable statesmen still hold forth about the eradication of poverty and the need for more aid to countries which cannot handle the money in a responsible way.[37]

> The busybody politicians are not without support. For instance Jeffrey Sachs, an eminent economist, has in *The End of Poverty* (2005) stood up for massive economic support to the LDCs. The basic idea is that poor countries must get help to climb to a critical point – the hump – a take-off point for self-supporting economic growth. Sachs accuses the West of mean stinginess and is passionately addressing our better selves. Such misdirected moralizing leads, as pointed out earlier, into a dead end. Sachs has already received an effective rejoinder from William Easterly – *The White Man's Burden: Why the West's Efforts to Aid the Rest Have Done So Much Ill and So Little Good* (2006). Unperturbed, Sachs is answering back with *Common Wealth: Economics for a Crowded Planet* (2008).

The cultural collision between the donor and the aid recipient is an established fact. Economic support has not brought about a turnaround in one single LDC. Development cooperation is a euphemism which tries to paper over the chasm between the widely diverging frames of reference. The first priority is to establish law and order, the basic conditions for economic growth. Such efforts are often sidelined or sabotaged by the local power brokers because it rarely serves their personal interests. How this equation could be solved will come up in the next chapter.

The overpopulation of many poor countries creates a chronic tension, externally and internally. Where subsistence agriculture is the norm, all available land is soon utilized. The gruesome showdown between the Tutsis and the Hutus in Burundi and Ruanda was related to the struggle for lebensraum in the countryside. Ethnical cleansing is the final consequence of the clash between cultures, races and economic interest in diverse combinations.

> Ethnic rivalry is the oldest cultural collision, and lurks under the surface even in civilized societies. The wholesale extermination of Jews

during the Second World War was a terrible regression into primitive tribal loyalty. In the former Yugoslavia, the atrocities were repeated in the same spirit, albeit on a smaller scale. Worse genocides have happened and are in offing in the overpopulated LDCs. The animosity emerges in no time but takes generations to overcome.

The collision between the expanding Western civilization and local cultures has been the main historic theme during the last five hundred years. The drama is now culminating. While modern technology and democratic values are spreading in ever wider rings, the old democracies are economically and demographically challenged by underprivileged nations. At home, our own identity is threatened by reproductive collapse and alien immigrants. Everywhere the future is equally uncertain.

Destructive cultural collisions are threatening the future of humanity. Negative historic experiences and deep-rooted prejudices are constantly disrupting constructive plus-sum play. To secure and extend the scanty trust capital is a formidable challenge. In the last chapters we will tackle these problems and try to distinguish safe routes between the numerous perils ahead.

Chapter 14
The mission of democracy

Only an empowered European Union can be an equal partner to the United States and carry its part of the responsibility for the future of democracy. A legitimate global government is an insoluble equation – a contradiction in terms. Instead we ought to aim for worldwide political self-organization. A group of major powers in peaceful cooperation could stand surety for international stability without loosing their sovereign status. Failed states have forfeited their independence and require a credible outside authority which can prepare the ground for a sustainable democracy. The Paris declaration of 1990 put an end to the cold war and presupposes only free elections, a market economy and respect for human rights. Within this framework, every democracy is free to realize itself in practical terms. Will the democratic mission succeed? This cannot be assured but there is no program more worthy of success.

14.1 Consolidating the core

In a democracy, domestic politics mostly overshadows foreign affairs. First and foremost, democratic rule must prove itself on its home turf. Here the ills and evils must be defined and confronted, here the values are reconsidered and the practical consequences played out. When democracy is marketed as an ideal form of government, we must first of all ensure that it can serve as a good example.

All well and good, but the cooperation of democratic states in a turbulent world is also essential. In this section the collaboration of the United States, the European Union and Japan is discussed. Every entity has its particular problems, but together they control the major part of the world's productive resources; the disproportion is even bigger in research and development. Together with their natural allies, they are well positioned to deal with current conflicts and threats.

Instead of close cooperation, the policing of the world and the attendant unpopularity have gladly been left to the United States. The country is today by far the strongest force in global politics, but its role as a world police is untenable in the longer term. By now the joints are creaking.

> Everywhere and particularly in the United States, success in the political zero-sum game implies that every opportunity to blacken an adversary is put to good use. Nowadays, an activist foreign policy is no vote-winner in democracies. The unavoidable sacrifices and reverses present a suitable target for the opposition which has a field day vilifying unjustified expenditure and shocking casualties.

In *Colossus: The Price of America's Empire* (2004), Niall Ferguson predicts that the United States will reject its mission as responsible imperialist. The country will soon return to relative isolationism if it does not get more support from other democracies. This would open the field for all kinds of bad behavior and engender a more dangerous world. A long-term democratic strategy would then be a futile undertaking when the so-called responsible governments were fully occupied in shuffling the jackass card to each other.

The European Union is in a key position but has its hands full with internal problems. Has-been European great powers strut, alone or in groups, around the international scene as if the good old days were here again. Global politics is still seen as a zero-sum game, a short term competition for influence and economic gain. National egoism seems to be the watchword for the EU-policy of many countries, a narrow-minded but infectious attitude. Until recently, opposing America almost became a conditioned reflex on the French model.[1]

> Already in 1957, Paul-Henri Spaak (1899–1972), Belgian statesman and general secretary of NATO, curtly stated: "there are only two kinds of countries in Europe today, the small ones who know it and the small who do not know". A healthy realism is eventually making its appearance, not least in France. Nicholas Sarkozy, the new President, distances himself from arrogant national self-sufficiency and stresses the role of the United States as the leading democracy in the world. France may be readying itself for a profound change.[2]

Only a united and empowered European Union can be an equal partner to the United States and take on its part of the responsibility for the future of humanity – liberty, justice, prosperity and security on a global scale. Such a democratic mission is, to my mind, the only way to protect our inalienable heritage. It is also the only passage to sustainable progress for less privileged groups and nations. Violent conversion is out of the question but unacceptable behavior has to be checked. A sufficient military preparedness exerts a salutary influence on potential troublemakers

The European Union has presently come close to a standstill even if the member countries stitched together a meager compromise on the Reform Treaty, a sort of quasi-constitution. It was promptly sabotaged by an Irish referendum, although Ireland owes the Union its present prosperity. The recruitment of new members is the one thing which keeps up the dynamics and that too is threatened by a xenophobic backlash. Internal consolidation is not necessarily at odds with enlargement. On the contrary, by continued growth the European Union has fulfilled its mission to expand and deepen the plus-sum game in our part of the world. Without this challenge, the Union would have drowned in qualified bickering about minutiae. Only a higher purpose can keep the Union together and turn the members into enduring plus-sum players.

> At present, the EU is in the grip of enlargement fatigue. Muslims evoke allergic reactions, which reflects on the negotiations with Turkey. This indicates a lack of trust in the vitality of our own values. A defense-oriented strategy vis-à-vis Islam is anyhow obsolete and behind time. There are approximately twenty million Muslims within the EU borders; the overwhelming majority are peaceful people who can hardly be expelled. The Muslims do not need to convert to Christianity but they can and they should become good citizens and democrats. Turkey provides a unique opportunity for the European Union to realize its mission. Olli Rehn, the Finnish EU Commissioner for Enlargement, is in *Europe's Next Frontiers* (2006) making a forceful plea for preserving the Turkish option.
>
> In a wider perspective, one can imagine a network of associated countries which would enjoy different degrees of close cooperation without participating in the joint decision making (Norway, Switzerland and Greenland are already in that position). A long list of candidates would range from the rather eligible, like Ukraine, Moldavia and Georgia, to the less plausible such as Russia, Israel and the Maghreb countries. A strong opinion within the EU countries believes that an associated status suffices for Turkey. This would seriously compromise the potential influence of the Union in the Near East and in the Maghreb. Turkey should be accepted in the EU. There are risks but to avoid risk-taking is often a greater risk.

Within the EU there is enduring pressure to harmonize taxation, social welfare, industrial working conditions and so on. Such legislation, at best, brings only marginal utility and sometimes it is outright harmful, tarnishing the image of the Union. A strict adherence to the principle of subsidiarity is the only viable policy. Instead of socio-political fine-tuning, the Union should concentrate on forging a common foreign and defense policy. In this area, the national ambitions are relics from bygone times and change is overdue.

> Common positions on foreign policy and security issues could be controversial but in due course they would create a distinct identity, internally as well as around the world. A community must clearly distinguish itself from its surroundings to earn the respect of its neighbors and the loyalty of its members. A joint appearance on the international scene would at one stroke put the European Union on an equal footing with USA. That would be in the best interests of the United States, too.
>
> A pan-European membership in NATO should be the self-evident first step in this direction. But the aversion of a few smallish countries to the American led coalition makes a breach in the European front and further undermines the influence of the European Union on NATO decisions and policies. The political leaders lack the will or the capability to turn around the conservative opinion in the countries referred to.
>
> Resistance to the integration of foreign relations and the armed forces is massive, though the Reform Treaty ventures a few hesitating steps in that direction. In trade, the EU-commission has a strong mandate but in foreign policy it is a supernumerary. The European Council of government heads, too, is devoid of power in these matters and mostly acts as a discussion club. A serious international crisis is needed to force a rethink among the peoples and the relevant bodies. For example, a single EU-representative in the Security Council of the United Nations would be a significant move.

We cannot have a Europe without Europeans. We sorely need nationally rooted movements which speak for the Union and consistently approach the political problems from the Union point of view. The preconditions are better than one could expect. A recent study shows that a European identity is in the offing, particularly among the young.[3] But constructive proposals are easily drowned by a cacophony of discord from injured special interests and short-sighted populists. A fresh initiative is called for from committed opinion leaders in the individual member countries. In democracies, a small group can eventually achieve a breakthrough if they strongly believe in a worthwhile cause.

The European Union is facing a historic choice. We can drift into an introverted, parochial stance, jealously protecting our local turf. Or we can set about to reform the decision making structure and confer a strong security and foreign policy mandate on the European Union. Immigration and aid to the LDCs should also be elevated to the EU-level. Then the Union could fully participate in preparing the ground for a better, democratic world. This would of course serve its own long-term interests and would require only good cooperation between the members of the Union – still a formidable moral challenge.

After the Second World War, Japan has concentrated on economic growth and kept a very low profile in foreign affairs. The Japanese have stubbornly stuck to their American-dictated constitution which prohibits the establishment of armed forces. Lately the interpretation of the law has been relaxed and an explicit change is in sight. Japan may eventually, like Germany, enter the international arena as a normal nation.

> An extended economic depression has induced the Japanese to re-evaluate their rules for the economic game, too. During Junichiro Koizumi's premiership, the rules and regulations were gradually adjusted and the positive effects of the liberalization have become apparent. But an affirmative foreign policy presupposes that Japan can get rid of its wartime stigma in the eyes of its neighbors.

The participation of Japan is required to maintain the democratic momentum in the region in cooperation with other stable democracies. Russia, too, has a presence in the Far East but it will probably assume a defensive posture; a definitive peace treaty with Japan is still outstanding. Still, Russia's membership in the G8 group, comprising the most influential democracies, implies that it is accepted as a democratic country – at a pinch.

> The G6 group was established in 1975 as an informal collaboration between the heads of state in France, Western Germany, Italy, Japan, the United Kingdom and the United States. (The idea was hatched in Helsinki over lunch during the Conference on Security and Cooperation in Europe.) Canada was invited in 1976, and the name was changed to G8 when Russia was taken on as a full member in 1998. The European Union is also represented by the Chairman of the Commission. The G8 group has no administration of its own; the host countries take their turn in handling the practicalities. Unfortunately, the G8 is hampered by the distorted member structure. One single representative for the European Union would do much to improve the balance.

Originally, the G8 group was focused on the coordination of financial policies but the agenda has been extended to a range of more controversial questions; in 2005 the group formulated an action plan to combat climate change.[4] The raucous and sometimes violent demonstrations during the meetings is a sure sign of growing influence. In any case, the G8 is an attempt to consolidate the forces of democracy. It leaves much to be desired, yet it is a beginning.

14.2 Major Powers in waiting

The political realities are in a state of flux. New major powers are in the offing with rising ambitions.[5] This does not constitute a security threat as long as totalitarian ideologies are kept at bay. There are reasons for cautious optimism. The market economy is becoming generally accepted – if not always in theory, then in practice. Democracy, too, is spreading but in many quarters democratic commitment is fickle and instabilities lurk under the surface.

China with more than 1.3 billion inhabitants is already a major power controlled by a party elite which calls itself communist – the only one-party state in the world of any distinction. The country is also the strongest contender for a super-power status besides the United States, which is producing frowns in Washington. A lot depends on the future development in China; its neighbors are already sensing that China is flexing its muscles.

> Nuclear weapons and missile technology are indispensable trappings for a major power; neither is conventional weaponry neglected. Taiwan is a sore point which comes in handy in regulating political tensions abroad. The relations with Japan are equally useful in manipulating domestic opinion. The demarcation line between Japan and China in the sea north of Taiwan is contested and the quarrel about the oil- and gas-rich area may still become ugly. The tussle for the potential oil finds around the Spratly Islands in the South China Sea is a long-running show with Vietnam, the Philippines and Malaysia as the main opponents. China has lately modified its stance towards the neighboring countries and the situation seems to be under control – as long as it suits China.

Today China is communist only in name, if that, and it has no ambitions to disseminate either Marxism, Maoism or socialism beyond its borders. The history of China indicates that the present regime will transform into a dynasty, headed by a nominally omnipotent Emperor/party chief, surrounded by a host of bureaucrats. As far as the power structure is capable of delivering enough material goods and goodies it is sitting pretty. Otherwise, the people start to grumble and the dynasty is deemed to have forfeited its heavenly mandate. The reforms tend to come too late and, if anything, hasten the revolutionary upheaval.

This scenario has been repeated in China over and over again, but times have now changed. There is no return from the market-oriented reforms which inevitably will transform the societal structure. Education is surging at all levels and the Chinese are open to foreign influences as never before. Foreign investment, domestic savings, industrial production and foreign trade have been growing in tandem, and the annual BNP-increase has for several years been spectacular, holding steady at around ten percent – with no sign of abating. China is sitting on a massive currency surplus and Chinese companies and sovereign funds are investing heavily abroad.

> The economy is racing ahead but difficulties are accumulating. The income differences are increasing and the countryside with its 800 million inhabitants is left behind. The peasants do not even own their land and the unemployed are threatening to deluge the cities, while working conditions and environmental control are in bad straits. The infrastructure is bursting at the seams and the state owned banks are not yet fully consolidated. Worst of all is the rising wave of corruption and administrative arbitrariness; the judiciary is still under development, to say the least. To top it all, the demographic situation is worrisome as a consequence of the successful one child policy.

China will, for sure, sort out the acute problems but setbacks are unavoidable if the administration is unwilling or unable to come to grips with the basic problems. Serious economic reverses are dangerous for a regime when its legitimacy is entirely built on increasing prosperity; internal feuding among the power brokers would add fuel to the fire. In such a case, the leaders can easily resort to nationalistic rants and posturing.

China has distanced itself from the mendacity and cruelty of Maoism but a clear repudiation of the past is not on the political agenda. Decision making is dominated by economic pragmatism and a rather moderate nationalism. Even so, the interests of the ruling party elite always come first, though confrontation with an ever more articulate public opinion may deliver a few surprises in the not too distant future.

India has close to 1.1 billion inhabitants and will probably surpass China around 2035 as the most populous country in the world. India is first in class among democratic less developed countries, but the economy has been lagging. While China after Mao's death discarded the obsolete Marxist dogmas, India is still hamstrung by considerable socialist ballast. Plenty has been heaved overboard but the economy is still trammeled by deep-seated political prejudices.

> Astoundingly, India enjoys less freedom of trade than China. In many sectors, industry is regulated in minute detail which provides feeding ground for an army of corrupt officials. The labor market is overregulated and inflexible. The bureaucracy is overstaffed and ineffective; everything takes much more time than in China. Foreign investment is on the increase but still only a fraction of the capital entering China.

Despite these handicaps, India has started to close the gap between its own and the Chinese economic growth rate. The countries have many things in common. The green revolution has secured the production of food, but the backward agriculture still employs the major part of the population. Cheap labor is obviously the main competitive weapon even if the supply of educated manpower is soaring. In both countries, the infrastructure is straggling and the banks are shaky. Nevertheless, both have managed to maintain respectable armed forces, including nuclear weapons.

Even if China demonstrates impressive economic dynamism, demography and democracy give India a strategic edge. However, the traditional caste system and newfangled socialist 'gains' are hampering development. If the country manages to shake off these historic burdens and release the inherent entrepreneurship of the population, nothing can prevent India from rising to the superpower class.

Brazil with its close to 200 million inhabitants is the uncontested number one of *Latin America*. But Brazilians speak Portuguese which could be a problem for the Spanish speaking countries, with Mexico (106 millions) and Colombia (43 millions) in the van. The situation is further complicated by Mexico's membership in NAFTA (North American Free Trade Area), dominated by the United States. A seemingly inexhaustible stream of irritants precludes the acceptance of USA as the guiding political light in the region.

> OAS (Organization of American States) was founded 1948 as a loose umbrella organization; only Cuba was excluded at a later stage. The United States has repeatedly attempted to improve the economic relations. The Free Trade Area of the Americas (FTAA) is the latest initiative. Talks started 1994 but have gone nowhere. Instead, bilateral deals have been concluded with Chile, Peru and the Dominican Republic

among others. The treaty with Colombia is presently held up in Congress and other negotiations are pending. Mercosur, a free trade area comprising Brazil, Argentina, Uruguay and Paraguay, was established as a counterweight but has been floundering.

Counting about 500 million inhabitants, Latin America should anyhow aspire to a seat among the major powers. In international forums, Brazil has assumed the position as spokesman for the third world, for instance in the World Trade Organization (WTO) and in the G20 group which is a contact group for the largest less developed countries. Even so it is difficult to see how the country could establish itself as a major power without the support of all Latin America. UNASUR (UNASUL is the Portuguese abbreviation), the Union of South American Nations is aiming at an extended free trade area but exists largely on paper. As it is, Latin America will continue to pull below its weight in world affairs.

Indonesia with 240 million inhabitants is the most populous Muslim country. The dominant Islamic faith is of a very moderate variety. The attempts to radicalize the population by sporadic terrorism have fizzled out. Indonesia has recently made significant progress towards a sustainable democracy and may soon be vying with Turkey for the top position in the Muslim league. The country is hardly pushing for major power status and is currently content with playing a leading role in ASEAN (Association of Southeast Asian Nations). The organization has ten member states and its main task is to facilitate trade. It also a counter to China's increasing dominance in the region.

Pakistan with 162 million inhabitants still features a rather high fertility (3.58). Its democratic credentials are meager despite a relatively free press and open access to the internet. Since its inception, the country has been balancing on the brink of military dictatorship and it has repeatedly crossed that line. Pakistan is the only Muslim country with nuclear weaponry and, with or without the consent of the authorities, it has contributed to the spread of the relevant technology to Iran, among other places. President Musharraf has worked in liaison with the United States in fighting terrorism but it made him deeply impopular.[6] His dictatorial powers are now a thing of the past and Pakistan is again making a try at democracy.

Musharraf's volte-face was a disappointment for al-Qaeda and a takeover in Pakistan is certainly still at the top of its wish list. The country would be an ideal base with its nuclear weapons and vast population. The potential instability poses a latent threat of civil war and the border disagreement with India does not help even if relations have been improving.

Pakistan exemplifies the dilemma of the Islamic states. The democratic legitimacy of the leaders is questionable or non-existent and they have to rely on the support of a corrupt elite and conservative mullahs. Diverse fundamentalists do their utmost to make life miserable for the rulers, but a seizure of power is unlikely; the Taliban victory in Afghanistan was an exception. The common people are uninformed and easily manipulated but have no yearning for Jihad, the holy war. The middle class is growing but has little political influence. The military and the secret police are the real guarantors of stability.

Today, the only ideologically undemocratic bastions in the world are the core countries of Mohammedan conservatism, each one in it own way. But even the Muslim lifestyle is eventually changing as traditions and beliefs are eroded and relaxed. No wonder that religious fanatics regard their world view as threatened, and are driven to desperate action. Their only hope is to provoke a religious war that would resurrect and activate the Ummah, the worldwide community of Muslims.

Such a united front is not in sight. Neither are building blocks at hand for a major Muslim power which could represent the legitimate interests of the Islamic states. Pakistan, Bangladesh and Indonesia will for now go their separate ways; in the end they might come together in a loose confederation with India as an anchor. For the Arab countries, unification looks easier but internal strife has deep roots and Iran is anyhow beyond the pale. Despite its oil riches, the Islamic world remains marginalized, increasing the mutual distrust and impeding the democratic mission.

14.3 Rogue and failed states

On our relatively ordered globe, there are still states which constitute a threat to the outside world. Despite their limited resources, they produce disproportionate trouble for the international community. Biological weapons will soon be within reach of most countries and the situation is getting worse when presumptive rogue states aim to obtain nuclear weapons. The use of weapons of mass destruction will, however, have serious repercussions for the domestic population; thus their main utility is blackmail.

IAEA (International Atomic Energy Agency) is supervising the production of fissionable material. The organization is backed by an international agreement (Treaty on the Non-Proliferation of Nuclear Weapons, NPT) which was ratified by all countries except India*, Israel, Pakistan and the Cook Islands (!). Unperturbed, North Korea delivered its notice of termination on January 10 2003 with immediate effect. This is typical of international agreements on knotty questions. The well-behaved countries do not really need any treaties and the bad boys just ignore them; either they do not sign up, or they cheat or revoke their participation whenever it suits them.

The earth will remain an insecure abode as long as criminal regimes have a free reign in procuring weapons of mass destruction. All the suspect states are controlled by small power elites which tenaciously cling to their positions and prerogatives. North Korea exemplifies the desperation of such gangs in the face of economic disaster; hazardous blackmail is the only way out. Irrational aggression can also be released by ideological frustration when a traditional value system is under threat.

The Shiah mullahs of Iran have evidently decided to get hold of nuclear weapons, not least to compete with Sunni Pakistan for the leadership of the Muslim world. The IAEA has repeatedly caught Iran for transgressions against the non-proliferation treaty. Presenting ridiculous evasions, Iran maintains the pretence of peaceful aims. The international community has so far been content with issuing protests; the mild sanctions of the Security Council are symbolic. No strong countermeasures are in sight and Iran will probably go nuclear, barring the unilateral intervention of Israel, as happened in Iraq when the French Osiris reactor was bombed to smithereens in 1981.

To forestall future nuclear attacks by rogue states, the United States is in the process of erecting a missile defense. Most of the world will remain open to nuclear blackmail and everyone is equally vulnerable to sophisticated terrorist attacks. There is not even an international organization to contain the threat of biological weapons. This might be as well in the light of the IAEA and NPT experience. Instead, friendly countries have established unofficial cooperation structures.

Most important of all, the terrorists should be denied a sanctuary in, or the support of any country. A breach of this principle is in itself a legitimate cause of war which should trigger appropriate measures by the Security Council or, in the case of decision paralysis, by some coalition of the willing. The role of the United States as the world cop has already been discussed. In fact, no other country has come for-

---

* India has recently become a de-facto signatory.

ward and embarrassingly few have been prepared to follow the sheriff in an international posse.

> The terrorist outrage of 9.11.2001 and the decisive action of the United States changed the attitudes to terrorism around the world. Violence against civilians can no more be justified by the struggle for freedom or independence; terrorism has become politically inexpedient. In Northern Ireland, the IRA/Sinn Fein choose to refrain from violence after many years of armed struggle, which opened the door to reconciliation. Neither Libya nor Syria wants to pose as terrorist sanctuaries any more. On the other hand, authoritarian regimes find it easier to suppress a legitimate opposition under the pretext of terrorism. The Andijan bloodbath in Uzbekistan in 2005 serves as an example.

To draw the line between right and wrong in this legal and moral quagmire is not an easy task. The military action in Afghanistan was supported by world opinion whereas the intervention in Iraq is controversial to say the least. Political and military considerations get in the way of putative strikes against Iran or North Korea, even if they would be justifiable. Trade boycotts are occasionally effective, provided that all the neighbors are committed. Waiting for a better international order we have to extemporize one day and one year at a time – hoping for the best and preparing for the worst.

Principally in Africa there are a number of states in different degrees of dissolution. These failed states are unstable and are mostly governed by dictators of variable longevity. In the absence of an outside intervention, the situation looks hopeless and no end to the sufferings of the people can be perceived. The streams of refugees multiply the problem. Liberia and Somalia have been discussed but unfortunately they are not unique. In the Congo, anarchy has for long been the normal condition, and Zimbabwe is heading in the same direction; Sudan, Sierra Leone and the Ivory Coast are on the fringe of civil war. Haiti is the most prominent failed state outside Africa.

> When genocide is imminent, the UN statutes prescribe immediate intervention but the Security Council has regularly acted too late and too feebly. The aborted intervention in Ruanda, when up to one million humans were slaughtered, is the biggest scandal in the history of the United Nations. East Timor was presented as a rare example of a successful UN-mission, but the country crashed soon after independence due to internal strife and still relies on foreign policing forces.

In Sudan the UN representatives have carefully avoided describing the bloodletting in Darfur as genocide to avoid exposing the lack of decisiveness. The AU (African Union) was constituted in 2002 with highflying goals but its operations, for instance in Somalia, have been inept. Resolute interventions by Great Britain (in Sierra Leone) and France (in the Ivory Coast) show that order can be restored with very limited means.

Many African countries are on the skids and totally dependant on outside support. The grip of incompetent central governments has contributed to the decay, but federalist constitutions along tribal lines have not fared much better. In any case, a durable democratization of the failed or collapsing states is impracticable without help from the outside world. But the present praxis is a glorious mess. On average, thirty different organizations vie for the opportunity to offer support to a less developed country. This cannot go on.

An authoritative European inquiry has mapped out the situation and produced a comprehensive report.[7] It concludes that the collapse of states is not a passing phenomenon but depends on the present international order – or rather the disorder. The report presents three scenarios: a malign one, a benign one and a third called the re-colonization scenario. Kosovo, Sierra Leone, the Ivory Coast, Afghanistan and Iraq are seen as relevant precedents for the last alternative.

"Contrary to nineteenth century colonization, a new trend towards shared sovereignty could be undertaken in negotiation with local populations and with a view to restoring security and welfare services that many of them have not known for a long time. This would imply not only a radical rethinking of post-1945 ideas concerning state sovereignty in the former Third World, but also the reappearance of a sense of international mission and/or duty in EU countries. It would require EU military forces to reorganize for a new type of mission that is neither old-fashioned war nor entirely humanitarian assistance."

The inquiry was published in December 2003 but created no response because it was simply silenced to death as politically incorrect. The ghosts of history are haunting the politicians. Most people with a say in these matters are tied to and benefit from the present hopelessly inefficient system, and nobody carries responsibility for the outcome; there is always somebody else to blame when things go wrong. Yet a resolute intervention would in many cases provide the best development aid and concurrently stem the migration pressure and all its unwelcome consequences.

Failed states have forfeited their sovereignty and require a credible outside authority which can reform the politics, create a capable administration and pave the way for sustainable democracy. A failed state could be adopted by one of the major democracies, for instance the EU or one of its member states, which would assume the responsibility for the political, economic and social development. Sovereignty would be suspended for a while, but the establishment of law and order, together with appropriate support efforts, should soon produce concrete results at the grass root level. The build-up of crucial trust capital would facilitate productive plus-sum play across the board.

An international mandate for such an adoption is difficult to imagine in the present political atmosphere. Neither can the acquiescence of the local power brokers be assured. But the most difficult task would be to recruit candidates for the guardianship mission. It is much easier to dole out money along the old lines. If the European Union or the whole international community could agree on the failure of the present policies then, at least, a sensible discussion would be possible.

State and nation building is a great challenge and the old colonial powers usually failed miserably. But India is an encouraging exception and the success of the United States in post-war Germany and Japan is equally remarkable. The intervention in South Korea was also successful but the Vietnam War was a serious reverse. In Afghanistan and Iraq the situation is wide open, but at least the people have a reasonable chance of building a better future. Most of the failed states in the world have in practice been abandoned by the international community. Temporary measures sometimes produce a false dawn which is again and again extinguished by violence and corruption. But hope lives eternally. In Liberia the election of President Ellen Johnson-Sirleaf in 2005 raised expectations, which have not yet come to grief.

In Bosnia and Kosovo the European Union has de facto assumed a re-colonialist responsibility and the same goes for Australia in the South-West Pacific.[8] A guardian state must exert uncontested control over its operational area to guarantee security and thus promote private investment. Its activities will be closely watched which should ensure fairness and keep the unavoidable use of force to a minimum. A protracted engagement is in nobody's interest. When the internal plus-sum game is initiated, the guardianship can step by step transform into a genuine partnership, democratic self-government and full sovereignty.

14.4 Global governance

From time to time, the dream of world domination has crossed the minds of psychopathic despots; its latest incarnation was the power-madness of Hitler, Stalin and Mao Zedong. Let us hope that such expressions of personal self-realization belong to bygone times. But the dream of world government persists in many minds even if no credible global constitution has been presented. The blessings of the idea itself are rarely denied. Only the implementation is seen as a problem.

I maintain that the legitimate global exercise of power is an unsolvable equation. Whatever way democratic principles are applied, a monopoly on forceful means is indispensable, as are enforceable rules for the administration, the judiciary and, above all, for the appointment and dismissal of those in power. Without such a structure society will fall apart. In the gigantic organization, corruption will grow like a cancer and will be ever harder to curb. Sooner or later the outcome will be stagnation, decay and breakdown.

> It would be interesting to carry out a strict game-theoretic analysis of the problems of a world government. It is hard to believe that a stable homeostasis could prevail in a worldwide society; change is what keeps societies on track. And without competition between nations there is no need for change in the long term. Imperial China in its self-sufficiency is an instructive simulation model for global governance. Time and again, the country was driven into anarchy by way of stagnation.

During a world government, liberty will crumble. No country can exit the political community and find its own way. Individuals are burdened with the same lack of alternatives; radically different environments would be non-existent. Creativity will be short-changed for conformity, truth seeking for political correctness. Without genuine alternatives, speechifying about cultural diversity becomes just that much lip-service. Even if democratic formality could be maintained for some time, any combination of unfavorable circumstances could bring on a state of weakness and indecision. Then the peoples will clamor for the certainties of a new, tranquil world and its irremovable potentates.

> Presently, the United Nations and its organs seem to be above the law; they cannot be touched in any court. Soldiers in the service of the United Nations are exempt from prosecution despite overwhelming evidence of breach of duty, misbehavior and outright crime. At least

those were the principles confirmed by a Dutch Court on July 10 2008. The broad immunity implied could be a foretaste of things to come.

Before proceeding, the need for global coordination should be analyzed in more detail. The avoidance of a new, utterly destructive world war occupies pole position. So far this calamity has been avoided by the otherwise cantankerous international community. Next in order are the unruly rogue states which have been dealt with in the previous section. Most of the constructive tasks are already attended to by existing international bodies.

> The reader has already been confronted with a multitude of unpronounceable mnemonics which designate international cooperative organizations. The list could be greatly extended but it is easier to point at the remaining gaps and weaknesses. The defense against asteroid impact requires more structured international collaboration. The management of climate change lacks an authoritative coordination organ. The IPCC does not live up to this role, but the World Trade Organization (WTO) could be the right body to impose a global carbon dioxide tax. The control of contagious diseases is a common task, especially when a pandemic is looming. And deep-sea fishing should be strictly regulated by an international body to avoid imminent overfishing.
>
> Like all public bureaucracies, the United Nations has an inbuilt tendency to acquire new tasks, to extend its organization and to expand its budget. There is no shortage of urgent problems which are deemed to require the intervention or at least investigation by the UN or its associated bodies. The syndrome, so well known at the national level, is reappearing in a global format; all the aberrations of socialist centralized authority are haunting us under the aegis of the United Nations.

It bears repeating that poverty is not an affliction which can be remedied by superordinate global institutions. The task must be dealt with locally or regionally, supported by factual help and prudent capital injections. The same goes for the associated problems of deforestation, water supplies, soil erosion and salinization, as well as other local environmental challenges. Small scale assistance in the form of education and other means of knowledge transmission are advisable, but massive monetary support is usually more of a hindrance than a help. The population issue, too, must be managed locally. Every country has to straighten out its own over- or underpopulation. Large scale migrations are always destabilizing and sometimes destructive.

Many UN-organizations carry out valuable work but the United Nations as a political instrument was a stillborn idea. In the aftermath of the Second World War, the ambition was to master all the world problems in one fell swoop. Yet real progress generally takes place as a sequence of small steps, one item at a time. That is what has happened within or without the framework of the United Nations. A number of voluntary but very useful cooperative vehicles have emerged. On the other hand, the efforts to strengthen the UN politically seem to be doomed. No major powers will submit to UN authority when even minor nations defy the Security Council without serious consequences.

Disregarding misgivings on principle, it seems practically impossible to construct a plausible political mechanism which would bolster the authority of the United Nations. The divergence in population, resources, power and democratic maturity locates both adequate representation and a responsible executive in never-never land. The UN court (International Court of Justice) has been depressingly powerless; its verdicts have been habitually ignored. The rise in pirate assaults off Somalia's shores is an ominous sign even though UNCLOS (United Nations Convention on the Law of the Seas) permits forceful intervention.

International justice is highly ambiguous and mostly dependant on the good will of the parties; a court without a police force at its disposal is actually a contradiction in terms. Even the proceedings against well-known mass-murderers, for example in Ruanda and Cambodia, have a deplorable tendency to fizzle out and turn into travesties of justice. A permanent International Criminal Court has been established to supplant the present ad hoc justice. The court is supported by more than one hundred nations, but the United States, China and Russia among others have so far refused to ratify the underlying treaty; the authority of the court will be correspondingly curtailed.

Instead of aiming at utopian goals, we can augment existing voluntary organizations. The WTO has been a success ever since its forerunner, GATT (General Agreement on Tariffs and Trade), was founded in 1947. China joined in 2001 and Saudi Arabia, Vietnam and Ukraine are the latest arrivals, with Russia on the verge of signing on. Soon only the international pariahs are absent.

There are many other examples of successful international plus-sum games which often feature a low media profile. The World Commission on Dams (WCD) was a collaborative project of 53 public, private and non-governmental organizations. The upshot was an extensive report (Dams and Development, 2000) analyzing about one thousand dam building projects, including detailed recommendations for the governments of the countries concerned. The mission was completed in a good two years.[9]

The ITU (International Telecommunication Union) was founded in 1865 and is an early example of international self-organization; national bodies are now receding into the background. The Internet has spontaneously spread across national boundaries and the World Wide Web provides access to a network of information sources. W_3C (World Wide Web Consortium) has taken on the role of a self-appointed global coordinator without any bureaucratic interference.

> Tim Berners-Lee invented the Web in 1989 when he worked for CERN, the European Organization for Nuclear Research; he has been the leader of W_3C since its beginning. The task of the Consortium is, according to its web site, to be a web for everyone on everything. A hotspot is the development of XML (Extensible Markup Language) which intends to facilitate information exchange on the web irrespective of format.
>
> The Consortium has more than 400 members and is managed by MIT/CSAIL (Massachusetts Institute of Technology, Computer Science and Artificial Intelligence Laboratory), ERCIM (European Research Consortium for Informatics and Mathematics) and the Keio University in Japan. The work is done by voluntary teams and supported by extensive consultations. The tiny budget keeps the membership fees at a very reasonable level – a few thousand dollars for institutions and smallish companies, big companies pay about ten times more.

Can international self-organization comprise political decision making, too? The answer is affirmative. The EU and NATO are the best examples. Can the cooperation become worldwide? In the motley progression of utopians, Immanuel Kant stands out as the most clearheaded. In *Zum ewigen Frieden** (1795) he puts forward three conditions for a workable global confederation. The first precondition is democratic regimes in all participating countries. Secondly, the cooperation must be founded on agreements between independent states. And finally, every country shall have the right to restrict immigration according to its own lights.

> In *The Shield of Achilles* (2002), Philip Bobbitt presents a thorough historic analysis of international jurisprudence and the strategic alternatives of the democracies in a world of new threats and conflicts. He concludes that international law and order can be ascertained only when the primary actors negotiate new treaties on a contingent, case by case basis. All-encompassing agreements are habitually vague and unenforceable to boot. In a later work, *Terror and Consent: The Wars for the Twenty-first Century* (2008), Bobbitt envisions an open world

---

* *Perpetual Peace* (on the web)

of 'market states' where the sovereignty of nations is eroded by their increasing interdependence and the global commitment to basic human rights. No more will wars focus on the destruction of an enemy but on its resurrection thus undermining the terrorist cause.

The G8 group referred to has perhaps the best chances to become the embryo for a worldwide political collaboration. The membership of China, India and Brazil is already under discussion and would render additional weight to its deliberations.[10] Further extrapolation opens up interesting perspectives. Ad hoc agreements between the major powers would gradually prepare a stable foundation for global co-operation and international jurisdiction. The United Nations would remain in the political margin but could serve as a forum for countries with a grievance. It would then function as world conscience and act as a superior court based on moral authority.

If we boldly assume global democratization and concomitant prosperity in the world, the consequence will be that economic strength will be distributed roughly in proportion to the population. If we furthermore presume regional self-organization on the EU-model, the world will be divided into perhaps a dozen political blocks. Everyone would be untouchable and sufficient onto themselves – no one would need to be anxious about their neighbors. In such an atmosphere it would be possible for these major powers to assume joint responsibility for the ways of the world without the burden of a formally superior entity. They would cover the overwhelming majority of the global population. The remaining small nations could find accommodation under the protection of a neighboring power.

14.5 A diverse humanity

In the foregoing, I have with supreme confidence presumed that a democratic mission will provide the solution to all the problems of the world. This postulate has two aspects. Firstly, is such a mission practicable? Secondly, would a democratized world meet the high expectations?

China is in key position regarding question number one. With China on board the wave of democratization would be well-nigh unstoppable. But where is China headed? Nobody knows, least of all the Chinese. Will the expanding middle class allow itself to be manipulated or will it press for influence through elected bodies? The Chinese leaders are already cautiously experimenting with local elections and media relaxation. Properly timed reforms could release the pressure and avoid a destructive explosion.

A benign development is looking increasingly probable as living standards are improving and the middle class is becoming more assertive. A pragmatic leadership of the communist party may be capable of accepting democratization by stealth, just as they did in introducing the market economy. The other alternative is social commotion with a very uncertain outcome.

> China's history is interspersed by violent outbreaks of popular discontent which time and again have precipitated regime shifts. Here an old French adage applies. The more things change, the more they stay the same. Genuine change requires time and patience, headlong upheavals tend to repeat or even magnify past errors in new guises. Mao was the latest exponent of this revolutionary reflex. His flagrant abuses and the attendant economic collapse provided the impulse for a gradual system shift initiated in 1978 by Deng Xiaoping (1902–97).
>
> Chinese culture has many features which are hard to reconcile with a democratic society, at least on the Western model. Respect for authority is deeply rooted and individual rights are basically subordinated to societal and collective interests, which all too often mean the interests of the ruling bureaucracy. Truth and liberty do not have the same intrinsic value as in Christian cultures but have habitually given way to the realities of power play; the rulers could usually carry on, untroubled by embarrassing revelations. The Confucian ideal is enlightened autocracy. Open confrontation is offensive and independent centers of power unacceptable. Initially a Chinese democracy will probably follow the Hong Kong or the Singapore rather than the Taiwan model.

The surrounding world can contribute to Chinese democracy by supporting all aspects of the mutual plus-sum game. Free trade and open information stimulates interaction and understanding as do contacts established in science, art and sport. China's inferiority complex is a liability; self-respect and respect for other nations goes hand in hand. The successful organization of the Olympic Games 2008 will hopefully consolidate Chinese self-esteem.

Otherwise not much can be done beyond China's borders to promote democracy. Nationalist posturing could be ignored but open aggression must be countered. There is a risk that the legitimate ambitions of a major power transform into an arrogant foreign policy. The surrounding world must make clear that this route is blocked. The cooperation of the democratic countries may still be severely tested. The European Union has followed the example of the United States and maintained the weapon embargo against China as a protest against the violations of human rights. So far, so good.

The Muslim world is the second big question mark for the future of a democratic mission. The Islamic theocracy is, for the time being, the only ideological alternative to democracy and its most militant followers adhere to the dream of world domination. Under pressure from the expanding secularization, they desperately fight back to provoke a religious war. This objective has so far been frustrated and the United States has mounted an ideological counteroffensive. Ill-advised or not, the main idea of the military interventions in Afghanistan and Iraq was (and is) to display the blessings of democracy for the Muslims.

> We have already delved into the difficulties of this task. Afghanistan was a failed country and the challenge was accentuated by ethnic splits and militant Islamic traditions; the country has always been ungovernable. Afghanistan represents a demanding test for external guardianship.
>
> In contrast, Iraq was a centralized, rogue state with relatively high living standards and corresponding self-esteem. Thanks to its oil, Iraq is economically well off but it is uncertain if the newly-established democratic regime can build up enough authority. Economically, Afghanistan will call for extended artificial respiration while in Iraq the politics needs outside buttressing. The road from anarchy or tyranny to democracy is long, winding and treacherous, however beneficent the guidance.

Nevertheless, the majority of the Islamic countries are rather stable even if many of them have an authoritarian government. They are no threat to their surroundings, neither is their disintegration imminent. The best policy is, without doubt, to stay on the sidelines and let time pass. Peaceful reform movements certainly deserve quiet support but in general we must trust the intrinsic strength of democratic ideas. Only exceptional circumstances can justify tough measures. And there is always the risk that the outcome of free elections is of the type 'one person, one vote, one time' with militant Islamists in the driver's seat. Algeria and Palestine provide examples of 'wrong' election results.

What would a reasonably democratic world be like? A democracy has the fundamental right to continuously redefine itself within a broad framework.[11] Free elections, a market economy and respect for human rights are the minimum prerequisites set forth by the Paris declaration of 1990, which formally put an end to the cold war.[12] Every democracy has to find its own forms for human cohabitation and realize its own plus-sum game – independently, or within the frame of a self-selected confederation, federation or something in between, like the European Union. The upshot will probably be a multitude of dissimilar democracies.

Democratic fundamentalism prescribes direct people power on the Athenian model, and the rise in education combined with electronic communication has improved the objective preconditions for direct democracy. But practical experience as well as theoretical considerations calls for great caution. At the crossroads of representative and direct democracy, the European Union has in its quasi-constitution rhetorically opted for 'participatory democracy'.

> A vast electronic assembly cannot negotiate compromises and may not be capable of taking difficult but necessary decisions (in representative democracies they are generally postponed beyond the next election). Populism is always lurking in the shadows, and an unfiltered popular opinion tends to vacillate between extremes. In the spring of 1938 the will of the Austrian people in a few weeks swung from enthusiastic support for independence to an equally great enthusiasm for submitting to Hitler.[13]
>
> A clear trend towards direct democracy is not on the cards. If anything, the core democracies have begun to de-politicize complex decisions. The value of money is too important to be left in the hands of unreliable politicians, not to mention a capricious popular vote. The trusted experts must, on the contrary, be protected against political interference; the independence of central banks is indeed approaching the level of the judiciary.

Every democracy will in due course learn from its own mistakes and perhaps also from the mistakes of others. Generalizations about different kinds of constitutions with highly variable election and judiciary systems, divisions of power and administrative rules are generally unproductive. The institutional background is historically conditioned, adapted to local circumstances and subject to the will of the people according to democratically accepted rules of the game. To predict the future outcome of human culture in all its expressions would be even more futile. The richness of variety will be enormous and the freedom of choice will fill the needs of every conceivable hue. If all goes well, the abundance will not be restricted to material utilities and pleasurable toys but also comprise a sufficient measure of good will.

> We are on our way towards a society where profit-seeking businesses encounter competition from voluntary and unpaid teamwork. Open

information platforms such as the Web, Linux and Wikipedia are striking examples. Private foundations already finance a significant part
of scientific research and high art, and public-private partnerships are
proliferating in many areas.[14] The collection of money is big business.
In the United States, a round two percent of BNP, about 250 billion
dollars, was donated to charitable purposes in 2004; regrettably abuses tend to increase in proportion.[15]

The hypothetical superpowers will be free to realize their intentions
within a broad framework of voluntary international agreements
which serve their joint superordinate interests – rogue states will not
be tolerated. If democracy is the dominant form of government, as we
hope, the risk of violent conflicts is much reduced; democracies will
hardly be at each others' throats. But this is not an indispensable condition. If all the superpowers have nuclear counter-strike capability
they can feel safe. In a nuclear war there are no victors; presumptive
world rulers are kept at bay.

Nevertheless, opportunities will remain for ill-intentioned people to
create havoc. An unpleasant super-virus could, for instance, throw a
spanner in the international cooperation machinery and perhaps create escalating conflict. But this is the price of liberty. Absolute security
is out of this world. The question also arises of whether world peace
is compatible with even a reduced nuclear capability. But trust is the
driver of disarmament, not the other way round. As time goes by, the
need for nuclear insurance will diminish and perhaps vanish. The main
point is that the nice boys must have the best weapons; a putative im-
perator should not be led into temptation.

The only threat to a superpower comes from the inside. If the plus-
sum game fails miserably, disintegration might be unavoidable. It is
not unthinkable, though less likely, that such a calamity could befall
a democracy. From this point of view too, the future of the European
Union is pivotal. A failure would make our part of the world impotent
and deprive us of control of our own affairs. Europe would also fail in
its mission as a guide for supra-national consolidation.

The EU has been the model for regional cooperation around the world.
NAFTA and ASEAN are rather well-established free trade areas whereas the AU (African Union) and UNASUR are still in the starting blocks.
A setback in Europe would further delay the indispensable consolidation on other continents.

In future, the competitive edge will emerge from a superior capability to play plus-sum games at all levels and in all contexts. A momentous challenge is to devise cooperative rules for the nations within a developing superpower structure. The experience of the European Union shows that it is a lengthy learning process – the US model cannot be copied outright. It will take time and time is short. Even if the nuclear threat recedes and the population explosion fizzles out, there are other known and unknown instabilities in the offing that may upset the political and ecological balance. There is no time to loose, either for the EU or for other potential superpowers.

Competition between the supranational power blocks would not necessarily cause political tensions; more probably it will exert a stabilizing effect. In any case it will be a driver of creativity and cultural diversity all around. We can already discern the first signs of noble competition, for example in space research and sports events. In an ideal world of competing democratic powers, human creativity should finally come into its own.

Culture potential grows roughly in proportion to the population involved in creative interaction. Though only a minor part of humanity has been offered full participation in the global plus-sum game, a remarkable upswing is already in evidence. When the majority get a chance to cooperate in real time we enter an era which defies our powers of prediction and even our imagination. The possibilities are boundless but the risks grow in proportion. When navigating in these treacherous waters, we lack adequate charts and are all the more dependent on a reliable moral compass.

Will we proceed in the direction indicated? It is not a certainty but I challenge whomsoever to present a program more worthy of success. Where are we headed? We have only the faintest idea. When do we arrive? We will never arrive. The key questions are these: Do we really believe in our own values? Are we ready to grasp the chance to build a better world which, for the first time in history, is within reach? Ultimately, our task is not to predict the future but to form it.

Chapter 15
The moral challenge

Everybody can contribute to the common fund of moral capital by te-
naciously searching a higher directive. Pragmatism is the tacit platform
for productive plus-sum play but pragmatism must, like democracy, be
steeped in a higher meaning. I am calling for a modern theology which
would integrate our essential insights and experiences in the light of
disparate beliefs. A democracy cannot work without democrats but
no superhumans are required to mold our future, only customary (or
uncustomary) civil courage. Faith in God, faith in the future and a
sound self-confidence are all connected, independent of religious or
ideological quibbles. It is so terribly simple. Openness and honesty
suffice – the good will to search for a shared truth. The love for and
of God cannot be distinguished from the love for thy neighbor, the
superior plus-sum game.

15.1 The faithful servant

It is time for closing the books. What is the sum total of what has been
said? I have enlarged on the need for moral capital in democracies,
but communities cannot possess morality. It is reserved for individual
human beings who not only cling to the common rules of the game
but want to do something more. The Good Samaritan in the Gospel of
St. Luke has become the epitome of the charitable human who volun-
tarily shoulders responsibility, inconvenience and expenses in helping
an alien in distress.

The choice of the Samaritan is simple. He could pass by, or stay and
help. If passing by, his lack of compassion would be manifest and if
morally endowed, he would feel guilty. But if one is part of a crowd,
the individual responsibility is diluted and it can happen that nobody
heeds the call for help, even if the greater part would act differently
when singled out. This is the dilemma of democracy. Refraining from
taking part, we become a member of the large class of free-riders who
deny society its wholehearted support. In the international community
the situation is much worse.

In *The Shield of Achilles*, Philip Bobbitt uses a nasty murder in Queens, New York, as a metaphor for the ineptitude of the international community confronted with the ethnic cleansing in the former Yugoslavia 1991–95. Kitty Genovese, a 29 year old bar manager, was stabbed in the middle of the night and finally murdered in a drawn-out process. Twice the murderer retreated, frightened by lights in the windows and shouts from the neighboring high-rise buildings. But when nobody appeared or called the police he came back and finished off the victim.

In Bosnia a similar situation prevailed. Years of crimes against humanity could pass without anybody intervening in earnest. Numerous organizations were engaged but for that very reason the atrocities could continue. I am citing Bobbitt: "No previous crises had been so flooded by helpful agencies: the European Union appointed mediators, offered peace plans, constitutions; the CSCE deployed its array of dispute resolution institutions; the UN was present to a degree that has, I believe, permanently damaged that institution; NATO was involved; and finally there was, of course, the Contact Group of the Great Powers." Currently, Sudan is playing hide and seek in Darfur with the international community.

Intrepid, independent yet loyal individuals constitute the gist, the moral fiber of every organization or society.[1] Democracies, in particular, are dependant on this scarce resource. Like salt in the food or yeast in the dough, such self-motivated citizens are a vitalizing force, actuating the commitment of their compatriots to a common cause. We owe our freedom and prosperity to the moral investments of bygone generations. But what happens if the salt loses its savor – if the quest for individual self-realization is strangling civic responsibility and threatens the very existence of future generations?

> The emphasis on the private is degenerating into unscrupulous egoism in the guise of a libertarian ideology. Anonymity eliminates the social control of our conduct and increases the scope for moral minus-sum games. Not without cause, alcoholics and drug addicts in group therapy have to be sincere to eliminate any self-deception. To confess our sins and repent has always been the road to edification and rehabilitation even though our diabolic pride revolts against the humiliation. Openness and honesty are and will remain the pillars of all plus-sum games.

These spiritual dilemmas will stay with us. There is no way to ensure the supply of moral capital. By common consent, we can try to make life easier for the genuine plus-sum players and render life more difficult for the free-riders. But who should take the initiative in such measures which do not serve the interest of a specific person or interest group but only the common weal. We are back at square one.

The latest advances in brain research point at a limited area in the frontal lobe as a center for superordinate coordination. Lesions in this area weaken self-control, long-term decision making and strategic learning. If the defect originates early in life, emotional detachment and a generally psychopathic personality may ensue. Religion too has been ascribed a specific address. In *The Ethical Brain* (2005), Michael Gazzaniga postulates a site in the temporal lobe because a type of epilepsy, which is rooted in this area, correlates with hyper-religious behavior. Psilocybin, the active component in hallucinogenic mushrooms, can also imitate ecstatic religious experience.[2]

Still, brain pathology is an undependable guide to our spiritual life. Other investigations show that the moral consciousness of intact persons cannot be localized in just one or even several limited regions. The frontal lobe is critical for the development of our personality but it is not the site of our moral faculties. Normally we feel, think and act with the sum total of our cerebral or rather our neural resources.[3] Brain lesions may be a cause for diminished sanity but common folks can hardly avoid responsibility for their actions, referring to their curtailed free will. A genetic as well as a neurological determinism must be rejected. The philosopher William James (1842–1910) concisely expressed the inbuilt paradox: "My first act of free will shall be to believe in free will".[4]

Puberty is a decisive period in personality development. That is when the foundations are laid for the world view of the mature person and guidelines are established for basic personal values. This character formation corresponds to a striking reorientation of the neurological wiring of the brain. A great number of neurons disappear which implies a consolidation of brain activity.[5] The adolescent cannot keep all options open any more but has to confront the existential challenge of the world, based on the scant information available.

As grown-ups we must, in any case, accept responsibility for both deeds and omissions. The strength and weakness of democracy is that it is neither better nor worse than its citizens. We are all carrying the ball – you, me, everyman. But can morality be produced by peer pressure? Should I be my brother's keeper? A lift of individual moral standards will anyhow make itself felt in public life by setting a good example, whereas decrees from above may appear only as hypocritical political correctness.

Victorian morality was the reaction of the middle class to the alcohol abuse and the laxity of mores which followed in the wake of the industrial revolution. The augmented social control can be verified in English statistics. During the second half of the nineteenth century, alcohol consumption dropped as did the proportion of births out of wedlock. The number of criminal offences, too, peaked around 1850.[6]

In the United States, prostitution was criminalized between 1910 and 1915 in most states on the initiative of WCTU (Women's Christian Temperance Union) – with negligible effect. The Voelsted act, which prohibited the consumption of intoxicating drinks, was passed 1919 and repealed 1933 when the country was inundated with illegal alcohol. In the name of women's liberation, Sweden has recently introduced legislation which criminalizes the purchase of sexual services while the 'sex worker' is declared innocent. The effect of such daft legislative interventionism is in doubt but its political correctness is beyond question.

Today, any restrictions on sexual liberty for men or women are off limits; pedophilia too is spreading despite the harsh legislation. We are recklessly wearing down our accumulated moral capital. The traditional norms have lost their steering power and are perceived as an unnecessary burden. 'Fuck you' has degenerated into an expletive but forthright expressions for sexual intercourse are studiously avoided in favor of sundry euphemisms. Love is the most abused word on our planet.

> Human needs can be ordered in a hierarchy with the physiological basic needs at the bottom.[7] Next come the social needs (identity, belonging, status) followed by the striving for self-realization. The transcendental needs are at the top of the hierarchy. They transcend the personal self and are fulfilled when serving your neighbor – that is all mankind – one way or another. The sexual drive is exceptional. It can be expressed at all levels of the hierarchy.

Sexual laxity reflects a meaningless chase after purpose in life and fritters away our aptitude for emotional plus-sum play, our most precious legacy. Everybody starts with a basic fund which must be managed. The Gospel of St. Matthew is unambiguously capitalistic.[8] It is not enough to preserve the moral endowment. The Lord is adamant that it must be increased, even multiplied and the over-cautious trustee is fiercely chastised. The Gospel urges us to play a consistent plus-sum game, to make the most of our preconditions, to create spiritual capital. Then morality will emerge by itself.

Yet no one is finally condemned. In the Gospel of St. Luke, the lost son is forgiven despite the indignation of the conscientious brother.[9] Once again modern democratic values are in amazing accord with the rather inconsistent instruction of the Gospels. Neither morality, nor justice, nor truth, nor love can be reduced to unequivocal mental constructs. The contradictions can be solved only case by case through good will. Human beings, strong as well as weak, need consistent demands *and* compassion, sanctions *and* forgiveness.

> Prominent personalities are capable of making a rod for their own back. The perfectionist strivings of Benjamin Franklin and Ludwig Wittgenstein have already been touched upon. William Gladstone (1809–98) was a perennial British Prime Minister and personified the morality and statesmanship of the Victorian epoch. In his old days he struggled in vain with the temptations of masturbation which is documented in his contrition-filled diaries.

Everyone is called to manage his or her basic fund of moral capital. In a democratic society we are blessed with the freedom to choose our own role, to play our own game and to stand up for our personal values. It is inevitable that we in practice largely work for the benefit of ourselves and our family, but the efforts should be compatible with superordinate interests. We are obliged to assume some responsibility for the common weal, according to our capabilities. This is a voluntary citizen tax which enriches life for the payer.

> Why should I contribute? My response (in The Spirit of the Game) is as follows: "The burden of evidence lies with you – why not you? Every able body is privileged, standing in for all those countless souls who cannot take part. You are only called upon to do your best, struggling for self-control, resisting everything except challenges … Self-indulgence and self-deceit are cowardly concessions; the game gets its merit from all the unpleasant truths accepted and from all the tempting moves passed by."

This somewhat lofty appeal may be naïve. At least it contradicts all worldly wisdom. But at bottom, a childish trust is the sole starting point for blessed play; genuine progress is always grounded in artless risk-taking, a kind of creative innocence and generosity. Only honest plus-sum play confers meaning and satisfaction, maybe even happiness to our life. The main point is not to succeed; failures build the bridges to the future. Samuel Beckett said it concisely: "Ever tried? Ever failed? Never mind. Try again. Fail better."

15.2 Value generation and re-generation

In primitive communities the rules of the social game – customs, norms and values – are accepted as such by the next generation. In their creative phase, high cultures generate new values which introduce more structure into society and create the necessary conditions for a superior plus-sum game. But past civilizations have regularly undermined the very preconditions of their existence or got stuck in unreliable quasi-homeostasis. The gradual decay and final breakdown went lock in step with social instability and environmental destruction. Only our Western culture exhibits a continual development of the game, which is about to envelope the great majority on our globe.

This dynamic has its price. Progress implies that many things are put in question, including norms and mores. The authority of the old generation is subverted, nothing is taken for granted and conventional morality is exposed to incessant corrosion. Even the central values are subject to criticism, reassessment and erosion. Every generation must redefine and recreate its moral base.

In *Generations: The History of America's Future*, William Strauss and Neil Howe analyze the interplay between successive generations in the light of the history of the United States. They distinguish four recurring types which follow each other in a cycle measuring 88 years (four times 22 years) and, in turn, put their hallmark on American society.

> The Idealists are moralistic world improvers and are succeeded by the cynical and hedonistic Reactives. They are followed by the Civics, an extrovert and pragmatic generation, which cleans up the mess of the cynics and is engaged in the implementation of the magnificent program of the Idealists. Finally, the hypocritical and opportunist Adaptives take over to be followed by a new generation of moralistic Idealists. Spiritual awakening alternates with disillusioned cynicism.
>
> A generation is defined as a cohort born during a 22 year period and is far from identical to a family generation. The American Civil War is considered an aberration and is the only exception allowed. Strauss and Howe expose themselves to falsification by making rather detailed predictions far into the future. The book appeared in 1991 and anyone interested can start to make preliminary comparisons.

The analysis in *Generations* builds on and confirms that youngsters are strongly influenced by their peer group (cf. chapter 1.4); otherwise the marked conformity of the cohorts would be hard to understand. The limited impact of the parents is also apparent. If anything, a spontaneous reaction to the values of the preceding generation can be observed. The world view of the grandparents seems to be better tuned to the life style of the grandchildren.

The ethical orientation is not made any easier by the ever faster rate of change in our way of life. The newly won sexual and material freedom cannot but expose traditional norms to wear and tear. In *The De-moralization of Society* (1995), Gertrude Himmelfarb maps out the continuous erosion of virtues and values in our Western societies. The dissolution of family ties, in particular, puts the emotional maturation of the rising generation at stake. Societal allegiance has weakened, too.

> In *The Great Disruption: Human Nature and the Reconstitution of Social Order* (1999), Francis Fukuyama has addressed this problem. The symptoms of ebbing social capital and societal trust in the United States during the second half of the twentieth century are annotated in considerable detail. But when facing the new millennium, Fukuyama strikes a more optimistic note and wonders if we are heading for a new moral revival in the mode of the Victorian breakthrough in the middle of the nineteenth century.

The United States is undergoing a moral reappraisal which exposes all the rifts in society. In Europe, sensitive antennae are required to detect weak signals in this direction. But I believe that ultra-liberalism has passed its best before date in Europe, too. Europeans, though, have not yet achieved a common consciousness which would provide a base for a passionate debate as well as for genuine solidarity within the Union.

Other parts of the world have been subject to considerable social stress when traditional values have run counter to the new economic and political realities. In the Far East, the Confucian norm system has proved remarkably resilient and flexible. Hinduism, for its part, comprises multifarious beliefs and has always been superbly assimilative of alien influences. The whole region is, in any case, marked by unprejudiced pragmatism; in practice immediate utility takes precedence.

Islam is more susceptible to the trauma brought on by the confrontation between the old and the novel. The ever shriller calls for orthodoxy, such as the reintroduction of *sharia,* can be interpreted as symptoms of desperation. Islam is losing its relevance in the current cultural reorientation. Western inspired nationalism is the political driving force in the Muslim world. The al-Qaeda terrorism, with its dreams of a new Caliphate and Islamic world rule, is a despairing protest against this state of affairs.

In *Globalized Islam: The Search for a New Ummah* (2004), Olivier Roy presents a systematic analysis of the Muslim dilemma. Islam is slowly but surely succumbing to secularization. This implies the inevitable separation of state and religion. Ummah, the all-encompassing community of Muslims, is nowadays imaginable only in a spiritual dimension. Particularly in the Diaspora, religious exercise becomes a personal challenge in a group of likeminded, in line with pious adherents of other persuasions.

> Muhammed Siddiqi (a conservative imam) says in his Ramadan sermon: "Do not succumb to drugs, narcotics or sexual perversions of fornication, adultery, homosexuality and pornography... Avoid divorces and breakdown of families. Protect yourself and your children from crimes, violence and gangs. Take care of your elderly. Teach your children how to be responsible citizens and good neighbors."[10]
>
> During her youth, Somalia-born Ayaan Hirsi Ali was an Islamic fundamentalist but today she is the most articulate spokeswoman for a radical Muslim liberalism. Her election to the Dutch parliament was proof of a political platform. She is openly critical of obsolete Muslim conservatism and she has had the temerity to take the sexual mores of the Prophet to task. In the controversy around the Mohammed caricatures, she was against any tokens of appeasement.[11]
>
> The Turkish author Orhan Pamuk stands for a more nuanced analysis. In his Nobel lecture he presents a collective self-diagnosis which touches the raw nerve of recent European history: "What literature needs most to tell and investigate today are basic fears of mankind: the fear of being left outside, and the fear of counting for nothing, and the feelings of worthlessness that come with such fears; the collective humiliations, vulnerabilities, slights, grievances, sensitivities, and imagined insults, and the nationalist boasts and inflations that are their next of kind... Whenever I am confronted by such sentiments, and by the irrational, overstated language in which they are usually expressed, I know they touch on a darkness inside me."[12]

To agree on religious freedom is easily done and it must be pushed as a general rule in every corner of the world – tolerance of intolerance should be banned! Everyday relations are more problematical. For us in the West immigration is a moral challenge. Good relations between culturally divergent people in close contact require a measure of good will among the established majority. The immigrants have to master the more difficult task of pulling their weight and gaining the trust of the surrounding people without losing their identity and self-respect. But time is needed, a lot of time to modify the attitudes on both sides and to identify the joint rules of the game.

The United States never had a proper immigration policy, possibly because almost everybody is a descendant of immigrants. This benevolent neglect could be the key to long-term integration. The newcomers have not been exposed to social security but instead they have had free access to the labor market. In Europe it is the other way around; immigrants are cared for but are often denied work, which poisons relations. Canada may represent a reasonable balance between laissez faire and government meddling.[13]

> The aliens in the oil-rich Arab states amount to a problem of quite another magnitude. In many countries, the imported foreign workers perform most of the manual work; in Dubai there are six times more foreigners than original inhabitants. The immigrants from Egypt, Yemen, India, Pakistan, Sri Lanka, Indonesia, the Philippines and so on are practically devoid of legal rights and can be expelled at short notice. They are regularly repatriated and replaced by new recruits to avoid permanent settlement.[14]

Cultural continuity is wholly dependant on the transmission of our spiritual legacy to future generations, preferably in an enhanced form. The first precondition is that we possess enough zest for life – faith, hope and love – to produce a new generation. Otherwise all talk about responsibility for the future is empty rhetoric, a mendacious flight from reality. Secondly, we must have a faith, something we stand for, providing a firm starting point for children and grandchildren during their own voyages of discovery.

> Lack of contact between parents and children disturbs the transmission of values between the generations. Such shortcomings certainly contributed to the weakness of the pre-revolutionary French high aristocracy. In general, the infants were dispatched to a wet nurse in the countryside and sometimes returned only as adolescents, when they were put in the hands of governesses and private tutors. (The world reformer Rousseau went one better in depositing every one of his five children in a foundling house where in all probability they met early deaths. Yet he had the nerve to write an influential book *Émile ou de l'education* about the exemplary upbringing of the young.).
>
> The same syndrome recurs in all forms of inherited privilege. Dynasties go downhill, fortunes are dissipated; great men (and women) are in the habit of neglecting their progeny. Democracies are not immune to this decadence. The offspring of well-known as well as less known personalities are perpetually berating us with their narratives of terrible childhoods and the sins of omission of their fathers and/or mothers. There are abundant sources for parent-fixated confession literature.

Our central values do not define detailed norms but express the sum total of a vague personal commitment. These meta-rules of the game are spontaneously applied in the daily round. The frame of reference is absorbed from the surroundings and our bad conscience is certainly socially conditioned. Even so we can interpret the rules of the game according to our own lights; every one can make a personal contribution to the common fund of moral capital. The precondition is that we untiringly look for a higher directive – how we do it is a private matter.

15.3 Moral capital

We should not wonder at the ubiquity of evil, war and conflict but rather at the fact that plus-sum games do dominate after all. The starting capital for our moral development is deposited in human nature (cf. chapter 1.3). Man has developed a unique cooperation morality which is based on indirect reciprocity, also called strong or aggressive reciprocity. To complement the semi-egoistic "help me and I will help you" a more forceful ethical code emerged: "I will help you and maybe somebody else will help me". This primordial tribal solidarity is expressed as social capital in every close-knit community.

In the anthology, *Moral Sentiments and Material Interests* (2005), Herbert Gintis et al. stress the point that strong reciprocity is a fundamental precondition for extended human plus-sum play. The key resource is our inclination to react against breaching the rules of the game. Foul and false play must lead to social sanctions; otherwise the plus-sum game will collapse.[15] Moral percipience and self-control calls for continual fine-tuning by feedback from the societal environment. To moralize is thus a civic duty – a bad conscience is our most precious asset.

> China is making a strong comeback from its ideological bankruptcy, but civic morality is yet to recover. The following episode speaks for itself (personal communication). A small group of activists decided to support local factory workers who suffered from disabling silicosis. They got hold of a lawyer who managed to extract a sizable compensation from the employer. Afterwards the workers declined to pay the lawyer – at least in Finland this would be past all sense of shame. Let us hope that the compassionate response to the victims of the 2008 Sichuan earthquake marks a turning point in civic moral awareness in China.
>
> A good friend of mine from California was once waiting for the train at the railway station in Zürich. Walking back and forth along the platform, he had a smoke and threw away the butt. After the next round he observed that an elderly gentleman was picking up the butt and put it in the waste basket. Rarely had he felt so ashamed. In a civic society, the sense of responsibility reveals itself, down to the slightest detail.

Our ability to perform in extended, exceptionally fruitful plus-sum play depends on public morality. Spontaneous solidarity is buttressed by ethical principles and agreed rules of the game; the concord crystallizes around abstract but attractive symbols – king and country, flag and fatherland. Constitutions, norms, and judicial systems are levers which augment our weak moral forces in steering the overarching plus-sum game. But the available moral capital sets a ceiling for the size and complexity of a society. Just like corporations, states tend to collapse if their ambitions exceed the moral resources.

While the production of morality is an elusive process, its erosion is all the more familiar. Success and prosperity beget arrogance and sloth while more and more people want a bigger slice of the cake – rights escalate while responsibilities and duties are curtailed. Power struggles come to the fore and all kinds of privileges proliferate – tax exemptions, sinecures, concessions, entitlements. The rot starts at the top and spreads until breakdown is imminent.

> Alexander VI of the Borgia family was Pope during 1492–1503. In fierce competition, he can be considered the most depraved of pontiffs. He showered ecclesiastic offices and estates upon his numerous children, pursued ruthless power politics and applied every means, including assassinations, to attain his aims. His successors were no less worldly. Small wonder that the Catholic Church lost its moral authority, which provoked a reformation and questioned the entire existence of the church.
>
> Irresolution rather than depravity is the mortal sin of political leaders. The personal conduct of Louis XVI was impeccable but as a leader he failed in a critical but by no means hopeless situation. The king reflected in a calamitous way the lack of decisiveness and moral fiber of the aristocratic elite. The French Revolution was overdue.

The destruction of the moral capital always precedes the collapse of government. The tax burden increases and the productive segments of the population lose out. The elite have betrayed their mission as stewards of the societal plus-sum game, a recurring pattern in world history. Only the modern democracies have so far managed to maintain and perhaps even to increase their moral capital despite the steadily rising living standards. Genuine democracies avoid great upheavals but instead move from one minor crisis to the next – a bewildering sequence of minuscule moral challenges.

Democracies are equipped with mechanisms for the resolution of divergent opinions but they lack definite preconceived goals; instead they accomplish a balancing act between demoralizing extremes. Fair play should be the guiding principle but the call for justice cannot be driven in absurdum. The weak must be supported but the strong should not be suppressed either. The immediate satisfaction of the citizens should not encroach on the legitimate interests of coming generations. Free-riders, cheats and crooks must be checked, but the human and civic rights of the citizens cannot be brushed aside. In the last analysis it is a question of a permanent conflict between the common interest and personal liberty, the collective versus the individual. In this contest the family, the basic unit of society, has come out as a rather poor relation.

The never ending settlement of these intertwined problems is the bread and butter of democratic politics. Democracies under construction cannot afford such luxury. Their scarce moral capital makes it a struggle to fulfill even a minimum of democratic criteria. The small number of plus-sum players may be overwhelmed by distrust between the factions that divide the population.

> The traditional hostility between clans, tribes or ethnic and religious groupings is a mighty challenge for wobbling democracies, say in Afghanistan and Iraq. Without an outside controlling power, the temptation to grab assets or political supremacy is hard to resist. The task of a responsible occupying power is to discourage such adventurousness until national loyalty is backed up by sufficient domestic forces, and the benefits of plus-sum play have become apparent.
>
> Most of the failing states do not enjoy the advantage of a determined outside intervention. They are abandoned in the midst of anarchy and internal fighting. A dismayed West keeps the system and the people floating by distributing money and food but shies away from assuming real responsibility. When the going gets too rough, the UN personnel are the first to leave, the killed and kidnapped excepted. The passive wait for democracy to emerge by itself is hardly compatible with true humanism or Christian compassion.

Today, the great majority of countries are at least nominally democratic but this does not guarantee good governance. The abuse of power is widespread, the police and the courts are often a travesty of justice. Extensive corruption may leave little room for honest entrepreneurs. When solidarity and loyalty is restricted to the family, the clan and the tribe, little moral capital is left over for nation-building.

It is vital that nations with democratic aspirations get relief and support. Massive economic assistance is not appropriate, at least not in the beginning. What is needed is political and moral backing from the established democracies. A cornered opposition, struggling for a better society, must not be left in the lurch but should be encouraged in every peaceful way.

> Unassuming but steadfast pursuits can make a big difference when the time and the place are right. The American Gene Sharp has supplied the reformists with democratic activist manuals (i.a. *The Politics of Nonviolent Action*, 1973; *From Dictatorship to Democracy*, 1993). The peaceable upheavals in Serbia, Ukraine, Georgia and Kirgizstan attest the importance of these writings for the reform movements. Russia's rulers have taken note and curbed the financing of popular movements from abroad. Unfortunately, no openings for democracy exist in totalitarian states like North Korea, Turkestan, Belorussia, Myanmar and Cuba.

In all democracies, the greatest challenge is to choose capable plus-sum players for handling the levers of public power. Demagogues and false prophets, that is intellectually dishonest persons of all categories, must be rejected. Instead we should trust people who deliver unpleasant truths and bitter medicines. But it takes its time before the appeal to factional interests becomes suspect, empty rhetoric disgusting and the electoral pork distasteful. The moral capital will grow only if citizens learn by their political mistakes and practice wholesome self-criticism. To cite John F. Kennedy's somewhat high-flown request: "Ask not what your country can do for you. Ask what you can do for your country".

New funds of moral capital are required to safeguard sufficient cohesion during the advance from a nation-state to a regional federation or confederation on the EU model. The European Union has successfully projected democracy to its surroundings and surpassed expectations in many other ways. But the feeling of community is still underdeveloped which seriously restricts the international influence of the Union.

> It is a scandal that the EU tolerates the well-nigh totalitarian regime of Alexander Lukashenka as a neighbor. The response has so far been limited to a denial of entry for the top brass. The United States has all the same passed the *Belarus Democracy Act* which stipulates trade sanctions and economic support for the opposition. Real political pressure by the European Union could make the position of the life-time president unsustainable.

The future of the European Union is still hanging in the balance. In many ways, the EU resembles an immature democracy. Most people favor broad cooperation but few are committed to the wider community. The Union is becoming the scapegoat for the failures of the national politicians while the voters persevere in their lack of interest. The Brussels bureaucrats have not made things better by occasionally overexploiting their mandates.

The breakdown of the Soviet Union opened a window of opportunity for expansion but simultaneously undermined the cohesion of the Union. The disappearance of the outside threat started the regression of the core countries into parochial nationalism and internal squabbling. One should be cautious when talking about historic turning points; here and now the future is always at stake. But we have forfeited a unique opportunity to create an exemplary form of government if the European nations insist on a sterile status quo and refuse to accept the challenge of an integrated Union.

Let's be honest: It is not a matter of detailed economic or political calculations but simply of cooperative morale. Are we capable of subordinating national interests, can we suppress atavistic emotions and are we up to the development of an overarching, supranational plus-sum game? All this calls for an increase of moral capital and would constitute one step on the road to sustainable global collaboration. A worldwide sense of community still belongs to the region of utopias. This is another good reason for Europe to concentrate its scarce moral resources on the EU project which today lies at the limit of our capability.

15.4 Global values

In the middle of the first millennium BC, a wave of spiritual awakening swept over Eurasia. Inspired prophets like Vardhamana Mahavira and Gautama Buddha in India, Laozi and Kong Fuzi (Confucius) in China, as well as Zoroaster*, Deutero-Isaiah and Socrates in the West were searching for a deeper meaning in existence and presented messages claiming universal validity.[16] The newly established 'axial' religions represented a dynamic world view and a fresh hope for suffering humanity. The tribal gods were deposed for good, and religious devotion was consolidated within a monotheistic framework. Personal virtue was enriched by an all-inclusive human dimension; right and wrong acquired a new import.

> The ten commandments of the Exodus were laid down sometimes around 1200 BC to affirm the domestic peace and the military power

---

* Recent research indicates that Zoroaster lived earlier but his ideas became influential only during the reign of Cyrus the Great (after 600–529 BC) of the unruly Israelite tribes. "Thou shalt not kill" applied only to kinsmen. Yahweh contemplated ethnic cleansing and no pardon was given to outsiders. Only during the age of the axial religions were concepts like justice, mercy and truth freed from their tribal context and became part of a universal ethic.

All the great civilizations are built on the legacy of this spiritual transformation. After all, mankind is endowed with a common ethical frame of reference. In the preceding chapter, I have envisaged a future global community, consisting of a small number of sovereign but collaborating states, federations or coalitions. The cooperation will, in the first place, be based on enlightened self-interest. A common value frame would nevertheless be desirable, and could even be an indispensable precondition.

The core democratic values enjoy at least lip service in the greater part of the world. But below the surface, the key concepts are incommensurable and confusion reigns. We are still inarticulate in a global perspective – with one important exception. In mathematics and the natural sciences, particularly, scientists communicate fluently unimpeded by divergent backgrounds. Their fraternity (and sorority) overcomes local prejudices because they have a common mission. A scientific approach certainly removes many obstacles for human understanding and serves as a starting point for global cooperation.

The reach of scientific thought is limited, though. Even our everyday communication requires a broader frame of reference. Practical utility has always been the guide in evaluating alternative modes of action. Pragmatism is the branch of philosophy, which relates truth and reality to utility – fruitfulness, functionality and success. The inventor and philosopher Buckminster Fuller (1895–1993) declared that the mark of real knowledge is that it helps to construct a better machine.

Pragmatism is an 'American' philosophy. The great names are Charles S. Peirce (1839–1914), William James, John Dewey (1859–1952) and Willard Quine (1908–2000). They held that every philosophy should be perceived as an empirically conditioned thought construct which is open to verification or falsification through human experience. Pragmatism is rooted in the theory of evolution and mathematical logic, spiced with a dose of fallibilism – nothing is completely certain but one can always move closer to the truth. Quine maintains that "the philosophy of science is philosophy enough".

For European philosophers, the disparagement of deductive and speculative thinking has been hard to digest. The contamination of the pure abstractions of philosophy with plain empiricism has been a stumbling block. The contrast between American can do mentality and European intellectual self-sufficiency reappears in philosophy. Fortunately there are bridge-builders, for instance Hans Joas, who in *Die Kreativitet des Handelns*(1992) and *Die Entstehung der Werte* (1997)* stands out as a European pragmatist. He wants to elucidate under which conditions core democratic values can arise and be maintained. He asks for example: "To what extent must the individual respect the social order which he expects to guarantee his personal rights?"

Pragmatism is the tacit framework for technical and economic development and for materialistic plus-sum play in general. In stable democracies, politics are distinguished by pragmatic considerations. The joint utility perspective checks the ubiquitous zero-sum impulse. International relations, too, thrive in an atmosphere of pragmatic rationality. The proffered draft for a global world order presumes only a few firmly rooted pragmatic values.

> Utilitarianism is an attempt to derive a generally acceptable and rational ethics from basic pragmatic principles. Jeremy Bentham (1748–1832) identified the good with maximal human happiness and John Stuart Mill (1806–73) elaborated the program into a full-blown philosophy. For all that, it does not provide any ethical guidance; if anything, our moral sensibility is blunted and dissipated. Happiness is an elusive concept which disappears in a fog of circular definitions. More to the point is to minimize pain, ill-fortune and unhappiness. Richard Rorty has in *Contingency, Irony, Solidarity* (1989) placed the elimination of cruelty and humiliation at the centre of his philosophical reasoning.

Pragmatism must, just like democracy, be filled with a deeper meaning; otherwise we cannot cope with our moral challenges. The strength and weakness of pragmatism is that contentious and emotionally loaded questions of principle are set aside. This is good thought economy but man is not for long content with his daily livelihood, even if supplemented with round-the-clock entertainment. We are searching for a role in a greater context, we are longing for a secure footing with a better overview and a deeper understanding. The demand for new world views and life styles has not fallen off, and the market for comprehensive and easily accessible salvation is very well supplied.

> Scientology, founded by Ron Hubbard in 1954, is a typical exponent of the trade.[17] With sovereign self-confidence it presents itself as a scientific and universal religion; the tolerance is equally remarkable: "Sci-

---

* In English *The Creativity of Action* and *The Genesis of Values*

entology is fully compatible with all existing major religions and does not conflict with those religions or their religious practices". No presumptive customers are deterred and scientology has actually become a good business. But the competition is unrelenting. Age-old Indian sagacity provides an attractive packaging for religious instant consumption; gurus and swamis are all the rage.

Medical humbug, too, has illustrious antecedents. Franz Anton Mesmer (1734–1815) took fashionable Paris by storm when he introduced his magnetic therapy. Mesmerism was considered a cure for everything from rheumatism, gout and asthma to epilepsy, paralysis and blindness(!), though venereal diseases were excepted. In 1784, a prominent commission including Franklin, Lavoisier and Guillotin branded mesmerism as fraud but the run did not abate.[18] An incredible gift for self-deception among high society was a portent of the approaching revolution. Alas, magnetic bracelets are still in vogue.

Hippocrates from Kós (c.460–375 BC) was the first to articulate a humane medical ethic. In our times, humanism has been the banner which well-meaning thinkers can gather around without coming to blows. It expands the narrow frame of pragmatism to encompass a principled benevolence to and respect for all fellow human beings. Humanism can be regarded as Christianity 'light' but it also incorporates the related values of other monotheistic religions. Despite that (or for that reason), humanism remains vague, tepid and provides little sense of direction. Humanism is indispensable but insufficient as a frame of reference.

> The weakness of humanism is that it makes man an idol, and does not admit his fundamental insufficiency – the reality of evil. To be nice to each other is not enough. And on which rational grounds is man set apart? Buddhists prescribe respect for all life and nature worshippers pay homage to an even wider range of objects. But these abstractions provide little guidance. We are all, in principle, friends of humanity and friends of animals and nature to boot, just as we are friends of peace and quiet. Most of us have nothing ill in mind, on principle. Yet bad things happen.

Superordinate global values must be kept within a narrow, pragmatic frame but nothing prevents us from positioning ourselves in relation to the existential questions which affect all mankind. Anthroposophy, Bahá'i and Christian Science are nineteenth century expressions of this striving. In *The Spirit of the Game*, I am calling for a different mode of truth-seeking, a modern theology with no strings attached. Its task would be to integrate our essential knowledge and experience in the light of divergent concepts of faith.[19]

"Besides historical experience, fundamental insights in the relevant sciences are the self-evident cornerstones of a modern theology, which should teach us to navigate in our value universe. Powered by the exponential growth in knowledge, mankind is hesitantly entering a new supercoalition which is capable of creative self-control down to the genetic base."

A modern theology cannot and should not strive for unanimity by compromise which would produce only lukewarm, vacuous syncretism, devoid of conviction and passion. Even so, we have every reason to ponder the conditions of our very existence, to come together to define and redefine what we consider holy or inalienable.[20] The hard-won insights into the workings of nature have created the capability to control our environment and to some extent ourselves, but they have also released the means of collective self-destruction, a *memento mori* for all of humanity. It is high time that we can find a way to meet in good faith so that the dialogue of the deaf is replaced by a plus-sum game at the highest level.

The vernacular is extraordinary flexible but it cannot cope with literally inexpressible issues. Literature, poetry as well as prose, is capable of transmitting in words implicit information, way beyond that explicitly conveyed. Forms and colors and pictures, still as well as moving, art in all its multiplicity takes the measure of man in his entire complexity. Music, the most abstract and most concrete of art forms, sets our psyche reverberating and helps us to become one with our innermost emotions.

The artist and the scientist have a common problem – how to simplify without distorting, how to condense and compress without deforming. Great art expresses truth as compelling beauty. The essence is communicated with optimal information economy; the work is perfected when nothing remains to be removed. Even if art usually has local roots, the highest manifestations can travel far beyond national or regional borderlines. The artistic idiom is, at bottom, a universal language which can help us to understand each other and find a common ground.

15.5 Play a plus-sum game!

The Empires have disintegrated; totalitarian ideologies are in full retreat; only the democracies are flourishing; that is the history of the twentieth century in a nutshell. The scent of victory was in the air and in some quarters the final triumph of democracy was promulgated. Nothing could be a greater error. Pride goes before fall and success contains the germ of future disasters. Democracy is the most difficult and demanding form of government. It does not need self-satisfaction but humility and continuous preparation for the ensuing challenges.

> The moral decay of the last century culminated in totalitarian hubris – communism and fascism. The corresponding brutalization of artistic criteria, especially in architecture, has raised less of a stir. Modernism arrived at an unholy alliance with post-war socialism; the concrete monsters in the suburbs look almost alike in the West and in the East. In art (and not only in art) the challenge of the new generation is to surpass or, if that seems impossible, to sideline or even dethrone their precursors. In this particular case, the easy way out was to deny the legitimacy of the aesthetic impulse. Artistic renewal does not imply that the old loses its value but rather the opposite.

Rash optimism and black pessimism are equally irresponsible. Against the background of a wide-spread cultural defeatism, I have stressed the almost limitless potential of human plus-sum play. The question remains as to whether we have the courage to seize the opportunity and live up to the challenge. The low fertility in many core democracies is a striking expression of internal decrepitude. Outside threats are mostly manageable but a permanent deficit in moral capital can only end in bankruptcy.

> Our greatest worry is, or should be, the skewed population pyramid which is wobbling on its shrinking base. The baby crash will in due cause create severe problems, not least in the care for senior citizens and the sick. Tax revenues will shrink while the costs of diverse entitlements are skyrocketing. Nowhere has this been taken seriously though the facts are on the table and many politicians are seeing the writing on the wall.[21] At the opposite end of the life cycle we are encountering another moral challenge. It can't be right to prolong the purely vegetative existence of many elderly people – a dignified death should belong to the basic human rights.

Democratic plus-sum play has no script; it can stall or go wrong. It is always a matter of improvisation with the accompanying slips – improvidence, unnecessary conflicts and waste of time. To cap it all, the actors perform in the full glare of publicity and the audience can enjoy all the gaffes and snafus.

It is no use blaming the politicians for their lack of perspective. It is the people who are responsible but the people rarely take the initiative. It is the task of the elite to be proactive: to identify the sore spots of society, to initiate a debate well in advance and to activate public opinion. This mission has been accomplished with regard to the climate threat but otherwise the track record is less impressive. The intellectual establishment is beholden to political correctness and generally clings to an obsolete, pseudo-radical world view – ignorance goes together with arrogance. If the leading stratum lacks credibility in the eyes of the people, the emergence of an informed public opinion is hampered. The transmission between the elite and the electorate has slipped out of gear.

In *The Future of Freedom: Illiberal Democracy at Home and Abroad*, Fareed Zakaria laments the irresponsible public opinion in modern democracies. When the public insists on participation in decision making, the authority of the political leadership is undermined. They do not lead any more but try desperately to follow the intentions of the electorate which are mapped in exquisite detail. If public opinion becomes a dominant power, the political process will become even messier and the responsibility ever fuzzier – Athens' classical democracy is haunting us.

This condition could be called the over-democratization of politics. It generates mistrust of politicians and is weakening the self-assurance of the democracies. The negative self-image is reflected in many European opinion polls. A recurring theme is that the government is incompetent and public affairs are a mess, but, as for me and my family, we are doing rather well. There must be something wrong with the optics of the political glasses.

To idolize popular opinion and make it into a measure of everything is to invite moral regress. If the public comes to believe that it always knows best, indiscriminate dissatisfaction with the governing bodies will pervade politics. The sense of fair play weakens and the political plus-sum game can fall apart when the lack of respect for the government is translated into wholesale contempt for a democracy, which cannot produce capable leaders. The choice between a vicious and a virtuous spiral, between a moral descent and ascent, remains forever open as it depends on our everyday conduct. Plain honesty should keep us on the narrow road whereas lying, slander, polemics, nay every nasty word poisons the plus-sum game and constitutes a step away from democracy.

The dictators of our times were extreme despisers of democracy. In their utter egocentricity they personify the worst in man and left behind countries in material and moral ruin. Self-deification is the logical consequence of their moral position which can be summarized in the dictum: Nothing means anything when I am dead. It is worth pondering that this sentence could be endorsed by all too many citizens even though it implies the total denial of responsibility – the death of God.

We have, free of charge, been blessed with much to be thankful for and to care for. I may sound like a revivalist preacher but it does not alter the fact that every new generation has to restrain its life appetites and recreate a durable morality in order to earn its freedom and prosperity. We must be prepared for reverses; neither natural disasters nor nuclear terrorists must shake our faith and thus destroy the long-term plus-sum game. Faith in God, faith in the future and a sound self-confidence are all interconnected, regardless of religious or ideological quibbles. The self-destructive alternative is unchecked conceit and limitless self-seeking – literally hopeless expressions of life ennui.

Our spiritual woes and temptations are the price of freedom but in exchange we have got a cornucopia of knowledge and unprecedented prosperity. Today we can, by the mediation of the market, trust the inputs of a multitude of perfectly strange people. Thanks to globalization, the radius of trustful cooperation is about to extend over the whole earth. Our challenge is to entice the majority of the human race into the complex network of material and intellectual plus-sum play – to make the poor productive.[22] The provisional end point for such a development could be called *metacapitalism*.[23] As most people achieve capitalist status, the surplus of resources transforms the capital from master to laborer. If we provide sufficient room for human enterprise, global prosperity will leave the realm of utopia.

The poor have few options. Only the rich can afford conscientious generosity and can assume long-term responsibility for the environment. Howsoever we judge modern democracies, they exhibit exceptional munificence towards the destitute within and without their borders. Wealth and human caring seem to go hand in hand – which should not be too surprising.

Through the eons, morality has been key to human cooperation and thus to the evolution of man. This is an incontestable fact. Moral relativists have an easier time in negating a rise in moral capital during historic times. The increase in material welfare is considered irrelevant or outright negative and bourgeois virtues are despised. In *The Moral Consequences of Economic Growth* (2005), Benjamin Friedman presents a convincing argument for his thesis that higher incomes make for better citizenship. In any case, a sustainable prosperity is wholly dependant on human collaboration; the successful plus-sum game becomes a fairly good measure of morality.

In *The Bourgeois Virtues* (2006) Deirdre McCloskey presents a passionate defense of the much decried capitalist values. "Profit is good not bad for our person and our soul" is a provocative statement. The extravagant honor of the old aristocracy has been converted to plain bourgeois honesty, which is hardly deplorable. I will give the last word on this subject to Alexis de Tocqueville: "Men cannot be cured of the love of money but they can be persuaded to enrich themselves only by honest means".

If we can mobilize enough morality, there are no limits to a grand plus-sum game where the vast majority of mankind is participating, body and soul. The specter of overpopulation is fading away and will disappear if everybody can and wants to take full responsibility for his and her offspring. If all the pieces are falling into place, every new citizen is an asset, not a burden. To speculate over the outcome of such a dynamic development is a vain undertaking. The direction and the route are important, valuable goals will appear during the voyage of discovery.

Like the market, democracy is always in the wrong, though it is continuously correcting itself. But we cannot have democracy without democrats. Here and now everything is at stake. No superhumans are needed to form our future. It is so terribly simple. The good will to search for a shared truth will suffice.

Every body has a place in the global interplay, nobody is indispensable but every one is called for. Concern, caring and compassion are expressions of humanity and testify that the next man is more than an instrument for our self-realization. This is an invaluable provision when we, with warm hearts and cool reason, try to work out our innermost beliefs in thoughts, in words and in deeds. The love for and of God in all its variations cannot be distinguished from the love for one's neighbor, the finest plus-sum game.

Acknowledgements

This book was first written in Swedish (I am a Swedish speaking Finn) and was published, together with the Finnish translation, in October 2007. The management and staff at The Finnish Business and Policy Forum EVA supported me in many ways during the gestation of the book. Many thanks to Martti Nyberg, Ilkka Haavisto and Hannu Kaseva in particular.

Janne Salonen provided insightful comments on the manuscript and Christina Lindqvist helped me out with the references and the bibliography. I am also thankful for the support of Christian Junnelius, Jukka Gronow, Bengt Stymne, Sören Lithell and Anders Björnsson.

The Challenge of Democracy is in essence an updated and slightly revised version of the Swedish original. Many thanks to Anthony Shaw, who took on the task of rectifying my English and also came up with valuable reflections on the text. The remaining linguistic shortcomings are entirely my fault. Mika Saloranta at Nordprint made the manuscript ready for printing and provided practical advice.

Finally I want to thank my family. My dear wife has without complaint accepted my long days, months and years at the computer. My children and grandchildren have also contributed in different ways. Rasmus and Anton Molander deserve special credit for helping me to reach out to an international audience. If the book becomes widely read it is not least due to their efforts.

Helsinki, October 2008
Gustav von Hertzen

Notes

Preface
 -de Tocqueville, Alexis *De la Démocratie en Amérique I-II* (1835–1840); in English *Democracy in America I-II* (1945)
 -von Hertzen, Gustav *The Spirit of the Game* (1993).

Chapter 1 **Human nature**
1. The relevant literature is extensive and partly controversial. Even so, a consensus is emerging. At this point I refer only to a few broad surveys which approach the problem from different angles.
 -Wilson, Edward O. *Sociobiology: The New Synthesis* (1975).
 -Eibl-Eibesfeldt, Irenäus *Die Biologie des Menschlichen Verhaltens* (1984).
 -Runciman, Maynard Smith & Dunbar eds. *Evolution of Social Behaviour Patterns in Primates and Man* (1996).
 -Wright, Robert *Nonzero: The Logic of Human Destiny* (2000).
 -Shennan, Stephen *Genes Memes and Human History* (2002).
 -Wilson, David S. *Darwin's Cathedral: Evolution, Religion and the Nature of Society* (2002).
2. The swift heritable changes in animal behavior have puzzled the geneticists for long. One possible explanation is the so-called Baldwin effect which is still disputed. See Weber & Depew eds. *Evolution and Learning: The Baldwin Effect Reconsidered* (2003). The main idea is that learned behavior acts as a guide for genetic changes; evolution thus acquires a preferred direction. New insights into epigenetic heredity, which is uncoupled from DNA, impart increased plausibility to such ideas. See for instance *Science* **319** (2008) 1781-1799 Special Section *Freedom of Expression*
 The major part of the genome is a closed book. The genes are expressed only at the right time, in the right place and in the right environment. Small changes in the regulatory system can have substantial effects on the phenotype and the behavior. The DNA double spiral is embedded in chromatin which plays a key role in this self-regulation. Chemical modification of the chromatin (and of the DNA itself) opens and closes the door to genetic expression. The profusion of regulatory RNA-snippets produces an additional level of complexity. About selective evolution in human populations see for instance Gary P. Nabhan *Why Some Like It Hot: Food, Genes and Cultural Diversity* (2004); Voight et al. *PloS Biology* March 7 (2006) *A Map of Recent Positive Selection in the Human Genome* on the web.
 The great question is if the genetic anchoring is exclusively achieved by the selection among the existing divergent genotypes, or if the somatic changes somehow carry over into the gametes; the cytoplasm of the egg cells can also transmit 'learned' information. It may be very difficult to separate the mechanisms but the swift evolution of behavior speaks for the latter alternative, even if it is hard to digest for dogmatic Darwinists. The environment may induce random change in specific parts of the regulatory system, providing additional raw material for selection. See Eva Jablonka & Marion J. Lamb *Evolution in Four Dimensions: Genetic, Epigenetic, Behavioral and Symbolic Variation in the History of Life* (2005); Viré et al. *Nature* **439** (2006) 871–874 *The Polycomb group protein EZH2 directly controls DNA methylation; Nature* **447** (2007) 396–440 *Epigenetics, Introduction and Reviews;* John Whitfield *Nature* **455** (2008) 281–284 *Postmodern evolution?* About the dog's genome, Hans Ellegren *Nature* **438** (2005) 745–746; Kerstin Lindblad-Toh et al. ibid: (2005) 803–819. About the

modification of chromatin, Shogren-Knaak et al.: *Science* 311 (2006) 844–847; Bannister & Kouzarides *Nature* 436 (2005) 1103–1106. About the continuous evolution of the human brain, Evans et al. *Science* 309 (2005) 1717–1720; Mekel-Bobrov et al. ibid: 1720–1722.

3. Inuktut (the Inuit language) and Romani (the language of the Roma) are well known examples. See also Arne Öhman *Science* 309 (2005) 711–713 *Conditioned Fear of a Face: A Prelude to Ethnic Enmity*.

4. Edvard Westermarck *The History of Human Marriage* (1891).

5. See for instance Lewis Wolpert *Six Impossible Things Before Breakfast: The Evolutionary Origins of Beliefs* (2006); Lee M. Silver *Challenging Nature. The Clash of Science and Spirituality at the New Frontiers of Life* (2006).

6. See Edward Hagen *The Bargaining model of Depression* in Peter Hammerstein ed. *Genetic and Cultural Evolution* (2003) p. 95–123. The hypothesis is referring only to mild depression, dejection and lack of motivation. Severe depression certainly has a different, physiological background.

7. If the relatedness is 50%, the benefit for the relative should be at least double the cost for altruism to pay off. Hamilton worked out the theory in detail and it is extensively verified empirically. He has written a scientific self-biography, *Narrow Roads of Geneland I-II* (1995, 2001), well worth reading.

8. See David Sloan Wilson *Darwin's Cathedral: Evolution, Religion and the Nature of Society* (2002).

9. John von Neumann & Oscar Morgenstern *Theory of Games and Economic Behavior* (1944) is the basic work of game theory. See also Robert Axelrod *The Evolution of Cooperation* (1984); Ken Binmore *Game Theory and the Social Contract I-II* (1998–2000); Herbert Gintis *Game Theory Evolving* (2000); Colin Camerer *Behavorial Game Theory* (2003).

10. See for instance Jane Goodall *The Chimpanzees of Gombe* (1986); Frans de Waal *Chimpanzee Politics* (2000).

11. See Desmond Morris *The Naked Ape* (1967). For a review of different aspects on this problem see *The Economist* December 18th (2003) *Human hair, the bare truth*.

12. See for instance Robert L. Trivers *Social Evolution* (1985) and *Natural Selection and Social Theory* (2002). The latter work is a compilation of scientific publications with comments by the author. Matt Ridley has written many easily accessible books about the origin of morality and human cooperation (see the bibliography). See also Bernhard, Fischbacher & Fehr *Nature* 442 (2006) 912–915 *Parochial altruism in humans*; Choi and Bowles *Science* 318 (2007) 636–640 *The Coevolution of Parochial Altruism and War* and the commentary by Holly Arrow *The Sharp End of Altruism* 581–582; Herrmann et al. *Science* 319 (2008) 1362–1367 *Antisocial Punishment across societies,* and the commentary by Herbert Gintis p. 1345.

13. See for instance J.P. Mallory *In Search of the Indoeuropeans* (1989). The proto-Indo-Europeans featured a markedly patriarchal society in contrast to many of the surrounding people. They were probably the first to domesticate the horse and to use it for pulling a chariot. From their origin somewhere to the north of the Black Sea, the Indo-Europeans spread all over Europe and Anatolia, Iran and Central Asia including India.

14. See for instance James Q. Wilson: *The Moral Sense* (1993). To my knowledge, the earliest use of the term "moral capital" occurs in this book (p. 221).

15. See Barbara Arredi et al. *The Peopling of Europe* in Michael Crawford ed. *Anthropological Genetics* (2007) p. 398–400.

16. Robert L Trivers *American Zoologist* 14 (1974) 249–264 *Parent-offspring conflict*. Reprinted in *Natural Selection and Social Theory* (2002) p. 123–153.

17. In 1928, the leading behaviorist John B. Watson advised mothers to avoid kissing, cuddling or hugging their babies to avoid spoiling them. These recommendations were officially embraced by Children's Bureau of the United States Department of Labor. See Otto Klineberg et al. *Students, Values and Politics* (1979).

18. See Judith Rich Harris *Psychological Review* 10, nr. 3 (1995) 458–489 *Where Is the Child's Environment? A group Socialization Theory of Development.*

19. See Edward O. Wilson *Sociobiology* (1975) p. 163–164. The figure 7-8 is very instructive.

20. See Wang et al. *Proceedings of the National Academy of Sciences* 103 (2006) No. 1, 135-140 *Global landscape of recent inferred Darwinian selection for Homo Sapiens*. According to this study the evolution of the human genome shows a steady acceleration from about 50 000 years ago to the present.

21. See for instance Paul Mellars *Nature* 432 (2004) 461–465 *Neanderthals and the modern human colonisation of Europe*; Paul Mellars *Nature* 439 (2006) 931–935 *A new radiocarbon revolution and the dispersal of modern humans in Eurasia*; Paul Mellars *Science* 313 (2006) 796–800 *Going east: New Genetic and Archeological Perspectives on the Human Colonization of Eurasia.*

22. In *Myths of the Archaic State* (2005) Norman Yoffee questions the partitioning of social development in definite predetermined stages.

23. In *The Greek Myths* (1955), Robert Graves interprets a substantial part of the Greek myths according to this schema.

24. See Steven A. LeBlanc *Prehistoric Warfare in the American Southwest* (1999).

25. See Napoleon A. Chagnon *Yanomamo*. (1992). The well-documented bellicosity of the Yanomamo has not been to everybody's taste. For a commentary see. *Science* 309 (2005) 227–228. See also Dan Jones *Nature* 451 (2008) 512–515 *Killer Instinct.*

26. See *Catholic Encyclopedia. Guarani Indians* and R.B. Cunninghame Graham *A Vanished Arcadia* (1998), Project Gutenberg, both on the web.

27. J. G. Frazer *The Golden Bough* (1922) is the classic text dealing with the mythical origin of regicide.

Chapter 2 The material base

1. See for instance Joe Mokyr *The Lever of Riches: Technological Creativity and Economic Progress* (1990) and *Long-term Economic Growth and the History of Technology* in Aghion & Durlauf eds. *Handbook of Economic Growth* (2003).

2. See for instance J. Diamond *Nature* 435 (2005) 283–284 *Geography and skin colour*; Carl Zimmer *TBRN News.Org* March 3 (2005) *The hobbit brain*; A review in *Science*, 309 (2005) 1717–1722 (Evans et al. *Microcephalin, a gene regulating brain size, continues to evolve adaptively in humans*; Mekel-Bobrov et al. *Ongoing adaptive evolution of ASPM, a brain size determinant in homo sapiens*; Latimer et al *Neutral ecological theory reveals isolation and rapid speciation in a biodiversity hot spot*). See also chapter 1, note 1.

3. The decisive role of man in the extermination of the paleofauna is uncontestable; a changing climate is not a tenable alternative. See for instance Barnosky et.al. *Science* 306 (2004) 70–75 *Review: Assessing the Cause of Late Pleistocene Extinctions on the Continents*. About Australia see Christopher N. Johnson 309 (2005) 255–256; Turney et al. PNAS USA doi:10.1073 (2008) and the comment of Jared Diamond in *Nature* 454, 836–837 (2008); Paul S. Martin: *Twilight of the Mammoths* (2005)

4. My chief source on the history of China is John King Fairbanks and Merle Goldman: *China: A New History* (1998).

5. See for instance Hugh Thomas *The Slave Trade* (1997).

6. Bronislav Malinowski *Argonauts of the Western Pacific* (1922).

7. My chief source on the history of money is Glyn Davies ed. *A History of Money from Ancient Times to the Present Day* (1996).

8. See John Maynard Smith *Evolution and the Theory of Games* (1982).
9. See G.F. Gause *The Struggle for Existence* (1934). G. von Hertzen has applied these ideas as a guide to company strategy (cf. chapter 4 ref. 13).
10. Richard Pipes *Property and Freedom* (1999).
11. In 1840 Pierre-Joseph Proudhon expressed the view that property is theft in *Qu´est-ce que la propriété?* (English translation *What is property?*). In *Theory of property* (1866) he says: "property is the strongest existing revolutionary force with an incomparable capability to resist the powers that be...private property... acts as a counterweight to the power of the state and guarantees the freedom of the individual."
12. R.L. Carneiro *Southwestern Journal of Anthropology*, **23**, nr 3 (1967) 234–243 *On the relationship between size of population and complexity of social organization.*
13. The cultural regress of the Tasmanians is archeologically documented but still somewhat controversial. See Lyndall Ryan *The Aboriginal Tasmanians* (1996), although it focuses on the fate of the Tasmanians after the contact with the Europeans.
14. Adrienne Mayor *Greek Fire, Poison Arrows & Scorpion Bombs: Biological and Chemical Warfare in the Ancient World.* (2003).
15. See for instance Maryanne Kowaleski *Local Markets and Regional Trade in Medieval Exeter* (1995); Fernand Braudel: (1979) *Les Jeux de l´echange. Civilisation materiell, economie et capitalisme XV-XVIII siecle* (English translation *The Wheels of Commerce* 1983).
16. About Anders Chydenius see Nordic Authors/Anders Chydenius, on the web
17. Schumpeters' most famous work is *Capitalism, Socialism and Democracy* (1942) where he predicts the demise of entrepreneurship in an increasingly socialized economy. See also Gunnar Eliasson et al. *The Birth, the Life and the Death of Firms* (2005)
18. Compare for instance Thomas Sowell *Conquests and Cultures: An International History* (1998).

Chapter 3 Political foundations

1. See for instance *Njál's saga* which was written down in the fourteenth century but is based on oral tradition from the twelfth century.
2. See for instance Simon Schama *The Embarrassment of Riches: An Interpretation of Dutch Culture in the Golden Age* (1987).
2a. See for instance Christopher Pendergast *The Fourteenth of July: And the Taking of the Bastille* (2008)
3. Until recently I was under the impression that I was the first person to put this sentence on paper in *The Spirit of the Game* (1993). But Lev Tikhomirov uses almost the same formulation in *Why I Ceased to Be a Revolutionary* (1895, in Russian). See Richard Pipes: *The Degaev Affair: Terror and Treason in Tsarist Russia* (2003).
4. See Hugh Brogan *Alexis de Tocqueville: A Biography* (2006),
5. See Winston Churchill: *The World Crisis* (1923).
6. See Max Jakobson: *Finland in the new Europe* (1988). After the fall of the Soviet Union I became acquainted with the Russian Ambassador, Juri Derjabin. During the old regime he had been a notorious fiend of Finland under the pseudonym Komissarov. His sweet-sour summary of our former relations was that Soviet and Finland were like Tom and Jerry.
7. See for instance Tony Judt: *Postwar: A History of Europe since 1945.* (2005)
8. See David McCullough: *Truman* (1992). See also Greg Behrman *The Most Noble Adventure: The Marshall Plan and the Time when America Helped Save Europe* (2007)

9. See for instance. John Lewis Gaddis *The Cold War: A New History* (2005).

10. See Arthur Koestler *The Invisible Writing* (1954). The book is the second part of Koestler's self-biography.

11. See the self-biographical work of Arvo Tuominen *Kremlin kellot*. (The bells of the Kremlin) 1956.

12. von Neumann and Morgenstern postulated that for every well-defined game there exists a contradiction-free set of rules, a 'constitution' which can solve all arising conflicts in an unambiguous way. But W.F. Lucas in due course falsified this hypothesis *Transactions of the American Mathematical Society* 137 (1969) 219–229.

13. Robert Putnam et al. *Making Democracy Work: Civic Traditions in Modern Italy* (1993).

Chapter 4 The foundations of morality

1. Holding this opinion, I am in good company. In *The Evolution of Morality* (2006) Richard Joyce has analyzed the concept of morality from a philosophical point of view and shows rather convincingly that an objectively 'correct' morality cannot be derived deductively or arrived at empirically in terms of evolutionary psychology. But see also for instance Martin Hollis, who in *Trust within reason* (1998) has approached the problem from a game-theoretic point of view. The conclusion is, as far as I understand, that reason will be a guide only if it understands its own limitations.

2. Kurt Gödel managed to construct a water-tight mathematical self-contradiction which in the vernacular corresponds to "this sentence is not true". This implies that neither the sentence nor its opposite can be the case and that mathematics is a logically incomplete system. The veracity of an infinite number of mathematical statements must remain an open question. The interested reader is referred to Douglas R. Hofstadter: *Gödel, Escher Bach: An Eternal Golden Braid* (1979).

3. See Ray Monk *The Duty of Genius* (1990) p. 361–384. Wittgenstein had intimated that he was one fourth Jewish, but in reality three of his grandparents were Jews.

4. See John Stephen Lansing: *Priests and Programmers: Technologies of Power in the Engineered Landscapes of Bali* (1991) and *Perfect Order: Recognizing Complexity in Bali* (2006). Fred Eiseman: *Rice and Ritual: Dewi Sri's Gift. Balivision* on the web (2004).

4a. See The University of Maine, *UMaine Today Magazine* – July/August 2003 *Lobster Lines* on the web

5. Jared Diamond relates the sad story in *Collapse* (2005) p. 79–119. See also Terry L.Hunt & Carl P. Lipo *Science* 311 (2006) 1603–1606 *Late Colonization of Easter Island*. A revised chronology indicates an early onset of environmental destruction and the raising of statues. See also a contribution by Jared Diamond in *Science* 317 (2007) 1692–1694 *Easter Island Revisited*.

6. See Michael Fellman *The Making of Robert E. Lee* (2000).

7. Alexis de Tocueville *Democracy in America II*, p. 336. de Tocqueville shows visionary perspicacity when he in 1840 could perceive a welfare dystopia which did not exist then even in an embryonic form.

8. See for instance. *The Financial Times* 21 August (2006) *Harris Poll of Adults in Five European Countries Reports on What People Think about Working Hours, Pensions and Retirement*

9. Karl Popper *On the sources of knowledge and ignorance. Encounter* September 1962. Republished 2006.

10. James Gleick *Chaos: Making a New Science* (1988) and Roger Lewin: *Complexity: Life at the Edge of Chaos* (1992) are popular introductions. Arkady Pikovsky, Michael Rosenblum, Jürgen Kurth *Synchronization: A universal concept in nonlinear dynamics* is more demanding.

11. The events are described in *Japanese American National Museum Quarterly* 9, no 3 (1994) 11–16.
12. For a game-theoretic exposition, see for instance Samuel Bowles: *Microeconomics: Behavior, Institutions and Evolution* (2004). See also Eric D. Beinhocker: *The Origin of Wealth: Evolution, Complexity and the Radical Remaking of Economics* (2006). Beinhocker expounds in detail the causal relations between prosperity, social structures and values, but eschews the concept of morality while C. D. Ellis provides an illuminating example of the value of moral capital in *The Partnership: The Making of Goldman Sachs* (2008).
13. See Gustav von Hertzen. *Att spela plussummespel. (Playing plus-sum games)* In Carlson, R. ed. *Strategier för att förtjäna pengar: Om affärsiden och andra SIAR-begrepp* (2000) p. 238–267 *(Strategies for making money: About the business idea and other SIAR concepts)*; see also Robert Frank *What Price the High Moral Ground? Ethical Dilemmas in Competitive Environment* (2005); the introduction in Deirdre N. McCloskey *The Bourgeois Virtues: Ethics for an Age of Commerce* (2006).
14. This assessment is not new. For instance according to Peter F. Drucker, integrity is the only indispensable quality of a leader. See *The Essential Drucker* (2001). See also Paul Babiak & Robert Hare *Snakes in Suits: When Psychopaths Go to Work* (2006) for the destructivity of cynical climbers.
15. See Gustav von Hertzen *The Cultor Story - The Path Abroad* p. 69–85 in Mannio et al. eds. *Our Path Abroad: Exploring Post-war Internationalization of Finnish Corporations* (2003)
16. See Wiklund et al. *The Hartwall/BBH-Case - The Dissolution of the Soviet Union as a Business Opportunity* p. 409–420 in Mannio et al. eds. *Our Path Abroad: Exploring Post-war Internationalization of Finnish Corporations.* (2003)
17. Gustav von Hertzen *Finnish Business and Policy Forum EVA Analysis* No. 5 (2008) *Management and Morality - An Overview.*
18. The public choice school was founded by James Buchanan and Gordon Tullock who published *The Calculus of Consent* in 1962 (Buchanan received the Nobel award in economics in 1986).
19. See Samuel Bowles *Science* 320 (2008) 1605–1609 *Review: Policies Designed for Self-interested Citizens May Undermine "The Moral Sentiments": Evidence from Economic Experiments.*

Chapter 5 Spiritual foundations

1. See Stacy Shiff *Great Improvisation: Franklin, France and the Birth of America* (2005).
2. See Fareed Zakaria *The Future of Freedom: Illiberal Democracy at Home and Abroad* (2003) p. 106–113. Zakaria provides examples for populist backlash in Indian democracy.
3. Ayn Rand's heroes in the *Fountainhead* (1943) and *Atlas Shrugged* (1957) are unconvincing as human beings but make for good copy. Her extreme position can be understood as a reaction to her first hand impressions of Bolshevism.
4. The argumentation appears in *Pensées* (1662), Pascal's last, unfinished work.
5. See Hannah Arendt: *Eichmann in Jerusalem: A Report on the banality of Evil* (1963).
6. See for instance. Fred P.M. van der Kraai *President Samuel K. Doe (1980–1990) The Master Sergeant-President in Liberia: Past and Present of Africa's Oldest Republic* (2006) on the web.
7. This reflection appeared only in a late edition published in 1790 (p. 237), 31 years after the original work.
8. The interested reader is also referred to Jaroslav Pelikan *Center of Theological Inquiry* (1997) *Reflections: The Predicament of the Christian Historian* on the web

9. See Adam Hochschild *King Leopolds Ghost: A Story of Greed, Terror and Heroism in Colonial Africa* (1998).

10. See Hartmut Mayer & Henri Vogt eds. *A Responsible Europe* (2006). The book is an attempt to map out the global responsibility and tasks of the European Union. See also Joseph Ratzinger: (the present Pope) *Europa, Seine Geistigen Grundlagen Gestern, Heute, Morgen* A lecture presented at the Bavarian representation in Berlin 28.11.2000

11. See for instance Ann Gibbons *The First Human: The Race to Discover our Earliest Ancestors* (2006). The author describes how the intense competition between the paleoanthropologists has led to mudslinging and restricted the exchange of information.

12. David S. Landes: *Revolution in Time: Clocks and the Making of the Modern World* (1983) p. 32–36.

13. Se Gustav von Hertzen: *The Spirit of the Game* (2003) p. 277–300.

14. In a posthumously published lecture by Max Weber: *Wissenschaft als Beruf. Schriften* p. 1894–1922 (1922), new edition 2002.

15. See also Gintis, Bowles, Boyd, Fehr eds. *Moral Sentiments and Material Interests: The Foundations of Cooperation in Economic Life* (2005)

16. See for instance Hsu et al. *Science* 320 (2008) 1092–1095 *The Right and the Good: Distributive Justice and Neural Encoding of Equity and Efficiency*

17. See Henrich et al. *American Economic Review* 91 (2) (2002) 73–78 *In search of homo economicus: Behavioral experiments in 15 small-scale societies*; Martin A. Nowak & Karl Sigmund *Nature* 427 (2005) 1291–1298 *Evolution of indirect reciprocity (a review)*; Henrich et al. *Science* 312 (2006) 1767–1770 *Costly Punishment Across Human Societies*

18. See Gustav von Hertzen: *The Spirit of the Game* (1993) p. 312-318.

19. See for instance Colin A. Ronan: *The Cambridge Illustrated History of the World's Science* (1983) p. 201–240.

20. See Jaakko Hintikka & Gabriel Sandu: *Game-theoretical Semantics* in Van Benthum, Ter Meulen eds. *Handbook of Logic and Language* (1997) p. 361–410. Gödel's insight in the incapability of mathematics to prove its own infallibility has the consequence that no truth criterion can prove its own veracity but must rely on a superordinate truth level, a meta-language which in turn can be 'gödelized' (cf. chapter 4, note 1). (My best regards to Jaakko – in 1953 we slept in adjacent beds in the academy for officers in the reserve.)

Chapter 6 Political zero-sum games

1. See for instance David Wiles *"Boss Tweed"* Wikipedia; *The Tammany Hall Machine* and *Tammany Hall NYC*, both on the web.

2. See *The Economist* January 18th (2005) *Money, Politics and More Money*.

3. See Gustav von Hertzen (2003) *The Cultor Story – The Path Abroad*. (cf. chapter 4, note 15)

4. In *Jack* (2001) Jack Welch, the long-time chief executive of General Electric, renders a fascinating insight into in the values and strategies of his company.

5. See Wikipedia *California electricity crisis*.

6. In *Economic Origins of Dictatorship and Democracy* (2006) Daron Agemoglu and James A. Robinson are presenting a political theory, based on the redistribution problem. They start with the assumption that economic class conflict is the only political driving force which facilitates the application of a rigorous but lopsided game-theoretic model.

7. See for instance Iain McLean: *Public Choice: An Introduction* (1987); James M. Buchanan och Richard A. Musgrave: *Public Finance and Public Choice: Two Contrasting Visions of the State* (1999). See also *The Concise Encyclopedia of Economics Public Choice Theory*.

8. Robert E. Hall & Alvin Rabushka *The Flat Tax* (1995). A measure of progressivity can be introduced by a basic deduction on the income. See also *The Economist* April 16th (2005). *The flat tax revolution.*

9. See Paolo de Renzio *QEH Working Paper Series* Working Paper Number 27 (2000) *Bigmen and Wantoks: Social Capital and Group Behaviour in Papua New Guinea* on the web.

10. The basic facts have not been contested. See for instance Wikipedia *Salvador Allende* which features an extensive discussion. The Parliament resolution, which preceded the Pinochet coup, is also a worthwhile read: *Agreement of the Chamber of Deputies* August 22, (1973). See also Karen Araujo and Paul Craig Roberts: *Chile: Two visions, the Allende-Pinochet era* (2006).

11. See Michael Reid *Forgotten Continent: The battle for Latin America's Soul* (2007).

12. See U.S. Senate *Lobbying Disclosure Act 1995.*

13. See Wikipedia *Weatherman (organization).*

14. *Archives Blast from the Past: Kicking up a Storm: The Legacy of Mark Rudd* (2003) on the web.

15. Dwight R. Lee and Richard B. McKenzie: *Helping the Poor Through Governmental Poverty Programs: The Triumph of Rhetoric over Reality* in Gwartney, Wagner eds. *Public Choice and Constitutional Economics* (1988).

Chapter 7 The economic plus-sum game.

1. In the United States, General Motors and Ford are on the skids and the federal fund for pension insurance (Pension Benefit Guaranty Corporation, PBGC) is wobbling.

2. OECD *Main Economic Indicators.* Conventional statistics do not include investments in education, R&D or marketing which distorts the comparison.

3. See *The Economist* January 27th (2005) *Nigeria: Democracy and its discontents; The Economist* October 27th (2005) *Nigeria: The fat of the land.*

4. See for instance Milton Friedman & Rose D. Friedman *Capitalism and Freedom* (1962) and *Free to Choose* (1980). See also the obituary in *The Economist* November 25th (2006) 87–88 *A heavyweight champ at five foot two.*

5. OECD *Main Economic Indicators.*

6. Johan Edqvist: *Sveriges Riksdag: Ledamöter inkl. ersättare,* (October 2005). Personal communication.

6a. It is encouraging that the Nobel Prize in economics in 2007 was awarded to Leonid Hurwicz, Eric Maskin and Roger Myerson for clarifying the design of the relevant mechanisms. See also Robert B. Reich *Supercapitalism* (2007)

7. See for instance David R. Henderson: *Japan and the Myth of MITI. The Concise Encyclopedia of Economics.*

8. The business idea concept was introduced in the 1970s by SIAR (Scandinavian Institute for Administrative Research) under the direction of Erik Rhenman (1933–1993). See for instance Erik Rhenman *Organization Theory for Long Range Planning* (1973); Richard Normann *Management for Growth* (1977); Christian Junnelius *Business Idea –The Cornerstone of Business Strategy* (2000).

9. See chapter 2, note 9. See also Berry J. Nalebuff & Adam M. Brandenburger *Co-opetition* (1996). For a Russian perspective see Alexander Martirosyan *Strategy Through People: The Basics of a Contributing Organisation* (2006).

10. See for instance Manuel Castells *The Rise of the Network Society* (1996) p.151–200; Castells & Himanen *The Information Society and the Welfare State. The Finnish Model* (2002) See also *Lean Tools, Toyota Production System (TPS)* on the web.

11. See Michael Porter & Elisabeth Olmstedt-Teisberg *Redefining Health Care: Creating Value-based Competition on Results* (2006).

12. In academic circles, too, a new paradigm has been initiated. See for instance Julian le Grand *Motivation, Agency and Public Policy: Of Knights and Knaves, Pawns and Queens* Oxford University Press (2003). Le Grand was one of Tony Blair's trusted advisers and his ideas reflect the aim to create a quasi-market for health care and education.

13. Buchanan, James, Devletoglou, A. & Nicos E *Academia in anarchy: An economic diagnosis* Basic Books (1970). See also *The Economist* September 10th (2005) *The brains business: A survey of higher education.*

14. An insider has rendered the chain of events as follows. The commission first proposed a carbon dioxide tax but was blocked by the aversion against any kind of tax decisions on the EU-level. The cap and trade regulation was approved despite the awkward quota system and the implied indirect taxation. In his latest book, *Making Globalization Work* (2006), Joseph E. Stiglitz presents the case for a global carbon tax. About the superiority of taxation as a steering device see for instance Richard Posner *Catastrophe: Risk and Response* (2004); William H. Schlesinger editorial *Science* 314 (2006) 1217.

15. See for instance Gwyn Prins and Steve Rayner *Time to ditch Kyoto, Nature* 449 (2007) 973–975.

16. See *U.S. Nuclear Regulatory Commission Fact Sheet on the Accident at Three Mile Island* (2000).

17. See for instance *US Death Rate Surged During Summer 1986. Causes Debated. Rachel's Environmental & Health News* #64, February (1988). Deaths due to pneumonia increased by 18.1 % and due to all infectious diseases with 22.5% compared with 1985.

18. World Health Organization *Media Centre Chernobyl: the true scale of the accident* (2005). International Atomic Energy Agency (IAEA) *Chernobyl's Legacy: Health, Environmental and Socio-economic Impacts* (2005). The main health hazards identified were psychological and psychosomatic.

19. According to *Svenska Dagbladet* 29.11. (2005). The official figures are much lower, a few thousands per annum.

20. Bertazzi et.al. *Epidemiology 8* (1997) 646–652. *Dioxin Update from Seveso;* J. Barton Sterling *Journal of Drugs in Dermatology* March-April (2005) *Dioxin toxicity and chloracne in the Ukraine; Science Encyclopedia, Dioxin – Toxicity* on the web.

21. See *Nature* 435 (2005) 1179–1186. *China's environment in a globalizing world.*

22. See for instance Wikipedia *CFC.*

23. See Jens Bjerre *The Last Cannibals* (1956) p. 31–38.

24. See *Friskolornas Riksförbund*, on the web. See also *The Economist* June 12th (2008) 69 *Private education: The Swedish model*

25. See *The Economist* June 28th (2008) 67–69 *Education reform: Top of the class*

26. See also Johan Norberg *In Defence of Global Capitalism* (2005).

27. International Organization for Migration (IOM), Press Briefing Notes – 7 February (2006) *Benin – Ministerial Conference of Least Developed Countries Focuses on Migrant Remittances.* About one half of the remittances are estimated to fall outside the official statistics.

Chapter 8 Law and justice

1. See Human Rights Watch May (2006) *Lost in Transition: Bold Ambitions, Limited Results for Human Rights Under Fox. Part V Law Enforcement: Ongoing Abuses that Undermine Public Security* on the web; Enrique Diaz-Aranda *Mexican Law Review* Number 6, July-December (2006) *Criminality and Criminal Law in Mexico: Where are we going?* on the web.

2. Annual report of the Finnish police *Rikostorjunta* (2004) (Crime protection)

3. The only time I have been indicted, I became the victim of a miscarriage of justice. I was fined for negligence in buying stock in breach of insider trading regulations. The court declared that I did not intend to make a profit but in view of my position as chairman of the supervisory board of the company, I should have been more careful in my trading. The letter of the law did not provide any grounds for the sentence but the court referred to preparatory work on the law and an obscure academic paper. The sentence was obviously contrary to law but my shocked lawyer counseled me to leave it at that. I followed his advice which was my mistake. Six months later the law was amended and explicitly declared that striving for profit was a precondition of criminality.

4. Reference.com *Japanese law* (2006), on the web.

5. Bill Stonehill *Japan Perspectives, Law in Japan* (2000), on the web

6. See Steve Bogira *Courtroom 302: A Year Behind the Scenes in an American Courthouse* (2005); *The Economist* February 3rd (2007) 58

7. See Simon Schama *The Embarrassement of Riches: In Interpretation of Dutch Culture in the Golden Age* (1987) p. 15–24. Schama is not wholly assured that this type of punishment was ever implemented.

8. *Misuse of Drugs Act* revised (1998). See also Wikipedia *Law of Singapore.*

9. See Alan A. Stone *American Psychiatric Press* (1984) 3–40 *Law, Psychiatry and Morality.* See also Wikipedia *Psikhushka.*

10. *California Penal Code* §374 et seq. (2004) (for cities). The punishment for littering is a $1000 fine but the implementation is rather slack.

11. See for instance *Venture Capitalists on the Streets. An interview with the Salvation Army´s National commander, W. Todd Bassett* on the web.

12. *CRIS Sweden* on the web

13. Essi Viding et al. *Journal of Child Psychology* 46 (2005) 592–597 *Strong genetic risk for psychopathic syndrome in children.*

14. J. Stevenson & R. Goodman *J. Psychiatry* Sept. Nr 179 (2001) 197–202. *Association between behavior at age 3 years and adult criminality.*

15. Robert E. Rector *The Myth of Widespread American Poverty. The Heritage Foundation, Policy Research & Analysis* Sept 18 (1998).

16. See Maurize Pinzon *New York News Network* April 16 (2004).

17. See Hartmut Mayer & Henri Vogt eds. *A Responsible Europe* (2006)

18. See Transparency International *The Kenya Bribery Index (2005; Mail & Guardian on line* 10 April (2006); *The Economist* February 10th (2005) *No End in sight to Kenya's corruption woes.*

19. See Amnesty International's *Report on Non-ID Palestinian Refugees in Lebanon* 05.10 (2005); Amnesty International: *Long Standing Suffering of Palestinian Refugees in Lebanon* 29.03 (2006).

20. See for Instance David Landes *The Wealth and Poverty of Nations* (1998).

Chapter 9 The fourth estate

1. See Wikipedia *United States journalism scandals.*

2. See for instance Encyclopedia Britannica *Brent Spar*; Dirk Maxeiner *Lessons from Brent Spar* Maxeiner & Miersch (2003) on the web. In 1998, the authoritative Oslo-Paris commission (OSPAR) decided that big platforms must be scrapped on land; the concrete structures can be excepted by special permission. At present, the value of steel scrap makes recycling profitable.

3. *Yearbook of International Organizations* 2006/2007 edited by the Union of International Assocations. K.G.Saur Verlag

4. See *The Economist* March 5th (2005) *Obituary: Peter Berenson.*

4a. See Pierre Rosanvallon *La contre-démocratie* for an in-depth analysis.

5. *The Economist* March 19th (2005) *Unbroken yokes: Niger decides not to free its slaves* and *Still with us.* See also Hugh Thomas *The Slave Trade: The Story of the Atlantic Slave Trade* (1997).

6. Helen Zumpe *Sprachlenkung im Nationalsozialismus*. Dokumentations- und Informationszentrum für Rassismusforschung e.V. (DIR) (2000) on the web.
7. See *United Nations Development Programme, Crisis Prevention & Recovery: Mine Action Update* (April 2004).
8. See *The Economist* December 2nd (2006) Technology Quarterly 3–4 *Cat and mouse*.
9. See *The Economist* April 22nd, (2006) Special section *Among the audience*.
10. See Wikipedia *Weblog*.
11. See for instance John B. Thompson *Books in the Digital Age* (2005).

Chapter 10 Democratic fallacies

1. Franz Schurmann et al. eds. *Imperial China* (1967).
2. See Nel et al. *Science* 311 (2006) 622–627. *Toxic Potential Materials at the Nanolevel*. The classic nano-technological text is K. Eric Drexler: *Engines of creation: The Coming Era of Nanotechnology* (1986) See also K.E. Drexler & C. Peterson: *Unbounding the Future: The Nanotechnology Revolution* (1991).
3. See Bill Kovarik *Mass Media and Environmental Conflict* (2002); Paul Frame *Radioluminescent Paint. Oak Ridge Associated Universities* on the web.
4. The relation between cancer and low doses of radioactive radiation has been controversial for long. For a dramatic hormetic effect see W.C. Chen et al. *Journal of American Physicians and Surgeons* 9, nr.1 (2004) 1–10 *Is Chronic Radiation an Effective Prophylaxis Against Cancer?* The cancer incidence of the radiated group was reduced by 97 % compared to the normal population! The authors encountered considerable difficulties in publication. See also Chandrasekara Dissanayake *Science* 309 (2005) 883–885 *Of Stones and Health: Medical Geology in Sri Lanka*. The author establishes that in many parts of Asia, no negative effects of natural radioactive radiation has been observed even with radiation 200 times the normal level. See also Wei and Sugahara. *Journal of Radiation Research,* 41 (suppl.) (2000) 1–76 *High background radiation area in China*; Myron Pollycove & L.E. Feinendegen *The Journal of Nuclear Medicine* 42, 9 p. 26–32N, 37N, a review (2001) *Biologic Responses to Low Doses of Ionizing Radiation: Part 2. Dose Responses of Organisms*.
5. See for instance Edward J. Calabrese & Linda A. Baldwin *Nature* 421 (2003) 691–692 *Toxicology rethinks its central belief: Hormesis demands a reappraisal of the way risks are assessed*..
6. See for instance Bruce N. Ames & Lois Swirsky Gold *Mutation Research* 447 (2000) 3–13 *Paracelsus to parascience: the environmental cancer distraction*..
7. St. Matthew 15: 17–20; see also St. Mark 7: 15–23. (King James's Bible)
8. See for instance A. Trevavas & D. Stewart *Plant Biology*. nr. 6 (2003) 185–190 *Paradoxical effects of chemicals in the diet on health Current Opinion*.
9. See for instance E. Isolauri et al. *Gut* 50 (2002) 54–59 *Probiotics: a role in the treatment of intestinal infection and inflammation?*; G.A. Rook & L.R. Brunet *Gut* 54 (2005) 317–320 *Microbes, immunoregulation, and the gut*.
9a. See for instance Emma Morris *Nature* 448 (2007) 860–863 *Making Room*
10. See Virtual Interpretative Center *Kennewick Man*, on the web.
11. *The Times-Democrat* 2nd November 1884. Can be found in *Occidential Gleanings*, volume II (1925).
12. See Ruth Brandon *The Spiritualists* (1983).
12a. Vincent Bugliosi *Reclaiming History: The Assassination of President John F. Kennedy* (2007). The book should be the final verdict on any conspiracy theories.
13. See Wikipedia *The Protocols of the Elders of Zion*.
14. CNS News.com January 07 (2005).
15. Energy Information Administration, US Department of Energy *Crude oil and Total Petroleum Imports* (April 2006).

16. See Melford Spiro *Gender and Culture: Kibbutz Women Revisited* (1979); see also J.Q. Wilson *The moral sense* (1993) p. 182–185.

16a. Karen Kidd *Natural Sciences and Engineering Research Council of Canada* 15.02.2007 *Fish Devastated by Sex-changing Chemicals in Municipal Wastewater,*.

17. The SCUM-manifest was written in 1966 by Valerie Solanas, a mentally instable part-time prostitute. She died in 1988.

18. About the Bonobo see Frans B.M. de Waal *Scientific American* March (1995) 82–88. *Bonobo Sex and Society,*

19. Several studies indicate the presence of so-called iatrogenic effects when the therapy is hurting more than its helps. See for instance Mayou et al. (2000) *ASR Annotation. Psychological Debriefing. Post-Trauma Acute Stress Reaction (ASR), Civilian Population* on the web. See also Richard J. McNally *Science* 313 (2006) 923–924 *Psychiatric Casualties of War.*

20. *National Comorbidity Survey Replication* is a statistical study under the aegis of National Institute of Mental Health together with Harvard University and University of Michigan. See *Science* 308 (2005) 1527.

21. *Lionel Robbins Memorial Lectures* 2002/3. on the web.

22. See *Bulletin of the World Health Organization* 79, 12 (2001) *Choosing to die – a growing epidemic among the young.*

23. Originally the characterization by Charles Maurice Talleyrand (1754–1838) of French aristocrats, returning from the 25 year exile with the Bourbons during the French revolution.

24. For the debunking of this line of argument see Dick Taverne: *The March of Unreason: Science, Democracy, and the New Fundamentalism* (2005); Ophelia Benson & Jeremy Stangroom *Why Truth Matters* (2006).

Chapter 11 The lessons of history

1. See for instance Peter Brown *The Rise of Western Christendom: Triumph and Diversity AD 200–1000* (1996)

2. Joseph A. Tainter *The Collapse of Complex Societies* (1988) p. 7–8.

3. J.Cramer et al. *Nature* 432 23 December (2004) 1020–1023 *Dating the Late Archaic Occupation of the Norte Chico region in Peru*: Commentary in *Science* 307 (2005) 34–35.

4. See Encyclopedia Britannica, *Pre-Columbian Writing*. The Inca state communicated by *khipu*, an intricate system of knots on cotton strings, but *khipu* does not qualify as a written language.

5. See Diamond *Collapse* (2005) p. 157–177. Cf. the literature review on p. 537–539; see also Yoffee *Myths of the Archaic State* (2005).

6. See David P. Chandler *A History of Cambodia* (2000). Every king wanted to build a temple (around forty in total) which preferably should surpass the predecessor's. About the water supply see *Science* 311 (2006) 1364–1368 *The End of Angkor*

7. Oswald Spengler *Der Untergang des Abendlandes* (1918–22); Arnold Toynbee *History of the World* (1934–54). Other significant contributions are for instance R.G. Collingwood (1889–1943) *The Idea of History* (appeared posthumously 1946) and Fernand Braudel (1902–1985) *Le Monde actuel, histoire et civilisations* (1963). I also want to call attention to *Kulturgeschichte der Neuzeit* (1927–1931) by Egon Friedell (1878–1938).

8. Joseph Needham (1900–1995) *Science and Civilization in China* (1954–2004) is a monumental work and a standard reference (the project is still work in progress). For an abridged presentation, see Colin A. Ronan *The Cambridge Illustrated History of the World's Science* p. 125–186 (1983). Needham idealizes Chinese science. The technical innovations were certainly path-breaking but they did not lead to the cumulative accumulation of knowledge and significant scientific insights.

9. Thomas Sowell *Conquests and Cultures: An International History* (1998) p. 330.
10. In India, the interaction between religious conceptions and social life is extraordinary complex. V.S. Naipaul *India: A Wounded Civilization* (1977) and *India: A Million Mutinies Now* (1990) provide illuminating examples of the social dynamics.
11. See Steven LeBlanc *Chaco Culture National Historical Park* Wikipedia (1999).
12. See Wikipedia *Mississippian Culture;* M. J. Heckenberger et al. *Science* 321 (2008) 1214–1217 *Pre-Columbian Urbanism, Anthropogenic Landscapes, and the Future of the Amazon*
13. See Encyclopedia Britannica *Ethiopia.*
14. See for instance Ata-Malik Juvaini *Genghis Khan: The History of the World-Conqueror* (1958); David Morgan *The Mongols* (1986). It has been calculated that one out of every 200 persons in Eurasia is a descendant of Djingis Khan. See Spencer Wells et al *American Journal of Human Genetics* 71, nr 3 (2002) 466–482 *A Genetic Landscape Reshaped by Recent Events: Insights into Central Asia.*
15. See for instance James J. Fox: *Harvest Of The Palm: Ecological Change in Eastern Indonesia* (1977). Fox compares two societies with an almost identical economic base but with different religious background. The outcome is two highly divergent social structures.
16. About the history of the Romany see for instance *The Patrin Web Journal, Timeline of Romani History.*
17. See Michael Reid *The Forgotten Continent: The Battle For Latin America's Soul* (2007). The book is an up-to-date companion to the tortuous history of the subcontinent. See also *Encyclopedia of Latin American History and Culture* (1996).
18. See Wikipedia *Antonio López de Santa Anna.*
19. To this day, regulations issued during the British colonial rule are in force in Pakistan. The city of Karachi is still using an exact copy of the colonial manual for the public works in Bombay. The title page reads as follows *"Bombay Public Works Department Manual, Volume 1: (Applicable in the province of Sind and useful for all concerned throug-out [sic] Pakistan)* Revised [?!] edition 2004". §40 in the manual is worthy of citation *in toto.* "When European officers and subordinates are killed or severely wounded by fanatics or others or meet with sudden or violent death in any very exceptional circumstances, particulars connected with the occurrence should be telegraphed to the Government of India [!] to enable early information to be given to the relatives and friends of those killed or injured."
20. Martin Meredith *The State of Africa: A History of Fifty Years of Independence* (2005) is my foremost source regarding the post-colonial history of Africa.
21. See for instance Ron Chernow *Titan: The Life of John D. Rockefeller* (1998). The oil magnate Rockefeller was the most successful of the economic empire-builders in the United States and, besides the steel baron Andrew Carnegie, also the most morally conscious. Robber baron is not a wholly adequate designation for these tough businessmen.
22. See for instance Anna Politkovskaya *Putin's Russia* (2004)
23. Robert L. Carneiro *Science* 169 (1970) 733–738 *A Theory of the Origin of the State;* Robert L. Carneiro *Proceedings of the National Academy of Science* 97 (2000) 12926–12931 *The transition from quantity to quality: A neglected causal mechanism in accounting for social evolution.*
24. See Yoffee *Myths of the Archaic State* (2005).

Chapter 12 Future perspectives

1. In 1984, a few eminent researchers founded the Santa Fe institute for the study of complexity in a cross-scientific perspective. Similar research centers have since

been founded in many places but a comprehensive complexity theory is not yet on the cards. Neither has futurology as a research object been convincingly staked out even if an extensive literature is already in existence. For the basics see for instance Wendell Bell *Foundation of future studies: Human science for a new era* (1996).

2. See for instance Peter Schwartz: *The Art of the Long View Planning (1996)* and *Scenarios* on the web. See also Dahlman, C. et al. eds. (2006) *Finland as a Knowledge Economy: Elements of Success and Lessons Learned.* World Bank Institute.

3. For a systematic analysis of the performance of political forecasters see Philip E. Tetlock *Expert Political Judgement: How Good Is It? How Can We Know?* (2005)

4. See also Elinor Ostrom *Policies that crowd out Reciprocity Action* in Gintis et al. eds. (2005) p. 255–275.

5. In November (2006), World Summit on the Information Society (WSIS) was concluded with a resolution which invited the United Nations to establish an Internet Governance Forum. The mandate of ICANN is supposed to remain intact.

6. In plants the basic photochemical reactions are very efficient, but the net production of organic material is generally low, of the order of 0.1 % of the solar input energy. A yield of 1 % is considered a breakthrough. See Long et al. Global Change Biology 14 (2008) 2000–2014. For the diverse possibilities to utilize renewable solar energy see for instance Kosuke Kurokawa ed. *Energy from the Desert: Feasibility of very large scale photovoltaic power generation system* (2003); Wall et al. eds. *Bioenergy* (2008); *The Economist* June 21st (2008) *The power and the glory: A special report on the future of energy.*

7. See Lu et al. *Nature* 440 (2006) 295 *Photocatalyst releasing hydrogen from water.*

8. See for instance Ragauskas et al. *Science* 311 (2006) 484–489 *The Path Forward for Biofuels and Biomaterials.* See also Y. Román-Leshkov et al. *Nature* 447 (2007) 982–985 *Production of demethylfuran for liquid fuels from biomass-derived carbohydrates.*

9. See for instance Judy D. Wall *Nature Biotechnology* 22 (2004) 40–41 *Rain or shine – a phototroph that delivers;* Lane & Schubert *Nature* 441 (2006) 274–279 *Batteries Not Included.*

10. See *Science* 309 (2005) 1168-1169 *Is the Friendly Atom Poised for a Comeback?; The Economist* June 3rd (2006) 81–82 *Nuclear Power: The Shape of things to come.*

11. See Krushelnick and Cowley *Science* 309 (2005) 1502–1503 *Reduced Turbulence and New Opportunities for Fusion.*

12. Richard Dawkins is better known for his expositions about the mechanisms of evolution. *The Selfish Gene* (1976) and *The Blind Watchmaker* (1986). *The God Delusion* (2006) is a tract based on an all out application of evolutionary psychology.

13. See for instance Mladen Pavičič: *Quantum Computation and Quantum Communication: Theory and Experiments* (2005).

14. Jan Kåhre *The Mathematical Theory of Information* (2002) structures the concept of information starting from simple axiomatic principles. See also Hans Christian von Baeyer *Information. The New Language of Science* (2003).

15. A classic text about this syndrome is A.R. Luria (1902–1977) *The Mind of a Mnemonist: A Little Book about a vast memory* (1968).

16. See for instance *The Economist* June 10th (2006) *Technology Quarterly* 20–21. *How to Build a Babel Fish.*

17. See Wikipedia *Transhumanism* (2006).

18. See for instance Lee M. Silver: *Remaking Eden: How Genetic Engineering and Cloning Will Transform the American Family* (1997).

19. See for instance Wikipedia *Wheat yields in developing countries, 1951–2004; Wheat yields in selected countries 1951–2004,*
20. See for instance *Science* **311** (2006) 1544–1546 *The Race for the $1000 Genome;* C. J. Arntzen *Science* **321** (2008) 1052–1053 *Using Tobacco to Treat Cancer.*
21. See Constance Holden *Science* **312**, 21 April (2006) 349 *Gene-Suppressing Proteins Reveal Secrets of Stem Cells; Nature* **441** (2006) 1059–1102 Insight *Stem Cell biology.*
22. See for instance Gregory Stock *Redesigning Humans: Our Inevitable Genetic Future* (2002) and Francis Fukuyama *Our Posthuman Future: Consequences of the Biotechnical Revolution* (2002). The books represent two diverging but well reasoned views – the former cautiously optimistic, the latter cautiously conservative. See also Gilbert, Tyler & Zackin: *Bioethics and the New Embryology: Springboards for Debate* (2005).
22a. See for instance Steven Weinberg *Cosmology* (2008), a rather demanding text.
23. Due to the Heisenberg uncertainty principle, the vacuum is full of virtual particles which are incessantly created and destroyed but also interact with real electrons, protons etc. The vacuum has an energy content which is connected to the cosmological constant. It can be measured and makes its appearance, for example, in the Casimir effect. However, a rough quantum-mechanical calculation arrives at values which are enormously bigger (10^{120}) than the measured one. This dizzying discrepancy between theory and reality is still unexplained. Something important is lacking in our interpretation of the relation between the micro- and the macrocosmos.
24. See for instance Freeman Dyson *Disturbing the Universe* (1979); Wikipedia *Terraforming* and *Red Colony.*
25. See for instance Ted Sargent *The Dance of Molecules: Nanotechnology is Changing our Lives* (2006)
26. Two entangled electrons form a boson. If the entangled electrons are separated and one of them interacts with a detector, the other one will turn into a fermion. If the original entangled pair is part of a sufficiently sensitive system this ought to be detectable. A space ship could then be equipped with a set of singled out but entangled electrons. By releasing specific electrons from the entanglement bank on board, a coded message could be instantly received on earth (or vice versa). This would not necessarily break against the principle that the velocity of light cannot be exceeded in transmitting information. The communication potential which is preserved during the slow progress of the space ship is sharply delimited. The communication does not imply any transfer of new information in an actual sense.
27. See for instance George Basalla *Civilized Life in the Universe: Scientists on Intelligent Extraterrestials* (2005).

Chapter 13 Threats galore

1. The single asteroid hypothesis is not unanimously accepted. In particular, the impact crater at Chicxulub presents several question marks. There may have been several, almost simultaneous impacts, perhaps from a disintegrated comet. The vast lava flows in the Deccan may have contributed to the mayhem.
2. For reviews of the asteroid threat see Richard Stone *Science* **319** (2008) 1326–1329 *Preparing for Doomsday* and *Cosmic Impacts* in *Nature* **453** (2008) 1157–1168. See also Robert Roy Britt *Space com.* 19 March (2002) *Asteroid Buzzes Earth Highlighting Cosmic Blind Spot.*
3. NASA, Near Earth Object Program, *The Torino Impact Hazard Scale;* Robert Roy Britt *Space Science* 27 December (2004) *Asteroid Watch: Odds of 2029 Collision Stuck at 1-in-40* on the web.
4. Leonard David *Space Science* 06 June (2002) *First Strike or Asteroid Impact? The Urgent Need to Know the Difference.*

5. B612 Foundation, on the web.

6. *Science* 312 (2006) 1327–1353 *Hayabusa at Asteroid Itokawa;* Eric Asphaug *Science* 316 (2007) 993–994 *The Shifting Sands of Asteroids.*

6a. See Douglas Erwin (2006) *Extinction: How Life on Earth Nearly Ended 250 Million Years Ago*

7. The mapping of the magma flows have only recently started in earnest. The flows cause the movements of the geological plates whereas the magnetic field around the earth is caused by fluid motion in the core. The field is occasionally reversed which weakens the shielding of the solar wind and the cosmic radiation, probably without serious consequences. The reversals occur at an average interval of 250,000 years but the with very large variations. The latest inversion occurred 750,000 years ago and the magnetic field strength is now decreasing.

7a. T.S. Murty et al. *ISET Journal of Earthquake Technology* December (2005) 227–236

8. The decrease in the carbon dioxide content is reflected in plant evolution. Many plant species (the so-called C4 plants) improved the efficiency of assimilation by developing a carbon dioxide pump to cope with the change. See Pagani et al. *Science* 309 (2005) 600-602 *Marked decline in atmospheric carbon dioxide concentrations during the Paleogene.* The latest sequence of ice ages may be due to the connection of North and South America by the Panama isthmus three million years ago which had an influence on oceanic circulation and thus the climate.

9. See for instance Raper & Braithwaite *Nature* 439 (2006) 311–313 *Low sea level projections from mountain glaciers and icecaps under global warming.*

10. See for instance Quirin Schiermeier *Nature* 439 (2006) 256–260 *A Sea Change.* For a more optimistic view see Patrick J. Michaels & Robert C. Balling Jr *The Satanic Gases: Clearing the Air about Global Warming.* Cato Institute (2000).

11. Friis-Christensen & Lassen *Science* 254 (1991) 698–700. *Length of the solar cycle: An indicator of solar activity closely associated with climate;* H. Svensmark, & E. Friis-Christensen *Journal of Atmospheric and Solar-Terrestrial Physics* 59, 11, July (1997) 1225–1232(8) *Variation of cosmic ray flux and global cloud coverage – a missing link in solar-climate relationships.* For a rejoinder see Paul E. Damon & Peter Laut: *EOS* 85, 39, 28 September (2004) *Pattern of Strange Errors Plagues Solar Activity and Terrestrial Climate Data.* For a supporting view see Svensmark et al. *Proceedings of the Royal Society A,* October 3, (2006) *Experimental Evidence for the role of Ions in Particle Nucleation under Atmospheric Conditions.*

12. *IPCC Fourth Assessment Report.* For an insightful comment see *The Economist* February 10th (2007) 86 *Climate change.*

13. See T.M.Wigley *Science* 314 (2006) 401–403, 452–454 *Pollute the Planet for Climate's Sake;* Oliver Morton *Nature* 447 (2007) 132–136 *Is this what it takes to save the world?;* Brian Launder & Michael Thompson eds. *Royal Society Publishing* October (2008) *Geoscale engineering to avert dangerous climate change.*

14. See Buesseler et al. *Science* 316 (2007) 567–569 *Revisiting Carbon Flux Through the Oceans's Twilight Zone.*

15. See Roger Angel *PNAS* 103, Nov 14 (2006) 17184–17189 *Feasibility of Cooling Earth with a Cloud of Small Space Craft near L1.*

16. See University of Minnesota, Extension Service (1999) *What's Happening to Tropical Forests?* See also Palm, Vosti, Sanchez, Ericksen eds. *Slash-and-Burn Agriculture: The Search for Alternatives* (2005).

17. Pekka Kauppi et al. *PNAS* 103 (2006) 17574–17579. *Returning forests analyzed with forest identity.*

18. See for instance *The Economist* April 23rd (2005) 78–80 *Environmental economics: Are you being served.*

19. See CDC *(Center for Disease Control and Prevention), Morbidity and Mortality Weekly Report (MMWR)* December 31 (1999); Donald A. Henderson *Nature* 447 (2007) 279–283 *Eradication: Lessons from the Past;* Wolfe, Dunavan, Diamond *Nature* 447 (2007) 279–283 *Origins of major human infectious diseases.*

20. See Leslie Roberts *Science* 312 (2006) 832–835 *Polio Eradication: Is It Time to Give Up.*

21. See James Chin *The AIDS Pandemic: The Collision of Epidemiology with Political Correctness* (2007).

22. See W.D. Hamilton *Narrow Roads of Geneland II: Evolution of Sex* (2001).

22a. See *Science* 321 (2008) 355–369 Special section: *Deadly Defiance*

23. See *Science* 310 (2005) Editorial p.17; News p. 28–29; Tumpey et al. p. 77–80 *Characterization of the Reconstructed 1918 Spanish Influenza Pandemic Virus; Science* 312 (2006) 379–397 Special Section *Influenza: The State of Our Ignorance.*

24. CDC *(Center for Disease Control and Prevention)* 10, No 11, November 2004 *Emerging Infectious Diseases. Women and Autoimmune Diseases.* About 80 % of patients are women.

25. See for instance M. G. Weinbauer: *Ecology of prokaryotic viruses. FEMS Microbiology Reviews* 28 nr (2004) 127–181. Larsen et al. *Limnol.Oceanogr.* 49 (2004) 180–190 *Spring phytoplankton bloom dynamics in Norwegian waters: Microbial succession and diversity;* Jean-Michel Claverie *Quantitative Biology* June 2005 *The 4th Algal Virus Workshop: Giant viruses in the oceans.*

26. Allander et al. *PNAS on line* September 6 (2005) *Cloning of a human parvovirus by molecular screening of respiratory tract samples.*

27. Hema Bashyam *The Journal of Experimental Medicine* 205, No. 1, 3 (2008) *An inflammating-enhancing virus;* Hong Qiu et al. *The Journal of Experimental Medicine* 205 No. 1 19–24 (2008) *Human CMV infection induces 5-lipoxygenase expression and leukotriene B$_4$ production in vascular smooth cells.*

28. See for instance Thorne et al. *Science* 311 (2006) 1780–1784 *Synergistic Antitumor Effects of Immune Cell-Viral Biotherapy.* See also chapter 12, note 19.

29. The source of the fertility data is *CIA World Factbook* 2008. All data are 2008 forecasts.

30. United Nation Population Division *World Population Prospects: The 2004 Revision. Highlights.*

31. *Public sector performance, SCP (Social and Cultural Planning Office), The Hague,* September (2004) *For the Lisbon process: Demography and the economy* on the web. See also Francesco C. Billari *National Institute Economic Review* No 194, October (2005) *Europe and its Fertility: From Low to Lowest Low; The Economist* February 11th (2006) *The fertility bust: Very low birth rates in Europe may be here to stay.*

32. Rahman, DaVanzo, Razzaque *Lancet* 358 (2001) 1051–1023 *When will Bangla Desh Reach Replacement-Level Fertility? The Role of Education and Family Planning Services.*

33. Cf. J. Wilson *The Moral Sense* (1993) p. 141–163.

34. See for instance Henry Bayman *The Secret of Islam: Love and Law in the Religion of Ethics.*

35. See *The Economist* May 20th (2006) 86–87. *Mass Hysteria: Telling the truth to the terrified.*

36. United Nations Development Programme (UNDP) Somalia. *Somalia Aid Coordination Body: Final Report Jan.Dec.* (2003) on the web.

37. See for instance Paul Collier *The Bottom Billion: Why the Poorest Countries Are Failing And What Can Be Done About It* (2007)

Chapter 14 The mission of democracy

1. France is, besides Great Britain, considered to be the most self-centered member of the European family. De Tocqueville knew his compatriots. "Thus the French are at once the most brilliant and the most dangerous of all European nations, and the best qualified to become, in the eyes of other people, an object of admiration, of hatred of compassion or alarm – never of indifference". *The Old regime and the French Revolution* (1856) p. 211

2. See for instance Nicolas Sarkozy *Testimony: France in the Twenty-First Century* (2007).

3. Wolfgang Lutz, Sylvia Kritzinger, Vegard Shirbekk *Science* 314 (2006) 425 *The Demography of Growing European Identity*. European Movement and JEF- Europe (Young European Federalists) are well-meaning organizations but they still lack visibility.

4. Se *G8 Gleneagles* (2005) Policy Issues, on the web.

5. See for instance Fareed Zakaria *The Post-American World* (2008)

6. Perez Musharraf has already written his self-biography *In The Line Of Fire: A Memoir* (2006)

7. *Failed and Collapsed States in the International System* A report prepared by The African Studies Centre, Leiden; The Transnational Institute, Amsterdam; The Center of Social Studies, Coimbra University; The Peace Research Center- CIP-FUHEM, Madrid. On the web.

8. For example RAMSI (Regional Mission to Solomon Islands) is a consortium, dominated by Australia. It has taken over the responsibility for nation-building in the Solomon Islands, which has been torn apart by tribal strife. See *Australian Government, Overseas Aid* on the web.

9. *The Report of the World Commission on Dams*, November 16 (2000) on the web.

10. See Risto E.J. Penttilä *IISS (International Institute for Strategic Studies) Adelphi Papers* 355 (2003) *The Role of the G8 in International Peace and Security*; Fratianni, Kirton, Rugman, Savona (ed.) *New Perspectives on Global Governance* (2005).

11. Max Weber made this point in 1919 in a lecture *Politik als Beruf* on the web.

12. *Charter Of Paris For A New Europe 1990: A new era of Democracy, Peace and Unity* on the web.

13. The Nobel Laureate Eric R. Kandel tells us in his self-biography, *In Search of Memory: The Emergence of a New Science of Mind* (2006), how he as an eight year old Jewish boy witnessed this astonishing metamorphosis.

14. See for instance P. Hawken, A. Lovins and L.H. Lovins *Natural Capitalism: Creating the Next Indistrial Revolution* (1999); A. Lovins et al. *Winning the Oil Endgame: Innovation for Profits, Jobs and Security* (2004)

15. See *The Economist* February 25th (2006) *The business of giving: A survey of wealth and philanthropy; Nature* 447 (2007) 248–254 *Biochemical Philanthropy*.

Chapter 15 The moral challenge

1. See Gustav von Hertzen *Cynics and Progress Motors* (1991). (Translated from *Organiserat entrepenörskap: Synpunkter på en företagarorganisation* 1974).

2. See Roland Griffiths et al. *Psychopharmacology* 187 (2006) 268–283 *Psilocybin can occasion mystical-type experiences having substantial and sustained meaning and spiritual significance*.

3. See for instance Alison Abbott *Nature* 410 (2001) 296–298 *Into the mind of a killer;* J. Greene and J. Haidt *Trends in Cognitive Sciences* 6, No 12 December (2002) *How (and where) does moral judgment work*.

4. A diary remark *The Letters of William James volume I* p. 147 (1920)

5. See Kendall Powell *Nature* **442**, 23 Aug (2006) 865–867 *How does the teenage brain work?*

6. See for instance William Acton: *Prostitution, Considered in its Moral, Social and Sanitary Aspects* 2nd ed. (1870); E. A. Wrigley ed. *Nineteenth-Century Society* (1972) p. 387–395; Eric Foner, John Arthur Garraty eds. *The Readers Companion to American History* (1991). About the historical background of the Victorian mind change see Ben Wilson (2007) *The Making of Victorian Values: Decency and Dissent in Britain 1789–1837.*

7. Maslow's hierarchy of values is the best known exponent for this approach. See Abraham H. Maslow *Motivation and Personality* 2nd ed. (1970).

8. St. Matthew 25;14–30.

9. St. Luke 15;12–32

10. See Roy *Globalised Islam* (2004) p. 215.

11. For example in an appearance in February 9th 2006 in Berlin "*Ich werde nicht die Klappe halten*" and "*Der Prophet war im Unrecht*" on the web. Ayaan Hirsi Ali has written a self-biography *Infidel* (2007). She has now moved to the United States.

12. Orhan Pamuk *My father's suitcase* Nobel lecture 2006 *Svenska Akademien* home page.

13. See David M. Thomas and Barbara Boyle Torrey eds. *Canada and the United States: Differences that Count* (2008)

14. See Migration Policy Institute (2004) *Labour Migration in Asia.* On the web.

15. See also Güreck et al. *Science* **312** (2006) 108–111 *The Comparative Advantage of Sanctioning Institutions.*

16. Karl Jaspers (1883–1969) was the first to notice the religious creativity around 500 BC in *Vom Ursprung und Ziel der Geschichte* (1953). He also introduced the concept of axial time.

17. See for instance Wikipedia *Scientology.*

18. See Stacy Schiff: *Great Improvisation: Franklin, France and Birth of America* (2005) p. 368

19. Gustav von Hertzen: *The Spirit of the Game* (1993) p. 412–419.

20. See for instance Stuart Kaufmann *Reinventing the Sacred: A New View of Science, Reason and Religion* (2008). The book can be understood as a contribution to modern theology (cf. chapter 5.5, p. 108).

21. See for instance Michael Balter *Science* **312** (2006) 1894–1897 *The Baby Deficit.*

22. Microcredits are a step in the right direction. They are given without collateral but are guaranteed by a small collective. Muhammad Yunus started the Grameen Bank in Bangladesh in 1983 and millions of poor people, mostly women, have since escaped poverty. Yunus got the Nobel Peace Award in 2006. Microbanking has since become a commercial success.

23. See Gustav von Hertzen *The Spirit of the Game* (1993) p. 404ff.

Bibliography

Acemoglu, D. & Robinson, J. (2006) *Economic origin of dictatorship and democracy* Cambridge University Press

Acton, W. (1857) *Prostitution: Considered in its Moral, Social and Sanitary aspects in London and in other large cities.* New edition, Cambridge University Press (1972)

Ali, A.H. (2007) *Infidel* Free Press

Araujo, K. & Roberts, P.C. (2006) *Chile: Two visions: The Allende-Pinochet era* TBA

Arendt, H. (1963) *Eichmann in Jerusalem: A Report on the Banality of Evil* Faber & Faber

Aristotle (fourth century BC) *Politica.* In English *Politics* on the web

Arredi, B. (2007) *The Peopling of Europe* In M. Crawford ed. *Anthropological Genetics* Cambridge University Press

Arrow, K. (1951) *Social choice and individual values* John Wiley

Axelrod, R. (1984) *The evolution of cooperation* Basic Books Inc

Baeyer, C. (2003) *Information: The Language of Science* Weidenfeld & Nicolson

Babiak, P. & Hare, R.D. (2006) *Snakes in Suits: When Psychopaths Go To Work* ReganBooks

Barash, D. & Barash, N. (2005) *Madame Bovary's Ovaries* Delacorte Press

Barrow, J. & Tipler, F. (1986) *The anthropic principle* Clarendon Press

Basalla, G. (2005) *Civilized life in the universe: Scientists on intelligent extraterrestrials* Oxford University Press

Baumeister, R. (1999) *Evil: Inside Human Violence and Cruelty* W.H.Freeman

Bayman, H. (2003) *The Secret of Islam: Love and Law in the Religion of Ethics* North Atlantic Books

Behrman, G. (2007) *The Most Noble Adventure: The Marshall Plan And The Time When America Helped Save Europe* Free Press

Beinhocker, E. (2006) *The Origin of Wealth: Evolution, Complexity and the Radical Remaking of Economics* Harvard Business School Press

Bell, W. (1996) *Foundation of future studies: Human science for a new era* Transaction Publishers

Benson, O. & Stangroom, J. (2006) *Why Truth Matters* Continuum International Publishing Group

Berry, W. (2000) *Life is a miracle: An essay against Modern Superstition* Basic Books

Binmore, K. (1994) *Game theory and social contract* I-II MIT Press

Bjerre, J. (1956) *The last cannibals* William Morrow

Bobbitt, P. (2002) *The Shield of Achilles: War, Peace and the Course of History* Knopf

Bobbit, P. (2008) *Terror and Consent: The Wars for the Twenty-First Century* Penguin books

Bogira, S. (2005) *Courtroom 302: A year behind the scenes in an American courthouse* Knopf

Bowles, S. (2004) *Microeconomics: Behavior, Institutions and Evolution* Princeton University Press

Brandon, R. (1983) *The spiritualists* Weidenfield and Nicholson

Braudel, F. (1963) *Le monde actuel, histoire et civilisation* Librairie Eugene Belin

Braudel, F. (1979) *Civilisation materiell, economie et capitalisme XV–XVIII siècle.* In English *The wheels of commerce* Cambridge University Press (1983)

Brogan, H. (2006) *Alexis de Tocqueville* Profile Books

Brown, P. (1996) *The Rise of Western Christendom* Blackwell Publishers

Buchanan, J & Musgrave, R. (1999) *Public Finance and Public Choice: Two Contrasting Visions of the State* MIT Press

Buchanan, J. & Tullock, G. (1962) *The calculus of consent*

Buchanan, J. et al. (1970) *Academia and anarchy: An economic diagnoses* Basic Books

Buchanan, J. et al. (1999) *Public finance and public choice* MIT Press

Bugliosi, V. (2007) *The Reclaiming of History: The Assassination of President John F. Kennedy* Norton

Burgess, A. (1962) *A Clockwork Orange* William Heinemann

Caldwell, C. (2004) *Hayek's Challenge: An Intellectual Biography* Unversity of Chicago Press

Camerer, C. (2002) *Behavioural game theory* Princeton University Press

Carlsson, R. et al. (ed) (2000) *Strategier för att förtjäna pengar: Om affärsidén och andra SIAR begrepp* Ekerlids forlag

Castells, M. (1996) *The rise of the network society* Blackwell

Castells, M. & Himanen, P. (2001) *The Information Society and the Welfare State. The Finnish Model* on the web

Chagnon, N. (1992) *Yanomamo* Hartcourt College Publications

Chandler, D. (2000) *A History of Cambodia* Westviev Press

Chernow, R. (1998) *Titan: The Life of John D. Rockefeller* Random House

Chin, J. (2007) *The AIDS Pandemic: The Collision of Epidemiology with Political Correctness* Radcliffe

Chydenius, A. (1766) *Den Nationale Winsten.* In English *National Profit and Loss* ChydenNet, on the web

Churchill, W. (1923) *The World Crisis* Thornton Butterworth

Clark, G. (2007) *A Farewell to Alms: A Brief Economic History of the World* Princeton University Press

Club of Rome (1972) *Limits to Growth* on the web

Collier, P. (2007) *The Bottom Billion: Why the Poorest Countries are Failing and What Can Be Done About It* Oxford University Press

Collingwood, R. (1946) *The Idea of History* Posthumously published and revised. New edition, Clarendon (1993)

Crawford, M. ed. (2007) *Anthropological Genetics* Cambridge University Press

Cunninghame, G. (1901) *A vanished Arcadia* Litrix reading room, on the web

Dahlman, C. et al. eds. (2006) *Finland as a Knowledge Economy: Elements of Success and Lessons Learned* World Bank Institute.

Darwin, C. (1871) *The Descent of Man* New edition, Penguin Classics (2004)

Davies, G. ed. (1996) *A History of Money from Ancient Times to the Present Day.* University of Wales Press.

Dawkins, R. (1976) *The Selfish Gene* Oxford University Press.

Dawkins, R. (1986) *The Blind Watchmaker* Norton.

Dawkins, R. (2006) *The God Delusion* Houghton Miffin

Diamond, J. (1997) *Guns, Germs and Steel* Norton

Diamond, J. (2005) *Collapse: How Societies Choose to Fail or Survive* Viking

Djilas, M. (1955) *The New Class: An Analysis of the Communist System* Harvest/ Hbj Book. New edition, Amazon (1983)

Donohue, J. et al. (2000) *The Impact of Legalized Abortion on Crime* Stanford Law School

Dostoyevsky, F. (1880) *Bratja Karamozovi.* In English *The Brothers Karamazov* Bantam Classics 1981

Drexler, K. (1986) *Engines of Creation: The Coming Era of Nanotechnology* Anchor Books

Drexler, K. & Peterson, C. (1991) *Unbounding the Future: The Nanotechnology Revolution* William Morrow

Drucker, P. (2001) *The Essential Drucker* Collins

Duncan, G. et al. (1984) *Years of Poverty, Years of Plenty.The Changing Economic Fortunes of American Workers and Families* University of Michigan Press

Dyson, F. (1979) *Disturbing the Universe* Harper & Row

Easterly, W. (2006) *The White Man's Burden: Why the West's Efforts to Aid the Rest Have Done So Much Ill and So Little Good* The Penguin Press

Eibl-Eibesfeldt, I. (1984) *Die Biologie des Menschlichen Verhaltens* Piper, Munich

Eliade, M. (1978–1985) *A History of Religious Ideas I–III* University of Chicago Press

Eliasson, G. (2005) *The birth, the life and the death of firms* The Ratio Institute, Stockholm

Ellis, C. D. (2008) *The Partnership: The Making of Goldman Sachs* Penguin Press

Erwin, D. (2006) *Extinction: How Life on Earth Nearly Ended 250 Million Years Ago* Princeton University Press

Etzioni, A. (1993) *The Spirit of Community* Touchstone

Etzioni, A. (1996) *The New Golden Rule* Basic Books

Etzioni, A. (2004) *From Empire to Community* Washington University

Fairbanks, J. & Goldman, M. (1998) *China: A New History* Harvard University Press

Fellman, M. (2000) *The Making of Robert Lee* Random House

Ferguson, N. (2004) *Colossus: The Price of America's Empire* Penguin Press

Florida, R. (2002) *The Rise of the Creative Class: And How It's Transforming Work, Leisure, Community and Everyday Life* Basic Books

Foner, E. et al. (1991) *The Readers Companion to American History* Houghton & Mifflin

Fox, J. (1977) *Harvest of the Palm: Ecological Change in Eastern Indonesia* Harvard University Press

Frank, R. (2005) *What Price the Moral High Ground? Ethical Dilemmas in Competitive Environments* Princeton University Press

Fratianni, M. et al. eds. (2005) *New Perspectives on Global Governance* Ashgate

Frazer, J. (1922) *The golden bough.* A one volume abridgement of the twelve volume work

Friedell, E. (1927) *Kulturgeschichte der Neuzeit*

Friedman, B. (2005) *The Moral Consequences of Economic Growth* Knopf

Friedman, L. M. (2002) *Law in America* Modern Library

Friedman, M. & R. (1980) *Free to Choose.* New edition, Harcourt (1990)

Friedman, M. (1962) *Capitalism and Freedom.* New edition, University of Chicago Press (2002)

Fukuyama, F. (1992) *The End of History and the Last Man* Free Press

Fukuyama, F. (1999) *The Great Disruption: Human Nature and the Reconstitution of Social Order* Free Press

Fukuyama, F. (2002) *Our Posthuman Future: Consequences of the Biotechnology Revolution* Picador

Furét, F. (1978) *Penser la Révolution française* Gallimard. In English *Interpreting the French Revolution* Press syndicate of the University of Cambridge (1981)

Gaddis, J. (2005) *The Cold War* Penguin Press

Gause, G. (1934) *The struggle for existence.* New edition, Dover publications (2003)

Gazzaniga, M. (2005) *The Ethical Brain* Dana Press

Gibbon, E. (1776–1789) *The History of the Decline and Fall of the Roman Empire.* New edition, The Folio Society (1983)

Gibbons, A. (2006) *The First Human: The Race to Discover our Earliest Ancestors* Doubleday

Gide, A. (1936) *Retour de l'U.R.S.S.* In English *Return from the U.S.S.R* Bolerium Books (1937)

Gilbert, S. et al. (2005) *Bioethics and the new embryology: Springboards for debate* Sinauer

Gintis, H. (2000) *Game theory evolving* Princeton University Press

Gintis, H., Bowles, S., Boyd, R., Fehr, E. eds. (2005) *Moral Sentiments and Material Interests: Foundations of Cooperation in Economic Life* MIT Press

Gleick, J. (1988) *Chaos: Making a New Science* Heinemann

Goodall, J. (1986) *The chimpanzees of Gombe* Harvard University Press

Grand le, J. (2003) *Motivation, Agency and Public Policy: Of Knights and Knaves, Pawns and Queens* Oxford University Press

Grass, G. (1999) *Kopfgeburten oder Die Deutschen sterben aus* Deutscher Taschenbuch Verlag

Graves, R. (1955) *The greek myths* Pelican books

Gwartney, J. et al ed. (1988) *Public choice and constitutional economics* JAI Press

Hagen, E. (2003) *The bargaining model of depression* In P. Hammerstein ed. *Genetic and cultural evolution of cooperation* p. 95–123. MIT Press

Hall, R. & Rabushka, A. (1995) *The flat tax* Hoover Institution Press

Hamilton, W. D. (1996) *Narrow roads to geneland I-II* W.H. Freeman Spectrum

Hawken, P., Lovins. A. & Lovins, L.H. (1999) *Natural Capitalism: Creating the Next Industrial Revolution* Little Brown & Co

Hayek von, F. (1944) *The Road to Serfdom*. New edition, Chicago University Press 1994

Hayek von, F. (1960) *The Constitution of Liberty* New edition, Chicago University Press 1978

Hayek von, F. (1988) *The Fatal Conceit* New edition, Chicago University Press 1991

Hertzen von, G. (1974) *Organiserat entrepenörskap: Synpunkter på en företagarorganisation* SIAR-S- 62. In English *Cynics and Progress Motors* SIAR (1979); Publica (1991)

Hertzen von, G. (1993) *The Spirit of the Game* Fritzes, Stockholm

Hertzen von, G. (2000) *Att spela plussummespel. (Playing plus-sum games)* In Carlson, R. ed. *Strategier för att förtjäna pengar: Om affärsiden och andra SIAR-begrepp* (2000) p. 238–267 (*Strategies for making money: About the business idea and other SIAR concepts*) Ekerlids förlag, Stockholm

Hertzen von, G. (2003) *The Cultor Story – The Path Abroad* p. 69–85 in Mannio et al. eds. *Our Path Abroad: Exploring Post-war Internationalization of Finnish Corporations* Taloustieto, Helsinki

Hertzen von, G. (2008) *Management and Morality – An Overview* EVA Analysis No. 5, Finnish Business and Policy Forum

Himmelfarb, G. (1995) *The De-Moralization of Society: From Victorian Virtues to Modern Values* Knopf

Hintikka, J. & Sandu, G. (1997) *Game-theoretical semantics*. In Van Benthum et al. eds. *Handbook of logic and language* 361–410, Elsevier

Hochschild, A. (1998) *King Leopolds ghost: A story of greed, terror and heroism in colonial Africa* Pan Books

Hofstadter, D. (1979) *Gödel, Escher, Bach: An Eternal Golden Braid* Basic books

Hollis, M. (1998) *Trust within Reason* Cambridge University Press

Huntington, S. (1996) *The Clash of Civilizations and the Remaking of World Order* Simon & Schuster

Ikegami, E. (2005) *Bonds of Civility* Cambridge University Press

Jablonka, E. & Lamb, M. (2005) *Evolution in Four Dimensions : Genetic, Epigenetic, Behavioral and Symbolic Variation in the History of Life* MIT Press

Jakobson, M. (1955) *Diplomaattien talvisota* WSOY. In English *The Diplomacy of the Winter War. An Account of the Russo-Finnish Conflict 1939–1940* Harvard University Press (1961)

Jakobson, M. (1988) *Finland in the New Europe*. New edition, Greenwood Publishing Group (1998)

Jaspers, K. (1953) *Vom Ursprung und Ziel der Geschichte*. In English *The Origin and Goal of History* Yale University Press (1955)

Jelinek, E. (1983) *Die Klavierspielerin*. In English *The Piano Teacher* Weidenfeld & Nicolson (1988)

Jelinek, E. (2000) *Gier. Ein Unterhaltungsroman* Rowohlt. In English *Greed. A Novel* Seven Stories Press

Joas, H. (1992) *Die Kreativitet des Handelns* Suhrkamp. In English *The Creativity of Action. Polity Press* (1996)

Joas, H. (1997) *Die Entstehung der Werte* Suhrkamp. In English *The Genesis of Values* Chicago University Press (2000)

Joyce, R. (2006) *The Evolution of Morality* MIT Press

Judt, T. (2005) *Postwar: A History of Europe since 1945* Penguin

Junnelius, C. (2000) *Business Idea – Cornerstone of Business strategy* Tallinn Technical University Press

Juvaini, A.-T. (1958) *Genghis Khan: The History of the World-Conqueror* New edition, University of Washington Press 1997

Kandel, E. (2006) *In Search of Memory: The Emergence of a New Science* Norton

Kant, I: (1795) *Zum ewigen Frieden* In English *Perpetual Peace* on the web

Kaufmann, S. (2008) *Reinventing the Sacred: A New View of Science, Reason and Religion* Basic Books

Kennedy, J.F. (1956) *Profiles in Courage* New edition, Perennial Classics (2000)

Klamer, A. (1990) *Conversations with Economist.* Rowman & Littlefield

Klineberg, O. et al. (1979) *Values and Politics* Free Press

Koestler, A. (1940) *Darkness at noon* Bantam Books

Koestler, A. (1954) *The invisible writing* The second volume of an autobiography covering 1932–1940. New edition, Stein & Day 1984

Kowaleski, M. (1995) *Local markets and regional trade in medieval Exeter* Cambridge University Press

Kurokawa, K. ed. (2003) *Energy from the desert: Feasibility of very large scale photovoltaic power generation system* James and James

Kåhre, J. (2002) *The Mathematical Theory of Information* Kluwer Academic Publishers

Landes, D. (1983) *Revolution in time: Clocks and making the modern world* Harvard University Press

Landes, D. (1998) *The Wealth and Poverty of Nations* Norton

Lansing, J. (1991) *Priests and programmers: Technological power in the engineered landscapes of Bali* Princeton University Press

Lansing, J. (2006) *Perfect order: Recognizing complexity in Bali* Princeton University Press

Laub, J. & Sampson, R. (2003) *Shared Beginnings, Divergent Lives: Delinquent Boys to Age 70* Harvard University Press

Layard, R. (2003) *Happiness: Has Social Science a Clue?* Centre for Economic Performance

Layard, R. (2005) *Happiness: Lessons from a New Science* Penguin Group

LeBlanc, S. (1999) *Prehistoric Warfare in the American Southwest* The University of Utah Press

Lee, D.R. et al. (1988) *Helping the Poor Through Governmental Poverty Programs: The Triumph of Rhetoric over Reality* in Gwartney, J. et al. eds. *Public Choice and Constitutional Economics* JAI Press

Lessing, D. (1962) *The Golden Notebook* New edition, Perennial Classics (1999)

Lewin, R. (1992) *Complexity: Life at the Edge of Chaos* University of Chicago Press

Lomborg, B. (2001) *The Sceptical Environmentalist* Cambridge University Press

Lomborg, B. (2007) *Cool It: The Skeptical Environmentalist's Guide to Global Warming* Knopf

Lorenz, K. (1963) *Das sogenannte Böse* In English *On Aggression* Harcourt (1966)

Lovelock, J. (2006) *The Revenge of Gaia: Why the Earth is Fighting Back – and How we Can Still Save Humanity* Basic Books

Lovins, A. B. et al. (2004) *Winning the Oil Endgame: Innovation for Profits, Jobs and Security* Rocky Mountains Institute

Lumsden, C. & Wilson, E. O. (1983) *Promethean Fire* Harvard University Press

Luria, A. (1968) *The Mind of a Mnemonist: A little book about a vast memory* Basic Books

Lyndall, R. (1996) *The Aboriginal Tasmanians* Allen & Unvin

Malinowski, B. (1922) *Argonauts of the western pacific* New edition, Cambridge University Press (1992)

Mallory, J. (1989) *In search of the Indoeuropeans.* Thames & Hudson

Maren, M. (1997) *The Road to Hell: The Ravaging Effects of Foreign Aid and International Charity* The Free Press

Martin, P. (2005) *Twilight of the Mammoths* University of California Press

Martirosyan, A. (2006) *Strategy Through People: The Basics of a Contributing Organisation* Book Surge

Maslow, A. (1970) *Motivation and Personality.* Harper & Row

Mauss, Marcel (1924) *Essai sur le Don* In English *The Gift: The Form and Reason for Exchange in Archaic Societies* Routledge (2006)

Mayer, H. & Vogt, H. (2006) *A Responsible Europe* Palgrave

Mayor, A. (2003) *Greek fire, poison arrows and scorpion bombs: Biological and chemical warfare in the ancient world* Duckworth

McCloskey, D. (2006) *The Bourgeois virtues: Ethics for an Age of Commerce* University of Chicago Press

McCullough, D. (1992) *Truman* Simon & Schuster

McLean, I. (1987) *Public choice: An introduction* Basil Blackwell

Meredith, M. (2005) *The State of Africa: A History of Fifty Years Independence* Free Press

Michaels, P. & Balling, R. C. (2000) *The Satanic Gases: Clearing the Air About Global Warming* Cato Institute

Mintzberg, H. (2004) *Managers not MBA:s: A hard look at the soft practice on managing and management practice* Berrett-Koehler Publishers

Mokyr, J. (1990) *The Lever of Riches: Technological Creativity and Economic Progress* Oxford University Press

Mokyr, J. (2003) *Long-term Economic Growth and the History of Technology* In Aghion, P. & Durlauf, S. eds. *Handbook of Economic Growth* University of California, Berkeley (2005)

Monk, R. (1990) *The Duty of Genius* Penguin Books

Montesquieu de C. (1748) *De l'esprit de lois* In English *The Spirit of laws* Cambridge University Press (1989)

Morgan, D. (1986) *The Mongols* Blackwell Publishing 1990

Morris, D. (1967) *The Naked Ape* McGraw-Hill.

Musharraf, P. (2006). *In the Line of Fire: A Memoir* Free Press

Nabhan, G. (2004) *Why some like it hot: Food, genes and cultural diversity* Island Press

Naipaul, V.S. (1977) *India: A Wounded Civilization* Knopf

Naipaul, V.S. (1990) *India: A Million Mutinies* William Heinemann

Nalebuff, B. & Brandenburger, A.M. (1996) *Co-opetition* Harper Collins Business

Neumann von, J. & Morgenstern, O. (1944) *Theory of Games and economic Behavior.* New edition, Wiley (1964)

Njál's saga (thirteenth century?) In English Penguin Books (1977)

Norberg, J. (2005) *In Defence of Global Capitalism* Centre for Independent Studies

Normann, R. (1977) *Management for Growth* Wiley

Nozick, R. (1974) *Anarchy, State and Utopia* Basic Books

Olson, M. (1969) *The Rise and Decline of Nations* Yale University Press

Ortega y Gasset, J. (1930) *La rebelión de las masas* In English *The Revolt of the Masses* Norton (1994)

Orwell. G. (1945) *Animal farm* Harcourt, Brace & Co

Palm, C. et al. (2005) *Slash-and-Burn Agriculture: The Search for Alternatives* Columbia University Press 302 .

Pascal, B. (1662) *Pensées* In English *Pensees* Kessinger (2004)

Pavičič, M. (2005) *Quantum computation and Quantum communication: Theory and experiment.* Springer

Pelikan, J. (1973–1990) *The Christian tradition I–V* The University of Chicago Press

Pendergast, C. (2008) *The Fourteenth of July: And the Taking of the Bastille* Profile Books

Penttilä, R. (2003) *The Role of G8 in International Peace and Security* IISS Adelphi Papers

Pikovsky, A. et al. (2001) *Synchronization: A universal concept in nonlinear dynamics* Cambridge University Press

Pipes, R. (1999) *Property and freedom* Vintage books

Pipes, R. (2003) *The Degaev affair: Terror and treason in tsarist Russia* University of Yale Press

Politkovskaya, A. (2004) *Putin's Russia* Amazon

Popper, K. (1945) *The Open Society and its Enemies* Routledge. New edition (2002)

Popper, K. (1962) Encounter, Sept. (1962) *On the sources of knowledge and ignorance* Republished, Library Books (2006)

Porter, M. & Olmstedt-Teisberg, E. (2006) *Redefining Health Care: Creating Value-based Competition on Results* Harvard Business School Press

Posner, R. (2004) *Catastrophe Risk and Response* Oxford University Press

Proudhon, P-J. (1840) *Qu'est-ce que la propriété?* In English *What is property?* Cambridge University Press (1994)

Proudhon, P-J. (1866) *Théorie de la propriété*

Putnam, R. (2000) *Bowling Alone: The Collapse and Revival of American Community* Simon & Schuster

Putnam, R. et al. (1993) *Making democracy work: Civic traditions in modern Italy* Princeton University Press

Rawls, J. (1971) *A Theory of Justice* Harvard University Press

Rector, R. (1998) *The myth of the widespread American poverty* The Heritage Foundation

Rehn, A. (2001) *Electronic potlatch – a study on new technologies and primitive economic behaviours* Kungliga Tekniska Högskolan, Stockholm

Rehn,O. (2006) *Europe's next frontiers* Nomos

Reich, R.E. (2007) *Supercapitalism* Vintage Books

Reid, M. (2007) *Forgotten Continent: The battle for Latin America's Soul* Yale University Press

Rhenman, E. (1973) *Organization Theory for Long Range Planning* Wiley

Ridley, M. (1996) *The Origins of Virtue* Penguin Books

Ridley, M. (2003) *Nature via Nurture* Fourth Estate

Ronan, C. (1983) *The Cambridge illustrated history of the world science* Cambridge University Press

Rorty, R. (1989) *Contingency, Irony, Solidarity* Cambridge University Press

Rosanvallon, P. (2006) *La contre-démocratie. La politique à l'age de la défiance* Senil

Rousseau, J-J. (1762) Le contrat social ou Principes du droit publique. In English *The Social Contract* Penguin (1968)

Roy, O. (2004) *Globalised Islam: The Search for a New Ummah.* Hurst & Company

Ruddiman, W. (2005) *Plows, Plaques and Petroleum: How Humans Took Control of Climate* Princeton University Press

Runciman, M. et al. eds. (1996) *Evolution of Social Behaviour: Patterns in Primates and Man* Oxford University Press

Ryan, L. (1996) *The Aboriginal Tasmanians* Allen & Unwin

Sachs, J. (2002) *The End of Poverty.* Barnes & Noble

Sachs, J. (2008) *Common Wealth: Economics for a Crowded Planet* Penguin Press

Sagan, F. (1954) *Bonjour tristesse.* New edition in English *Bonjour Tristesse* HarperCollins (2001)

Sargent, T. (2006) *The dance of molecules: Nanotechnology is changing or lives* Thunder's Mouth Press

Sarkozy, N. *Testimony: France in the Twenty-First Century* Pantheon Books

Schama, S. (1987) *The embarrassment of riches: An interpretation of Dutch culture in the golden age.* Collins

Schiff, S. (2005) *Great improvisation: Franklin, France and the Birth of America* Henry Holt & Co

Schumpeter, J. (1942) *Capitalism, Socialism and Democracy* New edition, Harper Perennial (1984)

Schurman, F. et al. eds. (1967) *Imperial China* Vintage Books

Schwartz, P. (1996) *The Art of the Long View Planning* Currency

Shannon, C. (1948) *The Mathematical Theory of Communication.* New edition, University of Illinois Press (1975)

Sharp, G. (1973) *The Politics of Nonviolent Action* Poeter Sergent Publisher

Sharp, G. (1993) *From Dictatorship to Democracy* Albert Einstein Institution

Shennan, S. (2002) *Genes, Memes and Human History* Thames & Hudson

Silver, L. (1997) *Remaking Eden: How genetic engineering and cloning will transform the American family* Avon Books

Silver, L. (2006) *Challenging Nature: The Clash of Science and Spirituality at the new frontiers of Life* Harper Collins

Smith, A. (1759) *The Theory of Moral Sentiments.* New edition, Kessinger (2004)

Smith, A. (1776) *An Inquiry into the Nature and Causes of the Wealth of Nations* on the web

Smith, J. M. (1982) *Evolution and the theory of games* Harvard University Press

Solanas, V. (1966) *SCUM Manifesto* on the web

Soto de, H. et al (1989) *The Other Path: The invisible revolution in the third world* Harper & Row

Soto de, H. (2000) *The Mystery of Capital: Why Capitalism Triumphs in the West and Fails Everywhere Else* Basic Books

Sowell, T. (1998) *Conquests and cultures: An International History* Basic Books

Sowell, T. (1999) The Quest for Cosmic Justice. Free Press

Sowell, T. (2007) Economic Facts and Fallacies Basic Books

Spiro, M. (1979) *Gender and Culture: Kibbutz Women Revisited* Duke University Press

Spengler, O. (1922) *Der Untergang des Abendlandes* In English *The Decline of the West* Oxford University Press (1991)

Spinoza, B. (1677) *Ethica Ordine Geometrica Demonstrata* In English *Ethics* Penguin Classics (1996)

Stiglitz, J. (2002) *Globalization and its Discontents* Norton

Stiglitz, J. (2006) *Making globalization work* Norton

Stock, G. (2002) *Redesigning Humans: Our inevitable Genetic Future* Houghton Mifflin

Strauss, W. & Howe, N. (1991) *Generations: The History of America's Future* William Morrow

Tainter, J. (1988) *The collapse of complex societies* Cambridge University Press

Taverne, D. (2005) *The March of Unreason: Science, Democracy and the New Fundamentalism* Oxford University Press

Tetlock, P. (2005) *Expert political judgment: How Good Is It? How Can We Know?* Princeton University Press

Thomas, D.M. & B. Boyle Torrey eds. (2008) *Canada and the United States: Differences that Count* Broadview

Thomas, H. (1997) *The slave trade* Simon & Schuster

Thompson, J.B. (2005) *Books in the Digital Age* Blackwell

Thucydides (late fifth century BC) *History of the Peloponnesian War* Random House (1982)

Tocqueville de, A. (1835–1840) *De la Democratie en Amerique I-II* In English *Democracy in America I-II.* New edition Random House (1945)

Tocqueville de, A. (1856) *L'Ancien Regime et la Revolution* In English *The Old Regime and the French Revolution. Anchor* Books (1955)

Toynbee, A. (1960) *History of the World.* New edition, Oxford University Press (1976)

Trivers, R. (1985) *Social evolution* Cummings Publishing Co

Trivers, R. (2002) *Natural selection and social theory* Oxford University Press

Tuominen, A. (1956) *Kremlin Kellot (The bells of the Kremlin)* Tammi, Helsinki

Waal de, F. (2000) *Chimpanzee Politics* Johns Hopkins University Press

Wall, J. D. et al. eds. (2008) *Bioenergy* ASM Press

Weber, B. & Depew, D. (2003) *Evolution and learning: The Baldwin effect reconsidered* MIT Press

Weber, M. (1922) *Politik als Beruf* in *Wissenschaft und Beruf* New edition, Duncker & Humblot (1996)

Weinberg S. (2008) *Cosmology* Oxford University Press

Welch, J. (2001) *Jack: What I've learned leading a great company and great people* Headline

Westermarck, E. (1891) *The history of human marriage* New edition, Macmillan (1921)

Wilson, B. (2007) *The Making of the Victorian Values: Decency and Dissent in Britain 1789–1837* Pergamon Press

Wilson, D. S. (2002) *Darwins Cathedral: Evolution, Religion and the Nature of Society* University of Chicago Press

Wilson, E. O. (1975) *Sociobiology: The New Synthesis* 25th Anniversary Edition, Harvard University Press 2000

Wilson, E. O. (1998) *Consilience: The Unity of Knowledge* Knopf

Wilson, J. Q. (1993) *The Moral Sense* Free Press

Wittgenstein, L. (1922–1923) *Tractatus Logico-Philosophicus.* New edition, Routledge (1974)

Wolf, M. (2004) *Why Globalization Works* Yale Nota Bene

Wolpert, L. (2006) *Six impossible things before breakfast* Faber & Faber.

Wright, R. (2000) *Nonzero: The Logic of Human Destiny* Pantheon Books

Yoffee N. & Cowgill, G. eds. (1988) *The Collapse of Ancient States and Civilizations* University of Arizona Press

Yoffee, N. (2005) *Myths of the archaic state* Cambridge University Press

Zakaria, F. (2003) *The future of freedom: Illiberal Democracy at Home and Abroad* Norton

Zakaria, F. (2008) *The Post-American World* Norton

Index

About Finland

In 1939-1940, Finland single-handed kept the mighty Soviet Union at bay; the aggressor had to content itself with a partial victory. Finland survived and pulled through the war and the vicissitudes of the post-war period, avoiding occupation and with an intact democratic system. Since then Finland has become a prosperous member of the European Union.

As a place to do business, Finland has regularly been rated at or near the top in international rankings. The same holds for lack of corruption and level of education. This cannot be a coincidence. There are important lessons that Europe and the rest of the world can learn from Finland.

Finland spends a lot on education, from primary school to the university level. In world-wide comparisons, Finnish schoolchildren cluster at the top in reading, mathematics and natural sciences. Despite a comprehensive health service and extensive social welfare, taxes are reasonable and have been consistently reduced.

High technology flourishes and Finland has one of the highest ratios of R&D expenditure in relation to BNP. Nokia is the flagship of Finnish industry with its spectacular expansion in mobile phones. Linus Torvalds, the father of Linux, is another exponent of Finnish entrepreneurship.